HANDBOOK ON

Hebrews through Revelation

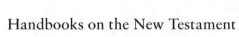

Handbooks on the New Testament

Benjamin L. Gladd, series editor

ALSO IN THIS SERIES:

Handbook on Acts and Paul's Letters
by Thomas R. Schreiner

HANDBOOK ON

Hebrews through Revelation

Andreas J. Köstenberger

Baker Academic

a division of Baker Publishing Group

Grand Rapids, Michigan

© 2020 by Andreas J. Köstenberger

Published by Baker Academic
a division of Baker Publishing Group
PO Box 6287, Grand Rapids, MI 49516-6287
www.bakeracademic.com

Paperback edition published 2022
ISBN 978-1-5409-6630-8

Printed in the United States of America

The Library of Congress has cataloged the hardcover edition as follows:
Names: Köstenberger, Andreas J., 1957– author.
Title: Handbook on Hebrews through Revelation / Andreas J. Köstenberger.
Description: Grand Rapids, Michigan : Baker Academic, a division of Baker Publishing Group, 2020. | Series: Handbooks on the New Testament | Includes bibliographical references and index.
Identifiers: LCCN 2019039577 | ISBN 9781540960184 (cloth)
Subjects: LCSH: Bible. Hebrews—Commentaries. | Bible. General epistles—Commentaries. | Bible. Revelation—Commentaries.
Classification: LCC BS2775.53 .K67 2020 | DDC 227/.06—dc23
LC record available at https://lccn.loc.gov/2019039577

To my students
past, present, and future

"I have no greater joy than to hear
that my children are walking in the truth."
(3 John 4)

Contents

Series Preface

The Handbooks on the New Testament are the counterpart to the well-received, four-volume set Handbooks on the Old Testament by Baker Academic. With the myriad of New Testament commentaries and introductions, why pen yet another series? The handbooks stand unique in that they are neither introductions nor commentaries. Most New Testament commentaries work in the trenches with verse-by-verse expositions, whereas introductions fly at forty thousand feet above the biblical text. This series lies between these two approaches. Each volume takes a snapshot of each New Testament passage without getting bogged down in detailed exegesis. The intent is for the reader to be able to turn to a particular New Testament passage in the handbook and quickly grasp the sense of the passage without having to read a considerable amount of the preceding and following discussion. This series is committed to summarizing the content of each major section of the New Testament. Introductory issues are not ignored (authorship, dating, audience, etc.), but they are not the focus. Footnotes, too, are used sparingly to keep the readers attuned to the passage. At the end of each chapter, the author includes a brief, up-to-date bibliography for further investigation.

Since the handbook focuses on the final form of the text, authors pay special attention to Old Testament allusions and quotations. The New Testament writers quote the Old Testament some 350 times and allude to it well over a thousand. Each author in this series notes how a good portion of those Old Testament allusions and quotations shape the passage under discussion. The primary audience of the handbook series is lay people, students, pastors, and professors of theology and biblical studies. We intend these volumes to find a home in the classroom and in personal study. To make the series more accessible, technical jargon is avoided. Each volume is theologically and pastorally informed. The authors apply their observations to contemporary issues within the church and to the Christian life. Above all, our prayer and desire is that this series would stimulate more study and serious reflection on God's Word, resulting in godly living and the expansion of the kingdom.

Benjamin L. Gladd

Author's Preface

It's been a wonderful challenge to comment succinctly on each of the so-called General Epistles and the book of Revelation. While the non-Pauline letters are often neglected, and Revelation has confounded many interpreters, these writings make an important contribution to the NT canon and merit careful study and application. While the placement of Revelation at the very end of the canon is not in question, the ancient manuscript tradition often places James, 1–2 Peter, 1–3 John, and Jude immediately following the book of Acts, which ties them more closely to the history of the early church, while Hebrews is often viewed as part of the Pauline corpus, whether the letter was written by Paul directly—a minority opinion today—or one of his followers.[1]

Placing the letters of James, Peter, John, and Jude in immediate proximity to Acts highlights the fact that each of these authors was an important figure in the early church. *James* was the leader of the Jerusalem church who presided over the so-called Jerusalem Council (Acts 15), which ruled on the delicate matter of criteria for gentile inclusion in the Christian community. *Peter* was the spokesman of the Twelve during Jesus's earthly ministry and was given "the keys to the kingdom" by Jesus (Matt. 16:19). He preached the first Christian sermon at Pentecost and presided over the inclusion of Jews and Samaritans into the early church (Acts 2:14–41; 8:14–25). Together with Paul, Peter is the leading character in the book of Acts and the main propagator

---

1. For all introductory matters regarding the books covered in the present volume, please consult Andreas J. Köstenberger, L. Scott Kellum, and Charles L. Quarles, *The Cradle, the Cross, and the Crown: An Introduction to the New Testament*, 2nd ed. (Nashville: B&H Academic, 2016). For the use of the OT in the books covered in this volume, see G. K. Beale and D. A. Carson, eds., *Commentary on the New Testament Use of the Old Testament* (Grand Rapids: Baker Academic, 2007). On the canonical status of the book of Hebrews, see also Gregory Goswell, "Finding a Home for the Letter of the Hebrews," *JETS* 59 (2016): 747–60.

of the message about the resurrected Jesus. *John* is the fourth evangelist and paired with Peter in both John's Gospel and the book of Acts (John 13:23–25; 18:15–16; 20:2–10; 21:7, 15–23; Acts 3–4; 8:14–25). In his Gospel, he stakes the claim of having been closest to Jesus during his earthly ministry, even closer than Peter (John 13:23; cf. 1:18; 21:20). Intriguingly, these same three men—James, Peter, and John, in the same order—are identified by Paul in his letter to the Galatians as "the pillars" of the early church (Gal. 2:9).

Jude, finally, like James, was Jesus's half-brother, one of the four sons of Joseph and Mary (Matt. 13:55; Mark 6:3; also called "Judas"). While not included by Paul among the "pillars," Jude was thus closely connected to both Jesus and James, the leader of the Jerusalem church, which not only tied him to the family of Jesus but also placed him in proximity to the apostolic circle. This family and apostolic connection made Jude, too, a suitable contributor to the NT canon. *Hebrews*, for its part, as mentioned, was often included alongside the other thirteen letters in the Pauline corpus, as it has been traditionally associated with the apostle Paul.

The book of *Revelation* brings closure to the biblical canon, providing a fitting bookend to the Scriptures by mirroring the opening book of Genesis. Together, these two books narrate God's initial creation of the universe and humanity on the one hand and the new creation on the other. In between these two bookends, the Bible tells the story of humanity's fall, a series of covenants made between God and his people, first with the nation of Israel (Abraham, Moses, David), and climactically, in keeping with prophetic prediction, in and through Jesus the Messiah (the new covenant). In this way, Revelation brings the biblical story to a fitting conclusion and depicts the eternal bliss of the redeemed in the presence of their covenant-keeping God and of Jesus, the lamb of God and lion of Judah.

Writing this book would not have been possible without the support of my partner in life and ministry, Margaret, who has been an incredible blessing to me over the course of our thirty years of marriage (and counting!). Whenever I'm asked to contribute to a useful project such as this, she wholeheartedly urges me to say "yes." You are truly more precious than rubies, my love! In addition, I'm grateful to the trustees of my institution, Midwestern Baptist Theological Seminary, and president Jason Allen for believing in me and for their generous support and encouragement. It means a lot. I'm also grateful to Benjamin Gladd for his enthusiastic invitation to contribute this volume to the series, and to the publisher, Baker Academic, for its excellence in producing this work. Thanks also to Drake Isabell for his help with the Scripture index.

The following handbook will cover the eight General Epistles and the book of Revelation in the order in which they appear in our English Bibles. While

I will briefly set the stage for each individual book in the respective chapter introductions, the bulk of my discussion will be spent plowing through the contents of each book. As the author of Hebrews states, "For the word of God is living and active, sharper than any two-edged sword, piercing to the division of soul and of spirit, of joints and of marrow, and discerning the thoughts and intentions of the heart" (Heb. 4:12). As a student of the Bible, I hope that as we journey through these portions of Scripture together, our hearts will be changed and our minds enlightened, for the glory of God and for our own good, and for the good of those with whom we'll share the fruit of our study. *Soli Deo gloria.*

Abbreviations

Symbol

//	parallels

Old Testament

Gen.	Genesis
Exod.	Exodus
Lev.	Leviticus
Num.	Numbers
Deut.	Deuteronomy
Josh.	Joshua
Judg.	Judges
Ruth	Ruth
1 Sam.	1 Samuel
2 Sam.	2 Samuel
1 Kings	1 Kings
2 Kings	2 Kings
1 Chron.	1 Chronicles
2 Chron.	2 Chronicles
Ezra	Ezra
Neh.	Nehemiah
Esther	Esther
Job	Job
Ps(s).	Psalm(s)
Prov.	Proverbs
Eccles.	Ecclesiastes
Song	Song of Songs
Isa.	Isaiah
Jer.	Jeremiah
Lam.	Lamentations
Ezek.	Ezekiel
Dan.	Daniel
Hosea	Hosea
Joel	Joel
Amos	Amos
Obad.	Obadiah
Jon.	Jonah
Mic.	Micah
Nah.	Nahum
Hab.	Habakkuk
Zeph.	Zephaniah
Hag.	Haggai
Zech.	Zechariah
Mal.	Malachi

New Testament

Matt.	Matthew
Mark	Mark
Luke	Luke
John	John
Acts	Acts
Rom.	Romans
1 Cor.	1 Corinthians
2 Cor.	2 Corinthians
Gal.	Galatians
Eph.	Ephesians
Phil.	Philippians
Col.	Colossians
1 Thess.	1 Thessalonians
2 Thess.	2 Thessalonians
1 Tim.	1 Timothy

2 Tim.	2 Timothy	2 Pet.	2 Peter
Titus	Titus	1 John	1 John
Philem.	Philemon	2 John	2 John
Heb.	Hebrews	3 John	3 John
James	James	Jude	Jude
1 Pet.	1 Peter	Rev.	Revelation

Secondary Sources

AB	Anchor Bible
AcBib	Academia Biblica
ACCS	Ancient Christian Commentary on Scripture
ACNT	Augsburg Commentary on the New Testament
ALGHJ	Arbeiten zur Literatur und Geschichte des hellenistischen Judentums
AnBib	Analecta Biblica
ANTC	Abingdon New Testament Commentaries
AUSS	*Andrews University Seminary Studies*
BBC	Blackwell Bible Commentaries
BBR	*Bulletin for Biblical Research*
BCBC	Believers Church Bible Commentary
BECNT	Baker Exegetical Commentary on the New Testament
BETL	Bibliotheca Ephemeridum Theologicarum Lovaniensium
BHGNT	Baylor Handbook on the Greek New Testament
Bib	*Biblica*
BJRL	*Bulletin of the John Rylands Library*
BR	*Biblical Research*
BSac	*Bibliotheca Sacra*
BTB	*Biblical Theology Bulletin*
BTCB	Brazos Theological Commentary on the Bible
BTCP	Biblical Theology for Christian Proclamation
BTNT	Biblical Theology of the New Testament
BTS	Biblical Tools and Studies
BZ	*Biblische Zeitschrift*
BZNW	Beihefte zur Zeitschrift für die neutestamentliche Wissenschaft
CBQ	*Catholic Biblical Quarterly*
CBR	*Currents in Biblical Research*
CJT	*Canadian Journal of Theology*
ConBNT	Coniectanea Biblica: New Testament
CTJ	*Calvin Theological Journal*
CTR	*Criswell Theological Review*
DBSJ	*Detroit Baptist Seminary Journal*
EBT	Explorations in Biblical Theology
EGGNT	Exegetical Guide to the Greek New Testament
ERT	*Evangelical Review of Theology*
EvQ	*Evangelical Quarterly*
ExpTim	*Expository Times*
FM	*Faith and Mission*

GNTE	Guides to New Testament Exegesis
GTJ	*Grace Theological Journal*
HNTC	Harper's New Testament Commentaries
HTR	*Harvard Theological Review*
IBRB	Institute for Biblical Research Bibliographies
ICC	International Critical Commentary
Int	*Interpretation*
IVPNTC	IVP New Testament Commentary
JBL	*Journal of Biblical Literature*
JETS	*Journal of the Evangelical Theological Society*
JMT	*Journal of Ministry and Theology*
JS	Johannine Studies
JSNT	*Journal for the Study of the New Testament*
JSNTSup	Journal for the Study of the New Testament Supplement Series
JTS	*Journal of Theological Studies*
LNTS	Library of New Testament Studies
MAJT	*Mid-America Journal of Theology*
MSJ	*The Master's Seminary Journal*
NABPRDS	National Association of Baptist Professors of Religion Dissertation Series
NAC	New American Commentary
NACSBT	New American Commentary Studies in Bible and Theology
NCB	New Century Bible
NCBC	New Cambridge Bible Commentary
NCC	New Covenant Commentary
NCCS	New Covenant Commentary Series
Neot	*Neotestamentica*
NIBC	New International Biblical Commentary
NICNT	New International Commentary on the New Testament
NIGTC	New International Greek Testament Commentary
NIVAC	NIV Application Commentary
NovT	*Novum Testamentum*
NovTSup	Supplements to Novum Testamentum
NSBT	New Studies in Biblical Theology
NTC	New Testament in Context
NTG	New Testament Guides
NTL	New Testament Library
NTR	New Testament Readings
NTS	*New Testament Studies*
NTT	New Testament Theology
PBM	Paternoster Biblical Monographs
PNTC	Pillar New Testament Commentary
PRSt	*Perspectives in Religious Studies*
PSTJ	*Perkins (School of Theology) Journal*
PTMS	Princeton Theological Monograph Series
RBS	Resources for Biblical Study
ResQ	*Restoration Quarterly*
RevExp	*Review and Expositor*

RTR	*Reformed Theological Review*
SB	Sources bibliques
SBJT	*Southern Baptist Journal of Theology*
SBLDS	Society of Biblical Literature Dissertation Series
SBLMS	Society of Biblical Literature Monograph Series
SBLRBS	Society of Biblical Literature Resources for Biblical Study
SNTSMS	Society for New Testament Studies Monograph Series
SP	Sacra Pagina
STDJ	Studies on the Texts of the Desert of Judah
TBT	*The Bible Today*
THNTC	Two Horizons New Testament Commentary
TNTC	Tyndale New Testament Commentaries
TrinJ	*Trinity Journal*
TT	*Theology Today*
TTC	Teach the Text Commentary
TTKi	*Tidsskrift for Teologi og Kirke*
TynBul	*Tyndale Bulletin*
UBC	Understanding the Bible Commentary
WBC	Word Biblical Commentary
WTJ	*Westminster Theological Journal*
WUNT	Wissenschaftliche Untersuchungen zum Neuen Testament
WW	*Word and World*
ZECNT	Zondervan Exegetical Commentary on the New Testament
ZIBBC	Zondervan Illustrated Bible Backgrounds Commentary
ZNW	*Zeitschrift für die neutestamentliche Wissenschaft und die Kunde der älteren Kirche*

CHAPTER ONE

Hebrews

Introduction

Author, Date, and Genre

The author of the Letter to the Hebrews is unknown.[1] However, the powerful message of the book of Hebrews does not depend on our knowledge of the author. Clearly, the early church decided that the contents of the book speak for themselves and bear the mark of divine inspiration; consequently, the church included the book in the NT canon. What is more, while *we* don't know who the author of Hebrews was, the original recipients of the letter almost certainly did (cf., e.g., 13:22)!

While the book's authorship is unknown, we can infer some interesting details about the circumstances surrounding the writing of this letter from the contents of the book. First, there is no mention of the destruction of the Jerusalem temple, which, according to the unanimous testimony of ancient sources, occurred in AD 70. Since mention of the destruction of the temple (if it had already occurred) would have greatly served to advance the writer's argument that the old sacrificial system and its institutions, now that Jesus had come, had been rendered obsolete, it is highly probable that the document was written prior to AD 70.

---

1. For an argument for Apollos as the author, see George H. Guthrie, "The Case for Apollos as the Author of Hebrews," *FM* 18 (2001): 41–56; for an argument for Luke as the author, see David L. Allen, *Lukan Authorship of Hebrews*, NACSBT (Nashville: B&H, 2010). Andrew W. Pitts and Joshua F. Walker, in "The Authorship of Hebrews: A Further Development in the Luke-Paul Relationship," in *Paul and His Social Relations*, ed. Stanley E. Porter and Christopher D. Land (Leiden: Brill, 2012), 143–84, argue that Hebrews constitutes Pauline speech material, recorded and later published by Luke.

Second, the author mentions that the "great salvation" in Jesus of which he speaks "was declared at first by the Lord" and "attested to us by those who heard" (2:3; I say, "*he* speaks," because, even though we don't know the name of the author, we do know that the author was male, based on the grammatical gender of the participle *diēgoumenon*, "telling," in 11:32). Thus, it appears that the author didn't count himself among the eyewitnesses of Jesus's ministry or the members of the apostolic circle. Rather, he seems to have been a second-generation believer who had received the apostolic message and was passing it on to others.

Third, while the book of Hebrews ends like a letter—with exhortations to obey the leaders of the church and to pray for Paul, as well as a closing benediction and final greetings (13:7–25)—the book doesn't start out like a letter. The epistles written by Paul, for example, typically follow the format, "Paul, an apostle, to [name of church or individual], grace and peace" (or a similar greeting; cf., e.g., 1 Cor. 1:1–3). By contrast, Hebrews begins more like an oral message, a sermon. In fact, while this is lost in English translation, the preface of Hebrews shows signs of careful rhetorical design, such as a pattern of alliteration in verse 1, which features as many as five words starting with the Greek letter *pi* (English "p"; see discussion at 1:1 below).

In addition, words of "speaking" and "hearing" replace the more customary terminology of "writing" and "reading," again suggesting that the letter adapts a series of oral messages. The author's closing remark, "I appeal to you, brothers, bear with my word of exhortation" (13:22), confirms this, since in the only other NT instance of "word of exhortation," Acts 13:15, the phrase refers to Paul's oral address in the synagogue of Pisidian Antioch. The cumulative evidence, therefore, points to the fact that the letter originated in a series of oral messages—sermons—that were later compiled and sent in the form of a letter, complete with an elaborate literary preface or introduction (1:1–4) and an epistolary conclusion (chap. 13).

Audience and Occasion

Who were the likely recipients of the letter? Again, several clues are embedded in the text and surrounding context. First, the title of the book is "[The Letter] To the Hebrews" (*PROS HEBRAIOUS*). While not part of the original, inspired text of the letter, the title is rather early and likely accurate in pointing to a predominantly (if not exclusively) Jewish readership. This is corroborated by the contents of the letter itself, which exhibits an extensive and impressive familiarity with the minutiae of the Jewish priesthood, the OT sacrificial system, and various OT liturgical practices.

2

Some have suggested that the likely audience were people such as the "great many of the *priests*" who "became obedient to the faith" mentioned early in Acts (6:7). While it is impossible to confirm this hypothesis conclusively, it is intriguing to think that the author may have addressed a Jewish-Christian congregation and its leaders who had come to believe that Jesus was the Messiah but had subsequently been tempted to revert to Judaism in the face of mounting persecution. This is also supported by the multiple "warning passages" throughout the book (e.g., 2:3–4; 6:1–6).

Moreover, we have good reason to believe that the letter was directed to a Christian congregation or group of house churches in the city of Rome, which at the time of writing was the epicenter of persecution of Christians under Emperor Nero, who reigned AD 54–68. The reference to "those who come from Italy" who "send you greetings" at the end of the letter seems to point in this direction (13:24). A Roman destination is also consistent with what we know of the later years of Nero's reign, during which he blamed Christians for the fire of Rome in AD 64 and had many of them executed.

It is likely that in the face of mounting persecution in the early or mid-60s AD some, if not many, Jewish believers—or potential believers—were tempted to retreat to the safer confines of Judaism, eliciting the author's warning, "How shall we escape if we neglect such a great salvation?" (2:3). Now that Jesus had come, died, risen, and "sat down at the right hand of the Majesty on high" (1:3), it was inconceivable that anyone could return to the old covenant system, which had been rendered obsolete by the finished cross-work of the Messiah and great eternal high priest, the Lord Jesus Christ.

Structure

The book of Hebrews presents one powerful, sustained argument for the superiority of the Lord Jesus Christ over the old covenant system of Judaism. Uniquely in the NT, the book focuses on the role of the Lord Jesus Christ as the great high priest of God's covenant people, who established a new covenant that supersedes the old by his death, in his blood (see, e.g., 10:19–22). The following table seeks to trace the author's argument in broad strokes.[2]

2. Cf. Cynthia Long Westfall, *A Discourse Analysis of the Letter to the Hebrews: The Relationship between Form and Meaning*, LNTS 297 (New York: T&T Clark, 2005), who argues for a tripartite division of Hebrews (1:1–4:16; 4:11–10:25; 10:19–13:16), "formally based on the two thematic discourse peaks in 4:11–16 and 10:19–25, which are formed by triads of hortatory subjunctives" (297). For surveys of structural proposals, see Barry C. Joslin, "Can Hebrews Be Structured? An Assessment of Eight Approaches," *CBR* 6 (2007): 99–129; Steve Stanley, "The Structure of Hebrews from Three Perspectives," *TynBul* 45 (1994): 245–71. A different breakdown is provided by Dennis E. Johnson, "Hebrews," in *ESV Expository Commentary*, vol. 12,

Characteristically, the closing section in a given unit often does double duty, functioning simultaneously as the opening section of the following unit.

Structure of Hebrews

Literary Unit	Content Summary	Transition
1:1–4:16	God's final revelation and salvation in his Son	4:11–16
4:11–10:25	Jesus as the great high priest and mediator of a new covenant	10:19–25
10:19–13:16	Jesus, who ran the race before us and suffered outside the camp	13:17
13:18–25	Epistolary closing	

Central Message

In the opening major unit, the author asserts that after a series of previous spokesmen—the OT prophets—God revealed himself "in these last days" by way of "a son" (1:1–2). The climactic nature of God's end-time revelation in his Son provides the major overarching framework for the assertion pervading the remainder of the unit—and indeed of the entire book—that Jesus is superior to all previous mediators of God's revelation and redemption. This includes angels, through whom, according to Jewish tradition, God gave the law to Israel (2:2). It also includes Moses, through whom God delivered Israel during the exodus and gave the law (3:1–6). It even includes Joshua, who led Israel into the promised land but failed to give the nation permanent rest from her enemies (4:8–10). What would have been particularly compelling for the writer's original Jewish audience is that the name "Joshua" in Greek is spelled precisely the same way as the name "Jesus" (*Iēsous*)![3] Thus, the argument runs essentially like this: What the former "Jesus" (Joshua) was unable to do—namely, to provide permanent rest and deliverance for God's people—the later "Jesus" (the Lord Jesus Christ) was able to do. This, in turn, perfectly sets up the discussion in the next unit regarding the superior, eternal high priesthood of Jesus Christ.

The second major unit in the book commences in 4:14 (in the midst of the transition section spanning 4:11–16) and is introduced as follows: "Since then we have a great high priest who has passed through the heavens, Jesus, the Son of God . . ." While the high priestly nature of Jesus was hinted at in the preface

---

Hebrews–Revelation, ed. Iain M. Duguid, James M. Hamilton Jr., and Jay Sklar (Wheaton: Crossway, 2018), 23, who identifies six major sections (1:4–2:18; 3:1–4:13; 4:14–7:28; 8:1–10:31; 10:32–12:17; and 12:18–29; note, however, that Johnson's outline on pp. 28–30 does not always correspond to this breakdown).

3. The author of Hebrews often quoted from the Septuagint (LXX), the Greek translation of the Old Testament. In this way, he was able to relate the wording in a given Old Testament passage to his own message, which was written in Greek as well.

("After making purification for sins, he sat down," 1:3), this is the first time in the book that Jesus's high priesthood is explicitly affirmed. The bulk of the middle section of the book is taken up with a detailed discussion and demonstration of Christ's superior priesthood. Over against the Levitical priesthood, which was limited in its nature and efficacy, the writer asserts, Jesus's priesthood is of a qualitatively different kind in that it was patterned after the priesthood of the enigmatic figure of Melchizedek (5:1–10; 7:1–28). As a result, Jesus became the mediator of a new, better covenant, which enables believers to draw near to God permanently in a way that OT believers were unable to do.

The third major unit, which is closer in length to the opening unit and shorter than the middle one, drives home the vital implications of Jesus's superiority over various OT figures—whether prophets, national deliverers, or priests—for the way in which believers ought to live. Starting in 10:19, the author addresses readers with a threefold exhortation: "Therefore, brothers, since we have confidence to enter the holy places by the blood of Jesus, by the new and living way that he opened for us . . . , and since we have a great priest over the house of God [cf. 4:14], let us draw near. . . . Let us hold fast the confession of our hope without wavering. . . . And let us consider how to stir up one another to love and good works" (10:19–24). Believers are surrounded by a great "cloud of witnesses" (i.e., OT believers exhibiting exemplary faith) and must run the race of faith while fixing their eyes on Jesus, who has already completed the race (12:1–2). They also should be willing to endure the type of suffering that inevitably ensues from following a crucified Savior (13:12–13).

Major Units in the Book of Hebrews

Literary Unit	Opening Declaration/Argument	Exhortation
1:1–3	"Long ago, . . . God spoke to our fathers by the prophets, but in these last days he has spoken to us by his Son. . . ."	"Therefore we must pay much closer attention to what we have heard, lest we drift away from it." (2:1)
4:14–16	"Since . . . we have a great high priest who has passed through the heavens, Jesus, the Son of God, . . .	. . . let us hold fast our confession."
10:19–25	"Therefore, brothers, since we have confidence to enter the holy places by the blood of Jesus, . . . and since we have a great priest over the house of God, . . .	. . . let us draw near with a true heart in full assurance of faith. . . . Let us hold fast the confession of our hope without wavering. . . . And let us consider how to stir up one another to love and good works."
13:17–25		"Obey your leaders and submit to them. . . . Pray for us. . . . Bear with my word of exhortation. . . ."

God's Final Revelation and Salvation in His Son (1:1–4:16)

Jesus Is Superior to Angels (1:1–2:18)

Often in the context of a current debate, we might say that "the final word on a given subject has not yet been spoken." Or, a TV moderator might tell a panel participant that she'll give him the "final word." What the author of the book of Hebrews asserts is that when it comes to the most important matter in human life following the fall—forgiveness and salvation from sin— the final word has already been spoken in the most definitive way possible. What's more, the final word was spoken by God himself—not in the various preliminary fashions we read about in the OT historical and prophetic books but in the person and work of the Lord Jesus Christ. To explain the manner in which God spoke this final word in and through Jesus, the author places the coming of the Son of God within the matrix of God's previous revelatory acts in OT times.

That said, the focus in chapters 1 and 2 of Hebrews is for the most part on Jesus's superiority to angels (see 1:5, 6, 7, 13, 14; 2:2, 5, 9, 16). Why is this the case? In part, at least, the answer lies in the Jewish understanding, only hinted at in the OT (cf. Deut. 33:2) but occasionally finding more explicit expression in the NT, that the law was given by God to Moses through angelic intermediaries (cf., e.g., Acts 7:38; Gal. 3:19). The law, in turn, ever since it was given at Mount Sinai, served as a sort of constitution for OT Israel, providing the nation with an overall ethic as well as with specific stipulations regarding the priesthood, worship, sacrifices, and many other matters of vital national and ritual importance.

While Paul at times draws attention to the limitations of the law, in many ways it was God's good gift to his people at that juncture in salvation history, providing his people with detailed instructions on how to live before him both corporately and individually. John hints at this when he writes in his prologue that "the law was given through Moses; grace and truth came through Jesus Christ" (John 1:17). Thus, the law was rightly held in very high esteem by God's people in OT times. In fact, their esteem for the law was so great that many argued that the law (Hebrew *Torah*) was eternal and already at God's side at creation (similar to wisdom; cf. Prov. 8). Many of the Psalms, likewise, attest to Israel's high esteem for the law and its perfection (see, e.g., Pss. 1, 19, and 119).

In light of this high regard for the law, it's no wonder that many in the first century expected that the law would always govern the ways of God's people, with the nation of Israel at the center. It is these assumptions that the author of the book of Hebrews challenges head-on. In the opening verse, virtually every word is significant, which is underscored by the author's use of alliteration: "At many times [*polymerōs*] and in many ways [*polytropōs*], long ago [*palai*], God, after speaking to the fathers [*patrasin*] by the prophets [*prophētais*], in these last days spoke to us by a son" (1:1, my translation). It is impossible to duplicate the rhetorical effect of this magnificent opening assertion in English translation, but the Greek is as momentous as it is memorable (my own feeble attempt at alliteration).

In the opening statement, the author contrasts "long ago" with "in these last days" (cf. Num. 24:14; Jer. 23:20; Dan. 10:14). Notably, the word "to speak" is constant; the contrast, however, is between God speaking by various *prophets* (plural) and his speaking by a *son* (singular). The repeated phrase "many" (*poly-*) in the expressions "at many times" and "in many ways" (two more plurals) stands in contrast with the absence of any such qualifications pertaining to God's *singular* "son" revelation. This son, the author adds, God appointed as heir of all things (a likely allusion to Ps. 2:8), and this son also served as the agent of God's creation, the Word through which (better, "whom") God spoke everything into being (1:2; cf. 11:3; John 1:2–3). Clearly, none of the OT prophets, while occupying a significant role as God's spokesmen, had such an exalted status as "the heir" (singular) "through whom" (singular) God created the world. (Note that the term "prophets" is likely rather broad and includes even OT figures such as Moses.) The book of Hebrews is also a superior form of revelation. God has spoken in his Son as testified through the apostles and the book of Hebrews.

Right at the outset, then, the author impresses on his audience, in a manner that is highly effective rhetorically, the superiority of Jesus, "the Son," over previous figures who served as intermediaries conveying communication from God to his people. In the remainder of his introduction, the author continues to develop the notion of Jesus's superior relationship with God and position in God's plan when he calls him "the radiance [*apaugasma*, only here in the NT] of the glory [*doxa*] of God and the exact imprint [*charaktēr*, only here in the NT] of his nature [*hypostasis*; cf. esp. Heb. 11:1, where ESV translates *hypostasis* as 'assurance']" and affirms that Jesus "upholds the universe by his powerful word" (1:3, my translation). The word denoting Jesus as the "exact imprint" of God's nature—presumably referring to his preexistent state—most likely conveys metaphorically the impression of a coin or seal. While upholding a distinction between God the Creator and Jesus the Son and Word of God, the author proffers an extremely high Christology—even prior to the destruction of the Jerusalem temple—and equates Jesus's and God's natures (what theologians call "ontology," or essential being).

That said, there are some scholars who deny that the author of Hebrews espoused a belief in Jesus's preexistence. They contend that the author is merely viewing Jesus within a framework of "wisdom Christology." According to these scholars, when speaking of Jesus being "the radiance of God's glory" and "the exact imprint of his nature," the author of Hebrews refers only to the human Jesus as the embodiment of wisdom, and references to Jesus's preexistence are to be taken only in a general and metaphorical sense. As the embodiment of divine wisdom, these scholars argue, Jesus also represents God's creative energy and saving intent. However, a plain reading of the first chapter of Hebrews and careful consideration of OT allusions suggest that the author creatively intersperses references to Jesus's preexistence, incarnation, and exaltation and holds both to the full humanity and to the full deity of Christ in proper balance and in relation to one another.

At this, the author takes a decidedly priestly turn when he speaks of (the incarnate) Jesus, "after making purification for sins," sitting down "at the right hand of the Majesty on high" (an allusion to Ps. 110:1, later quoted in 1:13 and several other times in the letter), "having become as much superior to angels as the name he has inherited is more excellent than theirs" (1:4; see also 8:1; 10:12; 12:2). By speaking of the purification (*katharismos*, used frequently in the Greek translation of Leviticus; cf., e.g., Lev. 8:15; 12:7–8; 13:6–7; 14:2; 15:13, 28; 16:19, 20, 30) for sins accomplished by Jesus, the author previews what will constitute a major topic of discussion in this letter—namely, Jesus's role as the great high priest who inaugurated a new covenant by his blood shed at the cross (see later uses of "cleansing" language in 9:13–14, 22–23; 10:2, 22; on the high priesthood of Christ, see 2:17; 3:1; 4:14; 5:1; 7:26; 8:1; 9:11). What is more, the fact that Jesus is depicted as having sat down—and in the past, at that—resoundingly underscores the definitive, once-for-all nature of the purification for sin he accomplished, which contrasts with the repetitive nature of sacrifices performed by Jewish priests under the OT sacrificial system in keeping with the nature of the Levitical priesthood (cf., e.g., 10:11). This contrast already hints at the fact that Jesus's priesthood was of a different kind, as the author will develop later on.

When the author speaks of Jesus having inherited (in the perfect tense, denoting an abiding result) a more excellent "name" than the angels, he uses the expression "name," as was common in Jewish parlance, as an embodiment of a person's identity, character, and role. Most likely, "name" here invokes the divine name YHWH (the so-called tetragrammaton), which God the Father shared with the Son as the exalted end-time Ruler of the universe (see the quotation of Ps. 102:25–27 in 1:10–12; see also the other three instances of "name," *onoma*, in 2:12; 6:10; and 13:15). After first mentioning angels in verse 4, the author continues to dwell on the topic of Jesus's superiority to angels for the remainder of chapter 1 and for much of chapter 2. In support of his argument, the author cites several OT passages, mostly from the book of Psalms.[4] He begins by adducing an exceedingly important messianic passage that surfaces repeatedly in the NT, namely Psalm 2:7, where God is cited as addressing an individual as follows: "You are my Son; today I have begotten you." Most likely, this does not refer to an eternal act of divine generation of God the Son by God the Father, but to the messianic appointment of the Son of God.

In typical "pearl-stringing" fashion—a common Jewish (rabbinic) practice of citing a whole cluster of Scriptures that all address a related topic—the author follows this reference to Psalm 2:7 with a reference to another exceedingly important OT messianic passage, 2 Samuel 7:14: "I will be to him a father, and he shall be to me a son." The author's point in both cases is that God did not appoint an angel to be the Messiah, nor did he place an angel in the messianic line as Son of David. Rather, this role was reserved exclusively for Jesus, whose stature before God is unrivaled and whose role in God's plan is unmatched. The author will later point out that part of the reason for this is that Jesus had to be not only fully divine but also fully human, a requirement no angel could ever fulfill.

In another contrast, the author, in conjunction with referring to Jesus as the "firstborn" (*prōtotokos*, not a reference to Jesus's actual birth but to his preeminence; cf. Rom. 8:29; Col. 1:15, 18; Rev. 1:5), cites Psalm 97:7 in 1:6, "Let all God's angels [or 'gods'] worship him" (implying that the object of the angels' worship is Jesus), while saying of the angels, "He makes his angels winds, and his servants flames of fire" (Heb. 1:7, quoting Ps. 104:4; my translation).[5] Jesus is therefore a proper object of worship, while the angels are not; their role is rather that of divine messengers (note that "angel," *angelos*, in the original Greek meant "messenger," whether angelic or human). While it may seem strange to some that people might actually worship angels, angels had taken on a very high role during the Second Temple period, which was characterized by the absence of direct divine revelation.[6] Paul's Letter to the Colossians

---

4. On the string of OT passages in 1:5–14, see Joshua W. Jipp, "The Son's Entrance into the Heavenly World: The Soteriological Necessity of the Scriptural Catena in Hebrews 1:5–14," *NTS* 56 (2010): 557–75, who argues that the event the catena describes—the Son's enthronement to the heavenly world—is critical for the logic of the author's argument regarding how humanity's salvation is accomplished.

5. The Hebrew of Psalm 97:7 has *Elohim*, "gods," which is translated in the LXX as *angeloi*, "angels." The author of Hebrews conflates the two ideas by choosing the wording *angeloi theou*, "God's angels."

6. "Second Temple" refers to the period between the rebuilt Solomonic temple in ca. 520 BC and the destruction of the same temple by the Romans in AD 70.

strongly speaks out against angel worship, implying that such was practiced by some (2:18), and the book of Revelation features an instance where the seer falls down to worship an angel, who at once sternly rebukes him, saying, "You must not do that! I am a fellow servant with you and your brothers the prophets, and with those who keep the words of this book. Worship God" (Rev. 22:9). In our day, angels have often become an object of strange fascination, exuding an aura of mystique. In our daily lives, most of us hardly ever think of angels (except perhaps at Christmas). Yet while the notion that every person has a guardian angel is not necessarily endorsed by Scripture, the Bible clearly attests to the reality of both fallen and unfallen angels, such as at the birth of Jesus as well as at his temptation and the resurrection. And while angels are God's servants and messengers and rank among his most wonderful creatures, they are creatures nonetheless, while Jesus, the Son of God, is uncreated and himself the agent of creation (cf. 1:2).

Verses 8–9 speak again of the Son's unique appointment—his messianic anointing—in God's plan: "But of the Son he says, 'Your throne, O God, is forever and ever; the scepter of uprightness is the scepter of your kingdom. . . . Therefore God, your God, has anointed you with the oil of gladness beyond your companions'" (Ps. 45:6–7). The author continues by contrasting God's creation, which will perish, with God—and the Son—who will remain and whose "years will have no end" (1:12, quoting Ps. 102:25–27). This again makes a clear distinction between God, the Creator, who is eternal, and the universe—including angels—which is created. There was a time when there were no angels (though the Bible does not record their creation), but God has always existed. And the Son, as "the radiance of the glory of God and the exact imprint of his nature" (1:3), is eternal as God is, while the angels have a beginning in time. What is more, not only is the Son ontologically superior to angels in terms of his essential being; his role as mediator of divine revelation and redemption is superior to that of angels. The author will shortly develop this point in greater detail.

Before wrapping up his argument thus far, the author plays his final trump card, citing a passage that was exceedingly important in the messianic teaching of Jesus and the early Christians—namely, Psalm 110:1. He writes, "And to which of the angels has he ever said, 'Sit at my right hand until I make your enemies a footstool for your feet'?" (Heb. 1:13). The answer to this rhetorical question, of course, is, "None." What's more, the citation of Psalm 110:1 here makes the mind of the alert reader wander back to the author's statement in the opening verses that Jesus, after making purification for sins, "sat down at the right hand of the Majesty on high" (1:3). The obvious implication is that, since Jesus *already* sat down at God's right hand, God has *already* made his enemies a footstool for his feet! Thus, the messianic prophecy of Psalm 110:1 has already been fulfilled in Jesus. At the same time, though, there remains a time at which God will utterly subject all of Jesus's enemies to him, per the book of Revelation. The author concludes this section by contrasting Jesus's role once more with that of angels, referring to them as "ministering spirits sent out to serve for the sake of those who are to inherit salvation" (1:14). In this sense, then, the angels are subservient even to humans, as their role is to serve them as directed by God (cf. 1 Cor. 11:10; 1 Pet. 1:12).

Use of the Old Testament in Hebrews 1:5–13

Hebrews	OT Passage	Quote
1:5a	Ps. 2:7	"You are my Son; today I have become your Father."
1:5b	2 Sam. 7:14	"I will be to him a father, and he shall be to me a Son."
1:6	Ps. 97:7	"Let all God's angels worship him."
1:7	Ps. 104:4	"He makes his angels winds, and his servants a fiery flame."
1:8–9	Ps. 45:6–7	"Your throne, O God, is forever and ever, the scepter of uprightness is the scepter of your kingdom. You have loved righteousness and hated wickedness; therefore God, your God, has anointed you with the oil of gladness beyond your companions."
1:10–12	Ps. 102:25–27	"You, Lord, laid the foundation of the earth in the beginning, and the heavens are the work of your hands; they will perish, but you remain; they will all wear out like a garment; like a robe you will roll them up, like a garment they will be changed. But you are the same, and your years will have no end."
1:13	Ps. 110:1	"Sit at my right hand, until I make your enemies your footstool."

The word "therefore" in 2:1 indicates a transition to the first of several "warning passages" in the book. The warning is against "drifting away" from "what we have heard," which is clearly implied to be the Christian gospel message: that Jesus died on the cross for our sins so that we can be saved by believing in him. In what follows, the author compares this message to the "message declared by angels"—namely, the law (see discussion above). Just as the Israelites were accountable to the stipulations of the law, the author uses an argument from the lesser to the greater, so people are accountable to the gospel of Christ now that Jesus has come and provided "such a great salvation" (2:3).

This message was proclaimed first by Jesus himself, then passed on by those who were eyewitnesses (cf. Luke 1:2; John 15:27; Acts 1:21–22), which apparently does not include the author of the book of Hebrews ("it was attested to *us* by those who heard," 2:3; see discussion in the introduction above). Undergirding the early Christian gospel preaching was God's own witness through "signs and wonders . . . and by gifts of the Holy Spirit," which presumably refers to the period of early Christian proclamation following the first Pentecost, which is narrated at some length in the book of Acts.

The author's point here is simply this: *Now that Jesus has come, and died, and risen, and the gospel message has been proclaimed far and wide, there is no going back to the Mosaic law.* This would be to "neglect such a great salvation"! Indeed, it is inconceivable that God would have gone to such lengths to send Jesus, and that Jesus would have endured such severe suffering to procure our salvation, and then for people to act as if all of this were of no consequence, living as if none of this had ever happened. The saving events surrounding the death and resurrection of Christ are too momentous in God's salvation-historical plan to be neglected and ignored.

Warning Passages in the Book of Hebrews

Hebrews	Exhortation
2:1–4	"How shall we escape if we neglect such a great salvation?" (v. 3)
3:7–4:13	"Today, if you hear his voice, do not harden your hearts." (3:7–8, 15; 4:7, quoting Ps. 95:7–8)
5:11–6:12	"Let us leave the elementary doctrine of Christ and go on to maturity." (6:1)
10:19–39	"Let us draw near with a true heart in full assurance of faith. . . . Let us hold fast the confession of our hope without wavering." (vv. 22–23)
12:14–29	"See to it that no one fails to obtain the grace of God." (v. 15)

Angels continue to serve as a sort of foil for the author's argument as he continues by asserting that "it was not to *angels* that God subjected the world to come" but to *Jesus*, "who for a little while was made lower than the angels" (2:5, 9). As proof, the author continues his string of Psalms quotations by invoking Psalm 8:4–6 (though he vaguely says his quotation is found "somewhere," 2:6). In so doing, he provides a messianic interpretation of this psalm, in particular the reference to the "son of man"—namely, Jesus, who was made "lower than the angels" for a little while—namely, the time of his incarnation and earthly ministry. What's more, the author notes that the period of Jesus's temporary choice of a status beneath the angels has now given way to "glory and honor" and a position of supreme authority. The author also adds that this temporary lowering of Jesus served God's purpose for Jesus: "that by the grace of God he might taste death for everyone" (2:9). In other words, for Jesus—"the radiance of the glory of God and the exact imprint of his nature" (1:3)—to die efficaciously for human sinners, he must be human himself. In this way, he can "taste death for everyone" (2:9)—though, of course, his vicarious, substitutionary atonement is *effective* only for those who believe.

Thus Jesus became the "founder" (*archēgos*) of our salvation (2:10; cf. 12:2; cf. 6:20, where Jesus is called a "forerunner," *prodromos*). In describing a salvation-historical necessity according to the plan of God, the author asserts that "it was fitting" that God, the sovereign Creator, "for whom and by whom all things exist, in bringing many sons to glory, should make the founder of their salvation perfect through suffering" (2:10). This, of course, does not imply that Jesus was somehow imperfect prior to his cross-death on our behalf. It does mean, however, that suffering is part of God's plan and suffering is the pathway to eventual glory (see 12:1–2). This doesn't mean only that Jesus procured our salvation once for all by suffering and dying on the cross for our sins; it also means that Jesus already traversed the way of suffering as our forerunner, so that we are called to follow in his footsteps and be prepared to endure suffering in this world as well (cf. 13:12–13; 1 Pet. 2:21–25). As Christians, we're called to suffer. Put differently, suffering is an inexorable part of our Christian calling. By suffering in his full humanity, Jesus not only died efficaciously for us; he also continues to point the way to how we should live as his followers for the remainder of our days on earth. God's desire in sending Jesus to suffer was not merely to procure our salvation; rather, his desire was to "bring many sons to glory" (2:10; "sons" in the original is gender-inclusive and includes women as well as men). "For he who sanctifies [presumably the Spirit] and those who are sanctified [believers] all have one source [God]" (2:11). This assertion is backed up by a series of three OT citations, Psalm 22:22, Isaiah 8:17 // 12:2, and Isaiah 8:18. All three passages highlight trust in God and the Messiah's identification with us as his "brothers" and "the children" God has given him.

Use of the Old Testament in Hebrews 2:12–13

Hebrews	OT Passage	Quote
2:12	Ps. 22:22	"I will tell of your name to my brothers; in the midst of the congregation I will sing your praise."
2:13a	Isa. 8:17 // 12:2	"I will put my trust in him."
2:13b	Isa. 8:18	"Behold, I and the children God has given me."

Hebrews 2:14 begins to drive home the author's argument that commenced in verse 5 following the warning passage of 2:1–4.

First, the phrase "not to angels," which began the literary unit in verse 5, is echoed by similar terms in verse 16: "not . . . angels." This inclusio (literary bookend) sets off verses 5–16 as a literary subunit containing a cohesive argument.

Second, the introduction to 2:14, "Since therefore," indicates that the author draws the necessary conclusion that follows from his argument in verses 5–13, which focus on the salvation-historical rationale for and the dynamic underlying Jesus's incarnation (cf. the phrase "it was fitting," v. 10; see above).

Third, the word "children" in verse 14 picks up the same word from the preceding OT quote in verse 13.

The argument in 2:14 is akin to what was already said in verse 9 ("because of the suffering of death . . . he might taste death for everyone"), except that here the author adds that "through death *he might destroy the one who has the power of death, that is, the devil.*" Thus, the angelic realm is part of God's salvation-historical theater and includes both unfallen angels and the devil. At the same time, the salvation Jesus procured is a transaction of which God is the source and humans are the beneficiaries.

The author thus canvasses the entire range of salvation-historical activity involving God, unfallen angels, Jesus, the devil, and humanity:

Cosmic Scope of Redemption in Hebrews

God: The source of salvation

Angels: The world is not subjected to them
Not the recipients of salvation

Jesus: Made a little lower than the angels
Tasted death for everyone
Destroyed the devil, who held power over death

Devil: Power over death destroyed

Humans: Beneficiaries of salvation

Jesus's death is not merely "for everyone"—that is, vicarious and substitutionary; it also breaks the devil's power over death and constitutes deliverance from "fear of death" and "lifelong slavery" (2:15). At this, the author brings closure to his argument in this portion of his letter by reiterating that it was not angels who were the beneficiaries of salvation but humanity, "the offspring of Abraham" (v. 16), whereby the author may be referring to Abraham not merely as the father of the Jewish people—though he certainly was—but more broadly as the ancestor of all those who would benefit from the salvation Jesus procured.

In 2:17, then, the author picks up on his statement in verse 11 ("That is why he is not ashamed to call them brothers") and anticipates the assertion in verse

18 by stating, "Therefore he had to be made like his brothers in every respect, so that he might became a merciful and faithful high priest in the service of God, to make propitiation for the sins of the people." Here, the author hints at the theme of Jesus's high priesthood, which he previously touched on in the introduction to the letter (1:3) and which will occupy much of the remainder of the letter. As a high priest, Jesus can sympathize with our frailty because he was tempted just as we are (v. 18).

Jesus Is Superior to Moses and Joshua (3:1–4:16)

"Therefore, holy brothers" in 3:1 introduces a new stage in the author's argument. "Holy brothers" is an interesting address; in 3:12, the address is simply "brothers." The phrase "who share in a heavenly calling" anticipates later references to believers' heavenly calling, such as the reference to Abraham as one who "was looking forward to the city that has foundations, whose designer and builder is God" (11:10) and the reference to other OT believers who desired "a better country, that is, a heavenly one" (11:16; cf. 12:23; 13:14). The author's burden in this section is to show that just as Jesus is superior to angels (chaps. 1–2), he is also superior to Moses and Joshua, God's servants who were instrumental in delivering God's people from bondage in Egypt and bringing them into the promised land.

The author urges his readers to "consider Jesus, the apostle and high priest of our confession" (3:1), continuing to hint at the theme of Jesus's high priestly office, upon which he will elaborate later in the letter. Just like Moses, Jesus was "faithful" over "God's house" (a metaphor for the stewardship entrusted to them), yet Jesus was counted worthy of greater "glory," or honor, than Moses, because he was faithful as a "son" rather than merely as a "servant," as Moses was (vv. 2–6). This analogy would have communicated effectively to a first-century Jewish audience familiar with the extended household in which a son had greater status and privileges than a mere servant. Developing the household analogy further, the author affirms that God—as well as Jesus—is the "builder" of the house (which makes Jesus both the builder and the son exercising faithful stewardship over the house), while believers are the house itself—if they hold fast to their confession and heavenly hope (3:6).

At this juncture (vv. 7–11), the author cites at length Psalm 95:7–11, introducing the OT quote with the phrase "as the Holy Spirit says." The remainder of chapter 3 and chapter 4—the second "warning passage" in the book—is given to a midrashic (commentary-style) exposition expounding the contemporary relevance of this psalm for the author's audience at their particular juncture of salvation history. The quote starts out with the word "Today" (3:7), and it is on this word, "today," that the author rests his main rhetorical emphasis, as verse 13 makes clear: "But exhort one another every day, as long as it is called 'today,' that none of you may be hardened by the deceitfulness of sin."

Three levels of time in salvation history are in play here: (1) the original setting in Moses's day and Israel's wanderings in the wilderness during the exodus from Egypt (Exod. 17:7; Num. 20:2); (2) the setting during the time of the psalmist, who called on his contemporaries not to harden their hearts as the Israelites did in the wilderness (Ps. 95); and (3) the setting of the author of Hebrews and the congregation to which he speaks or writes. Astutely, the author picks up on the fact that the wilderness Israelites didn't heed God's call not to harden their hearts toward him, and thus incurred divine judgment. This, he observes, occasioned the reiterated call by the psalmist.

Salvation-Historical Instances of "Today" in Hebrews

1. Israel during wilderness wanderings (Exodus, Numbers)

2. Israel at the time of the psalmist (Psalm 95)

3. The Jewish audience of the book of Hebrews (Hebrews)

And yet, the author asserts, in his day it is necessary for him to issue the call yet again. The "Hebrews" to whom he writes must not harden their hearts as Israel did in the wilderness, or divine judgment will inexorably ensue. All this is based on the author's underlying conviction that, in Scripture, God still speaks today.[7] He speaks through the Law (in the present case, the books of Exodus and Numbers), and he speaks through the Psalms (here, Ps. 95). These exhortations are not merely dead words of sheer antiquarian interest, intended for those who want to know what happened in the past. As the author will shortly assert, God's Word is "living and active"—through his Word, God continues to address his people, issuing warnings to them not to repeat past failures of God's people. For, as a later sage remarked, those who fail to learn from history are doomed to repeat it.

This, then, following the initial warning in 2:1–3 not to "neglect such a great salvation," is the second warning passage in this letter: "Take care, brothers, lest there be in any of you an evil, unbelieving heart, leading you to fall away from the living God" (3:12). In 2:4, the author had drawn attention to the way in which "God also bore witness by signs and wonders and various miracles and by gifts of the Holy Spirit"; in the present case, the Scripture-literate

7. Cf. Graham Hughes, *Hebrews and Hermeneutics: The Epistle to the Hebrews as a New Testament Example of Biblical Interpretation*, SNTSMS 36 (Cambridge: Cambridge University Press, 1979), who examines the author's understanding of the OT as God's Word before the coming of Christ and assesses the implications of this examination for contemporary hermeneutics.

reader is aware that wilderness Israel, likewise, received striking manifestations of God's miracle-working power through the "signs and wonders" performed by Moses prior to and during the exodus.

This assumption will be made explicit in a later warning passage, 6:1–8, which contains numerous allusions to the same period in the history of God's people, Israel's wilderness wanderings during the exodus. Both in Moses's and in Jesus's days, God's people received striking manifestations of God's power; and at both junctures, people were urged not to harden their hearts but to be receptive toward God's power being at work in front of their very eyes. And just as the psalmist called people back to trust in God's power, so the author of Hebrews issues a renewed call for God's people not to harden their hearts in view of the miraculous signs and wonders performed by Jesus and the apostles in the early days of the Christian movement. The substructure of the author's theology is therefore *God's recurring revelation in salvation history and our continuing need to be receptive toward that revelation, lest divine judgment ensue.*

Following the warning against falling away from "the living God" and being hardened by "the deceitfulness of sin" (3:13), the author affirms that his readers "have come to share in Christ" *if* they hold firm to their initial "confidence" (*hypostasis*; translated "assurance" at 11:1 ESV). At this, the author reiterates the initial verse in the OT Psalms quote (3:15; cf. vv. 7–8; Ps. 95:7–8). He reinforces his warning by using the generation of Israelites in the wilderness as an illustration. Let's ponder this analogy in a bit more depth. The wilderness generation was part of God's people Israel. They were God's chosen people. They had been delivered from bondage in Egypt. They had witnessed the signs and wonders performed by Moses. They had seen abundant evidence of the miracle-working power of God and received tangible expressions of his faithful provision—both manna and water—throughout their forty years of wandering in the wilderness.

And yet, because of their sinful rebellion and their hardened hearts toward their covenant-keeping God, they had failed to enter the promised land! This was the basis for the psalmist's exhortation to his contemporaries, and this is likewise the analogy appropriated and invoked by the author of Hebrews to his audience. Unlike Israel, his readers must not fall away from the living God by yielding to their sinful, unbelieving hearts. While they are ethnically Israelites, they must exercise faith in God if they are to enter his rest. This phrase—"enter my rest"—is the note on which the Psalm 95 quote ends in 3:11 and is the point the author drives home in verses 18 and 19. He will continue to explore the vital implications of this scriptural analogy in chapter 4.

In terms of biblical theology, "rest" is a theme that surfaces repeatedly in Scripture.[8]

First, it occurs in the creation narrative when God "rests" on the final, seventh day of creation (Gen. 2:2–3; the Hebrew term is *shabbat*, "Sabbath").

Second, it recurs in the Ten Commandments, where the Israelites are commanded to "remember the Sabbath day to keep it holy" by emulating God's creation example and refraining from work on the seventh day of the week (Exod. 20:8–11; reiterated in Deut. 5:12–14; and cited at 4:4).

Third, the book of Joshua ends on a note of "rest" as well. While the unbelieving generation of Israelites, including Moses, failed to enter the land God had promised to Abraham, Joshua his successor embarked on the conquest of the promised land: "Thus the LORD gave to Israel all the land that he swore to give to their fathers. And they took possession of it, and they settled there. And the LORD gave them *rest* on every side" (Josh. 21:43–44). At the end of Joshua's life, the inspired writer could sum up that "the LORD had given *rest* to Israel from all their surrounding enemies" (Josh. 23:1). We read that "not one word of all the good promises that the LORD had made to the house of Israel failed; all came to pass" (Josh. 21:45). Joshua assembled all the tribes of Israel and charged them to worship the Lord only; he made a covenant with the Lord at Shechem; and the patriarch Joseph's bones were brought from Egypt and reburied on a plot of land he had bought there (Josh. 24; cf. Heb. 11:22).

And yet, as the subsequent history of Israel reveals, starting with the book of Judges, the rest Joshua brings is anything but permanent. During the period of the judges, "everyone did what was right in his own eyes" (Judg. 21:25), and even though God later (reluctantly) gave Israel a king (first Saul, then David, Solomon, and others), the nation fell into disobedience, sin, and even idolatry, and foreign nations such as the Philistines repeatedly subdued the Israelites. Eventually, both the northern kingdom (Israel) and the southern one (Judah) succumbed to the Assyrians and Babylonians, respectively, and were taken into exile.

Fourth, it is for this reason that the writer of Psalm 95 can exhort his fellow Israelites not to harden their hearts "today" (i.e., in his day) as the unbelieving

---

8. See esp. Jon C. Laansma, *"I Will Give You Rest": The Rest Motif in the New Testament with Special Reference to Mt. 11 and Heb. 3–4*, WUNT 2/98 (Tübingen: Mohr Siebeck, 1997), who offers the contours of a biblical theology of "rest," placing both passages referred to in the title against the background of two OT themes: rest as related to the promised land and as tied to the OT theme of Sabbath. Cf. Judith Hoch Wray, *Rest as a Theological Metaphor in the Epistle to the Hebrews and the Gospel of Truth: Early Christian Homiletics of Rest*, SBLDS 166 (Atlanta: Scholars Press, 1988).

wilderness generation did, and why he can say that Israel did not, in fact, enter the rest that God had promised and that the nation initially appeared to enter in the days of Joshua.

Fifth, there is therefore a rest that God's people can enter following the coming of Christ—namely, salvation from sin on account of Jesus's atoning sacrifice. This "rest" is more overtly spiritual and not primarily tied to physical territory.

Sixth, this rest will be fully consummated and entered into when believers die and go to heaven and live forever in God's presence in the eternal state.

A Biblical Theology of Rest in Six Stages

1. God's rest from his work at creation
2. The Sabbath command in the Ten Commandments
3. Deliverance from bondage (the exodus) and rest in the promised land
4. Rest in the psalmist's day (not enjoyed by Israel in Joshua's day)
5. Salvation rest from sin through faith in Jesus's atonement
6. Final rest in heaven enjoyed by all believers

The biblical theme of "rest," therefore, is not static but dynamic and involves a prophetic dimension and redemptive-historical sequence. As the author of Hebrews puts it, "the promise of entering his rest still stands" (4:1). It is not enough to *hear* "good news," whether in the days of OT Israel or in the days of the writer's Hebrew audience; the message must be received in *faith* (4:2): "For we who have believed enter that rest" (v. 3). Remarkably, the expression "enter" refers to the present time, though doubtless the full consummation of believers' rest awaits their final entrance into God's presence in heaven.

At this, the author continues to explain the implications of the OT psalmist's message in Psalm 95, reiterating, in midrashic (commentary) fashion, that "it remains for some to enter" God's rest (4:6). This is true even at the present day from the vantage point of the writer of Hebrews (v. 6), which is why the invitation to enter God's rest "today" still stands—even in our day (v. 7)! Because Joshua failed to give God's people permanent rest, it remains for them to enter God's rest, "for whoever has entered God's rest has also rested from his works as God did from his" (v. 10). In this way, we see the above-mentioned six stages of the biblical theme of "rest" intersect.

Wrapping up his argument based on Psalm 95, the author proceeds to urge his audience, "Let us therefore strive to enter that rest, so that no one may fall by the same sort of disobedience" (4:11). In other words, learn a lesson from the negative experience of the wilderness generation. Don't presume upon God's mercy or your ethnic covenant membership. There's no substitute for heartfelt trust in God. The phrase "let us strive" conveys a considerable sense of urgency and elsewhere means, literally, "hurry" or "make haste" (e.g., 2 Tim. 4:9, 21).

The ground of the author's urgent appeal is that God's Word is living and active (4:12). In context, this doubtless refers to Psalm 95, of which the author has just offered a skillful, extended exposition on the basis of the conviction that God's Word still speaks today. In the present instance, the relevance of Psalm 95—specifically, the warning against unbelief in God's good news of salvation in Christ—was not exhausted by its original application but extends to the author's contemporary readers.

By the same token, the inference seems reasonable that the words of the author of the book of Hebrews bear relevance not only for his original audience but, as part of inspired, canonical Scripture, also continue to speak to God's people even today. Whether Jewish or non-Jewish, those hearing God's Word today should not harden their hearts but should receive the good news of salvation and forgiveness of sins in Jesus and so enter into God's rest. Conversely, God's wrath continues to rest on those who fail to receive the biblical message by faith (cf. John 5:24).

Jesus as the Great High Priest and Mediator of a New Covenant (4:11–10:25)

Jesus's High Priesthood after the Order of Melchizedek Introduced (4:11–5:10)

As mentioned in the introduction above, 4:11–16 serves as a bridge or transition between the author's argument in 1:1–4:16—namely, that God's final revelation and salvation have found full expression in his Son, the Lord Jesus Christ—and his assertion that Jesus is superior to previous mediators in salvation history, whether angels, Moses, or Joshua, so that the salvation Jesus brought is infinitely greater than that brokered by the law and the sacrificial system. In the section that follows, which constitutes the bulk of the remainder of the letter, the author will elaborate on this second aspect in further detail. Jesus is greater than Aaron, as well, in his service as the great high priest and mediator of a new covenant.

Consequently, 4:14 introduces the topic—previously hinted at in the introduction (1:3) and briefly touched upon in 2:17–3:1—that will occupy the author for the next several chapters: the high priesthood of Jesus: "Since then we have a great high priest who has passed through the heavens, Jesus, the Son of God . . ." Toward the end of this lengthy literary unit, the author will similarly transition to the next section: "Therefore, brothers, since we have confidence to enter the holy places by the blood of Jesus . . ." (10:19). Here, the author highlights the importance of holding fast to one's "confession" (*homologia*), echoing 3:1, where Jesus was identified as "the apostle and high priest of our confession" (the term *homologia* recurs in 10:23).

The reason for the author's appeal ("For," *gar*) is in 4:15 identified as the fact that we have a high priest who is able "to sympathize with our weaknesses," one "who in every respect has been tempted as we are, yet without sin." This assertion, made by way of a double negative—"We do not have . . . who is unable . . . ," a literary device called litotes, in which a strong positive assertion is couched in the form of denial of a negative assertion—essentially reiterates the author's similar argument in 2:14–18.

The exhortation that readers "with confidence draw near to the throne of grace, that [they] may receive mercy and find grace to help in time of need" (4:16) uses "throne" as a euphemism for God and "of grace" as a descriptor of the *source* of grace—namely, God. Because God *is* a gracious God, he is able to *dispense* grace (notice the repeated use of "grace"). As does 2:17, 4:16 features a form of the word "mercy," indicating that God in Christ is mindful of our need for gentleness, kindness, and compassion. Jesus's incarnation and his faithful and merciful high priestly service exemplify God's identification with sinners in their frailty and weakness.

By analogy, the author then explains the role of a high priest. First, he is "chosen from among men": he is a fellow human being (5:1a). Second, and relatedly, he is "appointed to act on behalf of men in relation to God," serving as a representative of his fellow human beings in relation to God (5:1b). Third, he is appointed to "offer gifts and sacrifices for sins" (5:1c). That is, a high priest's office is related specifically to the human problem of sin and the need to atone for sin by various gifts and sacrifices to God. Fourth, the author points out, a high priest's own "weakness"—not only his humanity and frailty but also his sinfulness—is an integral part and limitation of his high priestly office and role of dealing gently with those who are "ignorant" or "wayward" (5:2). Because of his own sinfulness, every human high priest is obligated to offer sacrifices not only for the sins of others but first for his own sins (5:3). What's more, no high priest is self-appointed; rather, he is appointed by God, "just as Aaron was" (5:4).

Based on these foundational and introductory observations in 5:1–4, the author then shifts his focus onto Christ and the nature of his high priesthood as greater than Aaron's. First, he points out that Christ, likewise, was not self-appointed but appointed to his high priestly office by God, citing Psalm 2:7: "You are my Son, today I have begotten you." Remarkably, by quoting this passage, the author repeats his first OT citation in this letter, in 1:5 (see discussion above), where he had used it to assert Jesus's superiority over angels. Here, he quotes the same Psalms passage to support his assertion that Jesus was appointed to his high priestly role by God, whereby Jesus was appointed as God's unique "Son," and "begotten" refers to his divine appointment as high priest. Then—no doubt rather strikingly and surprisingly for the original readers—the author adds a second OT quotation from another psalm, Psalm 110:4, asserting that Jesus is "a priest forever after the order of Melchizedek" (Heb. 5:6).

Melchizedek is a mysterious and highly enigmatic OT figure mentioned in Genesis 14:18–20, where he is identified as "king of Salem" who "brought out bread and wine" and served as "a priest to God Most High." This Melchizedek, we are told, blessed Abraham, who "gave him a tenth of everything." Intriguingly, this figure is mentioned in the OT elsewhere only in Psalm 110:4, a psalm of David, where he writes, "The LORD has sworn an oath and will not change his mind: 'You are a priest forever after the order [*taxis*] of Melchizedek.'" In the OT, it is the tribe of Levi—constituting the Levitical priesthood—that is appointed to furnish priests for Israel (cf. Num. 8; Deut. 18:1–8). Yet here, the author astutely picks up on the reference to an *eternal* priesthood patterned not after the Levitical priesthood but after a different pattern or order—namely, that of Melchizedek, of whom little is known other than what is said about him in Genesis 14.

The author of Hebrews skillfully exploits this latitude regarding the characterization of an eternal Melchizedekian priesthood. Intriguingly, this author was not the first to notice this enigmatic OT figure and to attach a certain significance to his role. A century or more earlier, the Qumran community, in one of the famous Dead Sea Scrolls, the Melchizedek Scroll (11QMelch), similarly featured Melchizedek in its literature (albeit as an angel, not an exalted human priestly figure).[9] For now, the author briefly explicates this connection to Melchizedek in 5:7–10, which is followed by an excursus on elementary matters of the faith and another "warning passage" in 5:11–6:20, at the end of which he returns to the topic of Melchizedek and develops it in much greater length in 7:1–28.

---

9. Cf. Eric F. Mason, *"You Are a Priest Forever": Second Temple Jewish Messianism and the Priestly Christology of the Epistle to the Hebrews*, STDJ 74 (Leiden: Brill, 2008), who discusses the background to Hebrews' central theme of Jesus's priesthood in the Qumran literature describing an eschatological priest and a heavenly Melchizedek.

Structure of Hebrews 5:6–7:28

Hebrews	Topic
5:6–10	Jesus a high priest after the order of Melchizedek (introduction)
5:11–6:20	Excursus on elementary matters of the faith (warning passage)
7:1–28	Jesus a high priest after the order of Melchizedek (exposition)

After his citation of Psalms 2:7 and 110:4 in 5:5–6 with reference to Jesus's appointment as God's Son and as an eternal high priest after the order of Melchizedek, the author intriguingly expands briefly on how Jesus's sonship and high priestly role were exhibited during the days of his incarnate earthly life (vv. 7–10). The reference to Jesus offering up "prayers and supplications, with loud cries and tears" may be to his prayer on the eve of the crucifixion in the garden of Gethsemane (cf. Matt. 26:36–56). There, Jesus asked God to deliver him, if possible, but added, "Nevertheless, not my will, but yours, be done" (Luke 22:42).

While God would certainly have been able to save Jesus from death, he chose not to do so in his sovereign providence and according to his will, so that Jesus could serve as our sinless substitute and die for our salvation. Nevertheless, Jesus "was heard because of his reverence" (5:7) in that God raised him from the dead after three days (cf. 13:20). While being a son, Jesus "learned obedience through what he suffered" (5:8); that is, he exemplified obedience to the divine will when suffering as a (sinless) human being. Once "made perfect" in this way—not implying any previous lack of perfection—Jesus "became the source of eternal salvation" to those who obey him (v. 9), having been designated by God as a Melchizedekian high priest.

Warning against Unbelief and the Certainty of God's Promises (5:11–6:20)

In 5:11–6:12, the author enunciates the third "warning passage" in the book (cf. 2:1–4; 3:7–4:13). The phrase "About this," which introduces 5:11–14, refers to Christ's eternal priesthood after the order of Melchizedek. The author here notes that he has much to explain in this regard—and in fact, as mentioned, he will do so shortly in 7:1–28. This connection between verse 11 and the preceding verses is often obscured in English versions, many of which start a new unit in verse 11, even inserting a new paragraph heading. However, in the original Greek, the phrase "concerning which or whom" at the beginning of verse 11 tightly connects verse 10 with verse 11 and binds the entire chapter 5 together.

That said, in what follows the author proceeds to digress because, he says, his teaching concerning the nature of Christ's eternal priesthood is "hard to explain" because his readers have become "dull of hearing" and thus require once again instruction about "the basic principles [*stoicheia*; elsewhere in the NT also in Gal. 4:3, 9; Col. 2:8, 20; 2 Pet. 3:10, 12] of the oracles [or words, *logioi*] of God" (Heb. 5:12). In what follows, the author identifies such basic principles as those including the following: (1) repentance from dead works and faith in God; (2) instruction about washings; (3) the laying on of hands; (4) the resurrection of the dead; and (5) eternal judgment (6:1–2). This is an intriguing list of Christian essentials that is somewhat unique to the context and audience of the book of Hebrews.

Elaborating on his rebuke of (some in) his audience, the author writes that they need "milk, not solid food" (5:12), implying that many of his recipients are mere baby Christians at best. He notes parenthetically that "everyone who lives on milk is unskilled in the word of righteousness, since he is a child" (*nēpios*, 5:13; cf. 1 Cor. 3:1; 13:11; Gal. 4:1, 3; Eph. 4:14). Not only are many of the readers mere infants in the Lord; it appears that they've been believers long enough to be mature, yet, tragically, their growth is stunted, and their maturity level not in keeping with their years in the faith. This shows that there is a reasonable scriptural expectation for believers to grow spiritually, just as people are expected to exhibit certain physical characteristics in keeping with their natural age. Similarly, there are people in our churches today who may appear to be long-standing Christians but who in terms of spiritual maturity are mere infants because they haven't grown in the faith the way they should have.

The mark of spiritual maturity, according to the author, is that such individuals "have their powers of discernment trained by constant practice [*hexis*, unique in the NT] to distinguish good from evil" (5:14). "Unskilled in the word of righteousness . . . distinguish good from evil" suggests that the primary emphasis here is on morality—that is, living a righteous life in keeping with scriptural teaching. The word "trained" in Greek is the word *gymnazō*, from the word *gymnos*, "naked," because in Greco-Roman culture athletes trained essentially naked (cf. 12:11; 1 Tim. 4:7). Similarly, the readers are exhorted later in the letter: "Let us . . . lay aside every weight, and sin which clings so closely, and let us run with endurance the race that is set before us" (12:1). The book also includes several warnings against spiritual laziness and self-indulgence (e.g., 12:7–11). Christians are to work off spiritual baby fat and grow in obedience and spiritual discernment. As Paul exhorted Timothy, "Train yourself for godliness; for while bodily training is of some value, godliness is of value in every way, as it holds promise for the present life and also for the life to come" (1 Tim. 4:7–8). In his second letter to Timothy, Paul affirms that it is "the sacred writings" (in the original context, the Hebrew Scriptures—that is, the OT) that are "profitable . . . for training [*paideia*] in righteousness" (2 Tim. 3:15–17).

In a related passage, Paul set "natural" against "spiritual" persons (1 Cor. 2:6–16, esp. vv. 14–15) and lamented that he could not address the Corinthians as "spiritual people" but only as mere "infants in Christ" (1 Cor. 3:1). "I fed you with milk, not solid food," Paul wrote, "for you were not ready for it. And even now you are not yet ready" (1 Cor. 3:2). In the Corinthians' case, they adhered to worldly conceptions of leadership and flocked to flashy orators rather than grasping the cross-inspired nature of Christian servanthood. The present passage bears an uncanny resemblance to Paul's instruction to the Corinthians, suggesting that the author of the book of Hebrews (whoever he was) was likely familiar with Pauline instruction, or, alternatively, that both Paul and the author of Hebrews drew on a common analogy using "milk/solid food" metaphors in urging Christians on to greater maturity (but contrast 1 Pet. 2:1–2: "Like newborn infants, long for the pure spiritual milk, that by it you may grow up into salvation," where Peter uses the same metaphor in a positive sense).

The reference to "repentance from dead works and . . . faith toward God" in 6:1 clearly is to Christian conversion. Conversion, of course, is absolutely vital, as it marks the initial act of turning from one's sin and embracing the salvation God provided in and through Christ. Yet, the author asserts, believers must not stop there. Conversion is just the beginning and should be followed by conscious steps taken to align one's life increasingly with the commands of Scripture. There are some churches today where preachers only preach basic, simple, evangelistic sermons with little (if any) substantial instruction on how believers are to live the Christian life amid the complex set of circumstances in which they find themselves. The present passage suggests that while it's important to urge unbelievers to convert to Christ, it's also vital to provide instruction on how to grow in Christ. Thus, preachers should provide *both* instruction for unbelievers to convert (evangelism) *and* instruction for believers to grow in their faith (discipleship).

The author's listing of component parts of the "elementary doctrine of Christ" in verse 2—"washings, the laying on of hands, the resurrection of the dead, and eternal judgment"—as mentioned, is unique to the present letter and may allow us a glimpse into the specific circumstances of the audience of the epistle. It's hard to know exactly what the author has in mind here, though the remainder of the letter may provide certain clues when it addresses matters related to washings or eternal judgment (see further the discussion below). In any case, the author notes that talking about such things is *not* what he intends to do at this point. Rather, he urges his readers to "leave the elementary doctrine of Christ and go on to maturity" (*teleiotēs*, 6:1, elsewhere in the NT only in Col. 3:14).

Going to the heart of this third "warning passage," the author's burden is that "it is impossible, in the case of those who have once been enlightened, who have tasted the heavenly gift, and have shared in the Holy Spirit, and have tasted the goodness of the word of God and the powers of the age to come, and then have fallen away, to restore them again to repentance, since they are crucifying once again the Son of God" (6:4–6). This is one of the most written-about and controversial passages in the entire book of Hebrews, as many scholars have claimed that the author in the present passage suggests that believers can lose their salvation, thus nullifying the Christian doctrine of the eternal security of believers, which seems clearly taught in other NT passages (cf., e.g., John 10:28–29; 2 Tim. 1:12; 1 John 5:13).

Several observations need to be made. First, clearly, this is a very stern warning. In context, it appears that at least some in the congregation to which the letter is addressed (and possibly, to whom the original series of sermons was preached) were wavering, contemplating a retreat to the safe confines of Judaism—a protected religion (*religio licita*) in the Greco-Roman world—and potentially shrinking back from the persecution that awaited them if they stepped out in clear commitment to the crucified Christ. In 10:34, the author mentions that some of the recipients had "joyfully accepted the plundering of [their] property" as part of that persecution. In the immediate context, the author says, "Though we speak in this way, yet in your case, beloved, we feel sure of better things—things that belong to salvation" (6:9).

Second, a distinction should be made between the congregation as a whole and individuals within the congregation. It appears that the congregation as a whole was a Jewish Christian community, most likely in Rome, that had embraced Christianity—implied by repeated exhortations for the readers to "hold fast [their] confession" (4:14; 10:23)—but that there may have been certain individuals in that congregation who had second thoughts, some of whom may never have trusted Christ savingly in the first place. For example, the author later writes, "And let us consider how to stir up one another to love and good works, not neglecting to meet together, *as is the habit of some*" (10:24–25). Thus, it appears that some who had previously gathered with this Christian community had more recently drifted away because of the cost of following Christ in the surrounding culture. Consequently, the author warns such individuals against "drifting away" and calls all true believers to stand firm.

That said, it is possible, if not likely, that those addressed were unbelievers in the congregation who had never truly placed their faith in Christ. If so, warning passages such as the present one would not stand in conflict with the assurance of believers (eternal security) clearly taught elsewhere in the NT.[10] Consider, for example, the possible parallel of those who "went out from us" but "were not of us; for if they had been of us, they would have continued with us" in one of the Johannine congregations (1 John 2:19). In that context, the "elder" (the apostle John) argues that, for a while, some people in the church appeared to be believers, but that their eventual departure proved that they had never been true believers in the first place. In any case, it is anachronistic to read the passage in light of more recent theological systems such as Calvinism or Arminianism, which present differing accounts as to whether a person can lose their salvation.

Third, the interpretation of the present warning passage hinges to a considerable extent on the sustained analogy or typology (historical comparison) underlying the author's argument. Arguably, the backdrop is provided by the exodus generation of Israelites, who wandered in the wilderness and eventually were not allowed by God to enter the promised land because of their unbelief.[11] The author has already addressed this issue at some length by providing a detailed midrashic exposition of Psalm 95 in chapters 3 and 4 (see discussion above). In the present warning passage, the same typology is at work and forms the basis of the illustration.

- "Those who have once been enlightened" (6:4) in the first instance likely refers to wilderness Israel, who walked by the "pillar of cloud" by day and the "pillar of fire" by night during the exodus (cf. Exod. 13:21–22), and in the second instance (the readers of Hebrews) to those who have, at least externally, seen the light of the gospel in those around them.

- Those "who have tasted the heavenly gift" (6:4) in the first instance refers to the Israelites who ate the manna, the "bread from heaven" provided by God daily to sustain them during their wilderness wanderings (cf. Exodus 16), and in the second instance to those who have witnessed

10. Cf. Wayne Grudem, "Perseverance of the Saints: A Case Study from the Warning Passages in Hebrews," in *Still Sovereign*, ed. Thomas R. Schreiner and Bruce A. Ware (Grand Rapids: Baker Academic, 2000), 133–82, who argues that the warning passages in Hebrews are consistent with the Reformed doctrine of the perseverance of the saints. More broadly, see Thomas R. Schreiner, *Run to Win the Prize: Perseverance in the New Testament* (Wheaton: Crossway, 2010), who argues for a Reformed view of perseverance that regards the warning passages as prospective warnings and as the mechanism of preventing believers from "falling away."

11. See Dave Mathewson, "Reading Heb. 6:4–6 in Light of the Old Testament," *WTJ* 61 (1999): 209–25, who argues that 6:4–6 should be read in light of the OT depiction of Israel's wilderness generation.

manifestations of the power of the Holy Spirit in the lives of those around them as they associated with them in the congregation.

- Those who "have shared in the Holy Spirit" (6:4), likewise, may refer to witnessing the power of God in the congregation at large—whether wilderness Israel in the first instance or the congregation to which the letter of the Hebrews is addressed in the second instance—without having personally been regenerated (though commentators differ on this). Certainly, the Israelites saw many "signs and wonders" performed by God through Moses prior to and during the exodus. The audience of Hebrews, likewise, had experienced in their midst how "God also bore witness by signs and wonders and various miracles and by gifts of the Holy Spirit" (2:4).

- Similarly, "have tasted the goodness of the word of God and the powers of the age to come" (6:5) may refer to the "great salvation" to which the author previously referred, which "was declared at first by the Lord" and had subsequently been "attested to us by those who heard" (2:3–4).

In terms of the big picture, the author presents wilderness Israel as a typical instance of unbelief that kept people from "entering God's rest" (see chaps. 3–4 above)—the promised land—and he shows that their fate can still prove instructive in the NT era. This is the exact same point made by the apostle Paul in a similar context in his first letter to the Corinthians (cf. 1 Cor. 10:1–13). Some in the Jewish Christian congregation in Rome were in danger of failing to enter salvation and their eternal rest in heaven because of unbelief, and to those people the author addresses a series of stern warnings. Since they were Jewish, they would find the example from the Hebrew Scriptures regarding wilderness Israel's unbelief most instructive and (hopefully) compelling. Too often, our problem has been that we've read the warning passages in Hebrews through the eyes of contemporary theological debates rather than in light of their original context.

Those who have "fallen away" after witnessing such striking manifestations of divine power, as both the wilderness Israelites had done and the unbelieving Hebrews in the present congregation were in danger of doing, cannot be "restored to repentance." They are in effect "recrucifying" Christ and "holding him up to contempt" (6:6). Paul makes a similar point when he writes to the Galatians that some there have ordered circumcision "only in order that they may not be persecuted for the cross of Christ" (Gal. 6:12), while he was resolved to boast in nothing "except in the cross of our Lord Jesus Christ"

(Gal. 6:14; cf. 1 Cor. 1–2). If any of us reject the one and only true remedy for sin provided by God in Jesus Christ—the cross—there remains no other hope of salvation. We cannot choose our own preferred way of salvation but only accept or reject the one and only way God himself has provided. As Jesus asserted, "I am the way, and the truth, and the life; no one comes to the Father except through me" (John 14:6). By rejecting the cross—God's way of salvation, and also an expression of God's inestimable love for sinners—we are rejecting the most precious gift the world has ever known.

In 6:7–8, the author illustrates his point with an agricultural metaphor: land that drinks the life-giving rains but produces only "thorns and thistles" is "worthless and near to being cursed" and in the end will be burned (an ominous allusion to hell, the eternal destiny that awaits those who persist in their rejection of Christ until their deathbed).

In 6:9, however, the author swiftly pivots to the assertion that, while the warning is real and the danger severe, he is "sure of better things—things that belong to salvation" in the case of (the majority of) his readers. This doesn't mean that the preceding warning is hypothetical; it is real in the case of those in the congregation who, while witnessing the power of God in the lives of those around them, have never trusted Christ and now are in danger of falling away. Rather, the author asserts that while the warning pertains to a certain segment of individuals in the congregation, he is convinced it does not apply to the (bulk of the) congregation as a whole. He is writing to a Jewish Christian congregation with several unsaved individuals within it (at least originally), who have now started to drift away (cf. 10:24–25).

When we consider the first-century context (i.e., the early to mid-60s AD), we see that it was vital to clarify that to continue in Judaism was no longer a viable option for those who didn't find a crucified Christ palatable, whether for theological reasons (continuing adherence to the law, objection to a crucified Messiah, etc.) or pragmatic reasons (the threat or reality of persecution). The Bible doesn't teach a two-covenant model, where, after the coming of Christ, people are able to either (1) believe in Christ for salvation or (2) continue to observe the law. This point had to be made forcefully: there was no going back to before Christ came. Now that he had come, trusting in him was mandatory, not merely optional! This was one of several defining moments in the early Christian movement—along with the Judaizing controversy addressed in Galatians—moments in which inspired writers defended and clarified the gospel against misunderstanding or misrepresentation.

In the same hopeful vein, the author proceeds to acknowledge the work and the love the readers have shown "for his name in serving the saints, as

[they] still do" (6:10). He urges the readers "to show the same earnestness to have the full assurance of hope until the end" (6:11). The NT consistently teaches that true believers persevere until the end (a teaching sometimes referred to as the doctrine of the "perseverance of the saints").[12] The book of Hebrews clearly teaches this truth, as does the entirety of the NT. By contrast, there may be those who are attracted to the gospel for a little while only to later lose interest and fall away. This is illustrated poignantly by Jesus's parable of the sower and the soils (e.g., Mark 4:1–20) and is also reflected in the nuanced presentation of "believers" in John's Gospel, where the evangelist makes clear that not all "faith" is saving faith; only genuine faith saves, and this, by definition, proves to be faith that perseveres in following Christ and in abiding by his word (cf., e.g., John 8:31). Thus, the readers are exhorted not to be "sluggish" (cf. 12:12–13) but to be "imitators of those who through faith and patience inherit the promises" (6:12). Later in the letter, the author will parade a series of OT figures—a veritable "cloud of witnesses" (12:1)—who exhibited exemplary faith worthy of emulation by NT believers (chap. 11). Note, however, that there is a certain tension as to whether OT believers attained what God promised; in 6:15, it is said that Abraham "attained the promise," whereas elsewhere the author affirms that OT believers didn't yet attain the promise but rather will receive their inheritance in the future when God's promises will be fulfilled (11:8–11, 17, 39).

The phrase "inherit the promises" at the end of 6:12 serves as a segue to the next section, which commences with the author's statement, "For when God made a promise to Abraham" (v. 13). In this way, the author moves back from wilderness Israel at the time of the exodus to God's promises to Abraham several hundred years earlier. Specifically, the author cites the promise enunciated in Genesis 22:17, "I will surely bless you, and I will surely multiply your offspring," which reiterated God's earlier promises to Abraham (cf. Gen. 12:1–3; 15). In the present instance, the author's emphasis falls on the fact that God swore an oath to Abraham *by himself*, "since he had no one greater by whom to swear" (v. 13). Not only was this oath final (v. 16) as an expression of "the unchangeable character of his [God's] purpose" (v. 17); it gives believers strong encouragement and hope (vv. 18–19). At this, the author pivots once again, this time back to the topic of Christ's eternal high priesthood according to the order of Melchizedek, a subject he previously introduced but that he will now develop at much greater length (6:20; cf. 5:6–10).

12. See, e.g., Thomas R. Schreiner and Ardel B. Caneday, *The Race Set before Us: A Biblical Theology of Perseverance and Assurance* (Downers Grove, IL: InterVarsity, 2001).

Jesus's High Priesthood after the Order of Melchizedek Explained (7:1-28)

Even though the author previously talked about Melchizedek by way of citing Psalm 110:4, the only reference to this figure outside the Genesis narrative, he now introduces Melchizedek more formally by giving details from his brief appearance in Genesis in conjunction with Abraham (cf. Gen. 14:18–20). This Melchizedek was (1) the "king of Salem" and (2) "priest of Most High God," who (3) "met Abraham returning from the slaughter of the kings and blessed him" (Heb. 7:1). Also, (4) Abraham rendered a tithe to him (7:2). So much for the facts.

Now, by way of interpretation, the author derives the following noteworthy conclusions from the mention of Melchizedek in Genesis: (1) "Melchizedek," translated, means "king of righteousness"; (2) also, "king of Salem" means "king of peace" (7:2). (3) The author draws attention to the fact that, as far as the Genesis narrative is concerned, Melchizedek has neither father nor mother. Clearly, this does not mean this figure is divine or eternal, yet according to the author, the lack of genealogy allows a certain parallel between Jesus, the Son of God, who is eternal, and Melchizedek, who has "neither beginning of days nor end of life" (7:3). In this way, Melchizedek's priestly service is not limited or genealogically constrained as that of the Levites but constitutes an eternal priesthood. In the end, the author is concerned not so much with Melchizedek himself as with the type of priest he was and the nature of priesthood he represented.

Melchizedek in Genesis and Hebrews

Hebrews	Genesis Description	Interpretation by the Author of Hebrews
7:2	Melchizedek	King of righteousness
7:2	King of Salem	King of peace
7:3	No father or mother	Eternal priesthood

Featuring Jesus as high priest according to the order of Melchizedek allows the author to give Jesus the central position he deserves in the Jewish readers' Christian faith while at the same time contextualizing Jesus's role within their own frame of reference—that is, one where the OT sacrificial system and priesthood appear to have been central. Engaging this framework, the author makes the point that Jesus is indeed a priest—yet one of a higher order, following not the Levitical pattern but that of Melchizedek. This, in turn, follows plainly, as he goes to great pains to show, from OT teaching— namely, the references to Melchizedek in Genesis and Psalm 110. In fact, the latter passage already states that Melchizedek's priesthood is eternal; hence this is not a new notion set forth by the author but rather one developed further in view of the intervening coming of Christ.

The author's argument is thus biblically grounded and substantiated. Not only does the author connect the dots between Genesis and Psalm 110 and draw out what is implicit in Psalm 110; he also relates Psalm 110 to the Levitical priesthood and demonstrates the superiority of the Melchizedekian priesthood over the Levitical one. In this way, the author enjoins his readers to place their faith in Jesus—not only as the Messiah and Son of God but also as the eternal high priest whose ministry far exceeds that of the Levites with their tedious, repeated sacrificial offerings, a point upon which he will shortly elaborate.

After formally introducing Melchizedek and drawing several interpretive conclusions, the author continues to extol the greatness of this mysterious and unique figure (7:4). In a sense, Melchizedek was greater even than Abraham, the author argues, as the latter rendered tithes to the former! While the Levites descended from Abraham, Melchizedek did not; in fact, Melchizedek transcended human descent in that his genealogy was unknown. Not only did Abraham give tithes to Melchizedek; Melchizedek blessed Abraham. Now the one who *receives* tithes is greater than the one who *gives* them, and the one who *blesses* greater than the one who *is blessed*. In both cases, therefore, Melchizedek proves to be greater even than Abraham.

What's more, the author argues that it might even be said that through Abraham, the Levites—Abraham's descendants—rendered tithes to Melchizedek, proving that Melchizedek is greater than the Levites, as the latter rendered tithes to the former: "For he [Levi] was still in the loins of his ancestor when Melchizedek met him" (7:10)—a very Jewish, rabbinic style of arguing. Through this extended exegetical and theological argument, the author demonstrates that *Melchizedek was superior to both Abraham and Levi, proving that the Melchizedekian priesthood was superior to the Levitical one.* The entire OT sacrificial system is now rendered obsolete.

Continuing his argument, the author notes that if the Mosaic law—and thus the Levitical priesthood—had been able to achieve "perfection" (i.e., provide eternal salvation), there would have been no need for another priest "after the order of Melchizedek" to arise (7:11). Yet a change of priesthood also means "a change in the law" (7:12). Specifically, Jesus, the new high priest after the order of Melchizedek, was not from the tribe of Levi but from the tribe of Judah—which was not a priestly tribe (7:13–14). That said, the author takes his argument to a higher level when he argues—based on Psalm 110:4, a passage he quotes here for the second time (7:17; cf. 5:6)—that Jesus's priesthood was ultimately not a function of his physical descent from Judah but derived from his eternal existence. In this way, Jesus is like Melchizedek, who, at least as far as the scriptural account is concerned, had "neither beginning of days nor end of life" and in this regard resembled "the Son of God" (i.e., Jesus), who "continues a priest forever" (7:3). Negatively speaking, a stipulation of the law is thus set aside (i.e., the Levitical priesthood) due to its "weakness and uselessness" (v. 18; i.e., its ineffectiveness in permanently removing sin and effecting eternal redemption and forgiveness); positively, a better hope is introduced that enables God's people to draw near to God (7:19). In this way, forgiven sinners are able to "draw near to the throne of grace" to "receive mercy and find grace to help in time of need" (4:16).

At this mention of a "better hope," the author returns to the subject of God's guaranteeing the fulfillment of his promise by swearing an oath by himself, a subject the author previously introduced in 6:13–20. The reason why the author does this is based on Scripture—and in fact on the following portion of the previously quoted Psalm 110:4, which reads, "The Lord has sworn and will not change his mind, 'You are a priest forever'" (7:21). Again, remarkably, the author's argument is based on solid exegesis of previous Scripture—the authoritative Hebrew Scriptures, in this case a psalm that also has an important prophetic dimension, predicting the type of priesthood characterizing Jesus the Messiah and Son of God. Since the book is addressed to "Hebrews" (i.e., Jewish Christians, or at least Jews), the author's argument displays an impressive array of innerbiblical exegesis, connecting the Law (Genesis, Leviticus) with the Psalms (Pss. 2, 95, 110, et al.), which, as mentioned, have important prophetic entailments as well. The author introduces yet another powerful concept: Jesus serving as the "guarantor" (*engyos*, 7:22, a word used only here in the NT) of a "better covenant" (*diathēkē*, 7:22, the first of sixteen references to "covenant" in Hebrews). In context, the "better hope" referred to in 7:19 is based on the "better covenant" inaugurated by Jesus.

Yet another advantage of Jesus's priesthood—based on its eternal nature—is that whereas the Levitical priesthood consisted of a long line of priests "who were prevented by death from continuing in office," Jesus occupies the priesthood permanently because he exists eternally (7:23–24). For this reason, Jesus can "utterly" (*panteles*; elsewhere in the NT only in Luke 13:11) save those who draw near to him as he continually exercises his mediatorial office and intercedes for them. Not only this, but as an eternal high priest, Jesus has two additional advantages: (1) he need not offer sacrifices for himself, since he—unlike mortal, sinful priests—is sinless; (2) he offered the ultimate sacrifice—his own life given for sinners at the cross—once and for all and thus no longer has need to bring any more sacrifices (7:27). Jesus's sacrifice is sufficient for all time! Concluding the present section, the author ends the way he started (cf. 7:20): with a reference to God's oath, per Psalm 110:4, made subsequent to the law, an oath that appointed the Son to his eternal priestly office. He has "been made perfect forever" (7:28)—a phrase that harks back to the reference to "perfection" in 7:11. But this does not imply that there was ever a time when Jesus was less than perfect.[13]

Nature of Jesus's Priesthood according to the Book of Hebrews

Hebrews	Advantages of Jesus's Eternal High Priesthood
7:20–22, 28; cf. 6:13–20	Confirmed by God's oath
7:27	No need to bring sacrifices for himself
7:27	Sacrifice was once for all

Jesus the Mediator of a New Covenant (8:1–10:25)

The beginning of a new subsection in the author's argument is clearly indicated by the introductory transitional remark in 8:1—a reader's dream—where the author summarizes his point thus far and moves on to the next stage in his argument: "Now the point in what we are saying is this: . . ." Thus far, the burden of the author's argument has been primarily to establish the type of *priesthood* held by Jesus—an eternal priesthood after the order of Melchizedek that is not subject to the various limitations of the Levitical priesthood. Now, the author seeks to build on his previous argument regarding the nature of Jesus's priesthood and to develop the topic of the *covenant* Jesus inaugurated by virtue of his superior priesthood (chaps. 8–10 contain 13 references to *diathēkē*, "covenant," out of 16 in Hebrews and 33 in the entire NT, a very high concentration).[14]

This is the point the author makes in 8:6: "But as it is, Christ has obtained a ministry that is as much more excellent than the old as the covenant he mediates is better, since it is enacted on better promises." The superiority of the new covenant established by Jesus over the old covenant (the law) established by Moses—of which the Levitical sacrificial system was a part—occupies the entire unit spanning from 8:1 to 10:25. And whereas the author's argument for

13. See David G. Peterson, *Hebrews and Perfection: An Examination of the Concept of Perfection in the "Epistle to the Hebrews,"* SNTSMS 47 (Cambridge: Cambridge University Press, 1982).

14. Gareth L. Cockerill, "Structure and Interpretation in Hebrews 8:1–10:18: A Symphony in Three Movements," *BBR* 11 (2001): 179–201, argues that 8:1–10:18 is best understood as a "symphony" in three movements (8:1–13; 9:1–22; 9:23–10:18) on the themes of sanctuary, sacrifice, and covenant, with the themes of sanctuary and covenant supporting the central theme of sacrifice.

Jesus's eternal priesthood was primarily based on Psalm 110:4, his argument for the superiority of the new covenant is based on Jeremiah 31:31–34, the only OT passage where the exact phrase "new covenant" occurs (though the *concept* is found in other prophetic passages such as Ezek. 36:24–27 as well). In fact, references to Jeremiah 31 frame the entire section, as they are found in 8:8–12 (the longest sustained OT quotation in the entire NT) and 10:15–17.

Underlying the author's description of Jesus's priesthood is the notion that it is carried out in heaven and that the operation of earthly priests is a mere shadow of heavenly realities (see esp. 8:4–5). There is a certain affinity here between the thought of the author of Hebrews and Greek philosophy such as that espoused by Philo of Alexandria, Egypt (20 BC–AD 50), though it is doubtful that the author of Hebrews held a Platonic philosophy according to which the earth is a mere copy (*hypodeigma*; cf. 9:23; see also 4:11, which the ESV translates as "sort") and shadow (*skia*; cf. 10:1; Col. 2:17) of ultimate reality.[15] More likely, the author once again bases his argument on the OT Scriptures, which he cites in 8:5, referring to the time when God instructed Moses to build the tabernacle "according to the pattern" God had shown him on Mount Sinai (cf. Exod. 25:40).

At this, the author proceeds to move to the subject of the superiority of the new covenant, citing Jeremiah 31:31–34:

> Behold, the days are coming, declares the Lord,
>> when I will establish a *new covenant* with the house of Israel
> and with the house of Judah,
>> not like the covenant that I made with their fathers
>>> on the day when I took them by the hand to bring them out of
>>> the land of Egypt.
> For they did not continue in my covenant. (Heb. 8:8–9)

The Mosaic covenant—made on Mount Sinai with the people of Israel at the exodus from Egypt—was faulty (8:8; the verb is *memphomai*, "to find fault"; elsewhere in the NT only in Rom. 9:19), in part because God's people didn't

---

15. This is the view of many, if not most, scholars, though there is lively debate as to the extent of indebtedness. See the discussion in Ronald Williamson, *Philo and the Epistle to Hebrews*, ALGHJ (Leiden: Brill, 1970). Stefan Nordgaard Svendsen, *Allegory Transformed: The Appropriation of Philonic Hermeneutics in the Letter to the Hebrews*, WUNT 2/269 (Tübingen: Mohr Siebeck, 2009), argues in favor of Philonic influence. But see Scott D. Mackie, *Eschatology and Exhortation in the Epistle to the Hebrews*, WUNT 2/223 (Tübingen: Mohr Siebeck, 2007), who prefers Jewish apocalyptic eschatology to Platonic cosmology, contending that spatial concepts in Hebrews such as "the coming world" are best understood in terms of the "age to come"—that is, temporally.

continue in that covenant. In addition, it was merely *external* and thus unable to effect obedience to the Mosaic regulations. As Jeremiah (cited here) continues,

> For this is the covenant that I will make with the house of Israel
>   after those days, declares the Lord:
> I will put my laws into their minds,
>   and write them on their hearts,
> and I will be their God,
>   and they shall be my people.
> And they shall not teach, each one his neighbor
>   and each one his brother, saying, "Know the Lord,"
> for they shall all know me,
>   from the least of them to the greatest.
> For I will be merciful toward their iniquities,
>   and I will remember their sins no more. (Heb. 8:10–12)

The two aspects highlighted here by the prophet Jeremiah (who prophesied during Israel's Babylonian exile in the sixth century BC), in which the new covenant will be superior to the old, are these: (1) God's law will be written on people's hearts, internally (a reference to the indwelling Holy Spirit), and (2) God will remember people's sins no more—that is, the forgiveness mediated through the new covenant is *definitive* and *complete*. The author will

Figure 1.1
Old Testament tabernacle

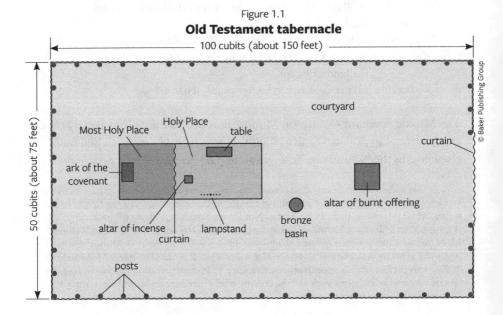

develop these points further in the following discussion. For now, he states the obvious—but nonetheless momentous—inference from Jeremiah's terminology: when referring to a future "new covenant," the prophet implies that the old covenant will at that time be rendered obsolete (8:13).

In chapter 9, the author rehearses details of the furniture found in the OT tabernacle (9:1–5). The "Holy Place" was furnished with a golden lampstand, a table, and the "bread of the Presence" (9:2; cf. Exod. 25:23–40; 37:17–24). Behind a curtain was the "Holy of Holies" (or "Most Holy Place"; Exod. 26:31–33), furnished with a golden altar of incense (Exod. 30:1–5; 37:25–29) and the "ark of the covenant" (Exod. 25:10–22), which contained an urn holding manna (food provided by God during the exodus), Aaron's rod, and the tablets of the covenant, and was topped by the cherubim (depictions of angels) and the mercy seat. After providing what may seem to be a rather detailed description, the author sums up, "Of these things we cannot now speak in detail" (9:5).

The reason why the author describes the tabernacle in some detail is that it represented the realm of operation of the OT Levitical priests. Although priests regularly entered the "Holy Place" to bring sacrifices, only the high priest entered the "Holy of Holies," and this only once a year (9:6–7). As the author observes, the fact that only the high priest was permitted to enter the "Holy of Holies" once a year indicates that direct access to God was unavailable to God's people in OT times. Against this backdrop, the author continually urges his readers to "draw near" to God now that Jesus, the great, eternal high priest, has opened a way by his once-for-all blood sacrifice on the cross. As the author makes clear, the presence of the first section, the "Holy Place," is "symbolic for the present age"—that is, shows that people are unable to enter God's presence directly apart from a mediator (9:9). In this interim stage in God's plan of salvation, priests had offered "gifts and sacrifices" that could not truly atone for sin but were performed only provisionally, "until the time of reformation" (*diorthōsis*, from the root *ortho-*, "straight," 9:10; not elsewhere in the NT).

All this changed with the coming of Christ. Hebrews 9:11–12 tells us that Jesus appeared "through the greater and more perfect tent" (referring to his body; cf. John 1:14, where the Greek word translated as "dwelt" means literally "tabernacled" or "tented"). He did not appear through the blood of goats and calves but through his own blood (this phrase appears toward the beginning of the sentence in the original Greek, for emphasis). When he came, as a high priest "of the good things that have come" (a vague expression, elaborated on below), he entered the holy places (plural) once and for all, securing an eternal redemption (*lytrōsis*, 9:12; elsewhere in the NT only in Luke 1:68; 2:38). The momentous declaration made in 9:11–12—that Jesus entered the holy places once for all to secure an eternal redemption—constitutes the climax thus far of the section that began in 8:1, where the author turned from Jesus's high priesthood to the covenant he instituted, and related the two themes to each other.

The declaration that Jesus secured an eternal redemption stands in stark contrast to the tedious nature of the OT priestly system with its sacrifices and offerings, which were many but nonetheless could never offer abiding redemption. Imagine what it would have been like to live in those days when sacrifices constantly needed to be brought, yet people always continued to sin and thus continually needed to bring ever more sacrifices, which nonetheless could never permanently atone for sin—a veritable cycle of futility! By contrast, now that Jesus has offered himself once for all, direct access to God has been opened and believers can draw near to God—and there is no more need for any sacrifices to be brought, because Jesus's sacrifice has been accepted by God once for all! This truly is the "great exchange," an expression of amazing grace and mercy on God's part toward otherwise hell-bound sinners.

Verses 13–14 simply draw out the distinction between the two kinds of blood in verse 12—the blood of goats and calves and Jesus's own blood. In a from-the-lesser-to-the-greater argument, the author asserts that if the former provided *temporary* "purification of the flesh," "how much more" will Christ's blood—an unblemished offering of himself "through the eternal Spirit"—purify believers' consciences *permanently*! In this way, they will be able to repent from "dead works" (part of the "elementary doctrine" of the Christian faith mentioned in 6:1) and serve the living God. Together with the reference to the Spirit in 10:29, the present passage constitutes a highlight in the author's theology of the Holy Spirit, whose work is linked with God's active speaking in and through Scripture (e.g., 9:8) and here closely connected with the atoning work of Christ on the cross.[16]

At this, the author picks up the topic of the new covenant, which has previously taken up most of chapter 8, where the author spoke of a "better" covenant (8:6) and referred extensively to the "new covenant" passage in the book of Jeremiah (8:8–12; cf. Jer. 31:31–34). Essentially, 9:1–14 thus serves as a plank in the author's argument that Jesus, the eternal high priest, came to inaugurate a new, better covenant—an argument he supports by contrasting Jesus's high priestly ministry with that of the OT Levitical priests. The opening phrase in verse 15, which can be translated "And for this reason" (*Kai dia touto*), drives home this point from the chain of argument in 9:1–14. The assertion that Christ is the "mediator" of a new covenant picks up on

---

16. On the pneumatology of the book of Hebrews, see Gregg R. Allison and Andreas J. Köstenberger, *The Holy Spirit*, Theology for the People of God (Nashville: B&H Academic, 2020).

the use of the same word, *mesitēs*, in 8:6 (elsewhere in the NT only in 12:24; Gal. 3:19–20; 1 Tim. 2:5). In 1 Timothy 2:5–6, Paul states emphatically that "there is one God, and there is one mediator between God and men, the man Christ Jesus, who gave himself as a ransom for all." Hebrews 12:24 reiterates that Jesus is "the mediator of a new covenant," whose "sprinkled blood . . . speaks a better word than the blood of Abel."

The concept of Christ as a unique mediator between God and humanity follows inexorably from the author's introduction to the book, where he contrasted Jesus with a multiplicity of previous mediators, whether OT prophets or angelic messengers. Although these previous figures had a genuine mediating function, Jesus is the mediator par excellence. The specific way in which Jesus exercised his mediatorial role was as an eternal high priest, and the specific offering he brought as a high priest was the sacrifice of his own blood. This blood, in turn, "speaks a better word"—Jesus's blood *speaks* (just as Abel is later said to "still speak," 11:4); that is, his sacrifice is effective in securing eternal redemption and is of abiding relevance for any who would be the beneficiaries of Jesus's substitutionary, high priestly, atoning death on the cross.

Likewise, Moses (through whom God gave the law), Joshua (who led Israel into the promised land), and the Levitical priests (who administered the OT sacrificial system) all had a genuine mediatorial role between God and his people in OT times, but their role, too, has been utterly eclipsed by the one mediator par excellence, Jesus Christ. Jesus's once-for-all sacrifice on the cross dwarfs all previous mediatorial acts by comparison and renders them merely preliminary to and anticipatory of what he accomplished. This is the grounds on which the author repeatedly urges his readers to trust in Christ and what he did for them on the cross (though, interestingly, the word "cross," *stauros*, occurs only once in Hebrews, at 12:2). To trust in the OT law and the OT sacrificial system, now that Christ has come and sacrificed himself, is woefully inadequate and utterly inexcusable. In fact, such neglect amounts to a rejection of Christ and his work and thus a "re-crucifixion" of Christ, which will result in the most severe consequences for any person who persists in unbelief (cf. 6:4–6).

Previous Mediators between God and Humanity Prior to Christ

Passage in Hebrews	Previous Intermediaries	Mediatorial Role
1:1	OT prophets	Mediated God's Word to his people
2:2; cf. 1:7–14; 2:5	Angels	Mediated God's law
3:5	Moses	Mediated God's law and led God's people
4:8	Joshua	Led God's people into the promised land
5:1–4; 7:11	Aaron, Levites	Brought sacrifices and offerings

The result of Jesus's mediation of a new covenant is that "those who are called may receive the promised eternal inheritance" (9:15a). Jesus's death redeems believers "from the transgressions committed under the first covenant" (9:15b)—that is, the Mosaic covenant, the law given at Sinai, including the Levitical priestly sacrificial system. In what follows, the author asserts the principle that even under the first covenant, "almost everything is purified with blood, and without the shedding of blood there is no forgiveness of sins" (9:22; cf. 9:18). Citing Leviticus 14:4 and Exodus 24:8, "This is the blood of the covenant that God commanded you," the author describes how Moses took the blood of sacrificial animals and sprinkled it, along with water, scarlet wool, and hyssop, on both the book of the law and the people, as well as on the tabernacle and the vessels used in worship (9:19–21). All this illustrates the principle of "life through death"—in the case of the OT sacrificial system, people lived on account of the death of a sacrificial animal.

Today, many find God's way of salvation involving the sacrifice of his one and only Son offensive. They contend that Jesus's death on the cross is in effect child sacrifice, the vestige of a primitive, antiquated religion that offends modern sensibilities. At the heart of Christian religion, these detractors contend, is the notion of God sending his Son to be sacrificed for others, which they reject as unacceptable for enlightened minds.[17] To this, the author of Hebrews would respond that from the first pages of Scripture and from the dawn of human history onward, the principle of "life through death (of another)" has a long and powerful pedigree. While this principle may militate against human rationality, it is deeply ingrained in the way in which a holy God and his justice are revulsed by human sin and rebellion. Rebellion against a holy, just God cannot simply be swept under the rug, nor can it simply be forgiven and forgotten without a proper transaction squarely facing and remedying the offense. As Paul explains in the book of Romans,

> But now [through the coming of Christ] the righteousness of God has been manifested apart from the law, although the Law and the Prophets bear witness to it—the righteousness of God through faith in Jesus Christ for all who believe. For there is no distinction: for all have sinned and fall short of the glory of God, and are justified by his grace as a gift, through the redemption that is

---

17. See, e.g., Steve Chalke, *The Lost Message of Jesus* (Grand Rapids: Zondervan, 2004), who says penal substitution is "a form of cosmic child abuse" (9). Those who are critical of and reject a penal substitutionary atonement (but may not use Chalke's exact language) include Joel B. Green and Mark D. Baker, *Recovering the Scandal of the Cross: Atonement in New Testament and Contemporary Contexts* (Downers Grove, IL: IVP Academic, 2000); J. Denney Weaver, *The Nonviolent Atonement*, 2nd ed. (Grand Rapids: Eerdmans, 2011); and John Goldingay, ed., *Atonement Today* (London: SPCK, 1995).

in Christ Jesus, whom God put forward as a propitiation by his blood, to be received by faith. This was to show God's righteousness, because in his divine forbearance he had passed over former sins. It was to show his righteousness at the present time, so that he might be *just* and the *justifier* of the one who has faith in Jesus. (Rom. 3:21–26; see also 1 Cor. 1–2)

The only way in which a holy God can forgive sins is through the death and shed blood of a sinless substitute.

In 9:23, the author returns to the topic of contrasting earthly copies with heavenly realities, a topic he introduced in 8:5–7. The underlying premise was that God showed Moses on Mount Sinai how to construct the tabernacle as a reflection of the heavenly sanctuary (cf. Exod. 25:40). Thus, the Levitical priests had an earthly priesthood, whereas Jesus exercises a heavenly one. Through his death, the author contends, Jesus entered into heaven itself in order to appear in God's presence on behalf of believers (9:24)! Whereas the high priest entered the earthly *copy* of the heavenly sanctuary—the "Holy of Holies"—once a year (though people themselves could never enter) with blood not his own, Jesus entered heaven itself by virtue of his own shed blood, yet he did so not repeatedly but only once (9:24–26).

The definitive nature of Jesus's vicarious sacrifice is underscored by the fact that he "appeared once for all at the end of the ages to put away sin by the sacrifice of himself" (9:26; cf. 1:2: "in these last days"). As the author asserted at the inception of his letter, "After making purification for sins, he [Jesus] sat down at the right hand of the Majesty on high" (1:3). The cross-work is complete! As the crucified Jesus says in John's Gospel, "It is finished" (*tetelestai*; John 19:30). The cross stood at the heart of Jesus's mission, so that Jesus could report to the Father toward the end of his days on earth, "I glorified you on earth, having accomplished the work you gave me to do" (John 17:4). While the work of Levitical priests was never finished, and needed to be repeated regularly and frequently, always remaining provisional and anticipatory of Jesus's own work "at the end of the ages," Jesus's work was once for all—done.

It is hard to exaggerate the contrast between the OT sacrificial system administered by the Levites and the new covenant ministry inaugurated by Jesus's blood. In conjunction with this, the author announces that at the final judgment, Jesus will appear a second time, "not to deal with sin"—his purpose at his first coming—"but to save those who are eagerly waiting for him" (9:27–28). And just as Jesus's first coming was definitive ("once for all"), so his second coming will be definitive as well: he will save those who have trusted in him and (the author implies) judge those who failed to put their trust in the finished work of Christ. For "it is appointed for man to die once, and after that comes judgment" (9:27). This is a sobering reality that every reader of this book—both ancient and modern—needs to face with utmost seriousness. The decision to trust Christ is made in this life; once a person dies, it is too late, and only judgment awaits that person—in case of unbelief, a Christless eternity apart from God's presence.

Figure 1.2

Jesus's activity in history (Hebrews 1:2; 9:26–28)

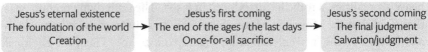

Jesus's eternal existence	Jesus's first coming	Jesus's second coming
The foundation of the world →	The end of the ages / the last days →	The final judgment
Creation	Once-for-all sacrifice	Salvation/judgment

The following paragraph (10:1–4) reiterates the author's argument that the law—which prescribes the Levitical system—is but a shadow (cf. 8:5) of "the good things to come" (i.e., eternal redemption in Christ; cf. 9:11: "But when Christ appeared as a high priest of the good things *that have come*"). If the sacrifices and offerings under the Levitical system had been efficacious, the author argues, why did the people on behalf of whom these sacrifices were brought continue to be conscious of their sin (10:2)? Why did they not truly feel forgiven? Why did lingering feelings of guilt and shame persist? In truth, the fact that these sacrifices must be brought annually furnished a continual reminder of people's experience of the reality of sin in their lives and the need for ongoing atonement (10:3). Like ancient Sisyphus in Greek mythology, who, in an exercise in futility, rolled a massive stone to the top of a mountain only to see it roll back down over and over again, ancient worshipers knew deep down inside that the Levitical system was ultimately inadequate: "For it is impossible for the blood of bulls and goats to take away sins" (10:4). Now we know that it must be a sinless human substitute—Jesus the Son of God, the God-man—who must shed his blood for the people, as the great, eternal high priest who performs his sacrifice once for all and then enters heaven to represent us before God and to open access to God for those who trust in him.

In support of his argument, the author adduces another psalm, Psalm 40:7–9, which prophetically describes the first coming of Christ: "Sacrifices and offerings you have not desired, but *a body* have you prepared for me. . . . Then I said, 'Behold, I have come to do your will, O God, as it is written of me in the scroll of the book'" (Heb. 10:5–7). As the author explains, the sacrifices and offerings mentioned at the onset of the quotation were offerings stipulated by the Mosaic law as part of the Levitical system. Christ's coming into the world in order to do God's will consisted of "the offering of the body of Jesus Christ once for all" (10:11). The eternal high priest offered his own body to God for his people!

This self-giving act, in turn, also effected the sanctification (or setting apart for holy service) of those who trust in Christ. The author previously asserted that the blood of Christ was to purify believers' "conscience from dead works to serve the living God" (9:14; cf. v. 13: "sanctify" [*hagiazō*]). Similarly, he asserts here that by God's will believers "have been sanctified [*hagiazō*] through the offering of the body of Jesus Christ once for all" (10:10). Thus, not only did the blood of Christ effect eternal redemption (9:12); it also effected spiritual sanctification—the setting apart of believers from sin for God's holy use. As the author affirms in the only previous reference to sanctification in the letter, "For he who sanctifies and those who are sanctified all have one source" (2:11; cf. 10:14, 29; 13:12)—namely, God.

This definitive, once-for-all setting apart would have been impossible under the old system; it has now been accomplished through the once-for-all sacrificial offering of Christ's body. In this context, it should be noted that Scripture attests to sanctification both as a definitive event that occurred in the *past* and as an ongoing *process*—Christian growth in maturity—that is predicated upon initial sanctification at conversion.[18] Just as the initial setting apart was by grace and was appropriated by faith, so progressive sanctification is by grace and is appropriated by faith as well. Thus, it was God's purpose in and through the first coming of Christ not only to redeem a people for himself but also to set this people apart for his holy service.

Concluding his argument in this main section (8:1–10:18), the author reiterates that while the Levitical priestly service could never permanently remove sin (10:11), Christ's once-for-all sacrifice did (10:12a). After this sacrifice, Jesus—his resurrection is implied—sat down at God's right hand (10:12b; cf. 1:3), waiting until the time at which his enemies will be made a footstool for his feet (a metaphor for the subduing of all spiritual forces opposed to God). This latter reference involves another allusion to Psalm 110:1, which the author has repeatedly cited in his previous argument, most notably in support of his argument that Jesus's eternal priesthood is patterned after that of Melchizedek (5:6; cf. 1:3, 13; Ps. 110:4).

The reference to believers' sanctification in 10:14 reiterates the statement in 10:10 already discussed above. Fittingly, this portion of the letter concludes with a partial quote of the passage from Jeremiah that the author quoted at

18. See on this David Peterson, *Possessed by God: A New Testament Theology of Sanctification and Holiness*, NSBT 1 (Grand Rapids: Eerdmans, 1995); Andreas J. Köstenberger, *Excellence: The Character of God and the Pursuit of Scholarly Virtue* (Wheaton: Crossway, 2011), chap. 3.

greater length at the beginning of this unit (10:15–16; cf. 8:8–12). The portion of Jeremiah cited here pertains to the end-time covenant the Lord will make with his people—now fulfilled in Christ—by which God will write his law onto people's hearts and minds and by which he will forgive them for all their sins. And where there is forgiveness, the author concludes compellingly, there is no more need for any offerings for sin (10:18).

Jesus, Who Ran the Race before Us and Suffered Outside the Camp (10:19–13:16)

Have Confidence in the Blood of Jesus; Don't Throw Away Your Confidence (10:19–39)

As mentioned in the introduction, 10:19–25 serves as a transitional statement between the previous section, dealing with the topic of Jesus as the great high priest and mediator of a new covenant (4:11–10:25), and the section that follows, concerning Jesus as one who ran the race before us and suffered outside the camp (10:19–13:16). The section is introduced by the phrase "Therefore, brothers" and directly addresses the readers by way of multiple exhortations on the basis of the sustained argument set forth by the author in the letter thus far, and in particular the section that this set of exhortations brings to a close. The basis on which the exhortations are given is twofold: "Since we have confidence to enter the holy places by the blood of Jesus, by the new and living way that he opened for us through the curtain, that is, through his flesh, and since we have a great priest over the house of God . . ." (10:19–21). That is, (1) Jesus provided direct access to God through sacrificing his body and shedding his blood for believers; and (2) Jesus holds a continual—eternal—high priestly office; that is, his office was not merely a matter of the past but is a continuing reality! In the original, the basic assertion "since we have" has two objects: (1) confidence to enter "the holy places" (i.e., God's presence) through Christ and (2) a great high priest over God's house (i.e., Christ). Our confidence is in Christ himself and in his role as mediator as well as in the once-for-all sacrifice he brought to God on our behalf.

On the basis of this twofold confidence, the author issues three exhortations:

1. "Let us draw near with a true heart in full assurance of faith." (10:22)
2. "Let us hold fast the confession of our hope without wavering." (10:23)
3. "Let us consider how to stir up one another to love and good works." (10:24)

Writing to the Hebrews—but with implications for all believers, Jew and non-Jew alike—the author writes that believers now have unprecedented access to God, a "new and living way" (10:20; resembling, one might add, only that enjoyed by Adam and Eve prior to the fall). They are therefore urged to take advantage of this access and to draw near to God "with . . . hearts sprinkled clean from an evil conscience and . . . bodies washed with pure water" (10:22). Depicted in sacrificial terms, this sprinkling and washing metaphorically refers to the atoning work and resulting cleansing from sin provided by Christ's death on the cross. Believers are to hold fast unwaveringly to their confession of Christ, since God, who issued the promise, is faithful (10:23). And, as an expression of this active adherence to their confession, believers are to live in close and loving community with one another rather than neglecting to meet, "as is the habit of some" (10:24–25). In context, this doubtless refers to some in the congregation to which the author addresses his letter who had drawn back from their association with Christ and his people due to the threat or reality of persecution. These Jews—possibly (some of them) former priests (given the unique prominence of priestly themes in this letter; see the introduction)—had apparently retreated to their Jewish system of beliefs (Judaism) and dissociated from both Christ and the assembly of believers. As discussed, throughout the letter we find several passages addressed to these individuals, warning them not to reject Christ and his work on their behalf, or terrible consequences would await, as they saw "the Day [of judgment] drawing near" (10:25).

At this, the author launches yet another severe warning (10:26–31). Continuing willfully in sin after receiving knowledge of the truth is deeply problematic, as there is no longer any sacrifice for sins; all that remains is the fearful expectation of divine judgment (10:26–27; cf. 9:27). While God is a God of love, he is also a God of righteousness and justice, and those who disregard his remedy for sin will have to bear the consequences. Thus, the author uses the prospect of divine judgment not as a scare tactic but as a motivating device to call people to repentance while there is still time—for the time will come when it will be too late.

Under the Mosaic law, the person who set aside the law was subject to death by the testimony of two or three witnesses (Deut. 17:6; cf. 19:15). The author uses very strong words in the following from-the-lesser-to-the-greater argument: "How much worse punishment, do you think, will be deserved by the one who has trampled underfoot the Son of God, and has profaned the blood of the covenant by which he was sanctified, and has outraged the Spirit of grace?" (10:29). It is jarring to think of anyone "trampling underfoot" (*katapateō*; cf. Matt. 5:13; 7:6; Luke 8:5; 12:1) the Son of God, just as it is unsettling to conceive of anyone "profaning" (literally, "consider common") the blood of the new covenant or "outraging" (*enybrizō*, unique in the NT) the "Spirit of grace" (i.e., the Holy Spirit, the Spirit who is the purveyor of divine grace).

The Spirit is outraged when Christ is trampled underfoot and the blood of the new covenant is considered of no consequence, because it is "through the eternal Spirit" that Christ "offered himself without blemish to God" (9:14). So close is the identification between Christ and the Spirit that when Christ is rejected, the Spirit is outraged! In support, the author cites OT Scripture according to which God will exact vengeance and judge his people (10:30; cf. Deut. 32:35–36). Indeed, it is a terrifying prospect "to fall into the hands of the living God" when one's sins are not covered by the blood of Christ (10:31). This is a powerful reminder of the holiness and righteousness of God in an age when the fear of God has largely vanished and many speak of God as "the man upstairs" or in similar terms and make light of God's authority and eternal judgment.

As in 6:9, the author pivots from a warning passage addressed to unbelievers in the congregation and turns to the congregation as a whole, made up mostly of believers: "But recall the former days . . ." (10:32). In those days after the gospel was initially proclaimed ("you were enlightened"), the congregation was subjected to suffering, whether directly or indirectly (10:33); they had mercy on those who were imprisoned for their faith, and they joyfully endured the confiscation of their property, knowing no one could take away their eternal inheritance (10:34), remarks that foreshadow the contents of chapter 11 (see below).

Apparently, this congregation that had started out so well had now weakened in its resolve to stand firm in their faith and witness and stood in need of encouragement "not [to] throw away [their] confidence, which has a great reward" (10:35); they were in "need of endurance" (10:36). The word used here for "confidence" (*parrēsia*) echoes the author's words in the opening exhortation of this literary unit (10:19), where he started by saying, "Therefore, brothers, since we have confidence [*parrēsia*] to enter the holy places [interestingly, here in the plural] by the blood of Jesus" (the word occurs elsewhere in Hebrews 3:6 and 4:16). Believers have every reason for confidence—not in themselves but in what Christ has done for them on the cross. Yet they must place their confidence in Christ and in the efficacy of his blood to atone for sin and, when facing persecution, they must not throw away this confidence but cling to it, in light of God's faithfulness to keep his promises (10:23) and the great reward that awaits them (10:35).

To drive home this encouragement and to ground it scripturally, the author cites Habakkuk 2:3–4, which asserts that God will come without delay in just "a little while" and that the "righteous one shall live by faith," yet God has no pleasure in the one who "shrinks back" (Heb. 10:37–38). The same passage in Habakkuk plays a prominent role in Paul's demonstration of God's righteousness in Christ in the letter to the Romans (1:16–17) and also in Galatians (3:11). While it may be a natural response to flinch when facing persecution, true believers ought to stiffen their resolve to follow the crucified and risen Christ when their faith is challenged and tested. Concluding this section, the author asserts that "we are not of those who shrink back and are destroyed, but of those who have faith and preserve their souls" (10:39). While persecution may lead to earthly loss, holding on to one's faith will lead to heavenly reward and the "preservation" (*peripoiēsis*, frequently rendered "possession"; cf. Eph. 1:14; 1 Thess. 5:9; 2 Thess. 2:14; 1 Pet. 2:9) of one's soul.[19]

The "Hall of Faith" (11:1–40)

At this, the author discusses at length those who in OT times had strong faith in God. These inspiring examples, he hopes, will encourage the Hebrews to whom the letter is addressed not to throw away their confidence but rather to persevere in their faith. It is remarkable that here OT believers are held up as examples for NT ones. This shows that, in essence, faith in God is the same in both Testaments (just as God, and Jesus Christ, are the same yesterday, today, and forever; cf. 13:8). Such faith has as its object the faithful, living God, who keeps his promises in Christ. In what follows, the author surveys the OT story line from creation to the exodus and the conquest of the promised land (11:1–31) and then more swiftly surveys the remainder of the OT period in the rest of the chapter (11:32–38) before transitioning to an exhortation to look "to Jesus, the founder and perfecter of our faith" (12:2).

Along the way, using the recurring phrase "By faith," sometimes multiple times when discussing one single character (e.g., Abraham: 11:8, 9; Moses: 11:23, 24, 27, 28), the author discusses Abel (11:4), Enoch (11:5), Noah (11:7), Abraham (11:8–19, with 11:13–16 providing a summary statement pertaining to all the OT characters mentioned up to this point), Sarah (11:11), Isaac (11:20), Jacob (11:21), Joseph (11:22), Moses (11:23–28), the people of Israel crossing the Red Sea (11:29), the conquest of Jericho (11:30), and Rahab (11:31). Clearly, the major emphasis falls on Abraham (twelve verses, though some of these, as mentioned, are broader in scope) and Moses (six verses), to whom eighteen out of thirty-one verses (or almost two-thirds of the

---

19. Cf. the "preservation theme" in the letters to Timothy and Titus, on which see Andreas J. Köstenberger, *Commentary on 1–2 Timothy and Titus*, BTCP (Nashville: B&H Academic, 2017), 444–45.

discussion) are devoted. Abraham and Moses and these other figures thus become prototypes, paradigms, and precursors of NT faith, a faith that is directed toward the God who promised and toward heavenly rather than earthly realities.

The "Hall of Faith" in Hebrews 11

Chap. 11	OT Event or Character	By Faith
3	Creation	Understand that universe was created by Word of God
4	Abel	Offered more acceptable sacrifice than Cain
5	Enoch	Taken up because he pleased God
7	Noah	Constructed an ark to save his household
8–19	Abraham	Obeyed when called; went to promised land; lived in tents; offered up Isaac; believed God could raise him back up
11	Sarah	Received power to conceive when past age of childbearing
20	Isaac	Invoked future blessings on sons Jacob and Esau
21	Jacob	Blessed sons of Joseph on his deathbed
22	Joseph	Anticipated exodus on deathbed, gave directions about bones
23–28	Moses	Hidden by parents at birth; identified with God's people; left Egypt; kept the Passover
29	People of Israel	Crossed the Red Sea
30	Joshua (implied)	Walls of Jericho fell
31	Rahab	Welcomed the spies
32	Gideon, Barak, Samson, Jephthah, David, Samuel and the prophets, etc.	Conquered kingdoms; enforced justice; obtained promises; shut lions' mouths; extinguished fires; escaped the sword; strong in weakness; mighty in war; defeated armies; received their dead by resurrection; endured torture, flogging, imprisonment; stoned; sawn in two; killed with the sword; destitute, afflicted, mistreated

Interestingly, the word "faith" (*pistis*) has only rarely been used up to now. Following three earlier references (4:2; 6:1, 12), the word is used three times toward the end of chapter 10 in anticipation of the extensive discussion of faith in chapter 11 (10:22, 38, 39). Similar to the way in which Habakkuk 2:3–4 proves foundational in the book of Romans (cf. 1:16–17), the passage serves as the OT foundation for the "Hall of Faith" exhibited in chapter 11, as it is quoted at the outset of the chapter (though this is easy to miss due to the chapter division). On the other end of the "faith chapter," the word is found only in 12:2 (with reference to Jesus) and one last time in 13:7 (with reference to imitating the faith of the congregation's leaders). The word occurs a couple of dozen times in chapter 11, often in the form of the introductory phrase "By faith" (*Pistei*).

The chapter opens with a remarkable definition of faith as "the assurance of things hoped for" and "the conviction of things not [yet] seen" (11:1). The word translated "assurance" literally means "substance" (*hypostasis*), which makes the important point that while faith itself is immaterial, in the spiritual realm faith is substantive as the *essence* of one's hope and future expectation. Faith is not merely wishful thinking or a weak hope against all odds, such as when a person says, "I hope so" (but knows something probably won't happen). No; faith is the confident stance taken toward something that, while yet future—and thus linked to hope—is eminently *real*. As Paul wrote to the Corinthians, faith and hope (as well as love) are related: "So now faith, hope, and love abide" (1 Cor. 13:13). The word *hypostasis* occurs elsewhere in this letter also in 1:3, where the author affirms that Jesus is the exact imprint of God's "nature," and in 3:14, where it is translated as "confidence." In the present passage, the author asserts that faith is the vehicle by which we grasp God's promises, the way in which we appropriate what is our hope and firm future expectation in Christ.

Faith is also the "conviction" of things not (yet) seen. While the noun for "conviction," *elengchos*, is unique in the NT, the verb *elengchō* is used with some frequency and has the strong force of "convicting" someone of something (such as sin; cf. John 16:8). Contrary to the common conception of faith as something less real than sight, the author asserts that faith is a strong conviction of the reality of the unseen realm, including future acts of God and the fulfillment of divine promises for believers, including receiving their eternal reward and inheritance. This is similar to Paul's statement, "For we walk by faith, not by sight" (2 Cor. 5:7), and echoes Jesus's statement, "Blessed are those who have not seen and yet have believed" (John 20:29). It is also similar to Peter's statement, "Though you have not seen him, you love him. Though you do not now see him, you believe in him" (1 Pet. 1:8).

Not only is faith strong in substance and confidence; it is also the attribute on account of which "the elders" or "ancients" (*presbyteroi*) were commended (11:2). Faith was the mark that distinguished them from others, the cardinal virtue that set these individuals apart from their contemporaries. Faith enables one to understand that God created the universe by his Word (11:3), a truth to be kept in mind in view of contemporary debates regarding creationism, theistic or nontheistic evolution, and intelligent design.[20] Faith prompted Abel to bring an offering that was more acceptable to God than

20. Cf. J. P. Moreland, Stephen C. Meyer, Christopher Shaw, Ann K. Gauger, and Wayne Grudem, eds., *Theistic Evolution: A Scientific, Philosophical, and Theological Critique* (Wheaton: Crossway, 2017).

that of his brother Cain, who subsequently murdered his brother (11:4). This statement helpfully illumines the OT narrative of this event, which simply states that "the LORD had regard for Abel and his offering, but for Cain and his offering he had no regard," without giving the reason why (Gen. 4:4–5). The author of Hebrews adds that Abel's life was not in vain: "Through his faith, though he died, he still speaks" (11:4).

Another OT exemplar of faith is Enoch, who was lifted into heaven without dying, though before being taken up by God, he was commended for being pleasing to God (11:5). The Genesis narrative states that "Enoch walked with God . . . 300 years"—apparently, he started walking with God when he fathered Methuselah, who turned out to be the proverbial longest-living human in history—affirming that "Enoch walked with God, and he was not, for God took him" (Gen. 5:21–24). Again, the author of Hebrews makes explicit that what pleased God was Enoch's faith. Parenthetically, he notes in verse 6 that "without faith it is impossible to please" God, for the one who draws near to him "must believe that he exists and that he rewards those who seek him." Thus, if it is said of anyone that he is pleasing to God, one may infer that this individual has faith. Conversely, if anyone lacks faith, he cannot please God (cf. James 1:3–8).

Another key OT exemplar of faith is Noah, who by faith—that is, trust in God's warning concerning future (and as of yet unseen) events—built a large ship (the ark) to save his family. In this way, he became an example of the "righteousness that comes by faith," extolled by Habakkuk (see 10:37–38 and the discussion above), as well as an example of "condemning the world" (i.e., exposing the world's unbelief). According to the author's central premise, God's Word speaks through the ages—it spoke creation into being; it speaks in the inspired scriptural accounts of events and lives of key individuals in human history; and it speaks through the covenants and promises of God to his people in ages past, which he intends to keep and which in Christ have already been fulfilled to a significant extent (though some aspects still await future fulfillment).

Abraham is widely known for his strong faith in God and so rightly occupies a central place in Hebrews' "Hall of Faith." The apostle Paul calls Abraham "the believer" (Gal. 3:9 NASB). It all started when Abraham was obedient to God's call to leave his native country and go to the place in a faraway land God promised to give him (Heb. 11:8; cf. Gen. 12:1–4). Out of sheer confidence in God—trusting in his promise, taking him at his word—Abraham went and lived in a foreign country, taking up temporary residence in tents (11:9; e.g., Gen. 12:8). The author elaborates that what motivated Abraham to do this was strong faith in the God who promised. Abraham was not attached to his surroundings; he let go of earthly attachments in order to pursue the heavenly city, "whose designer and builder is God" (11:10), and in this way became the paradigmatic "believer" in God.

The author is kind when he adduces Sarah as an example of faith even though the Genesis narrative indicates that she wasn't always exemplary in the way she responded. For example, when the Lord's promise to give Abraham an heir seemed to delay, Sarah gave her servant Hagar to her husband, and he slept with Hagar, who became pregnant; then Sarah put the blame for her unbelief on Hagar (Gen. 16:1–5)! Later, Sarah laughed when God renewed his promise and said her son would be born in a year, and she subsequently denied that she had laughed (18:9–15). Nevertheless, the author of Hebrews discerns that it was "by faith" that Sarah "received power to conceive" the promised son, considering the God "who had promised" to be "faithful" (11:11). In this way, Sarah serves as an example of an OT figure who persevered in her faith (cf. 1 Peter 3:5–6). As a result, God's promise to Abraham was fulfilled that he would make him "into a great nation" (Gen. 12:2; cf. Heb. 11:12) and that his descendants would be as numerous "as the stars of heaven and . . . as the innumerable grains of sand by the seashore" (cf. Gen. 22:17).

The giving of several specific OT examples is followed by a summary statement: "These all died in faith," whereby "these all" refers to Abel, Enoch, Noah, Abraham, and Sarah (11:13; cf. 11:4–12). The author's point is that none of these individuals saw the actual fulfillment of God's promise to them in their lifetime. As Jody Dillow—himself a man of great faith—once remarked in a sermon on this passage, these individuals merely greeted God's promises from a distance, saying, as it were: "Hello, promise!" During their earthly lives, they were "strangers" (*xenoi*) and "exiles" (*parepidēmoi*, 11:13; cf. Eph. 2:19; 1 Pet. 1:1; 2:11). They were seeking a "better country," a heavenly one, and indeed, one day they will enter God's city, which he—who is "not ashamed to be called their God"—has prepared for them (11:16).

Returning to the specific example of Abraham, the author resumes the narrative with perhaps the most striking instance of strong faith in Abraham's life (with the possible exception of his initial conversion and obedient following of God's call to leave his native country): his willingness to lay his son Isaac—the son whom God had promised—on the altar when tested, the famous Akedah (11:17; cf. Gen. 22:1–19). Even though God had told Abraham, "Through Isaac shall your offspring be named" (Gen. 21:12), he tested Abraham's faith and told him to offer up his son on Mount Moriah (22:1–2). As he had done when he first received God's call to leave his country and go to a land God promised to give him, Abraham responded with unquestioning obedience. The Genesis narrative simply says, "So Abraham rose early in the morning . . ." (22:3).

After a three-day journey, Abraham took his son Isaac, as well as firewood and a knife, and went up the mountain. When Isaac asked his father where the sacrificial lamb was that he was going to sacrifice, Abraham replied, "God will provide for himself the lamb" (22:8). Later, as Abraham was about to put the knife to his son, an angel stopped him, saying, "Now I know that you fear God, seeing you have not withheld your son, your only son, from me" (22:12). Looking up, Abraham saw a ram caught by its horns and offered it in place of Isaac (22:13). Again, the author of Hebrews reads between the lines of the Genesis narrative and reasons that, by implication, Abraham "considered that God was able even to raise him from the dead, from which, figuratively speaking [*parabolē*], he did receive him back" (11:19). Thus, two millennia prior to Jesus's resurrection, Abraham already believed in the God who could raise the dead! In this way, Abraham can serve as a prototype and example of resurrection faith even for NT believers, who lived on the other side of the resurrection of Jesus. The account of Abraham's faith in God when called to sacrifice his "only" son (Isaac, the promised son, was unique and distinct from Ishmael, the son who was the result of Sarah's unbelief; cf. Gal. 4:21–31) marks a high point in the chapter and serves elsewhere in the NT as a point of analogy, if not typology, for none other than God "giving his one and only Son," Jesus, to die on the cross for the sins of humankind (John 3:16). While the similarity is clear, the all-important difference is that Abraham didn't actually end up sacrificing Isaac, whereas Jesus did in fact sacrifice his own life on the cross.

Having covered Abraham's faith in great depth, the author moves much more quickly in discussing the faith of the other patriarchs, Isaac, Jacob, and Joseph (11:20–22). Isaac blessed his sons Jacob and Esau (Gen. 27:27–29, 39–40); Jacob blessed the sons of Joseph (48:8–20); and Joseph envisioned the exodus and gave instructions regarding reburying his bones in the promised land (50:25). In each case, the patriarch's actions display a forward-looking faith in anticipation of God fulfilling his promises. In this way, these figures serve as examples even for NT believers, who are called to trust God to fulfill all of his promises, including the second coming of Christ as well as their own reception of their final rewards and inheritance.

After this, the author again slows down and covers Moses and the period of the exodus and the conquest in greater detail (11:23–31). The following events are singled out for comment.

First, the author notes the faith of Moses's parents, which led them to hide the child for three months in defiance of Pharaoh's edict (11:23; cf. Exod. 1:15–16; 2:2).

Second, the author draws attention to Moses's own refusal as a young adult to be identified as the son of Pharaoh's daughter and his choice to identify instead with God's people, to be mistreated rather than indulge in the "fleeting pleasures of sin" (11:24–25; cf. Exod. 2:11–12). This example is particularly poignant in that it illustrates the exact choice the author wants the Hebrews to make, especially those who are wavering in their faith (see the discussion of the "warning passages" above). Just as Abraham already exhibited (NT) resurrection faith, so Moses in anticipatory fashion considered "the reproach [*oneidismos*] *of Christ*" superior to the treasures of Egypt as he looked to his heavenly reward (11:26). The author will later note that Jesus endured great hostility from sinners (12:3) and that Jesus "suffered outside the gate . . . outside the camp"—that is, in ignominy and shame—for God's people, and the author will call on the readers to likewise go "outside the camp and bear the reproach he [Jesus] endured" (13:12–13), as in fact some of them have already done (10:32–33).

Third, just as his parents were not afraid of Pharaoh's edict, Moses left Egypt rather than being afraid of Pharaoh's anger: he "endured as seeing him who is invisible" (11:27; cf. 11:23) and didn't give in to fear (cf. 1 Pet. 3:6). In both 11:23 and 11:27, the author calls Pharaoh "the king" rather than "Pharaoh," perhaps to make it easier for his readers to apply Moses's disposition to their own situation vis-à-vis the Roman emperor, King Nero (reigned AD 54–68). This parallel would be especially poignant if, as is likely, the letter is addressed to Christians in Rome, the empire's capital, where Nero was on the throne and persecution was mounting rapidly (cf. 1 Pet. 4:12). Again, the author implies that the readers should follow Moses's example and not succumb to fear but endure suffering "as seeing him who is invisible."

Fourth and finally, Moses commanded the people of Israel to observe the Passover (which serves as the type for the Lord's Supper) and to sprinkle blood on their doorposts in Egypt, so that the destroyer might "pass over" their house and not kill their firstborn (11:28; cf. Exod. 12:22–23). The readers were thoroughly accustomed to Passover, as they would have regularly celebrated it; the author's point here is that the celebration of the first Passover was prompted by faith in God's promise to deliver his people.

The author concludes the series of specific OT examples of faith from the period of the exodus and the conquest by mentioning more briefly three additional examples: (1) the crossing of the Red Sea (Heb. 11:29; cf. Exod. 14:15–31); (2) the conquest of Jericho, whose seemingly insurmountable wall collapsed after seven days (Heb. 11:30; cf. Josh. 6:1–21); and (3) the sparing of Rahab the prostitute, who had given shelter to the spies (Heb. 11:31; cf. Josh. 6:22–25). The "Hall of Faith" of chapter 11 is a great scriptural example of biblical theology where the author validates an abiding salvation-historical principle—that faith alone pleases God—by a string of selected instances demonstrating the underlying spiritual dynamic of faith. While faith is not always mentioned explicitly in the original passages of Scripture, the author skillfully shows that faith implicitly served as the consistent motivating factor prompting the choices made by key figures of the faith such as Abraham or Moses.

That said, the author at this point stops his selected biblical survey at Joshua 6, no doubt believing he has sufficiently made his point (like many preachers, if this was originally a sermon, he may have simply run out of time!). He fast-forwards to the time of the judges—mentioning Gideon, Barak, Samson, and Jephthah by name (while omitting other judges)—as well as to the period of the monarchy—mentioning David, Samuel, and the prophets (notice the interesting order of David being mentioned before Samuel). Remarkably, the list here closely resembles that found in 1 Samuel 12:11: "And the Lord sent Jerubbaal [i.e., Gideon] and Barak and Jephthah and Samuel" (though Samson is conspicuously absent from that list). Notably, Barak rather than Deborah is mentioned in both the present passage and 1 Samuel 12:11, suggesting that both the OT and the NT author considered him, not Deborah, to be the intended judge and military leader in this period (cf. Judg. 4–5).

Having listed the names in 11:32, the author is done with mentioning specific OT characters by name and instead lists a series of heroic acts prompted by faith, which need not be reproduced here (11:33–38). The chapter closes with the author's final enunciation of the key principle underlying his entire discussion: that all these individuals had forward-looking faith yet didn't yet receive what was promised. The message is clear: true, God-pleasing faith trusts in the promises of God often long before they become a reality, on the basis of nothing other than the faithful character of God. If God is faithful—and he is—he is worthy of our trust. What's more, the author notes that there is another reason why OT believers didn't yet receive what was promised: the fact that "apart from us [NT believers] they should not be made perfect" (v. 40). This shows the solidarity between OT and NT believers: both believe in the same God—the God who promised (Abraham), the God who delivered (Moses), and the God who keeps his promises (Jesus).

Jesus, Who Ran the Race before Us (12:1–29)

"Therefore"—the author now transitions to exhorting his readers based on the previous chapter, the "Hall of Faith." The ground for his exhortation is that "we are surrounded by so great a cloud of witnesses" (12:1)—namely, the individuals commended for their faith in chapter 11: Abel, Enoch, Noah, Abraham, Sarah, Isaac, Jacob, Joseph, Moses, Rahab, Gideon, Barak, Samson,

Jephthah, David, Samuel, and the prophets. All these people finished the race of faith, even though many of them (such as Rahab, Barak, or Samson) were far from perfect.[21] The author's exhortation is that his readers "lay aside every weight," as ancient runners would do, who ran practically naked. Metaphorically speaking, this refers to sin, "which clings so closely" (12:1). If believers shed the unnecessary weight of sin, they can run the race of faith that is set before them with endurance. As has been said before, the Christian life is not a sprint but a marathon, or at least a long-distance race. As Walt Henrichsen noted, "Many aspire, few attain." Many start out well, but not everyone who starts the race finishes it. This is why it is vital to confess our sins and to let God forgive and cleanse us by the blood of Christ, so we can have fresh and continual energy to run the race until at last we cross the finish line.

What's more, while we have a "cloud of witnesses"—OT believers—our main focus is to be none other than Jesus, "the founder and perfecter of our faith" (12:2). As the paradigmatic example for all believers—including the original readers of this letter—Jesus, for the joy ahead of him, endured the horrible agony of the cross, despite the public shame and humiliation it conveyed (note that 12:2 is the only place in the entire letter where the word "cross," *stauros*, is explicitly used). Yet today, Jesus is seated at God's right hand (12:2; cf. 1:3; Ps. 110:1). The author pleads with his readers to consider what incredible hostility Jesus endured from sinners, so that they, the readers, may not despair and give up (12:3). As it turns out, they've not yet had to suffer martyrdom (12:4).

In support, the author cites Proverbs 3:11–12, which urges God's people not to despise suffering as a form of God's purifying discipline (Heb. 12:5–6).[22] Divine discipline is evidence that we are God's children (12:8). Arguing from the lesser to the greater, the author points out that all of us were disciplined by our earthly fathers, albeit imperfectly; yet the discipline meted out by our heavenly Father is perfect—shall we not endure it all the more (12:10)? As in the case of athletes, discipline is painful at the time, but those who have been trained by it will share in God's holiness and reap "the peaceful fruit of righteousness" (12:10–11). The readers are therefore to stiffen their resolve to endure (12:12–13). They are to strive for peace and holiness (12:14) and not

21. For a study of the present passage in its Jewish and Greco-Roman background, see N. Clayton Croy, *Endurance in Suffering: Hebrews 12.1–13 in Its Rhetorical, Religious, and Philosophical Context*, SNTSMS 98 (Cambridge: Cambridge University Press, 1998).

22. Cf. Matthew Thiessen, "Hebrews 12.5–13, the Wilderness Period, and Israel's Discipline," *NTS* 55 (2009): 366–79, who argues that "children" in 12:5–13 should be interpreted in light of Jewish conceptions of Israel's experience in the wilderness, which instructs God's people that endurance during the process of discipline is required if they are to inherit the promised land.

grow bitter, be sexually immoral, or be unholy like Esau, who, incredibly, sold his birthright for a single bowl of stew and later, when overcome with remorse, found it was too late to change the outcome (12:15–17; cf. Gen. 25:31–34; 27:30–40).

In a grand finale (12:18–24), the author now solemnly writes that his readers have not come to the arresting sight of God's presence at Mount Sinai with its terrifying manifestations (cf. Exod. 19:16–19; cf. 20:18); they've instead come to Mount Zion and the heavenly Jerusalem, the new city of God, and to an innumerable host of angels in festive garments. They've come to the assembly of heaven, to God, who judges all people, and to "the spirits of the righteous made perfect" (12:23; i.e., those who ran the race of faith with endurance). Above all, they've come to Jesus, "the mediator of a new covenant" (v. 24; cf. 9:15), and to sprinkled blood that speaks "a better word" than that of Abel (cf. 11:4)—the blood of Christ. In this rousing finale, the writer engages in eloquent oratory befitting a preacher, enhancing the impression that this letter may have originated as a series of sermons given orally before they were written down in the form of a letter.

In one final "warning passage," the author adjures his readers not to "refuse him who is speaking"—God, who warns from heaven (12:25). In support, the author cites Haggai 2:6: "Yet once more I will shake not only the earth but also the heavens" (12:26). The purpose of such shaking, he explains, is that what cannot be shaken may remain (12:27). This entity that cannot be shaken is God's invincible, incomparable, immovable kingdom—his eternal rule. For this, believers should be grateful and offer God-pleasing worship "with reverence and awe" (12:28): "For our God is a consuming fire," a holy and "jealous" God who purifies and a righteous God who judges (12:29; cf. Deut. 4:24; 9:3).

Jesus, Who Suffered Outside the Camp (13:1–16)

Whereas 1:1–4:16 presented Jesus as God's final revelation and salvation, and 4:11–10:25 gave the heart of the author's argument—that Jesus is the great high priest and mediator of a new covenant—10:19–13:16 presents Jesus as the one who ran the race before us and who suffered outside the camp. We've seen how the author's exposition in 10:19–39 was followed by the extended illustration of the OT "Hall of Faith" in chapter 11, climaxing in the exhortation that his readers fix their eyes on Jesus, "the founder and perfecter of our faith" (12:1–2). Against the backdrop of several "warning passages," this exhortation is the undisputable high point of the entire epistle. In the present, concluding chapter (13), the author closes with a series of exhortations surrounding his statement in verse 12 that Jesus suffered outside the gate "in order to sanctify the people through his own blood," followed by the exhortation that his readers "go to him outside the camp and bear the reproach he endured" (v. 13). This is the last of a triad of references in the latter stages of the book enjoining believers to suffer the rejection Christ endured (*oneidismos*; 10:33; 11:26; 13:13).

In rapid succession, the author enjoins his readers

- to continue to show brotherly love (*philadelphia*, 13:1)
- to show hospitality to strangers (*philoxenia*, v. 2)
- to remember those who are in prison or mistreated (v. 3)
- to honor marriage and let the marriage bed (*koitē*) be undefiled (v. 4)
- to refrain from the love of money (*aphilargyros*) and be content (v. 5)

The author supports this last exhortation with two verses from Scripture, Deuteronomy 31:6 // 31:8 ("I will never leave you nor forsake you") and Psalm 118:6 ("The Lord is my helper; I will not fear; what can man do to me?"). Both verses provide strong encouragement and assurance that God is present with believers and that there is no need to fear human persecution.

In 13:7 and 13:17, readers are urged to "remember" and even "obey" their leaders (*hēgoumenoi*). The exhortation to remember the congregation's leaders need not imply that the leaders are no longer alive; it may rather encourage the readers to be grateful for them and to "imitate their faith" (v. 7). The assertion "Jesus Christ is the same yesterday and today and forever" is given in the context of a warning against being swayed by "diverse and strange teachings," with an oblique reference to "foods, which have not benefited those devoted to them" (13:8–9). This may point to the presence of false teachers who focused on dietary regulations from the Mosaic law rather than the gospel of "grace" (*charis*). The word, common in Paul, is fairly rare in Hebrews, occurring elsewhere only at 2:9; 4:16; 10:29; 12:15, 28 (translated as "grateful" in 12:28 ESV); and as a greeting at 13:25. Other NT references to similar challenges to the gospel in the early Christian movement are found in the book of Acts and several of Paul's letters (e.g., Acts 15; Col. 2:16–23; 1 Tim. 4:1–4).

At this, the author draws an analogy between sacrificial animals, which under the OT system were burned outside the camp, and Jesus, who likewise suffered outside the city of Jerusalem as a sign of the rejection he endured. Just as the author earlier called his readers to look to Jesus as they ran the race of the Christian life, he now calls on them to suffer the reproach, rejection, and persecution Christ had to endure (13:10–13).[23] Like the OT believers adduced in chapter 11, the readers are seeking the heavenly city (13:14; cf. 11:10, 16). Similar to Paul in Romans 12:1 and Peter in 1 Peter 2:5, the author then redefines the notion of "sacrifice" for NT believers. Rather than bringing physical animal sacrifices, they are to "continually offer up a sacrifice of praise to God, that is, the fruit of lips that acknowledge his name" (13:15). Christ has already brought the once-for-all sacrifice of his body on the cross. The only "sacrifice" left for believers to offer is that of lips acknowledging his name before others—holding fast to the Christian confession (the gospel) and not shrinking back from following the crucified Christ. In addition, believers are to perform good works and to share their possessions, "for such sacrifices are pleasing to God" (13:16; cf. Titus 2:14). In this way, believers follow through on their profession of faith by living selfless, sacrificial lives for the sake of others. It is clear that such good works are fueled by grace and not meritorious in any way (i.e., they don't add to what Christ has accomplished on the cross with regard to salvation).

Epistolary Closing (13:17–25)

Verse 17 could be taken as a conclusion to the previous section (13:1–16) or as the beginning of the epistolary closing. The exhortation to "obey" and "submit" to their leaders is one of the strongest NT passages referring to the authority of church leaders over their congregation (cf. 1 Thess. 5:12; 1 Tim. 5:17). The command to obey and submit to church leaders is grounded in the fact that they are "keeping watch over your souls" (*agrypneō*; elsewhere in the NT only at Mark 13:33; Luke 21:36; Eph. 6:18) and that they "will have to give an account" to God (13:17).

The request that the readers pray for him (13:18) makes clear that the original readers knew who the author was (even though we don't). Specifically, the author requests prayer "that I may be restored to you the sooner" (13:19), which could suggest (but doesn't necessarily mean) that he is currently in prison or otherwise detained from visiting them (most likely in Rome; cf. 13:23–24).

The magnificent benediction in 13:20–21 calls upon "the God of peace," who raised Jesus from the dead—Jesus, "the great shepherd of the sheep, by the blood of the eternal covenant"—to equip (*katartizō*; cf. 10:5 ["prepared"]; 11:3 ["created"]) the readers with everything they need to do God's will. In fact, it is God himself who is "working in us that which is pleasing in his sight,

---

23. This is similar to Paul, who repeatedly calls on Timothy to join him in his suffering (e.g., 2 Tim. 1:8).

through Jesus Christ" (13:20; cf. Eph. 2:8–10; Phil. 2:12–13). Not only did God provide salvation in his Son, the great, eternal high priest and mediator of a new and better covenant; the Son also is the primary agent of sanctification in believers, setting them apart spiritually and performing his sanctifying work in them through his Spirit (cf. 10:10, 14; see discussion above).

Added to the letter following the closing benediction is an "appeal" (*parakaleō*) by the author to his readers to bear with his "word of exhortation," which, in a case of transparent understatement, he has written to them "briefly" (13:22). Interestingly, the phrase "word of exhortation" (*logos tēs paraklēseōs*; cf. 6:18 ["encouragement"]; 12:5) occurs elsewhere in the NT with reference to a sermon or homily (Acts 13:15), which may suggest that the present letter originated as a series of sermons that were later brought together and sent in the form of an epistle (see introduction above). The epithet "briefly" applied to the present letter is intriguing, as the letter is one of the longer NT documents and presents a rather extended argument. Equally intriguing is the reference to "our brother Timothy"—no doubt the recipient of the two letters to Timothy included in the NT—who had recently been released from an otherwise unknown imprisonment (13:23). The added reference, "with whom I shall see you if he comes soon," suggests that he and the author were planning a joint visit to the congregation (which, as mentioned, is presumably located in Rome, the empire's capital). It is unclear whether this imprisonment is to be placed before, during, or after the writing of 1 Timothy (though hardly after 2 Timothy), yet in any case a time frame prior to the year 70 is a virtual certainty in light of the fact, as mentioned in the introduction, that none of the momentous events surrounding the Jewish revolt against Rome—including the destruction of the Jerusalem temple—are mentioned in the letter.

The letter closes with final greetings to the leaders (the third reference to these individuals after 13:7 and 17) and all believers. There are also final greetings from "those who come from Italy," a likely reference to believers who are with the author (whoever and wherever he is) and who send greetings back home to Rome, the letter's likely destination (Rome being the capital of Italy).

Hebrews: Commentaries

Allen, David L. *Hebrews*. NAC 35. Nashville: B&H, 2010.

Attridge, Harold W. *The Epistle to the Hebrews*. Hermeneia. Minneapolis: Fortress, 1989.

Bruce, F. F. *The Epistle to the Hebrews*. Rev. ed. NICNT. Grand Rapids: Eerdmans, 1990.

Cockerill, Gareth L. *The Epistle to the Hebrews*. NICNT. Grand Rapids: Eerdmans, 2012.

deSilva, David A. *Perseverance in Gratitude: A Socio-Rhetorical Commentary on the Epistle to the Hebrews*. Grand Rapids: Eerdmans, 2000.

Ellingworth, Paul. *The Epistle to the Hebrews*. NIGTC. Grand Rapids: Eerdmans, 1993.

France, R. T. "Hebrews." In *Hebrews–Revelation*, vol. 13 of *The Expositor's Bible Commentary*, rev. ed., edited by Tremper Longman III and David E. Garland, 17–195. Grand Rapids: Zondervan, 2005.

Guthrie, George H. *Hebrews*. NIVAC. Grand Rapids: Zondervan, 1998.

Hagner, Donald A. *Hebrews*. UBC. Peabody, MA: Hendrickson, 1990.

Heen, E. M., and P. W. D. Krey, eds. *Hebrews*. ACCS. Downers Grove, IL: InterVarsity, 2005.

Hughes, Philip Edgcumbe. *A Commentary on the Epistle to the Hebrews*. Grand Rapids: Eerdmans, 1977.

Johnson, Dennis E. "Hebrews." In *ESV Expository Commentary*, vol. 12, *Hebrews–Revelation*, edited by Iain M. Duguid, James M. Hamilton Jr., and Jay Sklar, 17–217. Wheaton: Crossway, 2018.

Johnson, Luke Timothy. *Hebrews: A Commentary*. NTL. Louisville: Westminster John Knox, 2006.

Koester, Craig R. *Hebrews: A New Translation with Introduction and Commentary*. AB 36. New Haven: Yale University Press, 2001.

Lane, William L. *Hebrews*. 2 vols. WBC 47A–B. Dallas: Word, 1991.

Schreiner, Thomas R. *Commentary on Hebrews*. BTCP. Nashville: B&H Academic, 2015.

Hebrews: Articles, Essays, and Monographs

Allen, David L. *Lukan Authorship of Hebrews*. NACSBT. Nashville: B&H, 2010.

Allison, Gregg R., and Andreas J. Köstenberger. *The Holy Spirit*. Theology for the People of God. Nashville: B&H Academic, 2020.

Barrett, C. K. "The Eschatology of the Epistle to the Hebrews." In *The Background of the New Testament and Its Eschatology*, edited by W. D. Davies and David Daube, 363–93. Cambridge: Cambridge University Press, 1956.

Bateman, Herbert W., IV, ed. *Four Views on the Warning Passages in Hebrews*. Grand Rapids: Kregel, 2006.

Bauckham, Richard, ed. *The Epistle to the Hebrews and Christian Theology*. Grand Rapids: Eerdmans, 2009.

Bauckham, Richard, Trevor A. Hart, Nathan MacDonald, and Daniel R. Driver, eds. *A Cloud of Witnesses: The Theology of Hebrews in Its Ancient Contexts*. LNTS 387. London: T&T Clark, 2008.

Black, David Alan. "The Problem of the Literary Structure of Hebrews: An Evaluation and Proposal." *GTJ* 7 (1986): 163–77.

Caird, G. B. "The Exegetical Method of the Epistle to the Hebrews." *CJT* 5 (1959): 44–51.

Chalke, Steve. *The Lost Message of Jesus*. Grand Rapids: Zondervan, 2004.

Chester, A. N. "Hebrews: The Final Sacrifice." In *Sacrifice and Redemption: Durham Essays in Theology*, edited by S. W. Sykes, 57–72. Cambridge: Cambridge University Press, 1991.

Cockerill, Gareth L. "The Better Resurrection (Heb. 11:35): A Key to the Structure and Rhetorical Purpose of Hebrews 11." *TynBul* 51 (2000): 215–34.

———. "Structure and Interpretation in Hebrews 8:1–10:18: A Symphony in Three Movements." *BBR* 11 (2001): 179–201.

Cody, Aelred. *Heavenly Sanctuary and Liturgy in the Epistle to the Hebrews: The Achievement of Salvation in the Epistle's Perspectives*. St. Meinrad, IN: Grail, 1960.

Colijn, Brenda B. "'Let Us Approach': Soteriology in the Epistle to the Hebrews." *JETS* 39 (1996): 571–86.

Cowan, Christopher W. "The Warning Passages of Hebrews and the Nature of the New Covenant." In *Progressive Covenantalism*, edited by Stephen J. Wellum and Brent E. Parker, 189–214. Nashville: B&H Academic, 2016.

Croy, N. Clayton. *Endurance in Suffering: Hebrews 12.1–13 in Its Rhetorical, Religious, and Philosophical Context*. SNTSMS 98. Cambridge: Cambridge University Press, 1998.

Decker, Rodney J. "The Intentional Structure of Hebrews." *JMT* 4 (2000): 80–105.

———. "The Warning of Hebrews 6." *JMT* 5 (2001): 26–48.

deSilva, David A. *Despising Shame: Honor Discourse and Community Maintenance in the Epistle to the Hebrews*. SBLDS 152. Atlanta: Scholars Press, 1995.

Emmrich, Martin. *Pneumatological Concepts in the Epistle to the Hebrews: Amtscharisma, Prophet, and Guide of the Eschatological Exodus*. Lanham, MD: University Press of America, 2003.

France, R. T. "The Son of Man in Hebrews 2:6: A Dilemma for Bible Translators." In *New Testament Theology in Light of the Church's Mission: Essays in Honor of I. Howard Marshall*, edited by Jon C. Laansma, Grant R. Osborne, and Ray Van Neste, 81–96. Eugene, OR: Cascade, 2011.

Gelardini, G., ed. *Hebrews: Contemporary Methods—New Insights*. Leiden: Brill, 2005.

Goswell, Gregory. "Finding a Home for the Letter of the Hebrews." *JETS* 59 (2016): 747–60.

Gray, Patrick. "The Early Reception of Hebrews 6:4–6." In *Scripture and Traditions: Essays on Early Judaism and Christianity in Honor of Carl R. Holladay*, edited by Patrick Gray and Gail R. O'Day, 321–39. NovTSup 129. Leiden: Brill, 2008.

Griffiths, Jonathan, ed. *The Perfect Saviour: Key Themes in Hebrews*. Leicester, UK: Inter-Varsity, 2012.

Grudem, Wayne. "Perseverance of the Saints: A Case Study from the Warning Passages in Hebrews." In *Still Sovereign*, edited by Thomas R. Schreiner and Bruce A. Ware, 133–82. Grand Rapids: Baker Academic, 2000.

Guthrie, George H. "The Case for Apollos as the Author of Hebrews." *FM* 18 (2001): 41–56.

———. "Hebrews." In *Commentary on the New Testament Use of the Old Testament*, edited by G. K. Beale and D. A. Carson, 919–96. Grand Rapids: Zondervan, 2007.

———. *The Structure of Hebrews: A Text-Linguistic Analysis*. New York: Brill, 1994.

Guthrie, George H., and Russell D. Quinn. "A Discourse Analysis of the Use of Psalm 8:4–6 in Hebrews 2:5–9." *JETS* 49 (2006): 235–46.

Haber, Susan. "From Priestly Torah to Christ Cultus: The Re-vision of Covenant and Cult in Hebrews." *JSNT* 28 (2005): 105–24.

Hagner, Donald A. *Encountering the Book of Hebrews: An Exposition.* Encountering Biblical Studies. Grand Rapids: Baker Academic, 2002.

Heil, John Paul. *Worship in the Letter to the Hebrews.* Eugene, OR: Wipf & Stock, 2011.

Horbury, William. "The Aaronic Priesthood in the Epistle to the Hebrews." *JSNT* 19 (1983): 52–59.

Hughes, Graham. *Hebrews and Hermeneutics: The Epistle to the Hebrews as a New Testament Example of Biblical Interpretation.* SNTSMS 36. Cambridge: Cambridge University Press, 1979.

Hughes, Philip Edgcumbe. "Doctrine of Creation in Hebrews 11:3." *BTB* 2 (1972): 164–77.

Hurst, L. D. *The Epistle to the Hebrews: Its Background and Thought.* SNTSMS 65. Cambridge: Cambridge University Press, 1990.

Isaacs, Marie E. "Hebrews 13.9–16 Revisited." *NTS* 43 (1997): 268–84.

———. *Sacred Space: An Approach to the Theology of the Epistle to the Hebrews.* JSNTSup 73. Sheffield: JSOT Press, 1992.

Jipp, Joshua W. "The Son's Entrance into the Heavenly World: The Soteriological Necessity of the Scriptural Catena in Hebrews 1:5–14." *NTS* 56 (2010): 557–75.

Jobes, Karen H. "The Function of Paronomasia in Hebrews 10:5–7." *TrinJ* 13 (1992): 181–91.

Johnston, Richard W. *Going outside the Camp: The Soteriological Function of the Levitical Critique in the Epistle to the Hebrews.* JSNTSup 209. London: Sheffield Academic, 2001.

Joslin, Barry C. "Can Hebrews Be Structured? An Assessment of Eight Approaches." *CBR* 6 (2007): 99–129.

———. "Christ Bore the Sins of Many: Substitution and Atonement in Hebrews." *SBJT* 11 (2007): 74–103.

———. *Hebrews, Christ, and the Law: The Theology of the Mosaic Law in Hebrews 7:1–10:18.* PBM. Carlisle, UK: Paternoster, 2008.

Kang, Dae-I. "The Royal Components of Melchizedek in Hebrews 7." *Perichoresis* 10 (2012): 95–124.

Käsemann, Ernst. *The Wandering People of God: An Investigation of the Letter to the Hebrews.* Translated by R. A. Harrisville and I. L. Sandberg. Minneapolis: Augsburg, 1984. First published 1957.

Kibbe, Michael. "Is It Finished? When Did It Start? Hebrews, Priesthood, and Atonement in Biblical, Systematic, and Historical Perspective." *JTS* 65 (2014): 25–61.

Köstenberger, Andreas J. "Jesus, the Mediator of a 'Better Covenant': Comparatives in the Book of Hebrews." *FM* 21 (2004): 30–49.

Laansma, Jon C. "The Cosmology of Hebrews." In *Cosmology and New Testament Theology,* edited by Jonathan T. Pennington and Sean M. McDonough, 125–43. LNTS 355. London: T&T Clark, 2008.

———. "Hebrews and the Mission of the Earliest Church." In *New Testament Theology in Light of the Church's Mission: Essays in Honor of I. Howard Marshall,* edited by Jon C. Laansma, Grant R. Osborne, and Ray Van Neste, 327–46. Eugene, OR: Cascade, 2011.

————. *"I Will Give You Rest": The Rest Motif in the New Testament with Special Reference to Mt. 11 and Heb. 3–4.* WUNT 2/98. Tübingen: Mohr Siebeck, 1997.

Laansma, Jon C., and Daniel J. Treier, eds. *Christology and Hermeneutics of Hebrews: Profiles from the History of Interpretation.* LNTS 432. London: T&T Clark, 2012.

Lane, William. *Hebrews: A Call to Commitment.* Peabody, MA: Hendrickson, 1998.

Lehne, Susanne. *The New Covenant in Hebrews.* JSNTSup 44. Sheffield: JSOT Press, 1990.

Leithart, Peter J. "Womb of the World: Baptism and the Priesthood of the New Covenant in Hebrews 10.19–22." *JSNT* 78 (2000): 49–65.

Leschert, Dale F. *Hermeneutical Foundations of Hebrews: A Study in the Validity of the Epistle's Interpretation of Some Core Citations from the Psalms.* NABPRDS 10. Lewiston, NY: Mellen, 1994.

Lindars, Barnabas. "Heavenly Sanctuary Mysticism in the Epistle to the Hebrews." *JTS* 62 (2011): 77–117.

————. "The Rhetorical Structure of Hebrews." *NTS* 35 (1989): 382–406.

————. *The Theology of the Letter to the Hebrews.* NTT. Cambridge: Cambridge University Press, 1991.

Mackie, Scott D. "Early Christian Eschatological Experience in the Warnings and Exhortations of the Epistle to the Hebrews." *TynBul* 63 (2012): 93–114.

————. *Eschatology and Exhortation in the Epistle to the Hebrews.* WUNT 2/223. Tübingen: Mohr Siebeck, 2007.

MacLeod, David J. "The Literary Structure of the Book of Hebrews." *BSac* 146 (1989): 185–97.

MacRae, George W. "Heavenly Temple and Eschatology in the Letter to the Hebrews." *Semeia* 12 (1978): 179–99.

Manson, Thomas W. "The Problem of the Epistle to the Hebrews." *BJRL* 32 (1949): 1–17.

Mason, Eric F. "The Epistle (Not Necessarily) to the 'Hebrews': A Call to Renunciation of Judaism or Encouragement to Christian Commitment?" *PRSt* 37 (2010): 7–20.

————. "Hebrews and the Dead Sea Scrolls: Some Points of Comparison." *PRSt* 37 (2010): 457–79.

————. *"You Are a Priest Forever": Second Temple Jewish Messianism and the Priestly Christology of the Epistle to the Hebrews.* STDJ 74. Leiden: Brill, 2008.

Mathewson, Dave. "Reading Heb. 6:4–6 in Light of the Old Testament." *WTJ* 61 (1999): 209–25.

McKelvey, R. J. *Pioneer and Priest: Jesus Christ in the Epistle to the Hebrews.* BZNW 159. Berlin: de Gruyter, 2008.

McKnight, Scot. "The Warning Passages of Hebrews: A Formal Analysis and Theological Conclusions." *TrinJ* 13 (1992): 21–59.

Meier, John P. "Structure and Theology in Heb. 1:1–4." *Bib* 66 (1985): 168–89.

————. "Symmetry and Theology in the Old Testament Citations of Heb. 1:5–14." *Bib* 66 (1985): 504–33.

Mitchell, Alan C. *Hebrews.* SP. Collegeville, MN: Glazier, 2007.

Moffit, David M. *Atonement and the Logic of the Resurrection in the Epistle to the Hebrews.* NovTSup 141. Leiden: Brill, 2011.

———. "Unveiling Jesus' Flesh: A Fresh Assessment of the Relationship between the Veil and Jesus' Flesh in Hebrews 10:20." *PRSt* 37 (2010): 71–84.

Moore, Nicholas J. "Jesus as 'the One Who Entered His Rest': The Christological Reading of Hebrews 4.10." *JSNT* 36 (2014): 1–18.

Morrison, Michael D. *Who Needs a Covenant? Rhetorical Function of the Covenant Motif in the Argument of Hebrews.* Eugene, OR: Pickwick, 2008.

Peterson, David G. *Hebrews and Perfection: An Examination of the Concept of Perfection in the "Epistle to the Hebrews."* SNTSMS 47. Cambridge: Cambridge University Press, 1982.

———. *Transformed by God: New Covenant Life and Ministry.* Downers Grove, IL: InterVarsity, 2012.

Pitts, Andrew W., and Joshua F. Walker. "The Authorship of Hebrews: A Further Development in the Luke-Paul Relationship." In *Paul and His Social Relations*, edited by Stanley E. Porter and Christopher D. Land, 143–84. Leiden: Brill, 2012.

Ribbens, Benjamin J. *Levitical Sacrifice and Heavenly Cult in Hebrews.* BZNW 222. Berlin: de Gruyter, 2016.

Richardson, Christopher A. *Pioneer and Perfecter of Faith: Jesus' Faith as the Climax of Israel's History in the Epistle to the Hebrews.* WUNT 2/338. Tübingen: Mohr Siebeck, 2012.

Rooke, Deborah W. "Jesus as Royal Priest: Reflections on the Interpretation of the Melchizedek Tradition in Heb. 7." *Bib* 81 (2000): 81–94.

Schenk, Kenneth L. "A Celebration of the Enthroned Son: The Catena of Hebrews 1." *JBL* 120 (2001): 469–86.

———. *Cosmology and Eschatology in Hebrews: The Settings of the Sacrifice.* SNTSMS 143. Cambridge: Cambridge University Press, 2007.

———. "Keeping His Appointment: Creation and Enthronement in Hebrews." *JSNT* 66 (1997): 91–117.

———. *Understanding the Book of Hebrews: The Story behind the Sermon.* Louisville: Westminster John Knox, 2003.

Scholer, John M. *Proleptic Priests: Priesthood in the Epistle to the Hebrews.* JSNTSup 49. Sheffield: Sheffield Academic, 1991.

Schreiner, Thomas R. *Run to Win the Prize: Perseverance in the New Testament.* Wheaton: Crossway, 2010.

Schreiner, Thomas R., and Ardel B. Caneday. *The Race Set before Us: A Biblical Theology of Perseverance and Assurance.* Downers Grove, IL: InterVarsity, 2001.

Silva, Moisés. "Perfection and Eschatology in Hebrews." *WTJ* 39 (1976): 60–71.

Small, Brian C. "The Use of Rhetorical *Topoi* in the Characterization of Jesus in the Book of Hebrews." *PRSt* 37 (2010): 53–69.

Son, Kiwoong. *Zion Symbolism in Hebrews: Hebrews 12:18–24 as a Hermeneutical Key to the Epistle.* PBM. Waynesboro, GA: Paternoster, 2005.

Stanley, Steve. "Hebrews 9:6–10: The 'Parable' of the Tabernacle." *NovT* 37 (1995): 385–99.

———. "The Structure of Hebrews from Three Perspectives." *TynBul* 45 (1994): 245–71.

Svendsen, Stefan Nordgaard. *Allegory Transformed: The Appropriation of Philonic Hermeneutics in the Letter to the Hebrews.* WUNT 2/269. Tübingen: Mohr Siebeck, 2009.

Swetnam, James. "Christology and the Eucharist in the Epistle to the Hebrews." *Bib* 70 (1989): 74–95.

———. "The Greater and More Perfect Tent: A Contribution to the Discussion of Hebrews 9:11." *Bib* 47 (1966): 91–106.

Swinson, L. Timothy. "'Wind' and 'Fire' in Hebrews 1:7: A Reflection upon the Use of Psalm 104 (103)." *TrinJ* 28 (2007): 215–28.

Thiessen, Matthew. "Hebrews 12.5–13, the Wilderness Period, and Israel's Discipline." *NTS* 55 (2009): 366–79.

Thomas, C. Adrian. *A Case for Mixed-Audience with Reference to the Warning Passages in the Book of Hebrews.* New York: Peter Lang, 2008.

Thompson, James W. "The New Is Better: A Neglected Aspect of the Hermeneutics of Hebrews." *CBQ* 73 (2011): 547–61.

Trotter, Andrew H., Jr. *Interpreting the Epistle to the Hebrews.* GNTE. Grand Rapids: Baker, 1997.

Vanhoye, Albert. *Structure and Message of the Epistle to the Hebrews.* SB 12. Rome: Editrice Pontificio Istituto Biblico, 1989.

Vos, Geerhardus. "The Priesthood of Christ in Hebrews." In *Redemptive History and Biblical Interpretation: The Shorter Writings of Geerhardus Vos,* edited by R. B. Gaffin Jr., 126–60. Phillipsburg, NJ: Presbyterian and Reformed, 1980.

Walser, Georg A. *Old Testament Quotations in Hebrews.* WUNT 2/356. Tübingen: Mohr Siebeck, 2013.

Westcott, B. F. *The Epistle to the Hebrews: The Greek Text with Notes and Essays.* Reprint. Grand Rapids: Eerdmans, 1977.

Westfall, Cynthia Long. *A Discourse Analysis of the Letter to the Hebrews: The Relationship between Form and Meaning.* LNTS 297. New York: T&T Clark, 2005.

Whitlark, Jason A. *Enabling Fidelity to God: Perseverance in Hebrews in Light of Reciprocity Systems in the Ancient Mediterranean World.* PBM. Milton Keynes, UK: Paternoster, 2008.

Williamson, Ronald. "Hebrews 4:15 and the Sinlessness of Jesus." *ExpTim* 86 (1974): 4–8.

———. "The Incarnation of the Logos in Hebrews." *ExpTim* 95 (1983): 4–8.

———. *Philo and the Epistle to Hebrews.* ALGHJ. Leiden: Brill, 1970.

Wray, Judith Hoch. *Rest as a Theological Metaphor in the Epistle to the Hebrews and the Gospel of Truth: Early Christian Homiletics of Rest.* SBLDS 166. Atlanta: Scholars Press, 1988.

Young, Norman H. "The Gospel according to Hebrews 9." *NTS* 27 (1981): 198–210.

CHAPTER TWO

James

Introduction

Author, Audience, Date, and Genre

While the author of Hebrews is unknown, we know the author of the letter of James very well. He is James, the half-brother of Jesus (Matt. 13:55) and leader of the Jerusalem church, and a "pillar" of the early church together with Peter, John, and, of course, the apostle Paul (Acts 15:13–21; Gal. 1:19; 2:9). This James should not be confused with James the son of Zebedee, brother of John the apostle, nor with James the son of Alphaeus, both of whom are mentioned in the NT apostolic lists; e.g., Matthew 10:2–4. Interestingly, James and his brothers accompanied Jesus on some of his early travels (e.g., John 2:1–13), though they were skeptical regarding his claims (7:1–9). Perhaps even as late as the crucifixion, James was not a believer, which would explain why Jesus entrusted the care of his mother to the apostle John, not James or one of his brothers (19:26–27).

As early as in the days immediately following the ascension, however, Jesus's brothers are found among those praying (Acts 1:14), and James, in particular, rose to prominence in the Jerusalem church and the early Christian movement at large. James was thus an important figure in the early church, and his words carried considerable weight, which should increase our respect for James's letter and compel us to take it even more seriously. Apart from his prominent position in the Jerusalem church, James's importance is also underscored by numerous allusions to Jesus's teaching, particularly in the

Sermon on the Mount.[1] While, as mentioned, James was likely not a believer when Jesus originally taught these truths, he apparently took note and, once he had come to faith, drew on his recollection of Jesus's teaching.

While prominent, James was also a controversial figure in that some, especially the so-called Judaizers, appealed to James in support of their teaching that gentiles ought to observe Jewish customs (such as circumcision) before being admitted into the church (cf. Gal. 2:12). Ironically, however, James himself ruled otherwise at the Jerusalem Council, insisting, "We should not trouble those of the Gentiles who turn to God" (Acts 15:13–21, esp. v. 19). At least prior to the council, in particular prior to the writing of Paul's letter to the Galatians (written ca. AD 49), these "Judaizers" seemed to try to pit James against Paul, though they ultimately failed in their effort to divide these two preeminent Christian leaders, which could have had devastating consequences for the unity of the early Christian movement. Even in Paul's letter to the Romans (written ca. AD 55–57), Paul still may be responding to the charge that he has no place for the law (Rom. 6–7). We'll discuss James's teaching on the relationship between faith and works further when commenting on chapter 2 of his letter below.

Turning from James the author to the letter James wrote, we note that James's epistle is in all probability the earliest NT letter, written most likely in the early or mid-40s AD. Together with the Jewishness of James, the early date gives the letter a distinctive Jewish-Christian flavor, which often causes Christian preachers difficulty, as they tend to "Christianize" the letter rather than allowing it to serve as an exemplar of early Jewish Christianity. The following characteristics underscore the Jewish nature of the book.

First, the opening greeting is "to the twelve tribes in the Dispersion" (1:1), most likely referring to Jews living in the Diaspora—that is, in exile away from Palestine amid the Greco-Roman world. Note also the reference to a "meeting place" using the Jewish term "synagogue" (*synagōgē*, 2:2). Second, the examples of faith James adduces come largely from the OT—Abraham (2:21; who is called "our father"), Rahab (2:25), the prophets (5:10), Job (5:11), and Elijah (5:17)—and the letter includes several OT quotations and allusions (e.g., 2:8, 23; 4:6).

Third, James's primary ethic is grounded in OT wisdom (see esp. 4:13–18), though, as mentioned, he also alludes to Jesus's teaching multiple times. What is unusual for a NT letter is that James refers to Jesus only twice in his entire epistle (1:1; 2:1). The reference to "our Lord Jesus Christ, the Lord of

---

1. See Andreas J. Köstenberger, L. Scott Kellum, and Charles L. Quarles, *The Cradle, the Cross, and the Crown: An Introduction to the New Testament*, 2nd ed. (Nashville: B&H Academic, 2016), table 17.1 (p. 803).

glory" in 2:1 displays, though, a remarkably high Christology, particularly at such an early juncture in the Christian church. The abundance of references to OT wisdom and the relative paucity of direct references to Jesus suggests that James's audience was Jewish and continued to live out their faith within an OT framework while believing that Jesus was the Jewish Messiah. This constitutes a remarkable parallel to the audience of the letter of Hebrews, discussed above, though unlike the audience of Hebrews, James's readers were likely not in Rome. Note that in Hebrews, too, the "Hall of Faith" in chapter 11 consists of OT believers.

I noted above that Hebrews doesn't start out like a letter, though it concludes like one. When it comes to James, the opposite is the case: the epistle starts out like a letter but doesn't end like one. In fact, there is no real ending at all, whether a final greeting, closing benediction, or some other concluding section. Instead, the letter seems to break off rather abruptly with the statement that the person who restores a wandering soul from death "will cover a multitude of sins" (5:20). This suggests that the epistolary genre in NT times was not adhered to rigidly by the NT writers but allowed a certain amount of flexibility. The body of the letter itself, as we'll discuss shortly below, consists of multiple cycles of exhortation, most likely to a group of congregations that were characterized by various types of challenges, whether standing firm in temptation, showing partiality to the rich, or neglecting the importance of works as evidence of genuine faith. Thus James, the half-brother of Jesus, wrote this letter in the early or mid-40s AD to a group of Jewish-Christian congregations to exhort those believers to live in keeping with OT wisdom and the ethical teaching of Jesus.

Structure

The opening of James's letter is very succinct and consists of a single verse (1:1). In the body of the letter, which consists of the remaining epistle (no closing), the address "my brothers" (*adelphoi mou*) or a variation thereof recurs in 1:2, 1:16, 1:19, 2:1, 2:5, 2:14, 3:1, 4:11, 5:7, 5:12, and 5:19. In some cases, exhortations are introduced by one or several rhetorical questions (2:14; 3:13; 4:1; 5:13–14) or the direct address "Come now" (4:13; 5:1). As mentioned, there is no real conclusion to the letter.

The references to "my brothers" (or an equivalent) and other introductory phrases present themselves as follows:

James	Introductory Phrase	Topic
1:2	My brothers	Trials and temptations
1:16	My beloved brothers	God the source of every good gift

James	Introductory Phrase	Topic
1:19	My beloved brothers	Doers of the word, true religion
2:1	My brothers	Warning against partiality toward the rich
2:5	My beloved brothers	Partiality toward the rich (continued)
2:14	My brothers	Relationship between faith and works
3:1	My brothers	Warning regarding stricter judgment of teachers Exposition on nature of true wisdom
4:1	What causes quarrels and what causes fights among you?	Warning against friendship with the world Submit to God, resist devil, repent
4:11	Brothers	Warning against judging one's brother
4:13	Come now, you who say . . .	Warning against arrogant planning
5:1	Come now, you rich	Direct exhortation addressed to the rich
5:7	Brothers	Call to steadfastness and patience
5:12	My brothers	Warning against swearing
5:13, 14	Is anyone among you suffering? Is anyone cheerful? Is anyone among you sick?	Pray Sing praise Elders pray, anoint; confess sins to one another
5:19	My brothers	Restore the errant brother

While at a first glance it may seem hard to discern a flow and structure in James's letter and it may appear that the epistle essentially consists of a series of loosely-strung-together exhortations, closer scrutiny reveals that James typically issues an instruction or warning to the congregation and subsequently elaborates on this piece of instruction in the form of a sort of excursus.[2] If this understanding of James's method and procedure is basically on target, a tentative outline of his letter would present itself as follows:

James	Main Contents
1:1	Letter opening
1:2–18	Instruction on dealing with trials and temptations
1:19-27	Excursus on practicing one's faith and true religion
2:1-13	Warning against preferential treatment of the rich
2:14-26	Excursus on the relationship between faith and works
3:1-12	Warning against many becoming teachers

2. Robert L. Plummer, "James," in *ESV Expository Commentary*, vol. 12, *Hebrews–Revelation*, ed. Iain M. Duguid, James M. Hamilton Jr., and Jay Sklar (Wheaton: Crossway, 2018), 229, speaks of James's "staccato style." He provides a similar outline as the one proposed here, except that he subdivides some of the units further into subunits (i.e., 1:2–18 into 1:2–11 and 1:12–18; 4:1–17 into 4:1–12 and 4:13–17; and 5:7–20 into 5:7–12 and 5:13–20; see ibid., 223–25). For a discussion of various proposals regarding the literary plan of James's letter, see Köstenberger, Kellum, and Quarles, *The Cradle, the Cross, and the Crown*, 813–15.

James	Main Contents
3:13-18	Excursus on the contrast between earthly and heavenly wisdom
4:1-17	Warning against covetousness, slander, and arrogant planning
5:1-6	Warning to the rich against greed or injustice
5:7-20	Concluding call to patience and prayer in suffering

Central Message

In many ways, James assumes a role akin to that of an OT prophet who issues a series of warnings and exhortations to his readers in order to shake them from their complacency and stir in them a thirst for righteousness. The ethos of the letter may therefore be best characterized as a *wake-up call to a complacent church*. In many ways, James calls his readers to repent and to put their faith into practice rather than paying mere lip service to their Christian confession. This is not only remarkably similar to the role of OT prophets in ancient Israel; it also serves as a call for the church of today, in particular in the West, to wake up from its complacency and to repent and act out its (otherwise merely nominal) Christian confession. In relation to the message of Hebrews, we may therefore say that James exhorted his readers to act out their Christian confession, while the author of Hebrews exhorted his readers not to shrink back from their confession but to hold fast to it in the face of mounting persecution.

Doubtless the most frequently discussed topic pertaining to James's letter is the relationship between faith and works, especially in comparison to the teaching of Paul on the same subject (2:14–26; cf., e.g., Gal. 3). We will discuss James's message in this regard in greater detail when covering the relevant portion in James's letter below. In short, the question revolves around the apparent contradiction between James's and Paul's respective emphases. While James seems to insist that works are necessary and that faith by itself is not enough, Paul seems to teach salvation by faith alone apart from any works. In fact, both James and Paul adduce the very same passage—Genesis 15:6—to argue what appear to be diametrically opposite points: James, that Abraham was justified by works and not merely by faith (2:23); Paul, that Abraham was justified by faith apart from works (Gal. 3:6)! In fact, James seems to flatly contradict what later, during the Reformation, became one of the core truths of Christianity (the so-called *solas*, from Latin, meaning "alone")—*sola fide*, or "faith alone"—when he says that "a person is justified by works *and not by faith alone*" (2:24). It will be important, therefore, to think through the relationship between these two teachings when discussing 2:14–26 below. For now, it will suffice to note that James makes an important contribution to the

NT teaching on the relationship between faith and works, in particular with his emphasis on the necessity of works accompanying true faith.

Letter Opening (1:1)

At the outset, James—the half-brother of Jesus (see introduction above)—identifies himself as "a servant of God and of the Lord Jesus Christ." In so doing, he places God and Jesus Christ in parallelism and on par with each other, implying the deity of Christ (this is also suggested by the title "Lord," *kyrios*, which regularly in the OT refers to Yahweh). Also, while he could have identified himself in relation to Jesus as a member of his natural family, James opts instead to call himself "a servant . . . of the Lord Jesus Christ." This displays remarkable humility and shows proper deference and devotion to Jesus Christ. While Jesus was James's half-brother in that they shared the same mother, he was also—and more importantly—his Lord and Master.

The recipients of James's letter are identified as the "twelve tribes in the Dispersion"—that is, Jewish people living in the Diaspora—scattered in exile away from Palestine somewhere in the Greco-Roman world. "Twelve tribes" is reminiscent of ethnic Israel, while "Dispersion" invokes the Jewish experience following the Assyrian and Babylonian exiles subsequent to the disintegration of the monarchy. The word "greetings" (*chairein*) is precisely the same as that used in the circular letter resulting from the Jerusalem Council, which was led by this same James (Acts 15:23).

Instruction on Dealing with Trials and Temptations (1:2–18)

Without any opening prayer or thanksgiving, James turns at once to exhortation. The first words in the original Greek are perhaps for emphasis, "all joy," though what follows is unexpected. Addressing the congregation as "my brothers" (doubtless including female members of the congregation as well), James in his opening salvo exhorts these Jewish Christians to "count it all joy" when they "meet trials of various kinds" (1:2). The word translated "trials" (*peirasmos*) can mean either external trials or testing, or internal temptation; the term recurs in 1:12, where James writes, "Blessed is the man who remains steadfast under trial, for when he has stood the test he will receive the crown of life." The cognate verb *peirazō* is translated "to tempt" four times in 1:13–14. The same phrase, "various trials" (*peirasmos poikilois*), is found in 1 Peter 1:6, also in the context of testing (1 Pet. 1:7), most likely conveying persecution for the faith (for Pauline references, see 1 Cor. 10:13; Gal. 4:14; 1 Tim. 6:9; cf. Heb. 3:8).

The fact that James starts his letter with a reference to enduring various kinds of trials and the testing of believers' faith suggests that this may have been a real issue in the congregation(s) to which he writes and that these Christians had need of steadfastness when their faith was tested. The theme of testing opens and concludes the first of James's exhortations in this letter (1:2–4, 12–15). In fact, even the intervening material may be related to this theme (i.e., the need for wisdom in vv. 5–8 and the disparity between the lowly and the rich in vv. 9–11). In keeping with the range of meaning of the word *peirasmos*, therefore, the "trials of various kinds" mentioned in 1:2 may include both external testing and internal temptation (see further vv. 12–16 below). In either case, such trials test a person's faith, and the God-intended effect is steadfastness in character. This is different from the common adage that "what doesn't kill you makes you stronger." James doesn't merely talk about mental toughness; he encourages growth in our ability to trust in God when facing adversity.

A person who has learned to respond to sudden, unexpected challenges in a Christlike manner is strong in character, or, as James puts it, such a person is "perfect" (*teleios*; see below) and "complete" (*holoklēros*, elsewhere in the NT only in 1 Thess. 5:23), "lacking in nothing" (1:4). This description echoes Jesus's words in the Sermon on the Mount, "You therefore must be perfect, as your heavenly Father is perfect" (Matt. 5:48). Of course, perfection is elusive for sinful human beings, but the idea here is not literal perfection but proven character—that is, spiritual maturity that comes from years of practice and character formation (later in James, see 3:2; cf. 1 Cor. 2:6; Phil. 3:15; Col. 1:28; 4:12; Heb. 5:14).

Now some may object that they lack the *wisdom* called for in trying situations; note that the word "lack" (*leipō*, elsewhere in James only in 2:15 and in the NT in Luke 18:22; Titus 1:5; 3:13) connects 1:4 ("lacking in nothing") and verse 5 ("lacks wisdom"). For James, this is no valid excuse, for such a person should simply ask God—that is, pray—whose nature is such that he "gives generously," not only to some but "to all," and who does so "without reproach"—and the person in need of wisdom will receive it (again, James's statement echoes Jesus's saying in the Sermon on the Mount, "Ask and it will be given to you," Matt. 7:7; cf. Matt. 7:8–11). Now some believe wisdom will somehow magically pop up in a person's head or heart and an otherwise foolish or ignorant person will suddenly be infused with an injection of divine, supernatural wisdom. A more likely interpretation of this passage, however, is that God will *develop* wisdom in such a person over time as part of a process on their journey.

James issues one caveat, however: such prayer for wisdom must be offered in *faith*, not doubt (*diakrinō*), because a person who doubts will receive nothing from God; such a person is "double-minded" (*dipsychos*; literally, "two-souled," similar to schizophrenic or bipolar) and "unstable [*akatastatos*; elsewhere in the NT only in 3:8, there translated "restless"] in all his ways" (1:5–8). Again, James's words echo those of Jesus, who said, "Truly, I say to you, if you have faith and do not doubt [*diakrinō*], . . . even if you say to this mountain, 'Be taken up and thrown into the sea,' it will happen. And whatever you ask in prayer, you will receive, if you have faith" (Matt. 21:21–22). Nothing will be impossible for those with mountain-moving faith! James's analogy to one who doubts is that of "a wave of the sea that is driven and tossed by the wind," which may invoke the (frequently turbulent) weather on the Sea of Galilee, to which the Gospel narratives amply attest.

At this, James addresses one specific problem in the congregations to which he writes: preferential treatment of the rich (1:9–11). He will return to this topic at some length at least twice later in his letter (2:1–7; 5:1–6). In this first early mention, his focus is on encouraging the poor and exhorting the rich: the "lowly" brother (*tapeinos*) should "boast" in his exaltation—esteeming the privilege of lacking material possessions, so he is more keenly aware of his dependence on God's provision—while the rich (the word "brother" may be implied here) should boast in his "lowliness" (*tapeinōsis*). Note the play on words between "lowly" and "lowliness," a feature often lost in translations such as the ESV that translate *tapeinos* with "lowly" and *tapeinōsis* with "humiliation." Apparently, James addresses both the poor and the rich in the congregation as "brothers"—that is, believers—and exhorts each of them to take an appropriate stance toward God amid their material circumstances (1:9–10). Both, whether rich or poor, ought to recognize their dependence on God. To drive home the transitory nature of wealth, James, in conjunction with an OT allusion (Isa. 40:6–7), uses an illustration from the hot climate of Palestine, where the sun with its scorching heat withers the vegetation; the same fate will come upon the rich: their wealth will "fade away" (*marainō*, unique in the NT) as they go about their business (1:11).

Returning to the way in which he started this portion of the letter, James now elaborates on his opening statement that believers should count it "all joy" when they encounter various kinds of trials (1:3). At the outset, James wrote that steadfastness rendered a person "perfect and complete, lacking in nothing" (1:4). Now he elaborates that a man who remains steadfast under trial is "blessed" (*makarios*), perhaps invoking Jesus's Beatitudes in the Sermon on the Mount (Matt. 5:3–12). This person, having stood the test, "will receive the crown of life"—that is, his promised heavenly reward (1:12).

Similarly, Paul speaks of "the crown of righteousness" (2 Tim. 4:8; cf. 1 Cor. 9:25), and Peter of "the unfading crown of glory" (1 Pet. 5:4). The "crown" (*stephanos*) was a victor's prize awarded in athletic contests in the ancient world; underlying the conception of an athletic context is the NT writers' confidence that those who remain steadfast under trial and endure until the end will receive a spiritual reward from God in heaven. James closes this exhortation with a clarification: temptation is never from God; rather, it is one's own desire—first conceived, then giving birth in the form of sin—that tempts a person (1:13–15). Again, Jesus's words in the Lord's Prayer come to mind: "Lead us not into temptation [*peirasmos*]" (Matt. 6:13).

In a rather stern rebuke, James tells his readers not to be deceived (1:16; note the warnings against self-deception in 1:22 and 26): God does not change, and every good gift comes from him, or "from above," a characteristic Jewish circumlocution referring to the divine name (1:17; cf. 3:15, 17; John 3:3, 7). God is good! He can never be the source of evil; temptation arises from an evil heart. It did so originally in mysterious fashion in the heart of Lucifer, who wanted to be like God, and through Lucifer (turned Satan) infected the human race when Satan promised Eve in the garden that if she ate the forbidden fruit, she and her husband would be like God (Gen. 3:5).[3] By tempting Eve in this way, Satan cast doubt on God's goodness, implying that God intended to withhold something from her and her husband that he knew would be beneficial for them. In this way, Satan deceived the woman (2 Cor. 11:3; 1 Tim. 2:14). James doesn't want his readers to be deceived in a similar way (not implying that James necessarily had Satan's deception of Eve at the fall in mind, though this is not impossible). Jesus had similarly asserted, "If you then, who are evil, know how to give good gifts to your children, how much more will your Father who is in heaven give good things to those who ask him!" (Matt. 7:11). As a specific example of such a good gift, Luke adduces the Holy Spirit (Luke 11:13); James here adduces the new birth brought about by "the word of truth" (1:18; cf. 1 Pet. 1:23; 2 Tim. 2:15), rendering the readers "firstfruits" (*aparchē*)—another agricultural metaphor referring to the first produce of the season—of God's creatures (cf. Rom. 16:5; 1 Cor. 16:15; 2 Thess. 2:13).[4]

---

3. See Isaiah 14:12 (though not all scholars agree that this reference to the "Day Star" is to prefall Satan).

4. Plummer ("James," 235) notes that firstfruits "alludes to OT laws mandating that the earliest part of the agricultural harvest be offered in gratitude to God in anticipation of the expected remainder of the harvest (Exod. 23:19; Lev. 2:12; Num. 18:12)," which would have reminded James's readers that they were only among the first of many more believers the Lord would gather into his fold.

Excursus on Practicing One's Faith and True Religion (1:19–27)

Introduced by the phrase "My beloved brothers," which both begins this new exhortation (1:19) and concludes the previous one (1:16), James continues his convicting, prophetic-style exhortation. Essentially, he challenges his readers to put their religion into practice by being "doers of the word" and to practice "true religion." The opening exhortation to "be quick to hear, slow to speak, slow to anger," is firmly rooted in OT wisdom (1:19; see the book of Proverbs). The OT repeatedly affirms that God himself is slow to anger (Exod. 34:6; Num. 14:18; Neh. 9:31; Ps. 86:5, 15; Joel 2:13); how much more should people be slow to get angry: "for the anger of man does not produce the righteousness of God" (1:20; cf. Eph. 4:26 citing Ps. 4:4)? James also urges his readers to put away all "filthiness" (*ryparia*, not elsewhere in the NT) and rampant evil and to receive the "implanted" (*emphytos*; not elsewhere in the NT) word with meekness.[5]

Having mentioned the "word of truth" at the end of the previous exhortation (1:18), and now speaking of the "implanted word" (1:21), James sets the stage for talking about being "doers of the word, and not hearers only" (1:22). Again, Jesus's words at the end of the Sermon on the Mount ring in one's ears: "Not everyone who says to me, 'Lord, Lord,' will enter the kingdom of heaven, but the one who does the will of my Father who is in heaven. . . . Everyone then who hears these words of mine and does them will be like a wise man who built his house on the rock" (Matt. 7:21–27). Hearing without application is tantamount to self-deception. James gives the example of a man who looks himself in the mirror and then walks away and immediately forgets what he looked like (1:23–24). Conversely, the person who peers into (*parakyptō*; elsewhere in the NT in Luke 24:12; John 20:5, 11; 1 Pet. 1:12) the "perfect law of liberty" and puts it into practice will be blessed (*makarios*; cf. 1:12; see also 5:11) in his doing. Here we already see an emphasis on action that will inform James's words on the relationship between faith and works in chapter 2 that have given rise to much discussion and have caused some (such as Martin Luther) to dismiss James's teaching and have caused many to see a contradiction (or at least tension) between James's teaching and that of Paul (more on this soon). In light of the pervasive and demonstrable influence of Jesus's teaching on James, however, we would argue that James's teaching is perfectly aligned with that of Jesus and that both merely stress the importance of putting one's faith into practice and warn against false professions of faith without adequate follow-through.

---

5. "Implanted" is reminiscent of the language of some of Jesus's parables, such as the parable of the sower and the soils (Mark 4:1–20 and parallels).

Concluding his second exhortation, James, in 1:26 and 27, three times uses the rare term "religious" (*thrēskos*; only here in the NT) or "religion" (*thrēskeia*; used elsewhere in the NT only in Acts 26:5 with reference to Judaism and in Col. 2:18 with regard to angel worship). Anyone who professes to be religious but fails to control his tongue is self-deceived (1:26; cf. 1:16, 22; James will later devote an entire chapter to this topic; see James 3 below).[6] "Pure and undefiled religion," according to James, in keeping with OT teaching involves care for orphans and widows (cf., e.g., Pss. 10:14, 18; 68:5; Isa. 1:17; Jer. 22:3) as well as keeping oneself "unstained" (*aspilos*; elsewhere in the NT only in 1 Tim. 6:14; 1 Pet. 1:19; 2 Pet. 3:14)—spotless, unpolluted, uncontaminated—from the world (1:27). This kind of Christian piety calls for, on the one hand, separation from the world's evil and a resolute commitment not to get entangled in unrighteousness and, on the other, an active expression of Christian social concern for the helpless—orphans and widows. Orphans, of course, were in desperate need due to their loss of father and mother; widows, too, were often in dire straits financially in the ancient world due to the loss of their husband and needed financial and other support (cf. esp. 1 Tim. 5:2–16).

The present passage serves as a potent reminder for Christians today not to neglect putting their faith into practice in tangible ways and helping those who are needy, such as the unborn, children, or the victims of sex trafficking, to name but a few concrete examples. In recent years, there has often been a debate between (liberal) advocates of the "social gospel" and those who focus on the spiritual message of the gospel (salvation and forgiveness of sins). James is helpful here in that he affirms both the need for spiritual regeneration (1:18, 21) and the need for tangible expression of social concern (1:26–27). Spiritual and social dimensions of the Christian faith go together, James reminds us, and either one without the other—whether regeneration without social concern or social concern without regeneration—is inadequate, to say the least. As mentioned, James will have more to say about this topic in his next chapter.

Warning against Preferential Treatment of the Rich (2:1–13)

In chapter 1, James exhorted his audience regarding their need to stand firm when their faith was tested, whether by external or internal challenges (1:2–18). As part of this opening exhortation, James also touched on the proper attitude for the lowly and the rich (1:9–11). His second exhortation pertained to believers' need to practice "true religion"—that is, to live out their faith with

---

6. See Dan G. McCartney, "Self-Deception in James," *CTR* 8, no. 2 (2011): 31–43.

authenticity and integrity (1:19–27). Putting their faith into practice involved tangible expressions of social concern, such as caring for orphans and widows, in keeping with OT teaching. While chapter 1 does not contain any explicit references to Jesus (apart from the opening reference in v. 1), we've seen that James's teaching is thoroughly grounded in Jesus's teaching, especially in the Sermon on the Mount (Matt. 5–7). This is perhaps nowhere more apparent than in James's insistence that believers must be "doers of the word, and not hearers only," which closely parallels the closing words of the Sermon on the Mount (1:22; cf. Matt. 7:21–27). In addition, James's teaching is regularly built off of OT teaching, such as his words on caring for orphans and widows (1:27; e.g., Isa. 1:17).

Chapter 2, introduced with the phrase "My brothers" (cf. 1:2; see also "My beloved brothers" in 1:16, 19; 2:5), opens with the only major reference to Jesus in the entire letter. Elaborating on his previous comments on the lowly and the rich (1:9–11), James exhorts the readers to "show no partiality" (*prosōpolēmpsia*) as they profess faith "in our Lord Jesus Christ, the Lord of glory" (2:1). The syntax is somewhat awkward in the original language, which literally says, "our Lord Jesus Christ of glory." Again, James urges his readers to act in the congregation in keeping with the true nature of their faith, contending that showing partiality toward the rich is incompatible with God's character (cf. Rom. 2:11: "For God shows no partiality"; Eph. 6:9; Col. 3:25). "Lord of glory" is a highly exalted expression applied to Jesus Christ, especially this early in the first century, perhaps only a decade after Jesus died, rose, and ascended into heaven (see 5:7). While James, as mentioned, frequently echoes and draws on the teachings of the earthly Jesus, he here (and in 1:1) makes clear that he views Jesus as presently exalted and having moved past his earthly ministry into his heavenly state.[7]

Again, this is no new teaching; the law was already very clear on this matter: "You shall do no injustice in court. You shall not be partial to the poor or defer to the great, but in righteousness shall you judge your neighbor" (Lev. 19:15). Applying this set of principles to congregational life, James gives the example of a rich man wearing a gold ring and fine clothing being given a good seat in the congregation while a poor man is told to "stand over there" (2:2–3). This, James argues, is undue discrimination and an outflow of "evil thoughts" (2:4). God has chosen the poor to be "rich in faith" and "heirs of the kingdom" (2:5). Again, the teaching of Jesus immediately comes to mind: "Blessed are you who are poor, for yours is the kingdom of God" (Luke 6:20;

---

7. On the theology, Christology, and eschatology of James, see Köstenberger, Kellum, and Quarles, *The Cradle, the Cross, and the Crown*, 821–22.

cf. Matt. 5:3); also, the citation of Isaiah 61:1 in Luke 4:18: "The Spirit of the Lord is upon me, because he has anointed me to proclaim good news to the poor." Jesus's teaching, in turn, is congruent with OT teaching regarding the poor (e.g., Prov. 19:17). The point is that for God it makes no difference whether or not a person has material possessions. God looks at the heart and at a person's character (cf. 1 Sam. 16:7). Therefore, in our congregations we should not be blinded by material wealth but rather look at people the way God looks at them—for who they are regardless of power, status, and prestige in this world.[8]

In fact, roles will often be reversed in God's kingdom, and the poor be found better prepared to enter than the rich. Jesus said, "Truly, I say to you, only with difficulty will a rich person enter the kingdom of heaven. Again I tell you, it is easier for a camel to go through the eye of a needle than for a rich person to enter the kingdom of God" (Matt. 19:23–24). James added that showing preference to the rich was ironic also in that it was the rich who exploited the readers and dragged them into court, even blaspheming God's name (2:6–7). Why, then, honor the rich and dishonor the poor? This is another penetrating, prophetic word of James that is applicable also to today's church, which is rife with materialism and where preferential treatment is often given to those of means or worldly status. At best, the poor are treated as cases of benevolence, but they are rarely accepted as members of equal standing in the church. The same applies to other people of low status in society such as immigrants, ethnic minorities, and those of another race.

James has already called the law "the perfect law, the law of liberty" (1:25; cf. 2:12 below); now he speaks of "the royal law according to the Scripture"— that is, the command to love one's neighbor as oneself (2:8; cf. Lev. 19:18; the word for "royal" is *basilikos*, used in Acts 12:21 to refer to Herod's "royal robe").[9] Jesus himself said, "There is no other commandment greater than these" (Mark 12:31), listing this command second after the command to love God with all one's heart, soul, mind, and strength (cf. Deut. 6:5). According to James—who is still on the topic of undue preferential treatment in the church—showing partiality toward the rich is in fact a violation of the biblical command to love one's neighbor (2:9)! This is a brilliant and fascinating

8. For a treatment of James's ethical teaching, including that on social issues, see Andrew Chester, "The Theology of James," in *The Theology of the Letters to James, Peter, and Jude,* by Andrew Chester and Ralph P. Martin, NTT (Cambridge: Cambridge University Press, 1994), 16–45. See also Peter H. Davids, *A Theology of James, Peter, and Jude,* BTNT (Grand Rapids: Zondervan, 2014).

9. For a discussion of the reference to Lev. 19:18 in 2:8, see D. A. Carson, "James," in G. K. Beale and D. A. Carson, eds., *Commentary on the New Testament Use of the Old Testament* (Grand Rapids: Baker Academic, 2007), 998–1001.

application of OT teaching to the NT era and serves as a case study of early Christian ethics. In condemning preferential treatment, James minces no words: partiality is not merely an excusable but understandable lapse or minor offense; it is "sin" (*hamartia*) and amounts to a transgression of the law (2:9).

In keeping with standard rabbinic teaching—including that of Jesus—James proceeds to make the case that anyone who breaks one commandment has broken the entire law (2:10; cf. Matt. 5:18–19; Gal. 5:3; cf. Deut. 27:26).[10] No one can say, "I've only committed adultery, but I haven't murdered anyone (or vice versa), so I'm OK." It's obvious that we must keep both commandments (cf. Exod. 20:13–14); Jesus's teaching on both subjects—murder and adultery—in the Sermon on the Mount is relevant here (Matt. 5:21–30).[11] Therefore, James urges his readers to "speak and . . . act as those who are to be judged under the law of liberty," warning that those without mercy will be judged without mercy—yet "mercy triumphs over judgment" (2:11–13).[12] As Jesus said, "Blessed are the merciful, for they shall receive mercy" (Matt. 5:7), himself reflecting OT teaching (e.g., Mic. 6:8 NIV: "love mercy"). Therefore, God's people should be merciful toward others and not treat people based on their social status. As if these words were not convicting enough, James continues to drive home his point yet further when he asks the provocative question, "What good is it, my brothers, . . . if a brother or sister [note that here a 'sister' is mentioned explicitly] is poorly clothed and lacking in daily food, and one of you says to them, 'Go in peace, be warmed and filled,' without giving them the things needed for the body . . . ?" (2:14–16). The obvious answer to this rhetorical question is that such faith is worthless and in fact hypocritical. Again, Jesus made the same point emphatically in one of his end-time parables when he said that whenever his followers gave a needy person food, drink, or shelter or visited someone in prison, it was as if they had done it for Jesus himself (Matt. 25:31–46).

10. For more detailed discussion and primary references in extrabiblical (including rabbinic) literature, see the standard commentaries—e.g., Douglas J. Moo, *The Letter of James*, PNTC (Grand Rapids: Eerdmans, 2000), 113–17.

11. For a discussion of the use of the OT in 2:11, see Carson, "James," 1001–3. The commands not to murder and not to commit adultery are the sixth and seventh commandments in the Decalogue (the Ten Commandments), the second tablet, so Jesus and James naturally start with these. Cf. the words in Matt. 19:18 spoken by Jesus, who likewise starts with the commands not to murder, not to commit adultery, not to steal, and not to bear false witness, before backtracking to the command to honor one's father and mother and citing the command to love one's neighbor as oneself.

12. Plummer ("James," 248) notes that James's words here are reminiscent of the spiritual lesson imparted by Jesus in his parable of the unmerciful servant in Matt. 18:32–35.

Excursus on the Relationship between Faith and Works (2:14-26)

At this, James moves from the specific example of rendering practical assistance to the poor to dealing with the broader theological question: *What is the relationship between faith and works?*[13] It is interesting to note how theology here arises out of a practical issue rather than the other way around. The problem of people in the church doing nothing about the predicament of the poor raises the question of the legitimacy and authenticity of their profession of Christian faith. Does inaction in the face of the need of others in our midst invalidate such a faith profession? One thinks of Jesus's parable of the good Samaritan, which drives home the point that a person's neighbor is any person in need (Luke 10:25–37). In that parable, it was not the religious professionals—priest or Levite—who passed the test but a lowly Samaritan. The message is clear: merciful action speaks louder than pious words. In fact, pious words not backed up by merciful action are empty, hollow, and hypocritical.

Returning to James's question in 2:14, therefore ("What good is it, my brothers, if someone says he has faith but does not have works?"), we see that James answers his own question in verse 17: "So also faith by itself, if it does not have works, is dead." Dead! Those are strong words. James anticipates that some will not readily accept such a stern verdict, so he engages in dialogue with an imaginary interlocutor in what follows: "But someone will say, 'You have faith and I have works.'" He retorts, "Show me your faith *apart* from your works, and I will show you my faith *by* my works" (2:18). When the relationship between faith and works is put in such terms, it is clear that faith is revealed *by* a person's works, while it is a virtual impossibility to show one's faith without any tangible expression in the form of concrete actions. Such faith may exist, but it can't be shown or validated, since the validation of one's faith consists of works done in faith. Citing the Jewish Shema—affirming the characteristic Jewish monotheistic belief that God is one (Deut. 6:4)—James brushes this profession aside, retorting that even "demons believe—and shudder!" (2:19). In other words, mere intellectual assent to orthodox doctrine unaccompanied by heartfelt, faith-inspired action is inadequate and nonsalvific.

As biblical proof, James cites the OT example of Abraham "our father" (indicating the Jewish nature of his audience), who, according to James, was

---

13. Plummer ("James," 250) notes the inclusio between 2:16 and 2:24 and observes that James here provides an "illustration of useless faith" (vv. 15–17) and "correcting an interlocutor" (vv. 18–20), and proceeds to the examples of Abraham (vv. 21–24) and Rahab (v. 25). For a basic discussion, see Köstenberger, Kellum, and Quarles, *The Cradle, the Cross, and the Crown*, 822–25.

"justified by works" when offering up his son Isaac (2:21; cf. Gen. 22:1–19, esp. v. 9).[14] Interpreting the dynamic underlying Abraham's actions, which are not fully spelled out in the Genesis narrative (which simply says that at God's command, "Abraham rose early in the morning," took the needed supplies for an offering, and set out for Mount Moriah with two young men and his son Isaac, in Gen. 22:3), James observes that in Abraham's case, "faith was *active along with his works*, and *faith was completed by his works*" (2:22). This is the kind of faith that justified Abraham in the eyes of God, and the statement in Genesis 15:6, "Abraham believed God, and it was counted to him as righteousness" (2:23), which James cites at this point, should be interpreted in that vein and that context rather than being taken out of context (the main context here being Gen. 22) and implying that faith can be separated from works validating such faith. Faith is primary but works will—and must— inexorably follow. This kind of active faith, James argues, was what commended Abraham to God and resulted in Abraham being called a "friend of God" in subsequent OT Scripture (2:23; cf. 2 Chron. 20:7; Isa. 41:8).

At this, James summarizes his argument: "A person is justified by works *and not by faith alone*" (i.e., by faith artificially severed from associated and accompanying faith-inspired actions; 2:24). Of course, no one would want to insist on such "dead" faith in any case; what is faith worth if not being practically demonstrated in actual deeds? The two obviously belong together. One is almost tempted to appropriate Jesus's words, originally given in the context of marriage and divorce, and to apply them to the present question: "What therefore God has joined together [i.e., faith and works], let not man separate" (i.e., artificially dichotomize by disjunctive thinking or theological reasoning; Matt. 19:6 // Mark 10:9). In closing, James adds a second example, that of Rahab the prostitute, who likewise was "justified by works" when sheltering the spies scouting out the promised land (2:25; cf. Josh. 2:1, 4, 15; 6:17). James ends his discussion of the relationship between faith and works with a poignant analogy: Just as "the body apart from the spirit is dead, so also faith apart from works is dead" (2:26). And based on James's compelling argumentation, who would disagree?

In fact, many disagree. As mentioned, James's treatment of the relationship between faith and works in 2:14–26 is by far the most-discussed passage in the entire letter among scholars. Often, the problem is that people start with what the apostle Paul says on this subject—especially in the letter to the Galatians—and then compare James's teaching to that of Paul. The problem with this is, in part, that James wrote first—would it therefore not

14. See the discussion of this passage at Heb. 11:17–19 above.

be more appropriate to start with James and to subsequently compare Paul with James? I would argue that this would be a better procedure to follow. In fact, this is what I've done above (notice that there is no reference to Paul's teaching). If James wrote in the early to mid-40s AD, several years prior to Paul's letter to the Galatians and the Jerusalem Council, it will be helpful to be mindful of James's context before situating Paul's theological argument in Galatians in its context.

Specifically, James, as mentioned, is an exemplar of early Jewish Christianity, still very much grounded in OT teaching. This is why the argument from Abraham in Genesis 15:6 and Genesis 22 is so important, because James hopes that it will prove compelling for his Jewish readers, some of whom may have previously interpreted Genesis 15:6 differently. Against interpretations of Genesis 15:6 out of context, James shows that, when that verse is read in light of the following narrative, particularly Genesis 22, Abraham's faith—the one that was credited to him by God as righteousness—was not a "dead" faith (i.e., one unaccompanied by faith-inspired action) but one that led to one of the most striking expressions of OT faith—Abraham's willingness to offer up his son Isaac, the son God had promised and given, in fulfillment of the Abrahamic covenant (cf. Gen. 12:1–3). In this regard, it will be very profitable and instructive to read what the author of the book of Hebrews (also written to Jewish believers) says about this same set of passages:

> By faith Abraham obeyed when he was called to go out to a place that he was to receive as an inheritance. And he went out, not knowing where he was going. By faith, he went to live in the land of promise. . . .
> By faith, Abraham, when he was tested, offered up Isaac, and he who had received the promises was in the act of offering up his only son, of whom it was said, "Through Isaac shall your offspring be named." *He considered that God was able even to raise him from the dead, from which, figuratively speaking, he did receive him back.* (Heb. 11:8–9, 17–19)

Of course, the difference is that the author of Hebrews holds Abraham up as an example of *faith*, while James holds him up as an example of *works* (albeit ones that were inspired by strong faith). But this is more a function of the different kinds of pastoral situations the two authors are addressing than it is evidence of a different (or even conflicting) theological outlook. In the case of Hebrews, the congregation was tempted to drift away from their Christian confession; in that context, the author argues that in truth, even OT believers had the kind of faith that now was to be exemplified as faith *in Jesus* (Heb. 12:1–2). In James's case, the congregation insisted they had faith while showing preferential treatment to the rich and failing to care for the poor and needy in their midst. In that context, James argues that mere professions of faith alone are not enough—they must be accompanied by works on the part of those who, in keeping with the teaching of Jesus, are "doers of the word and not hearers only" (1:22). In the end, both authors advocate the necessity of an active, living faith that is based on God's promises and that results in action ("works").

Turning to Paul, he, too, spoke into a unique pastoral context—namely, the teaching of the so-called Judaizers in the Roman province of Galatia (part of modern Turkey) several years after James had written his letter. Paul's purpose for writing his letter to the Galatians is evident from his comment at the outset of the letter, "I am astonished that you are so quickly deserting him who called you in the grace of Christ and are turning to a different gospel" (Gal. 1:6). What was this "different gospel"? In short, it was the teaching by so-called Judaizers that Christians were required to follow Jewish customs such as circumcision. While "Jesus Christ was publicly portrayed" before the Galatians "as crucified," Paul had to ask them the pointed question: "Did you receive the Spirit by works of the law or by hearing with faith?" (3:1–2). Scholars vigorously debate the meaning of the phrase "works of the law" in this and other Pauline passages. In any case, Paul's concern was that adding circumcision to the requirements for salvation, on top of faith, didn't merely change the gospel; it utterly subverted it, rendering the crucifixion ultimately unnecessary. If salvation could be attained by keeping the law, why did Christ have to come and die? As a result, Paul was adamant that all people—Jews as well as gentiles—were justified by faith, not by keeping the law (3:7), in accord with the core message of both the law, as exemplified in Genesis 15:6, and the prophets, as exemplified in Habakkuk 2:3–4, passages he cites in both Galatians and Romans (written a few years later).

Does Paul, then, contradict James's teaching as outlined above? This is the case only if their assertions are pressed to conform their literal wording to each other. The spirit of each writer is that both sought to instruct believers in their respective pastoral realms to live out their faith in a God-pleasing manner. In James's case, he must press professing believers to act out their faith in keeping with their Christian commitment, urging them on to "active faith," faith resulting in works. In Paul's case, he must defend the gospel against undue additions, insisting that no one can add to what Christ did for them on the cross; salvation is by faith alone through grace alone. While a necessary outflow of faith, works are not part of the gospel—what people must do in order to be saved. All that is required in response to God's work in Christ on the cross is faith in the crucified and risen Messiah and his finished cross-work. When Jewish people asked Jesus, "What must we do to do the works God requires?" he simply responded by saying, "This is the work of God, that you believe in him whom he has sent" (John 6:28–29). With this, both James and Paul would have whole-heartedly agreed.[15]

Warning against Many Becoming Teachers (3:1–12)

Perhaps there is a connection between James's discussion of the thorny theological subject of the relationship between faith and works and his exhortation starting in 3:1: "Not many of you should become teachers, my brothers." Paul at times could be harsh when it came to would-be teachers, such as when he remarked in his first letter to Timothy that "certain persons . . . have wandered away into vain discussion, desiring to be teachers of the law, without understanding either what they are saying or the things about which they make confident assertions" (1 Tim. 1:7). In other words, those self-appointed teachers didn't know what they were talking about! Elsewhere, Paul warns against appointing elders prematurely and stipulates that they be "able to teach" and be "able to give instruction in sound doctrine and also to rebuke those who contradict it" (1 Tim. 3:2, 6; Titus 1:9). The fallout of false teaching can be devastating for the church. As Jesus said, "The truth will set you free" (John 8:32), but, alternatively, false teaching enslaves and brings people into bondage.

The reason James gives for why being a teacher should be considered a position for the select few is that "we who teach [including himself among those who teach] will be judged with greater strictness" (3:1). Paul implies as much when he writes to Timothy, "Do your best to present yourself to God as one approved, a worker who has no need to be ashamed, rightly handling the word of truth" (2 Tim. 2:15). His references to God's approval and to not needing to be ashamed both conjure up the notion of God's end-time judgment for teachers. As teachers and preachers of God's Word, we're responsible and accountable for our hermeneutics and the accuracy of our teaching and will one day give an account for what we've taught and preached. As James points out, all of us stumble in many ways, but the person who doesn't slip up

---

15. See also the wonderful balance in Paul's statement on the same issue in Ephesians: "For *by grace* you have been saved *through faith* . . . not a result of works, so that no one may boast. For we are his workmanship, *created* in Christ Jesus *for good works*, which God prepared beforehand, that we should walk in them" (2:8–10). So, Paul is saying, we were not saved *by* works but *for* works. On the subject of grace in the NT and in particular in Paul's writings, see also John M. G. Barclay, *Paul and the Gift* (Grand Rapids: Eerdmans, 2017).

in what he *says* is a "perfect man" (3:2; cf. 1:4 regarding steadfastness under trials).

In fact, it's amazing just how hard it is to control a body part as small as our tongue! James aptly illustrates this with several poignant examples:

- bits put in the mouth of horses (3:3)
- a very small rudder steering a ship (3:4)
- a small fire setting ablaze a large forest (3:5)

Virtually every animal—beast and bird, reptile and sea creature—can be, and has been, tamed by humanity; but no one can tame the tongue (3:7–8).[16]

Here is what James says about the tongue:

- It boasts of great things (3:5).
- It stains the whole body (3:6).
- It sets on fire the entire course of life and is itself set on fire by hell (3:6).
- It is untamable (3:7–8).
- It is a restless evil, full of deadly poison (3:8).
- With it we bless God and curse people made in God's image (3:9).[17]

Again, James uses several colorful and culture-appropriate illustrations as to why it is improper for an instrument such as the tongue to become the vehicle of two diametrically opposite actions (both blessing and cursing):

- a spring producing both fresh and salt water (3:11)
- a fig tree bearing olives or a grapevine producing figs (3:12)
- a salt pond yielding fresh water (3:12)

Clearly, in the natural realm such incompatible results or fruits are impossible and inconceivable. Yet, paradoxically, it is not so with the tongue: it utters both blessings and curses. James's point in his various illustrations, however, is that while this is possible, it should not be so. Things have changed very little in the last couple millennia since James wrote. People still say offensive things on Twitter and lose their job or political office over it. Husbands still

16. Plummer ("James," 269) notes that in v. 7 James harks back to the categorization of animals in four major classes (cf. Gen. 1:20–21, 24–25).

17. Plummer ("James," 269) observes that in v. 8 James mirrors terminology found in the Psalms (e.g., Pss. 5:9; 12:2; 140:3). See also Dale C. Allison, "Blessing God and Cursing People: James 3:9–10," *JBL* 130 (2011): 397–405.

stick their foot in their mouth and hurt their wives with insensitive remarks. And preachers still say things from the pulpit that get them into trouble years later and in some cases even force their resignation. Especially those of us who are teachers should resolve to guard our tongue with all our might since we have a greater responsibility and accountability due to our more public and more visible position.

Excursus on the Contrast between Earthly and Heavenly Wisdom (3:13–18)

At this point, James extols the many virtues of wisdom (*sophia*; 3:13–18; the list somewhat resembles Paul's list in Phil. 4:8).[18] He distinguishes the "meekness of wisdom" from "bitter jealousy and selfish ambition" leading to "disorder" and "every vile practice" (vv. 14–16).[19] Earthly "wisdom" is "unspiritual" and "demonic" (*daimoniōdēs*, only here in the NT; 3:15) while "wisdom from above" (i.e., God-induced wisdom) is characterized by the following seven attributes, most of which start with either the letter *alpha* (*a*) or *epsilon* (*e*), which would have facilitated memorization or at least memorability (v. 17):

1. pure (*agnos*; as an attribute of women, Titus 2:5; 1 Pet. 3:2)

Followed by a triad of Greek words starting with the letter *epsilon*:

2. peaceable (*eirēnikos*; elsewhere in the NT only in Heb. 12:11; cf. James 3:18)
3. gentle (*epieikēs*; cf. Phil. 4:5; 1 Tim. 3:3; Titus 3:2; 1 Pet. 2:18)
4. open to reason (*eupeithēs*; only here in the NT)

Then another triad with words in the second and third example starting with the letter *alpha*:

5. full of mercy and good fruits (another agricultural metaphor; cf. 5:7, 18)
6. impartial (*adiakritos*; only here in the NT)

18. William Varner, "The Main Theme and Structure of James," *MSJ* 22 (2011): 115–29, argues that 3:13–18 constitutes the peak of the letter, highlighting James's primary concerns. See already George H. Guthrie, "James," in *Hebrews–Revelation*, vol. 13 of *Expositor's Bible Commentary*, rev. ed., edited by Tremper Longman III and David E. Garland (Grand Rapids: Zondervan, 2005), 206, who posits a macrochiasm with 3:13–18 at the center.

19. Plummer ("James," 264) notes that James's words here are reminiscent of Jesus's denunciation of the Pharisees in Matt. 12:33–35.

7. sincere (*anypokritos*; love, Rom. 12:9; 2 Cor. 6:6; 1 Pet. 1:22; faith, 1 Tim. 1:5; 2 Tim. 1:5)

The overriding quality of wisdom is peace, which is mentioned three times in the last two verses (3:17–18).

Every one of us would do well to confront our natural tendency toward envy, greed, jealousy, and selfish ambition and to reflect on the above list of attributes of wisdom. It's also worth remembering that wisdom is personified in the book of Proverbs as a woman (e.g., Prov. 1:20–33) and presented as an attribute of God at creation (8:22–31). In conjunction with James's remarks on teachers earlier in the chapter, it's worth reflecting on the fact that teaching is more than imparting knowledge; more importantly, it requires wisdom. Thus, teachers in James's day and in ours are set on notice that theirs is a more taxing task that requires great wisdom and self-control (taming of the tongue). This sets the bar very high for teachers in the church and calls for diligent self-examination as well as careful screening of suitable candidates in the church.

Warning against Covetousness, Slander, and Arrogant Planning (4:1-17)

Chapter 4 starts with a rhetorical question. Apparently, James was aware of conflict in the congregations to which he wrote. Previously in this letter, he tackled the issue of dealing with trials and temptations and the need to care for orphans and widows, warned against giving preferential treatment to the rich, and advised against many wanting to become teachers. Perhaps a clue to the underlying motivation for addressing the topic of "quarrels" (*polemoi*; cf. Matt. 24:6 and parallels; our English word "polemic" is derived from this word) and "fights" (*machai*; elsewhere in the NT in 2 Cor. 7:5; 2 Tim. 2:23; Titus 3:9) amid the congregation is the fact that James has just mentioned the need for "the meekness of wisdom" and cautioned against "bitter jealousy and selfish ambition in your hearts" (3:13–14). Perhaps there is a connection between 3:13–18 and chapter 4 that is masked by the chapter division.

James is quick to answer his own question: the reason for these conflicts is that people's passions (*hēdonē*; cf. v. 3 below; see also Titus 3:3; 2 Pet. 2:13 [ESV: "pleasure"]; our English word *hedonism* is derived from this word) are waging war within them. Covetousness—breaking the tenth commandment (cf. Exod. 20:17)—leads to "murder," not necessarily literal murder, but manifestations of hatred, jealousy, and anger (again, cf. Jesus's teaching in the Sermon on the Mount: Matt. 5:21–26). When people want to have something they're not supposed to have and can't have it—perhaps it belongs to someone else already—negative emotions churn them up inside and incite them to quarrel; we know that all too well from our own experience. But there is a simpler way to go: asking God (cf. 1:5)! "You do not have, because you do not ask" (4:2).

One problem, therefore, is a failure to ask God—the giver of "every good gift and every perfect gift" (1:17)—when we want something. Yet mere asking is not enough; sometimes we ask but don't get what we want because we ask with the wrong motivation—to "spend" (*dapanaō*; cf. Mark 5:26; Luke 15:14) it on our passions (4:3; cf. James's earlier comments on being tempted by one's own desire, 1:13–15). The right way to respond to an unfulfilled desire, then, is to examine one's motivations and make sure we ask God with the proper motivation and for the right reasons. James already charged his readers with murder ("so you murder," 4:2); now he says they're adulterers as well: "You adulterous people!" (4:4).[20] By way of merism (parts representing the whole), breaking the sixth and seventh commandments, as well as the tenth, represents breaking the entire law, as James himself pointed out earlier (2:11). Again, what he has in mind is not literal but spiritual adultery—"friendship with the world," which amounts to enmity with God. In support, James cites two passages from Scripture: "He yearns jealously over the spirit that he has made to dwell in us" (4:5; source is unclear) and "God opposes the proud but gives grace to the humble" (4:6; Prov. 3:34; also cited in 1 Pet. 5:5). The former reference most likely doesn't refer to the Holy Spirit but to the spirit God infused into humanity through Adam (cf. Gen. 2:7). James's two points are that (1) God is jealous for our right heart motivation; and (2) God opposes pride while prizing humility.

At this, James, in characteristic fashion, unleashes a series of exhortations in rapid-fire succession, in several cases also spelling out the result of proper action (all verbatim quotations from 4:7–10):

- Submit yourselves therefore to God.
- Resist the devil, and he will flee from you.
- Draw near to God, and he will draw near to you.

---

20. The grammatical gender in the Greek is feminine, so that one could translate this, "You adulteresses!" (NASB; see also CSB, ESV, and NLT footnotes). Cf. Hosea 3:1, where God implies that Israel has committed spiritual adultery in keeping with the OT portrayal of God as Israel's spiritual husband (e.g., Isa. 54:5; Jer. 2:2; see discussion in Plummer, "James," 268).

- Cleanse your hands, you sinners.
- Purify your hearts, you double-minded (cf. 1:8).
- Be wretched and mourn and weep (anticipating 5:1).
- Let your laughter be turned to mourning and your joy to gloom.
- Humble yourselves before the Lord, and he will exalt you.

James proceeds to address an infraction of yet another commandment, the ninth, not to bear false witness against another (4:11; cf. Exod. 20:16). Judging another person is tantamount to elevating oneself to the position of judge, James argues. However, "There is only one lawgiver and judge"—God—"who is able to save and to destroy" (4:12). It is therefore inappropriate and presumptuous to judge one's neighbor.

Speaking of presumptuousness, it's likewise presumptuous to plan one's activities pridefully as if one were in charge of one's own destiny ("Come now, you who say," 4:13). Apparently, this was the custom of merchants in James's day, who said, "Today or tomorrow we will go into such and such a town and spend a year there and trade and make a profit" (4:13). Problem is, while planning out the next entire year, they didn't even know what tomorrow would bring (4:14). To engage in presumptuous medium- or long-range planning with this kind of prideful attitude overlooks the fact that our life is but "a mist that appears for a little time and then vanishes" (4:14).[21]

Does this mean that all planning is evil? Not at all. It's all a matter of humility and proper disposition toward God: "Instead you ought to say, '*If the Lord wills*, we will live and do this or that'" (4:15).[22] Planning, therefore, is good and necessary; *presumptuous*, prideful planning is evil. It's both boastful—asserting fallaciously that one is in control—and arrogant (4:16). The principle, therefore, is this: "Whoever knows the right thing to do and fails to do it, for him it is sin" (4:17).

In practice, there is often a fine line between proper and presumptuous planning. For this reason, we should ask God to examine our motives (cf. Pss. 26:2; 139:23–24; Prov. 16:2; Jer. 17:10) and to help us submit ourselves and our plans to him for his divine alteration (if necessary) and approval. As James identified himself at the beginning of his letter, I am "a servant of God" and as such accountable to him. Therefore, we should not act as though we are accountable to no one and can go and do as we please without submitting

21. Plummer ("James," 273) observes that the "brevity and contingency of human life . . . is a common motif in the OT (Pss. 39:5; 102:3; 144:4; Job 7:7)."

22. Plummer ("James," 274) notes the equivalent Latin phrase, *Deo volente* (D.V.), used by some to indicate that they will engage in a certain action "if the Lord wills."

our plans to him and humbling ourselves before him to receive our orders from "the Lord Jesus Christ" (cf. 1:1).

Warning to the Rich against Greed or Injustice (5:1–6)

Using the same introductory formula as in 4:13 ("Come now"), James proceeds to challenge the rich, returning to a topic he previously broached in 1:9–11 and 2:1–7, where he mentioned that the rich oppressed the poor and dragged them into court (2:6). Again, the chapter division between chapters 4 and 5 may mask the internal connection between 4:13–16 and chapter 5. Speaking of merchants engaging in presumptuous planning, in part perhaps out of greed ("make a profit," 4:13), may have led James to address the rich more directly in the following remarks in chapter 5: "Come now, you rich." In addition, many commentators argue that the group in 5:1–6 (outside the church) is distinct from the group in 4:13–17 (inside the church). As in the case of the merchants in 4:13–16, James frontally challenges this group of people in a blunt manner reminiscent of prophets such as Elijah or John the Baptist. James's challenge to the rich is to brace themselves for the miseries (*talaipōros*; elsewhere in the NT only in Rom. 3:16 in a citation of Isa. 59:7; the related verb is found in 4:9) that will come upon them.

James's withering denunciation of the rich in 5:2–6 again recalls Jesus's similar stern warnings to the rich in the Sermon on the Mount when he said, "Do not lay up for yourselves treasures on earth, where *moth* and *rust* destroy and where thieves break in and steal, but lay up for yourselves *treasures* in heaven, where neither moth nor rust destroys and where thieves do not break in and steal" (Matt. 6:19–20). James similarly speaks of riches that have rotted and garments that are *moth*-eaten; gold and silver have *rusted*; the rich have "laid up *treasure* in the last days" (5:2–3). In addition, James now elaborates on the oppression of the poor at which he had previously only hinted (2:6). The rich had defrauded the laborers (who had mowed their fields) of their proper wages, but their cries had now reached the ears of "the Lord of hosts" (5:4; cf. Isa. 5:9). John the Baptist had similarly excoriated various groups of people in his day with prophetic zeal for justice (Matt. 3:7–10; Luke 3:7–14). The sin of the rich is that of self-indulgence (*spatalaō*, 5:5; elsewhere in the NT only in 1 Tim. 5:6). While others suffered, they opportunistically exploited the plight of others to enrich themselves ("You have fattened your hearts in a day of slaughter," 5:5; cf. Jer. 12:1–4). In addition, they had engaged in literal murder, condemning (cf. the reference to "dragging the lowly into court";

cf. 2:6) and killing the righteous person who could not or chose not to resist them (5:6).[23]

Social justice often constitutes a blind spot in the evangelical church today. Christian churches and other organizations presume upon the work of church members or employees and expect them to work for free or for minimal pay. Institutions co-opt the work of their employees and make it their own without proper credit (or remuneration) being given. Power is used to oppress (or at least protect one's power) rather than to serve and lead. Self-promotion masks as altruism, and pious posturing invokes the "Great Commission" or other noble-sounding aims and purposes. Truly, the human heart is wicked and deceitful; greed and selfish ambition will not die unless they are exposed, repented of, and renounced. As always, Jesus set the example: he who "had nowhere to lay his head" (Luke 9:58); he who "though he was rich, yet for your sake became poor so that you by his poverty might become rich" (2 Cor. 8:9; see Paul's discussion in 1 Cor. 9 and 2 Cor. 8–9). While we may not consider ourselves rich, we still should be careful not to exploit others in the church or other social contexts.

Concluding Call to Patience and Prayer in Suffering (5:7–20)

After addressing merchants (4:13–17) and the rich (5:1–6) directly ("Come now"), James returns to address his "brothers," that is, the members of the congregation(s) to which he writes (5:7). He calls them to be long-suffering and patient until the coming (*parousia*) of the Lord (i.e., Jesus Christ; cf. 1:1; 2:1; see also the reference to the "crown of life" in 1:12 and the discussion below). As is common in the NT, James cites the farmer as an example of patient waiting for the harvest (5:7; cf. 2 Tim. 2:6). "Establish your hearts," he urges (*stērizō*; cf. Rom. 1:11; 16:25; 1 Thess. 3:2, 13; 2 Thess. 2:17; 3:3; 1 Pet. 5:10; 2 Pet. 1:12), for the Lord's coming "is at hand" (*engizō*, to approach, draw near; 5:8; cf. 4:8; Rom. 13:12; Heb. 10:25; 1 Pet. 4:7).

The prospect of Jesus's return should encourage believers to renew their efforts to stand firm and wait patiently for their final deliverance. Admittedly, James wrote this almost two millennia ago, and Jesus has yet to come back, but Peter reminds us not to be like those who discard the prospect of Jesus's coming, because with God a thousand years are like a single day (2 Pet. 3:8; cf. Ps. 90:4). Looking at it this way, only a couple days have passed since James penned his epistle! Again, James's teaching here echoes Jesus's end-time parables exhorting his disciples to patient waiting for his return and faithful service in the interim (see, e.g., Matt. 25).

23. For a discussion of the OT use in 5:4–6, see Carson, "James," 1009–11.

Not only is Jesus's return at hand; so is the final judgment. Therefore, believers should not "grumble" (*stenazō*; cf. Heb. 13:17) against one another, so as not to incur the judgment of the divine Judge, who is already "standing at [literally, 'before'] the door," a potent metaphor conveying the imminence of God's judgment (5:9). As Paul affirms, "We will all stand before the judgment seat of God," and "each of us will give an account of himself to God" (Rom. 14:11–12). This should be ample motivation to be careful to focus on preparing an account of our lives before God on the last day rather than getting sidetracked by worrying about the faults of others. We can be assured that they, too, will have to give an account of their lives to God, and so we can be content to leave the judgment of others to him!

James has already adduced the farmer as an example of patience above (5:7). Now he adds a second example—namely, the OT prophets, who serve as examples not only of patience in general but specifically of patience in suffering (v. 10). We consider these individuals who remained steadfast "blessed" (*makarizō*, "consider blessed," the verb form of the more commonly used adjective *makarios*, "blessed"); this comment reminds the reader of James's opening statement, "Blessed is the man who remains steadfast under trial," with reference to receiving "the crown of life" (1:12). Interestingly, it appears that James considers Job a prophet, as he now adduces him specifically as an example of patience in suffering (5:11).

James adds that, "above all," his readers ("my brothers") should not swear—whether by heaven or earth or anything else—but simply "let [their] 'yes' be 'yes' and [their] 'no' be 'no'" (5:12; i.e., keep their word), again recalling Jesus's teaching in the Sermon on the Mount: "Do not take an oath at all, either by heaven, for it is the throne of God, or by the earth, . . . or by Jerusalem. . . . Let what you say be simply 'yes' or 'no'" (Matt. 5:33–37). The resemblance is undeniable. In so many ways, it seems James is trying to convey the essence of Jesus's teachings on many important and relevant topics to his readers.

As at previous occasions (2:14; 3:13; 4:1), James starts a new subunit with a question or series of questions, and, in this case, he supplies the answers as well (5:13–14; sort of having a Q&A with himself as a way of instructing his readers):

Is anyone among you suffering?   Let him pray.

Is anyone cheerful?   Let him sing praise.

Is anyone among you sick?   Let him call for the elders of the church.

James has addressed the topic of suffering in 5:10–11; he now adds further instructions. The appropriate response to suffering is prayer to God—not complaining, retaliation, or another form of human sinful reaction. The appropriate response to happiness, good news, or some other positive disposition or event is not to brag, gloat, or exalt oneself in some other way, eliciting jealousy or even hatred from others, but to praise God. Whether we encounter good or bad, our response should always be God-focused—whether in the form of prayer or praise.

That said, James posits a third scenario—sickness. This, too, is a form of suffering. Yet rather than merely praying in solitude, such a person should call the elders (note the plural, supporting the notion that the early church held to a plurality of leadership) and have *them* pray over the person as a group, representing the assembly of believers as a whole. In addition, James advises that elders anoint the sick person with oil, most likely an ancient practice, but one that most churches today no longer observe (though the Roman Catholic Church made this practice one of its seven sacraments, namely, the Last Rites). The expectation is that the elders' prayer, offered in faith, will restore the health of the person who has fallen sick; if the sickness is a result of sin, the person will be forgiven (assuming repentance). James makes this explicit by calling, in the immediately following statement, for mutual confession and reciprocal prayer for healing (5:15–16).

Again, while the Roman Catholic Church has elevated confession to a sacrament, administered by a priest, most Christian churches in the non–Roman Catholic tradition have neglected such confession. Yet while not without its perils, and open to abuse, confessing one's sins to one another is an important part of mutual accountability and a vital safeguard against falling into sin. As believers, we've been given the authority to declare that another person's sins are forgiven on the basis of the finished cross-work of Christ and their heartfelt repentance and renewed trust in Christ (cf. Matt. 18:18; John 20:23).

Marshalling another OT example, James adduces the OT prophet Elijah as proof that "the prayer of a righteous person has great power" (5:16–18). Preceding and following his major confrontation with the prophets of Baal, when dealing with Ahab king of Israel, Elijah prayed, first, that it might not rain, and it didn't, and a severe famine ensued; later, he prayed that it would rain, and it did (1 Kings 17:1; 18:42–45; cf. 18:1). While it may not be possible, even for people of great faith, to duplicate this feat literally today, the fact that God heard and answered Elijah's prayer in OT times in such an unusual way demonstrates that prayer can be very powerful, in part because of the person praying (Elijah was a righteous man and a prophet of God), but more importantly because God is the all-powerful God who controls the universe.

The letter closes rather unexpectedly with a final important piece of encouragement. Whoever restores a fellow church member who has temporarily strayed from the truth, presumably because of falling into sin ("brings back a sinner from his wandering," 5:20), will save (or preserve; cf. 1 Tim. 2:15; 4:16) his soul from death and "cover a multitude of sins" (cf. 1 Pet. 4:8; a likely allusion to Prov. 10:12).[24] In the previous scenario, James asserted that "the prayer of faith will save the one who is sick, and the Lord will raise him up. And if he has committed sins, he will be forgiven" (5:15). It is possible that the two scenarios are related. If so, 5:19 does not start a new paragraph but should be read with verses 13–18. The one important difference, however, seems to be that in verse 14, it is the person calling the elders of the church, whereas in verse 20, it is another person who brings a sinner back from his wandering. Nevertheless, even if the scenarios are not identical, they may still be related.

At this, James's letter ends on a hopeful note of a soul being saved from death and a multitude of sins (presumably committed by the person being restored) being covered. At the end of the letter, we catch a glimpse of the leadership structure of the congregation—a group of elders, as was common in the Jewish synagogue—and some of its practices: prayer, praise, care for those who are sick, and confession of sins. Throughout the letter, we've heard about the rich and the poor, about wealthy merchants, and about suffering for one's faith. We've heard James's instructions about the need for endurance, patience, wisdom, and prayer in the context of his eschatology, which affirms the expectation of Jesus's imminent return. While explicit references to Jesus are rare, the backdrop of Jesus's teaching, especially in the Sermon on the Mount, is almost ubiquitous. In addition, James's teaching is grounded in OT teaching, as is apparent on a conceptual level (wisdom), in explicit OT quotations, and through OT examples such as Abraham, Rahab, Job, and Elijah. Above all, James urges his readers, ancient and today, to put their faith into practice in the form of an active "faith that works."

James: Commentaries

Adamson, James B. *The Epistle of James*. NICNT. Grand Rapids: Eerdmans, 1976.

Allison, Dale C., Jr. *James: A Critical and Exegetical Commentary*. ICC. London: Bloomsbury T&T Clark, 2013.

Blomberg, Craig L., and Mariam J. Kamell. *James*. ZECNT. Grand Rapids: Zondervan, 2008.

Davids, Peter H. *The Epistle of James*. NIGTC. Grand Rapids: Eerdmans, 1982.

Dibelius, Martin, and Heinrich Greeven. *James: A Commentary on the Epistle of James*. Hermeneia. Philadelphia: Fortress, 1976.

24. See Carson, "James," 1012.

Hort, F. J. A. *The Epistle of St. James*. London: Macmillan, 1909.

Johnson, Luke Timothy. *The Letter of James*. AB 37A. New York: Doubleday, 1995.

Laws, Sophie. *The Epistle of St. James*. HNTC. New York: Harper & Row, 1980.

Martin, Ralph P. *James*. WBC 48. Waco: Word, 1988.

McCartney, Dan G. *James*. BECNT. Grand Rapids: Baker Academic, 2009.

McKnight, Scot. *The Letter of James*. NICNT. Grand Rapids: Eerdmans, 2011.

Moo, Douglas J. *James: An Introduction and Commentary*. TNTC. Downers Grove, IL: InterVarsity, 2015.

———. *The Letter of James*. PNTC. Grand Rapids: Eerdmans, 2000.

Painter, John, and David A. deSilva. *James and John*. Paideia. Grand Rapids: Baker Academic, 2012.

Plummer, Robert L. "James." In *ESV Expository Commentary*, vol. 12, *Hebrews–Revelation*, edited by Iain M. Duguid, James M. Hamilton Jr., and Jay Sklar, 219–86. Wheaton: Crossway, 2018.

Reicke, Bo. *The Epistles of James, Peter, and Jude*. AB 37. Garden City, NY: Doubleday, 1964.

Ropes, James Hardy. *A Critical and Exegetical Commentary on the Epistle of St. James*. ICC. New York: Scribner's Sons, 1916.

Varner, William. *James: A Commentary on the Greek Text*. Philadelphia: Fontes, 2017.

Vlachos, Chris A. *James*. EGGNT. Nashville: B&H Academic, 2013.

James: Articles, Essays, and Monographs

Aletti, Jean-Noël. "James 2,14–26: The Arrangement and Its Meaning." *Bib* 95 (2014): 88–101.

Allison, Dale C. "Blessing God and Cursing People: James 3:9–10." *JBL* 130 (2011): 397–405.

Baker, William R. "Searching for the Holy Spirit in the Epistle of James." *TynBul* 59 (2008): 293–315.

Bauckham, Richard. *James: Wisdom of James, Disciple of Jesus the Sage*. NTR. New York: Routledge, 1999.

Chester, Andrew, and Ralph P. Martin. *The Theology of the Letters to James, Peter, and Jude*. NTT. Cambridge: Cambridge University Press, 1994.

Chilton, Bruce, and Craig A. Evans, eds. *James the Just and Christian Origins*. NovTSup 98. Leiden: Brill, 1999.

———. *The Missions of James, Peter, and Paul: Tensions in Early Christianity*. NovTSup 115. Leiden: Brill, 2005.

Chilton, Bruce, and Jacob Neusner, eds. *The Brother of Jesus: James the Just and His Mission*. Louisville: Westminster John Knox, 2001.

Davids, Peter H. "God and the Human Situation in the Letter of James." *CTR* 8, no. 2 (2011): 19–29.

———. "Theological Perspectives on the Epistle of James." *JETS* 23 (1980): 97–103.

———. *A Theology of James, Peter, and Jude*. BTNT. Grand Rapids: Zondervan, 2014.

Deppe, Dean B. *The Sayings of Jesus in the Epistle of James.* Chelsea, MI: Bookcrafters, 1989.

deSilva, David A. *The Jewish Teachers of Jesus, James, and Jude: What Earliest Christianity Learned from the Apocrypha and Pseudepigrapha.* Oxford: Oxford University Press, 2012.

Fiorello, Michael D. "The Ethical Implication of Holiness in James 2." *JETS* 55 (2012): 557–72.

Hartin, Patrick J. "Call to Be Perfect through Suffering (James 1,2–4): The Concept of Perfection in the Epistle of James and the Sermon on the Mount." *Bib* 77 (1996): 477–92.

———. *James of Jerusalem: Heir to Jesus of Nazareth.* Interfaces. Collegeville, MN: Liturgical Press, 2004.

Johnson, Luke Timothy. *Brother of Jesus, Friend of God: Studies in the Letter of James.* Grand Rapids: Eerdmans, 2004.

Kamell, Mariam J. "The Implications of Grace for the Epistle of James." *Bib* 92 (2011): 274–87.

Kirk, J. A. "The Meaning of Wisdom in James." *NTS* 16 (1969): 24–38.

Kloppenborg, John S. *James, 1 & 2 Peter, and Early Traditions.* JSNTSup 478. London: T&T Clark, 2014.

Knox, W. L. "The Epistle of St. James." *JTS* 46 (1945): 10–17.

Lockett, Darian R. *Purity and Worldview in the Epistle of James.* JSNTSup 366. London: T&T Clark, 2008.

Mayor, Joseph P. *The Epistle of St. James: The Greek Text with Introduction, Notes and Comments, and Further Studies in the Epistle of St. James.* London: Macmillan, 1913.

McCartney, Dan G. "Self-Deception in James." *CTR* 8, no. 2 (2011): 31–43.

Morgan, Christopher W. *A Theology of James: Wisdom for God's People.* EBT. Phillipsburg, NJ: P&R, 2010.

Niebuhr, Karl-Wilhelm, and Robert W. Wall, eds. *The Catholic Epistles and Apostolic Tradition: A New Perspective on James to Jude.* Waco: Baylor University Press, 2009.

Nienhuis, David R. *Not by Paul Alone: The Formation of the Catholic Epistle Collection and the Christian Canon.* Waco: Baylor University Press, 2007.

Painter, John. *Just James: The Brother of Jesus in History and Tradition.* Minneapolis: Fortress, 1999.

Varner, William. "James as the First Catholic Epistle." *Int* 60 (2006): 245–59.

———. "The Main Theme and Structure of James." *MSJ* 22 (2011): 115–29.

Wall, Robert W. *Community of the Wise: The Letter of James.* NTC. Valley Forge, PA: Trinity Press International, 1997.

Wall, Robert W., and David R. Nienhuis. *Reading the Epistles of James, Peter, John, and Jude as Scripture.* Grand Rapids: Eerdmans, 2013.

Ward, Roy Bowen. "Partiality in the Assembly: James 2:2–4." *HTR* 62 (1969): 87–97.

———. "The Works of Abraham: James 2:14–26." *HTR* 61 (1968): 283–90.

Webb, Robert L., and John S. Kloppenborg, eds. *Reading James with New Eyes: Methodological Reassessments of the Letter of James.* LNTS. New York: T&T Clark, 2007.

CHAPTER THREE

1 Peter

Introduction

Author, Audience, Date, and Genre

Moving from James to another "pillar" of the NT church, we come to the first letter by the apostle Peter.[1] Peter was the leader and spokesman of the Twelve, Jesus's group of apostles. He was also the leader during the initial stages of growth of the early church, preaching the powerful sermon at Pentecost, with the result that many Jewish and other people were saved (Acts 2), and later bearing witness to the Sanhedrin that had recently been complicit in putting Jesus on the cross (Acts 3–4). Peter was also instrumental in bringing the Samaritans into the fold (Acts 8), as well as the first gentile, Cornelius, after Peter received a vision directing him to do so (Acts 10–11).

The present letter finds Peter addressing a group of "elect exiles of the Dispersion" in the Roman provinces of Pontus, Galatia, Cappadocia, Asia, and Bithynia (1:1). At a first glance, this designation sounds similar to James's address "to the twelve tribes in the Dispersion" (1:1), though the content of Peter's letter makes it unmistakably clear that his readers are gentiles, not Jews. Thus, Peter speaks of his recipients' "futile ways inherited from [their] forefathers" (1:18) when calling them to conduct themselves "with fear throughout the time of [their] exile" (1:17). Paradoxically, he urges his readers, "keep your conduct among the Gentiles honorable" (2:12; cf. 4:3)—paradoxically, because

---

1. The Petrine authorship of 1 Peter is not seriously disputed. Irenaeus is the first church father to explicitly attribute the letter to Peter. Eusebius cites 1 Peter as the only undisputed letter among the General Epistles (though not included in the Muratorian Fragment).

they themselves are gentiles! Yet, according to Peter, they are gentiles no more. Now that they have converted from idol worship to Christ, they have assumed a new identity, analogous to the identity of OT Israel: once they were not a people, but now they are the people of God (2:10).

It may seem strange that Peter, the apostle to the Jews (Gal. 2:7–8), is now found working among gentiles, but this is what seems in fact to be the case. Several decades have passed since the days of Jesus's earthly ministry and even since the days of the first Pentecost and the days when the gospel first came to Samaria and Cornelius, and it appears Peter's ministry has expanded to include gentiles in more remote Roman provinces as well.

Peter's first letter was most likely written in the early 60s AD. In 4:12, Peter ominously warns his readers concerning a "fiery trial" that is about to come upon them, and the entire epistle is laced with references to suffering. The letter places Peter in Rome—though he uses the code word "Babylon" (5:13), referring to the evil reigning world power of the day—the traditional site of Peter's eventual martyrdom not many years later, in keeping with Jesus's prediction (John 21:19). Mark, the second evangelist, is with Peter in Rome, which accords with early tradition that Mark wrote his Gospel in Rome for the church there (5:13).

The references to mounting suffering suggest that not only has persecution set in from their local communities in Asia Minor, but additional persecution is clearly on the horizon. This persecution is going to be increasingly intense, which points to a time in the early 60s AD, perhaps in the year 62 or 63, prior to the fire of Rome in AD 64, which Emperor Nero used to scapegoat Christians. This, in turn, triggered fierce persecution that led to the martyrdom of many ordinary believers and also conspicuous leaders such as the apostles Peter and Paul (ca. AD 65 or 66). Most likely, Peter, being in Rome, sees persecution coming and is writing his letter to the outskirts of the Roman Empire to warn believers in those provinces that persecution is on its way in order to prepare them to stand firm and trust in God's ultimate end-time deliverance. That the letter is authentically Petrine is suggested, among other things, by the reference to himself as "a fellow elder and a witness of the sufferings of Christ" (5:1).

Structure

The letter opening follows the standard formula: "Peter, an apostle . . . to . . . grace and peace . . ." (1:1–2). The letter closing identifies Silvanus (a longer form of Silas: he also served as Paul's associate—e.g., Acts 15:22, 32) as the carrier of the letter or, perhaps less likely, as Peter's amanuensis and concludes the letter rather tersely (5:12–14).[2] The body of the letter starts with an opening thanksgiving ("Blessed be the God and Father . . ."; 1:3–12), followed by an exhortation to holiness (1:13–21) and fervent Christian love (1:22–25) and an exposition of (gentile) believers' new identity as the people of God (2:1–10).

The address "Beloved" (*agapētoi*) then opens a new section in 2:11 that harks back to the opening address of the readers as "elect exiles" (1:1), calling believers "sojourners and exiles." In this way, Peter reiterates the fact that believers are only resident aliens on this earth, as it were—their true home is heaven—and so they should separate themselves from the world and live holy lives. What follows is a *Haustafel* (house table), or household code, instructing believers how to conduct themselves in their various roles as Christian citizens (2:13–17), servants (2:18–25), wives and husbands (3:1–7), and finally believers in general (3:8–12). On the basis of the conviction that God is a God of order who has assigned everyone specific roles and responsibilities in relation to one another, Peter urges submission to God-ordained authorities in every area of life—the political arena, the economic realm, and the domestic sphere. In each of these areas, God is pleased by submission to earthly authorities. While this is a sensitive subject, and certainly in no way condones abuse, Peter does stress that Christ serves as an example of righteous suffering at the hands of the unrighteous, and believers may be called to follow in his steps (2:21–25, with frequent reference to Isaiah 52:13–53:12). In this context, Peter elaborates on believers bearing witness in the surrounding culture by suffering for doing what is right (3:13–22), again calling them to separate themselves from their former, gentile lifestyle (4:1–6). The section that began in 2:11 concludes in 4:7–10 with an opening reference to the "end of all things" being near and a closing doxology.

The opening phrase in 4:12, "Beloved," harks back to 2:11, which began with the identical address. Here, Peter speaks of an imminent "fiery trial" and calls believers to "[suffer] as a Christian" (*Christianos*; 4:16, one of the first instances of this word in the NT; cf. Acts 11:26). At this, Peter exhorts first the elders as one who himself is an elder (5:1–5), then those who are younger

---

2. Peter's use of an amanuensis (scribe) in writing either 1 or 2 Peter may explain, at least in part, some of the stylistic differences between the two letters. Many scholars contend that 2 Peter is pseudonymous (not actually written by Peter but by someone else under Peter's name), but in many ways 2 Peter is actually more personal (e.g., the opening attribution to "Simon Peter," 2 Pet. 1:1), and 2 Peter, similar to 2 Timothy in Paul's case, seems to convey the character of a last testament or final charge prior to Peter's martyrdom. E. Randolph Richards, "Silvanus Was Not Peter's Secretary: Theological Bias in Interpreting διὰ Σιλουανοῦ ἔγραψα in 1 Pet. 5:12," *JETS* 43 (2000): 417–32, argues that 1 Pet. 5:12 only identifies the letter carrier and not the secretary and thus cannot legitimately be used to appeal to Silvanus as the reason for the differences in Greek style between 1 and 2 Peter.

(5:5), and finally all people to practice humility toward one another (5:6–7). A series of final exhortations concludes with a second doxology (5:8–11, esp. v. 11; cf. 4:10). Based on these observations regarding the flow and organization of the letter, we arrive at the following proposed outline:[3]

1 Peter	Content
1:1–2	Letter opening: Peter to elect exiles in the dispersion
1:3–2:10	Thanksgiving, call to holiness and love, and believers' new identity
2:11–4:11	Exhortation to sojourners and exiles (including household code)
4:12–5:11	Exhortation to suffer as Christians in all humility
5:12–14	Letter closing: by Silvanus, from Rome, with Mark

Central Message

Clearly, the #1 theme pervading the entire epistle is Christian suffering. As Christ's close follower, Peter was "a witness of the sufferings of Christ" (5:1). He commends Jesus as the supreme example of Christian suffering, the one in whose footsteps Christians should follow, and he uses language reminiscent of the suffering servant featured in Isaiah 53 (2:21–25; 3:18; 4:1). Not only does Peter uphold Jesus as the ultimate example of how to suffer righteously; he puts Christian suffering within an end-time context and framework, repeatedly referring to the Christian hope of future salvation at the "revelation of Jesus Christ" (i.e., the second coming; e.g., 1:5, 13; 5:4).

Christian living and suffering is therefore fueled by "a living hope" (1:3, 13) and trust in a righteous and just Creator and Judge who will vindicate righteous sufferers and bring about the final judgment and rewards in his own appointed time (2:23; 5:4). What is more, any such suffering is only "for a little while" (1:6). The overall gist of Peter's letter is perhaps best summarized by the concluding assurance: "And after you have suffered for a little while, the God of all grace, who has called you to his eternal glory in Christ, will himself restore, confirm, strengthen, and establish you" (5:10).

Letter Opening: Peter to Elect Exiles in the Dispersion (1:1–2)

While the Letter to the Hebrews and the Epistle of James were written to Jewish Christian congregations, Peter's first letter is addressed to a predominantly

---

3. C. Samuel Storms offers a similar outline, though he further subdivides 4:12–5:11 into 4:12–19 and 5:1–11. Storms, "1 Peter," in *ESV Expository Commentary*, vol. 12, *Hebrews–Revelation*, ed. Iain M. Duguid, James M. Hamilton Jr., and Jay Sklar (Wheaton: Crossway, 2018), 297–98.

non-Jewish group of believers.[4] This may be surprising, as Peter is known as the apostle to the Jews (in contrast to Paul, the apostle to the gentiles— i.e., non-Jews). Yet while Peter, who of course himself was Jewish, started out as the leader of the twelve apostles, the core group of the church, and preached the Pentecost sermon in Jerusalem (Acts 2), he apparently also had a ministry among non-Jews in the decades following the initial establishment of the church. Introducing himself as "an apostle of Jesus Christ"—which distinguishes him from both the author of Hebrews and James, Jesus's half-brother—Peter addresses his first letter to the "elect exiles of the Dispersion" in the vast area covered by the provinces of Pontus, Galatia, Cappadocia, Asia, and Bithynia (1:1; see figure 3.1).[5]

Figure 3.1
The recipients of 1 Peter

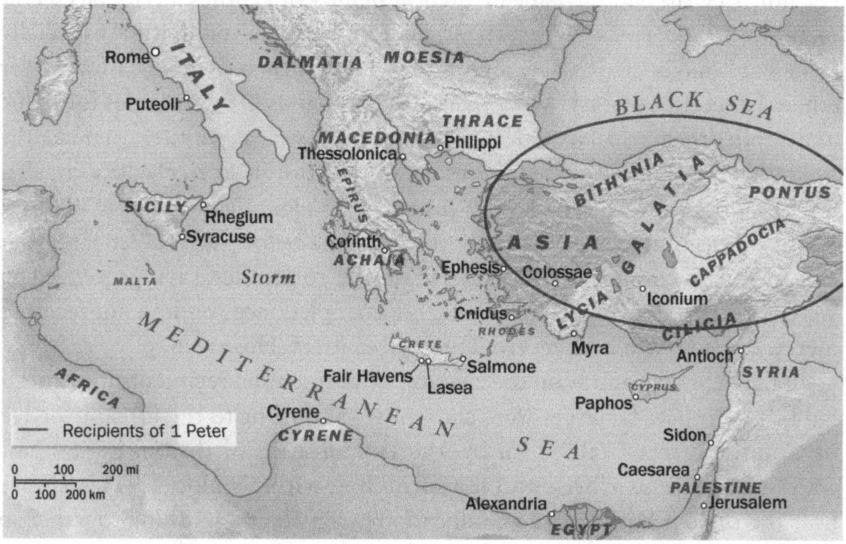

Peter's self-identification as "an apostle" is very humble; he was not just any apostle, but the leader and spokesman of the Twelve. "Elect exiles" is

4. Note, for example, that Peter repeatedly in the letter refers to the recipients' former way of life in a way unlikely to apply to Jews (1:18; 4:3).
5. Note that Acts 16:7 indicates that the apostle Paul attempted to go to Bithynia, but the Spirit of Jesus prevented him from doing so. Peter H. Davids, *A Theology of James, Peter, and Jude: Living in Light of the Coming King*, BTNT (Grand Rapids: Zondervan, 2014), makes a strong case for a largely gentile readership for 1 Peter (102–6) and provides excellent social-historical background to explain why Christians would have been persecuted in a Greco-Roman context (112–20). See also Mark Wilson, "Peter's Christian Communities in Asia Minor," in *Lexham Geographic Commentary on Acts through Revelation*, ed. Barry J. Beitzel (Bellingham, WA: Lexham, 2019), 604–18.

most likely metaphorical and strikes two related notes: (1) these believers were among God's chosen people (a designation reserved in the OT for ethnic Israel); and (2) they were scattered across the Greco-Roman world, reminiscent of Jewish people being scattered (in the so-called Diaspora) following the Assyrian and Babylonian exiles. Both designations, therefore, identify the recipients of Peter's letter with OT Israel, yet in such a way that the scope of the terms "elect" and "exile" is expanded to include all of God's people, not only Jews. In this way, the identity of gentile believers is couched in terms that in the OT were used to describe the people of Israel. What is more, "exile" intimates that the earth is not ultimately these believers' home but that they are only temporary residents in this world (cf. 1:17: "the time of your exile"; 2:11: "sojourners and exiles").[6]

It may appear that Peter here espouses a replacement theology—that is, teaching that the church made up predominantly of gentiles has replaced ethnic Israel in God's plan—yet such a conclusion would be premature, especially since Paul makes clear elsewhere in the NT that there remains a future for ethnic Israel (Rom. 9–11). More likely, Peter expands OT categories for Israel and applies them to all of God's people, Jews as well as gentiles, to make the point that the church now represents a new salvation-historical entity consisting of all believers who believe in Jesus Christ regardless of ethnic identity. This will become clear especially in chapter 2 below, where Peter applies categories used exclusively for Israel in the OT to gentiles, saying, "Once you were not a people, but now you are God's people; once you had not received mercy, but now you have received mercy" (2:10; cf. Hosea 1:6, 9).

In 1:2, Peter expounds on the election of his (gentile) recipients in trinitarian fashion: these believers were chosen (1) "according to the foreknowledge of God the Father," (2) "in [or by] the sanctification of the Spirit," (3) "for obedience to Jesus Christ and for sprinkling with his blood." This shows how the three persons of the Godhead are aligned and working together in salvation: God the Father foreknew believers; Jesus Christ died on the cross, shedding his blood for our sins; and the Spirit set us apart and sanctifies us for God and his holy use (though the order here is God the Father—Spirit—Jesus Christ, perhaps so as to end climactically with Jesus Christ). It's worth reflecting on the fact that, according to Peter, we're chosen, redeemed, and sanctified for obedience to Jesus Christ! Also, we can't contribute anything to the Triune Godhead's work of salvation: we're the recipients of God the

---

6. John H. Elliott, *A Home for the Homeless: A Sociological Exegesis of 1 Peter, Its Situation and Strategy* (Philadelphia: Fortress, 1981), argued that the addressees are real resident aliens from a "conversionist sect" whom Peter encourages by insisting on their distinctive communal identity, but he unduly downplays the spiritual and theological dimension of the passage.

Father's election, the Spirit's sanctification, and Jesus Christ's redemption. Peter will develop the theology of 1:2 in the conclusion of the first major unit of the body of his letter in 1:19–21 below. The standard greeting "Grace and peace" concludes the letter opening.

Thanksgiving, Call to Holiness and Love, and Believers' New Identity (1:3–2:10)

Thanksgiving (1:3–12)

The body of the letter opens with thanksgiving in the form of a blessing of "the God and Father of our Lord Jesus Christ" (1:3), which continues until verse 12, where Peter moves on to exhortation. In the Greek original, the definite article governs both nouns "God" and "Father," binding the two expressions together with reference to one person (the so-called Granville Sharp rule). No doubt based on his own personal experience, Peter extols God's "great mercy," according to which "he has caused us to be born again" (all one word in the Greek, *anagennēsas*, from *anagennaō*, a verb that appears in the NT only here and in 1:23). Together with the apostle John (John 3:3–7), Peter underscores the vital importance of a new, spiritual birth in the lives of believers at conversion (closely related to regeneration; cf. Titus 3:5). As Jesus told Nicodemus, the "teacher of Israel" and Jewish rabbi, "You [plural, referring not only to Nicodemus but to the Jewish people in general] must be born again" (John 3:3, 5, 7; cf. 1:12–13). The necessity of spiritual rebirth is grounded in the prophetic vision of a spiritual renewal and cleansing to be brought about by God in the messianic age (see esp. Ezek. 36:24–27). While this expectation was mostly corporate, referring to Israel as a nation (cf. Ezek. 37, Ezekiel's vision of the valley of dry bones), there was an important individual component as well (cf., e.g., Jer. 31:31–34; see also Dan. 12:1–2).

This new birth spoken of by Peter was "to a living hope through the resurrection of Jesus Christ from the dead" (1:3). Peter's readers were suffering, or at least suffering was on the horizon, so hope was vital as they held on to their faith. From the inception of the church, Peter and the other apostles preached that Jesus had risen from the dead (Acts 2). Peter himself was among the first to see Jesus risen, and did so repeatedly. This is reported by, among others, the evangelist Mark, who was with Peter when he wrote this letter (5:13; cf. Mark 16:7: "But go, tell his disciples and Peter"; 1 Cor. 15:5). The apostle John, another one of Peter's close associates and fellow apostles, reports that Peter and nine other apostles saw the risen Jesus on the night of the resurrection, again a week later (now also including Thomas), and then a third time by the

Sea of Galilee, where Peter had gone back to fishing. At that third occasion, Peter had the no-doubt-unforgettable experience of hauling in a net "full of large fish"—153 fish, to be exact—that Jesus had helped Peter and his six fishing buddies catch (20:19–21:14). John also reports that after breakfast the risen Lord Jesus took Peter aside and asked him three times if he loved him, commissioning him to shepherd Jesus's "sheep." Jesus also predicted that in his old age Peter would die a martyr's death (21:15–19). Peter was also among the disciples who received the "Great Commission" from the risen Jesus to go and make disciples of all the nations (Matt. 28:18–20).

All of these eyewitness reports underscore that Peter had firsthand experience of what he was talking about: "the resurrection of Jesus Christ from the dead." Here, Peter points out the benefit of Jesus's resurrection for believers—it enabled their new, spiritual birth to a "living hope." What's more, that living hope is further specified as an "inheritance" (*klēronomia*, only here in 1 Peter; cf. Eph. 1:14, 18; Col. 3:24; Heb. 9:15) that is "imperishable, undefiled, and unfading" and "kept in heaven" for believers (1:4). Note that believers' "hope" and "inheritance" are also linked in Paul's teaching (Eph. 1:18). The three attributes of our inheritance—imperishable (*aphthartos*; cf. 1:23; 3:4; applied to God in Rom. 1:23; 1 Tim. 1:17), undefiled (*amiantos*; cf. Heb. 7:26; 13:4; James 1:27), and unfading (*amarantos*, unique in the NT; cf. *amarantinos* in 1 Pet. 5:4)—are alliterated and in the original Greek all start with the letter *alpha* (a so-called *alpha* privative), designating what the inheritance is *not*: it won't perish, it won't be defiled, and it won't fade. That is, our inheritance isn't affected by death, evil, or time—it is permanent, glorious (Eph. 1:18), and eternal (cf. Heb. 9:15). While our inheritance is still future, it is well worth waiting for and striving toward!

At the end of 1:4, Peter transitions to the second-person plural "you," addressing his readers directly, assuring them that their inheritance is secure, as it is kept (the perfect participle conveys a settled state) in heaven for them (a divine passive, implying the person keeping our inheritance is God). Believers themselves are "being guarded" (*phrouroumenos*, a present participle, conveying a continual progressive process of preservation; cf. Gal. 3:23; Phil. 4:7) by God's power through faith (*pistis*, the first reference to faith in this letter) "for a salvation ready to be revealed [*apokalyptō*] in the last time" (1:5). This reference is part of Peter's concerted attempt to set the readers' present suffering and experience within an end-time framework (cf. the use of the verb *apokalyptō* at 1:12; 5:1 and of the noun *apokalypsis* at 1:7, 13; 4:13), so much so that some have called 1 Peter an "apocalyptic epistle."[7] In fact, the

---

7. Cf. Peter H. Davids, *The First Epistle of Peter*, NICNT (Grand Rapids: Eerdmans, 1990), 15–17, who also refers to Robert L. Webb, "The Apocalyptic Perspective of First Peter" (unpublished ThM thesis, Regent College, 1986).

"apocalyptic" vocabulary is particularly pronounced in the opening portion of Peter's letter and is used in conjunction with various concepts such as believers' salvation, faith, and hope:

- 1:5: Believers' *salvation* is "ready to be revealed [*apokalyphthēnai*] in the last time."
- 1:7: Genuine, tested *faith* will "result in praise and glory and honor" at the revelation (*apokalypsis*) of Jesus Christ (i.e., the second coming).
- 1:12: It was revealed (*apekalyphthē*) to the prophets that they were serving later generations of believers.
- 1:13: Believers are to set their *hope* completely on the grace to be brought to them at the "revelation" (*apokalypsis*) of Jesus Christ (i.e., the second coming).

Notably, it is not believers who guard their own salvation; rather, they're being guarded by God's *power* (*dynamis*), with *faith* being the means by which they appropriate God's power. What is more, believers' salvation is here presented not from the vantage point of having been accomplished in the past (though this is certainly true), or as being experienced in the present (though this is true as well), but from a future vantage point (the preposition *eis*, "for," frequently conveys a future purpose or goal; cf. 1:2: obedience; v. 3: living hope; v. 4: inheritance; v. 5: salvation). While it may be surprising at first to hear Peter speak of salvation (*sōtēria*) as yet future, the NT does affirm that salvation has a past, present, and future dimension: in the past, Jesus saved us when he died for us on the cross; in the present, we're being saved in the sense of being preserved and sanctified; and in the future, we'll experience complete and final salvation and deliverance from the power of Satan and from the presence of sin in our lives when Jesus returns and takes us to be with him forever. In the present context, verse 5 introduces the notion of our future salvation; after this Peter focuses on the present dimension of salvation in verses 6–8 (including trials and testing) before returning to our future salvation in verse 9. Finally, Peter discusses the past background of our salvation in verses 10–12.

In English translations, verse 6 is often rendered as a new sentence, "In this you rejoice," though in the original Greek verse 6 continues the previous clause: "for a salvation ready to be revealed in the last time, *in which you rejoice* . . ." This shows the continuity in Peter's thought and underscores the fact that verses 3–12 form a literary unit and contain a coherent, sustained string of argument. This can be seen also in that the salvation mentioned in verse 5 continues to serve as the subject of verses 6–12, as is apparent from the introduction to verse 10 (a sort of excursus or digression): "Concerning this salvation." The entire unit is pervaded by Peter's exhortation that believers not focus on their present experience of suffering but on their future salvation and inheritance—that they live by faith and in hope of a certain future reality which ought to inform their present disposition. This is also the core message of verse 6: "In *this* [ultimately encompassing all that Peter wrote in vv. 3–5] you rejoice" (cf. v. 8 below). The lives of suffering believers should be characterized by faith, hope, and even joy (cf. Phil. 4:4, 7: "Rejoice in the Lord always. . . . And the peace of God . . . will *guard* [*phroureō*; cf. 1 Pet. 1:5] your hearts and your minds in Christ Jesus")!

This joy can remain unperturbed by the experience of "various trials"— "for a little while" (*oligon*, 1:6; cf. 5:10), "if necessary" (*deon*; cf. Acts 19:36).[8] "For a little while" is set in contrast to the "unfading" inheritance kept in heaven for believers (cf. v. 4); it would have been tremendously encouraging, comforting, and reassuring for these believers to be reminded of the fact that our present suffering will last only for a fraction of the time we will enjoy our eternal inheritance with God. "If necessary" affirms that, in the ultimate analysis, suffering is God-ordained, or at least God-permitted; all of human life unfolds under the sovereign umbrella of God's saving and sanctifying purposes. What is this purpose? This is made explicit in verse 7: it is the testing of our faith, to be understood not so much in terms of passing a test as one might take in school but in terms of refining our faith and making it more enduring. Such tested faith is even "more precious than gold," which, though it can be refined by fire, ultimately perishes (note that "fire" is a common emblem for divine judgment; e.g., Heb. 12:29). By contrast, faith endures and will become the cause of praise, glory, and honor accruing to God at the second coming of Jesus Christ.

Although Peter, the author, was a close follower of Jesus during his earthly ministry, he is mindful that his readers have never seen Jesus with their own eyes (cf. John 20:29). And yet they love him and believe in him and are filled with "inexpressible" joy (*aneklalētos*, unique in the NT) and glory (*doxazō* used in the passive voice; literally, "are glorified"; v. 8). In this way, believers attain (*komizō*; cf. esp. several references in Hebrews to obtaining the promise: 10:36; 11:19, 39) the "goal" (*telos*) of their faith, the salvation of their souls

---

8. On the persecution of Christians in the provinces where the recipients lived, see Eckhard J. Schnabel, "The Persecution of Christians in the First Century," *JETS* 61 (2018): 543–44. Schnabel contends that the persecution at that time took on primarily the form of verbal abuse, as suggested by words such as "slander" (2:12; 3:16), "disparage" (3:16), "malign" (4:4), and "reproach" (4:14).

(v. 9). Thus, believers should live their present lives in light of their future goal. Their salvation was procured in the past by Jesus's finished work on the cross; it has been appropriated by them by faith, which currently sustains them in the midst of various trials; but it will be fully experienced, consummated, and realized only when Jesus returns.

At this point, Peter briefly elaborates upon "this salvation" (1:10–12). It was the object of the prophets' diligent inquiry (note that Peter uses as many as three different Greek words to convey the intensity of the prophets' search: *ekzēteō, exeraunaō* [unique in the NT], *eraunaō* [cf. Rom. 8:27; 1 Cor. 2:10], vv. 10, 11). Specifically, the prophets inquired as to "what person or time the Spirit of Christ in them was indicating [*dēloō*; cf. 2 Pet. 1:14; see also Heb. 9:8; 12:27] when he predicted the *sufferings* of Christ and the subsequent *glories*" (v. 11; note the plurals). Remarkably, the Holy Spirit and his activity in OT times are here referred to as "the Spirit *of Christ*," and that Spirit is said to have been "in" the prophets as they inquired as to "the sufferings of Christ and the subsequent glories." Remarkably as well, Peter makes clear that the same Spirit was at work both in the OT prophets predicting the Messiah's sufferings and glories and in "those who preached the good news" to Peter's readers "by the Holy Spirit sent from heaven" (v. 12). This underscores the essential continuity between the OT prophetic message looking forward to the Messiah and the NT apostolic message—the gospel—proclaiming that this Messiah had now suffered and died and risen and been exalted (cf. the reference to "the Holy Spirit sent from heaven" subsequent to Christ's ascension to heaven). Thus, both prophets and apostles served NT believers by predicting and proclaiming the Messiah's suffering and salvation, and salvation history centers on the gospel of the suffering and glorious Messiah, the Lord Jesus Christ.

Peter closes his elaboration on the salvation of believers with the intriguing comment that, while not direct beneficiaries of salvation, even angels long to peer into (*parakyptō*; cf. Luke 24:12; John 20:5, 11; James 1:25) these matters surrounding the gospel proclaimed by those infused with the Holy Spirit (v. 12). Thus, the section closes the way it started: although believers' inheritance is "kept in heaven" (1:4), the gospel was preached to them by the Holy Spirit "sent from heaven" (1:12). In all this, Peter strives to impart to his readers who experience present suffering a heavenly perspective. Heaven is real. It is every bit as real as the various trials believers are presently experiencing, and it is infinitely more lasting and enduring. Adopting such a heavenly perspective will help them persevere in their faith and live in hope and be filled with inexpressible joy as they anticipate receiving their full share of salvation when Christ returns.

Call to Holy Living (1:13–21)

"Therefore" (*dio*) in 1:13 signals a major transition in the letter, moving from an exposition of the biblical framework for suffering—the believer's living hope (noun) and heavenly inheritance—to a call to action based on this reality (verb). Just as in verse 3, in which Peter speaks about God's action of causing believers to be born again "to a living hope" (cf. 1:21; 3:15), he now in verse 13 urges his readers to "set [their] hope" (cf. 3:5; 2 Pet. 1:12; 1 Tim. 4:10; Heb. 11:1) fully on Christ and the grace they will receive at the second coming. Future hope and future grace ought to motivate them to "gird up the loins of your mind" (KJV) for action (*anazōsamenoi*, an aorist participle, indicating preceding action).[9] Having prepared themselves for action, believers should be sober-minded (*nēphontes*; cf. 4:7 and 5:8; 1 Thess. 5:6, 8; 2 Tim. 4:5) and place their hope perfectly or completely (*teleios*; unique in the NT) on the grace to be brought to them at the future revelation (*apokalypsis*) of Jesus Christ.[10] In this way, Peter continues to operate within his future-oriented framework laid out in verses 3–12.

What specific kind of action is Peter urging his readers to take? Addressing them as "obedient children," he wants them not to be "conformed" (*syschēmatizō*, elsewhere in the NT only in Rom. 12:2, where Paul calls on his readers not to be "conformed to this world" but rather to be transformed in their way of thinking) to the passions to which they were formerly subject in their ignorance (*agnoia*, clearly referring to gentiles; cf. Eph. 4:18; Acts 17:30). Rather, Peter exhorts his readers to emulate the holy character of God in all their conduct. In characteristic fashion, Peter first issues his command and subsequently follows it up with scriptural support. In the present case, he quotes the Levitical holiness code: "You shall be holy, for I am holy" (1 Pet. 1:19, citing Lev. 11:44; cf. 19:2; 20:7, 26). Remarkably, as mentioned in the introduction, Peter here cites an OT injunction originally addressed to Israel and broadens its scope, reapplying it to all of God's people, including Peter's predominantly gentile audience. Peter will continue to use this kind of hermeneutic when discussing the identity of God's people in chapter 2. In fact, in the next verse, Peter once again invokes the term "exile"—again, originally applied to Israel— and speaks of his (gentile) readers' "time of . . . exile" (v. 17; cf. 1:1, above, when Peter addressed his readers as "elect exiles"; see also 2:11; 4:12 below).

---

9. The metaphor of "girding one's loins"—i.e., preparing oneself for action—so characteristic of the portrait of Peter in the Gospels—is lost in some English translations (such as the ESV). Elsewhere the related verb *zōnnymi* is used in the NT only with reference to Peter (John 21:18 [twice]; Acts 12:8).

10. See discussion of Peter's "apocalyptic" language above.

This designation invokes Israel's distinct identity in the midst of pagan nations during OT times, which the Jews maintained even when scattered into exile following the Assyrian and Babylonian captivities. While a remnant returned to the Holy Land, the majority did not, establishing Jewish settlements all across the Greco-Roman world, including meeting places for worship (synagogues) that later served as ideal initial points of proclamation for Paul and the early church (see the book of Acts).[11] While the Jews lived in literal, physical (geographical) exile, converted gentiles lived in spiritual exile—that is, as resident aliens in a world that subsequent to their conversion to Christ was no longer their true home.[12] Paul similarly wrote to the Philippians, "But our citizenship is in heaven" (Phil. 3:20). This distinct spiritual identity necessitated a spiritual separation from the world, a distancing from customary and characteristic gentile immorality and a life of holiness in keeping with God's own character and his purpose for all his redeemed people, not only for their own sake but also for the sake of their bearing witness in the unbelieving world around them. Thus, a life of holiness, for Peter, is a key part of believers' mission in this world, both individually and corporately.

The reference to God as judge continues the eschatological orientation pervading the letter (1:17). Believers should conduct themselves "with fear" (*phobos*) during their time of exile in this world, mindful that God ("the Father") is the one who "judges impartially [*aprosōpolēmptōs*, unique in the NT] according to each one's deeds." In other words, God is no respecter of persons; while it is our nature to expect God to give preferential treatment to us just because it is we whom he is dealing with, God is impartial (cf. James 2:1). At this point, Peter reminds his gentile readers that they were "ransomed from the futile ways inherited from [their] forefathers" (again, something he would never have said to Jews) "not with perishable things such as silver or gold, but with the precious blood of Christ," as that of an unblemished, spotless lamb (1:18–19; cf. 1:2). The value of silver and gold pales in comparison

---

11. There are thirty-four references to synagogues in Luke-Acts, nineteen of which are in the book of Acts. These include synagogues in Damascus, Pisidian Antioch, Iconium, Thessalonica, Berea, Athens, Corinth, and Ephesus. Cf. Anders Runesson, Donald D. Binder, and Birger Olsson, *The Ancient Synagogue from Its Origins to 200 CE: A Source Book* (Boston: Brill, 2008), 45.

12. In addition, writers such as N. T. Wright point out that even in Israel, there was a sense in the first century AD that while a remnant had returned to the Holy Land, Israel was still in spiritual exile. However, Wright's thesis is the subject of extensive scholarly discussion. See, e.g., James M. Scott, ed., *Exile: A Conversation with N. T. Wright* (Downers Grove, IL: InterVarsity, 2017). See also Carey C. Newman, ed., *Jesus and the Restoration of Israel: A Critical Assessment of N. T. Wright's "Jesus and the Victory of God"* (Downers Grove, IL: InterVarsity, 1999); and Christoph Heilig, J. Thomas Hewitt, and Michael F. Bird, eds., *God and the Faithfulness of Paul: A Critical Examination of the Pauline Theology of N. T. Wright* (Minneapolis: Fortress, 2017), 181–206.

with the unsurpassed redemptive value of Christ's precious blood (cf. 1:4: imperishable, undefiled, unfading)!

Whereas God had foreknown Christ "before the foundation of the world" (i.e., from eternity; cf. 1:1), Christ was revealed (*apokalyptō*) in (literally) "the last of times" on account of "you" (again addressing the readers directly; 1:20). For it was God who not only foreknew Jesus and sent him as an atoning sacrifice for sin but also raised him from the dead and "gave him glory" (i.e., exalted him), so that Peter's readers' faith and hope should be in God (1:21). Note the references to hope and faith at the outset of the letter in 1:3 and 5 and the reference to "love" in verse 22 below, completing the triad of "faith, hope, and love" (cf. 1 Cor. 13:13). Peter's words in 1:19–21 provide a fitting conclusion to the first portion of his letter, which started out in similar terms, with references to God's foreknowledge of believers. Here he speaks of God foreknowing Jesus—specifically his atoning sacrifice as well as his resurrection and exaltation—and also foreknowing the believers' sprinkling with Christ's blood (1:2). All in all, Peter's presentation is thoroughly Jewish— God's holiness, Christ's sacrifice as the unblemished, spotless lamb, God's people in exile—yet he here contextualizes the Christian message, framed in Jewish terms, for a gentile audience.

Call to Love (1:22–2:3)

Continuing with the logic of his previous exhortation to holy living in 1:13–21, Peter now extends his exhortation by issuing a call to *love*. As in verse 13, he starts with preceding action: "Having purified your souls by your obedience to the truth . . ." (1:22). Again, this language harks back to the letter's opening, where Peter spoke of believers having been chosen "for obedience to Jesus Christ" (1:2). Later, Peter spoke of the salvation of believers' "souls" being the goal of their faith (1:9). Believers, of course, are able to "purify their souls" (*agnizō*, a sacrificial term; cf. John 11:55; Acts 21:24, 26; 24:18; James 4:8; 1 John 3:3) only on the basis of the precious blood of the unblemished and spotless lamb, the Lord Jesus Christ, who ransomed believers from their life of sin (1:18–19). Nevertheless, this purification is not merely a matter of passive receiving but also a matter of active faith. Obedience to the truth also entails purification from sin.

Yet purification from sin is not an end in itself; it occurs for the purpose of sincere (*anypokritos*; with regard to love, cf. Rom. 12:9; 2 Cor. 6:6; with regard to faith, cf. 1 Tim. 1:5; 2 Tim. 1:5; with regard to wisdom, cf. James 3:17) brotherly love, which springs from a "pure heart" (1:22). Since they have been born again, "not of perishable seed but of imperishable seed"

(1:23), believers should love one another "earnestly" (*ektenōs*; cf. 4:8; see also Luke 22:44; Acts 12:5, both with regard to prayer). The reference to being born again in verse 23 recalls the opening thanksgiving stating that God, "according to his great mercy," caused believers to be born again to a "living hope" (1:3). Here, Peter points out that our new birth should result in sincere love of our fellow believers in Christ. The contrast between perishable and imperishable marks the third time Peter speaks in those terms (cf. 1:7 with regard to faith; 1:18–19 with regard to Christ's blood; here, in 1:23, with regard to the "living and abiding" Word of God as the instrument of believers' regeneration).

Again, Peter first states his point in 1:23 and subsequently provides his scriptural support, in the form of OT Scripture (1:24; citing Isa. 40:6, 8). While grass withers, and flowers fade, the "word of the Lord remains forever." While in the original instance Isaiah's statement referred to Yahweh's word in general, Peter here, in the form of a rabbinic technique commonly referred to as *pesher*—that is, by way of contemporary application ("this . . . is that")—applies the Isaianic reference to the gospel that was preached to his readers: "And *this* [i.e., "the word of the Lord"] is *the good news* that was preached to you" (1:25; cf. 1:12). In this way, once again Peter establishes essential continuity between the word of the Lord to Israel in the prophet Isaiah's day and the gospel preached to God's people (in the present case, the gentiles) in his own day.

Call to Grow in Salvation and to Come to the Rejected Cornerstone (2:1–10)

Following the same pattern as in 1:13 and 1:22, Peter starts the new subunit with a precondition (conveyed by an aorist participle)—"Put away all malice and . . ."—followed by a command (imperative), "Long for the pure spiritual milk," and then he adds the desired result, "that by it you may grow up into salvation" (2:1–2; note that "salvation" was mentioned previously at 1:9 and 10). In order for believers to grow in their salvation, they have to be nourished by "pure spiritual milk," which in context most likely refers to the "living and abiding word of God" mentioned in 1:23.

To be nourished by the word of God, they must first put away a whole handful of ungodly activities: malice (*kakia*), deceit (*dolos*; cf. 2:22; 3:10; Rom. 1:29), hypocrisy (*hypokrisis*; cf. 1 Tim. 4:2), envy (*phthonos*; cf. 1 Tim. 6:4; Titus 3:3; James 4:5), and slander (*katalalia*; see 2:12; cf. 2 Cor. 12:20). The word "all" is used in conjunction with the first, second, and fifth of these vices; see the similar lists in Ephesians 4:31 and Colossians 3:8.

All of these evil characteristics flow from a wicked, sinful heart and result in negative dispositions and actions toward others:

- wanting others to fail (malice)
- manipulating, tricking, or misleading others (deceit)
- engaging in pretense, purporting to be someone other than who one truly is (hypocrisy)
- resenting others for what they have and wanting those things for oneself (envy)
- speaking negatively and untruthfully about others, impugning their character (slander; cf. 2:12, which makes clear that the believers themselves are on the receiving end of slander by those around them)

Believers in Christ must turn away from such evil and avail themselves of the "pure spiritual milk" of God's Word ("pure" translates *logikos*, which can also mean "proper" and is found elsewhere in the NT only in Rom. 12:1, whereas "spiritual" renders *adolos*, which is part of a wordplay with *dolos*, "deceit," in v. 1, and is not found elsewhere in the NT). As believers turn away from evil and are nurtured by God's Word, they will "grow up into salvation"—that is, grow into spiritual maturity in Christ (i.e., be sanctified), just as infants are nourished by their mother's milk and gradually grow into physical maturity. Again, Peter first lodges his assertion and then follows it up with scriptural backing, in the present case Psalm 34:8: "Taste and see that the Lord is good" (2:3).

The new sentence in most English translations in verse 4 masks the fact that in the original language the verse is closely tied to the preceding verse: "If indeed you have tasted that the Lord is good, *to whom you come . . .*" In the following unit, 2:4–11, the Greek word *kyrios*, "Lord," which in the first instance (Ps. 34:9, cited in v. 3) referred to Yahweh (God the Father), is reapplied to Jesus Christ (2:4; cf. 1:23). He was "a living stone [*lithos*] rejected by men but in the sight of God chosen and precious" (2:4; cf. 1:3: "living hope"). While Peter is a man of action (note the multiple instances of *anastrophē*, "conduct"; 1:15, 18; 2:12; 3:1, 2, 16), he is careful to consistently ground his teaching theologically in the OT Scriptures.

In so doing, Peter uses the OT in multiple ways, including direct quotation (e.g., 1:16, 24–25), allusion (e.g., 2:3, 12), pearl-stringing / *gezerah shawah* (e.g., "stone citations"; 2:4–11), and reference to OT characters (e.g., 3:5–6).

At the outset of his letter, Peter had identified his *readers* as "chosen exiles" (*eklektos*; 1:1); now he says *Jesus* is "chosen" (*eklektos*; 2:4; cf. 2:6, 9) and "precious" (*entimos*; 2:4; cf. 2:6; Luke 7:2; 14:8; Phil. 2:29; cf. *timios*, "precious," in

Use of the Old Testament in 1 Peter

1 Peter	OT Passage	Content
1:16	Lev. 11:44	Be holy, for God is holy
1:24–25	Isa. 40:6, 8	The word of the Lord abides forever
2:3	Ps. 34:8	The Lord is good
2:6	Isa. 28:16	Jesus is the cornerstone
2:7	Ps. 118:22	Jesus is the cornerstone
2:8	Isa. 8:14	Jesus is the stumbling stone
2:9a	Exod. 19:5–6; Isa. 43:20	Chosen race, royal priesthood, holy nation, people for God's possession
2:9b	Isa. 43:21; cf. 42:12	God's people called to proclaim his praises
2:10	Hosea 1:6, 9–10; 2:23	Once not a people, now the people of God
2:12	Isa. 10:3	Day of visitation
2:18–25	Isa. 53:4–6, 9, 12	Jesus is the suffering servant
3:5–6	Gen. 18:12	Sarah called Abraham "my lord"
4:18	Prov. 11:31	Dismal outlook for ungodly and sinners

1:19) in God's sight. Again, Peter first lodges his assertion (2:4), paraphrasing a set of OT passages, and then follows up with a formal citation of Scripture (cf. 1:15–16, 23–25; see below). Before moving on to Jesus, however, Peter draws an analogy: just as Jesus is a "living stone," so believers are "living stones" (in the plural), who are being built up (*oikodomeō*) as a "spiritual house" (i.e., a temple) and "holy priesthood" (*hierateuma*) to offer "spiritual sacrifices" pleasing to God through Jesus Christ (2:5).

As he has done previously (1:1, 15–16), but now much more extensively, Peter here draws on a matrix of OT terms and concepts (temple, priesthood, sacrifices) and applies them to his gentile readers and all NT believers, indicating the fulfillment of these realities for his audience. Rather than focusing on a physical building or structure (the OT temple), Peter here points out that the church is *believers* who are being "built up" in Christ. Elsewhere in the NT, Paul speaks similarly of believers as "members of the household of God, built on the foundation of the apostles and prophets, Christ Jesus himself being the cornerstone, in whom the whole structure, being joined together, grows into a holy temple in the Lord" (Eph. 2:19–21). He also presents the church as the body of Christ, with believers serving as individual members of that body (e.g., Rom. 12:3–8; 1 Cor. 12–14; Eph. 4–5).

Peter's words in 2:4–5 are followed by a series of "stone citations" which in their characterization of Jesus as both *cornerstone* and *stone of stumbling* echo Jesus's similar usage (2:6–8; cf. Matt. 21:42 // Mark 12:10 // Luke 20:17).

Peter previously made the same point when speaking to the Sanhedrin (the Jewish ruling council) in the early days of the church (Acts 4:11). Paul, too, drew on the same set of OT passages in his letter to the Romans (Rom. 9:32–33; cf. Eph. 2:20). In this catena of "stone passages," Peter invokes multiple OT passages primarily from Isaiah and the Psalms, presenting Jesus, in keeping with OT messianic prophecy, as, paradoxically, both a cornerstone (cf. Isa. 28:16; Ps. 118:22) and a stumbling stone (cf. Isa. 8:14). In the present context, Peter does this in conjunction with calling upon his readers to associate with ("come to") Jesus, who is both the cornerstone in God's plan—having ransomed them with his precious blood (1:18–19)—and the stone over which his opponents stumble. This, in turn, implies that believers, too, will be called upon to suffer rejection with Christ as they identify with him in this world.

Peter is quick to point out that those who stumble over Christ because they disobey the word do so because they were "destined" or "appointed" to do so (a divine passive, implying God's agency; 2:8). In this, he aligns closely with other NT writers such as John or Paul who likewise in similar contexts make clear that God is sovereign even over human sin (e.g., John 12:38–41; Rom. 9:6–33). "But you" (the personal pronoun, *hymeis*, denotes emphasis) in verse 9 marks a contrast between those who stumble over Christ and the readers, whose identity Peter now describes in terms appropriated directly from the foundational OT passage, Exodus 19:5–6, supplemented by several other relevant OT passages (Isa. 42:12; 43:20–21; Hosea 1:6, 9–10; 2:23).

The fact that Peter here cites Exodus 19:5–6 is significant as the passage presents the new nation of Israel at Sinai at the giving of the law following the exodus from Egypt. The fact that Peter cites Isaiah 43:20–21 and Hosea 1:6, 9 is also significant as these passages envision a restored Israel following the exile and even the inclusion of gentiles into the orbit of God's people. In spiritual continuity with OT Israel, Peter's gentile readers are (2:9–10):

- *a chosen race* (Isa. 43:20: "my chosen people"): cf. 1:1 (believers); 2:4 (Jesus): the church transcends earthly racial boundaries, and believers are a spiritual "race" united by faith in Christ, the rejected cornerstone
- *a royal priesthood* (Exod. 19:6: "kingdom of priests" or "priestly kingdom"): cf. 2:5 ("a holy priesthood" offering spiritual sacrifices): the Reformers developed this notion into their teaching on the priesthood of all believers over against the Roman Catholic Church's notion of priests as a separate class and the clergy-laity distinction[13]

13. On the priestly theme in Scripture, see Andrew S. Malone, *God's Mediators: A Biblical Theology of Priesthood*, NSBT 43 (Downers Grove, IL: InterVarsity, 2017). But see also John H.

- *a holy nation* (Exod. 19:6: "to me . . . a holy nation"): the church is set apart spiritually from the world, transcending earthly national boundaries
- *a people for God's own possession* (Exod. 19:5: "my treasured possession among all peoples, for all the earth is mine"): believers are distinct from the world and uniquely the Lord's, set apart by him and for him
- *called to proclaim the excellencies of him who called them out of darkness into his marvelous light* (Isa. 43:21: ". . . the people whom I formed for myself that they might declare my praise"; cf. Isa. 42:12): believers are to serve as God's witnesses out of gratitude for his forgiveness and redemption from moral darkness and sin
- *those who previously were not God's people, had not received his mercy; now are God's people and have received mercy* (Hosea 1:6, 9–10; 2:23): although in Hosea, those who were "not my people" were estranged gentiles, and in OT times gentiles as a group were not included in God's compass of salvation (though the prophets envisioned a time when this would change), Peter here applies the passage to gentiles who are not estranged and who have received salvation

All of this should evoke profound gratitude in Peter's gentile readers, and in all of God's people today. We are chosen by God, precious in his sight, set apart for his holy purposes, called to be his witnesses as those who have been called out of spiritual darkness into his marvelous light, included among God's people even though we were previously far off. All of this perfectly sets up the next unit, starting in 2:11, which urges Peter's readers to abstain from sin, calling on them in their identity as "sojourners and exiles" in this world—resident aliens whose true home is in heaven with God. While on this earth, they are called to identify with Christ, to live holy, spiritually set-apart lives, and to witness to God's breathtaking rescue operation: salvation in Christ, the unblemished, spotless lamb of God and the cornerstone in God's plan of salvation.

Exhortation to Sojourners and Exiles (2:11–4:11)

Submission to Earthly Authority (2:11–3:12)

The introduction "Beloved" (which recurs in 4:12; *agapētoi*) in 2:11 introduces the second major unit in the letter (following 1:3–2:10). Peter's address of

---

Elliott, *The Elect and the Holy: An Exegetical Examination of 1 Peter 2:4–10 and the Phrase* βασίλειον ἱεράτευμα, NovTSup 12 (Leiden: Brill, 1966), who denies that priesthood is a primary concern in 1 Pet. 2:4–10 and that the community as a whole—not the function of individual members—is the focus of the passage. Christians as a whole are a body of priests in continuity with the elect people of Israel who were a kingdom of priests.

the readers as "sojourners" (*paroikos*; cf. Acts 7:6: Abraham's offspring; 7:29: Moses in Midian; Eph. 2:19: paired with *xenoi*, "strangers," with salvation-historical reference to gentiles) and "exiles" (*parepidēmos*; cf. 1:1; Heb. 11:13: paired with *xenoi*, "strangers," with reference to OT believers such as Abel, Enoch, Noah, Abraham, Isaac, and Jacob) is reminiscent of his opening identification of the recipients of the letter as "elect exiles." Remarkably, the reference in Hebrews applies the terms "strangers" and "exiles" even to Abraham and the patriarchs, which shows that these terms are all-encompassing for believers—whether Jews or gentiles—who live by faith in God's promises and look forward to their eternal heavenly home.[14]

Peter's burden continues to be that his readers—who, as mentioned, are predominantly if not exclusively gentile—live spiritually set-apart, God-honoring lives in the midst of their immoral gentile surroundings. Toward that end, he urges them to keep away from "passions of the flesh," which "wage war" (*strateuomai*) against the soul (*psychē*, 2:11; cf. 1:9, 22). The word translated "wage war" literally refers to what soldiers do (e.g., Luke 3:14; 1 Cor. 9:7; 2 Tim. 2:4), though Paul (2 Cor. 10:3; 1 Tim. 1:18), James (James 4:1), and Peter (in the present passage, 2:11) all use the expression in a figurative sense to refer to the internal struggle people experience and the spiritual warfare in which God's servants are engaged. The clear message here is that fleshly passions are detrimental to a person's soul and that we're engaged in a fierce struggle (or at least should be) combating our own sinful tendencies and predispositions.

Ironically, Peter then calls upon his readers—who themselves are gentiles—to "keep [their] conduct among the Gentiles honorable" (literally, "good," *kalos*; 2:12; cf. the reference to "good deeds" later in the same verse). This indicates that those gentiles now, as Christians, are no longer gentiles but have a new identity—as Peter developed at length earlier in this chapter (cf. 2:4–10)—and thus are called to transcend the immorality of their physical surroundings by their spiritual conduct (*anastrophē*; cf. 1:15, 18; 3:1, 2, 16). Their strategy should be to silence their opponents—who slander them as evildoers (cf. 2:1)—by their good deeds, so that their opponents "glorify God on the day of visitation" (2:12, an allusion to Isa. 10:3), a reference to the final day of judgment, when everyone will be called to give an account to God for all their works. Peter's words here echo those of Jesus, who told his followers: "You are the light of the world. . . . In the same way, let your light shine

14. Elliott, *Home for the Homeless*, has proposed that these terms also have a sociological dimension in that believers in that day were literally homeless and ostracized in the world in which they lived, but he unduly neglects the salvation-historical dimension that is clearly primary in Peter's characterization of believers' existence in this world.

before others, so that they may see your good works and give glory to your Father who is in heaven" (Matt. 5:14–16). We should adopt the same strategy today and live in keeping with our identity and calling as "salt of the earth" and "light of the world" (cf. Matt. 5:13–14).

Following the introduction of the new subunit in 2:11, verse 13 launches into an embedded house table or household code, which will occupy the remainder of this chapter and the beginning of the following chapter (2:13–3:7), with 3:8–12 serving as a summary and transition to what follows. The head command introducing the house table is this: "Be subject [*hypotassō*] . . . to every human institution" (*ktisis*, which can mean "creature," as in Rom. 1:20, but here means "institution"). The structure of the household table, tied closely to the verb *hypotassō*, is as follows:

Household Code in 1 Peter 2:13–3:7

1 Peter	Form of *hypotassō*	Content
2:13	Submit (imperative)	"Be subject . . . to every human institution"
2:18	Submitting (participle)	"Servants, being subject . . . to your masters"
3:1	Submitting (participle)	"Likewise, wives, being subject to your own husbands"

In this way, the head command, "Submit to every human institution," is first applied to government (2:13–17) and then extended to two other types of human relationships, slaves and masters (2:18–25), and wives and husbands (3:1–7). In terms of persons addressed, the focus is squarely on those who are called to submit—that is, citizens, slaves, and wives; there is no address to government officials or slave masters, and only one verse is directed toward Christian husbands (3:7). Strikingly, embedded in the household code in 2:21–25 is a lengthy rationale for why Christian slaves should submit to their masters: they should imitate Christ's example and follow in his footsteps, mindful of the way in which he endured suffering on the way to the cross. Note also that 2:19–20 begins and ends with the phrase "This is grace"—that is, "This is met with divine approval and will receive a divine reward"—enclosing the exhortation to suffer for doing good.

Special emphasis in the household code is laid on bearing up under abuse or suffering from unbelieving authorities, whether emperors or governors, slave masters, or unbelieving husbands. In this regard, Christian freedom is expressed in voluntary submission to human authorities—whether a Roman tyrant (the Emperor Nero [reigned AD 54–68] was on the throne when Peter wrote) or a harsh slave master—rather than rebelling against them and asserting one's independence, a response that is profoundly countercultural.

Similarly, Christian wives are to seek God's approval rather than the culture's in the way they submit to their unbelieving husbands and also in the way they dress with regard to hairstyle, jewelry, and clothes. That said, contrary to first-century culture, Christian wives need not submit to their husbands when it comes to adopting their religion (a remarkable exception), but otherwise they should be devoted, modest, and submissive wives.

Submission to Authorities in 1 Peter

Passage	Submission to
2:13	Government
2:18	Workplace (even cruel ones)
3:1	Husbands (even unbelieving ones)
3:5–6	Abraham (by Sarah)
3:22	Christ (by spirit world)
5:5	Elders (by younger men, and others)

In 2:13–18, first, Peter calls on Christians to submit to the governing authorities, thus silencing the misinformation spread by some first-century opponents of Christianity that the movement was inherently subversive (see the charges brought against Jesus and later Paul, addressed particularly in Luke-Acts). Rather, Christians were law-abiding citizens who honored those in authority (cf. Paul's similar teaching in Rom. 13:1–7; Titus 3:1). The unit begins and ends with a command to submit to (or "honor") the emperor (2:13, 17). Likewise, Christians are to honor local governors (*hēgemōn*; cf. Matt. 27:2, 11, 14, 15, 21, 27; 28:14; Luke 20:20: Pilate; Acts 23:24, 26, 33; 24:1, 10: Felix; Acts 26:30: King Agrippa; cf. Jesus's prediction that his followers would stand before and bear witness to "governors and kings," Matt. 10:18; Mark 13:9; Luke 21:12). Peter's rationale is that every human authority is ultimately instituted by God, "sent by him to punish those who do evil and to praise those who do good" (2:14). Rather than challenging those in authority, believers should "silence the ignorance of foolish people" by doing what is good (2:15).

Peter follows up by making the paradoxical point that while believers are free, they shouldn't use their freedom as a cover-up (literally, "veil") for evil, but rather as "servants" or "slaves of God" (*doulos*). Peter concludes the first part of the household code with four succinct injunctions, each featuring an imperative with an object: "Honor everyone. Love the brotherhood. Fear God. Honor the emperor." In this way, he makes honoring the emperor a subset of honoring everyone (the first and last injunctions). In between these two commands to "honor," Peter calls on believers to "love" the brotherhood (*adelphotēs*; elsewhere in the NT only in 5:9), no doubt a higher standard, and to "fear" God (*phobeomai*), also a higher standard than that of paying honor and respect to human authorities. That said, as Peter himself had asserted earlier over against the Jewish Sanhedrin, the command to honor those in authority is not absolute: "We must obey God rather than men" (Acts 5:29; cf. 4:19–20).

After this, Peter, second, in 2:18 moves on to instructions to servants (*oiketai*; elsewhere in the NT only in Luke 16:13; Acts 10:7; Rom. 14:4), which, as mentioned, contain an excursus on the example of Christ (2:21–25). The connection to the head command in 2:13, "Be subject . . . to every human institution," as mentioned, is made clear by the participial form of the verb "submit" (*hypotassomenoi*; literally, "submitting") in verse 18. Whereas today we would universally recognize that slavery is not God-honoring and often downright evil—no human should own another human—there have been various forms of slavery across human history, and Peter's point here is simply that for Christian servants or slaves to submit to their (unbelieving) masters is God-honoring because it is done "for the Lord's sake" (2:13) and submission to earthly authorities ultimately honors him.

Peter raises the bar even higher when he calls on servants to be subject not only to masters who are good and gentle but also to those who are unjust or harsh (2:18; *skolios*; elsewhere in the NT only in Luke 3:5; Acts 2:40; and Phil. 2:15). This, Peter points out in 2:19 and reiterates at the end of 2:20, is "grace" (*charis*)—a "gracious thing" to do—when a person is mindful of God and bears up under sorrows or griefs, suffering unjustly (2:19); conversely, no credit is due when a person suffers for sinning (2:20). This assertion already triggers the memory of Isaiah's depiction of the Messiah—Jesus—as a "man of sorrows and acquainted with grief" (Isa. 53:3). Sure enough, the fact that Peter has this passage of Scripture in mind is confirmed by the following elaboration on Christ's example of suffering in 2:21–25.

Remarkably, Peter's point here is not the redemption itself that Jesus procured by dying for our sins on the cross but the way in which Christ suffered, which Christians should imitate and emulate: "For to this you have been called, because Christ also suffered for you, *leaving you an example* [*hypogrammos*, unique in the NT], so that you might follow in his steps" (2:21). Peter's following description invokes at the same time portions of Isaiah's song of the suffering servant (Isa. 52:13–53:12) as it recalls the depiction of Christ's suffering in the Gospel passion narratives. Peter himself is a major eyewitness to these events and is "a witness of the sufferings of Christ" (cf. 5:1). At this point, Peter slides into poetry, which is at times lost in English translation, in that verses 22, 23, and 24 each start with the relative pronoun "who" (*hos*), describing the way in which Christ suffered in an exemplary manner (ESV is altered to show this parallelism):

- "who committed no sin, nor was deceit found in his mouth" (2:22)
- "who when reviled did not revile in return, when suffering did not threaten, but continually entrusted himself to the one who judges righteously" (2:23)
- "who himself bore our sins in his body on [or "to"; the object "the tree" is accusative, not dative) the tree [*xylos*—i.e., the cross],[15] so that having died to sins we might live to righteousness, by whose wounds you were healed" (2:24)

Peter concludes his exhortation by noting, "You were straying like sheep, but now have returned to the Shepherd [*poimēn*] and Overseer [*episkopos*] of your souls" (2:25, *psychē*; cf. 1:9, 22; 2:11).[16] In midrashic (commentary-style) fashion, Peter here creatively weaves through Isaiah's suffering servant song, not always in Isaianic order, incorporating several portions in his own depiction of the messianic suffering of the Lord Jesus Christ. If Isaiah's servant song is divided into five sections, it appears that Peter draws primarily on the third section, in the center of the song (Isa. 53:4–9).

Use of Isaiah 53 in 1 Peter 2:21–25

1 Peter	Jesus the Suffering Servant	Isaiah
2:22	No deceit was found in his mouth	53:9
2:23	He did not open his mouth, remained silent	53:7
2:24	He bore our sins	53:4, 6, 12
2:24	By his wounds we are healed	53:5
2:25	We went astray like sheep	53:6

In many ways, therefore, 2:21–25 serves as the theological high point of the household code in 2:13–3:7 (or through 3:12), if not the entire letter—a high point similar in import to Paul's description of Christ in Philippians 2 (where the emphasis is on Jesus's humility). In this way, Peter holds up before believers the ultimate example of one who suffered unjustly. If Jesus bore up under such incredible, unjust suffering, entrusting himself to God and not

15. Cf. Peter's use of the same term in Acts 5:30 and 10:39, a powerful corroboration of both the Petrine authorship of 1 Peter and the historical accuracy of the book of Acts. Note also the allusion to Deut. 21:23 (cf. Gal. 3:13).

16. Translations in 2:21–25 are my own based on the wording and word order in the original Greek.

taking revenge into his own hand, how much more should his followers be content to imitate Christ's conduct and leave righteous judgment to God? In this way, believers can continue to extend Christ's redemptive mission (cf. the word *kai*, "also," in 2:21; 3:18). Peter will return to this matter once more in 3:18 below. In this way, believers extend the fulfillment of Isaiah 53 beyond the suffering servant and become part of God's redemptive plan and purposes for others.

For now, third, Peter continues the household code by providing instructions (mostly) for wives of unbelieving husbands (3:1–7). Again, Peter connects this set of instructions to the preceding house table by the participle "submitting" (*hypotassomenai*). What is in view here is not the submission of all women to all men but rather the submission of a wife to "her own husband." While Paul elsewhere addresses himself to women of *Christian* husbands (Eph. 5:21–23; Col. 3:18), Peter here, in keeping with his emphasis on "hard" cases and on suffering for doing what is right throughout the household code and in fact the entire letter, speaks primarily (though not exclusively) to women of *unbelieving* husbands, "so that even if *some* do not obey [*apeitheō*; cf. 2:8; 4:17] the word, they may be won without a word by the conduct of their wives" (3:1; note the wordplay on "word": they disobey the *word* [i.e., of God] and may be won without a *word* [i.e., from their wives]). Peter's counsel here is similar to the principle enunciated later in general terms at 3:14–15.

Notice that there is no word here of *abusive* husbands; Peter only mentions that "some" husbands may not be believers. The best way to overcome their resistance, Peter counsels, is for Christian wives to let their conduct do the talking (cf. the example, invoked in 2:23 above, of Christ, who quietly continued to entrust himself to God). Such husbands, Peter holds out hope, may be won to Christ "when they see [their wives'] respectful and pure conduct" (3:2). The translation "see" hardly does justice to the unusual word used here, *epopteuō*, which refers to careful and perceptive observation and is used elsewhere in the NT only in the previous reference in the present letter, at 2:12, where Peter urges his readers to keep their conduct honorable in their gentile surroundings so that when people revile them, those same people may perceive (*epopteuō*) their good deeds and glorify God. "Respectful" renders the literal "in fear" (which is due ultimately to Christ; cf. Eph. 5:21; see also, similarly, Paul's words in Eph. 5:33), while "pure" translates the word *hagnos* (used in a similar context in Titus 2:5; cf. 2 Cor. 11:2).

Peter's encouragement to wives—remember, Peter himself was married (see the reference to Peter, the other apostles, and the half-brothers of Jesus having believing wives in 1 Cor. 9:5; note also the references to Peter's mother-in-law in the Gospels [Matt. 8:14; Mark 1:30; Luke 4:38])—is that they focus on inner rather than external beauty: a "gentle and quiet spirit" rather than elaborate hairstyles, gold jewelry, or expensive clothing (3:3–4). This was standard instruction for women in the first century in the Jewish and Greco-Roman world alike and remains applicable today. It is in part a matter of stewardship: What do we spend the bulk of our time doing, and what do we spend most of our money on? Having our hair done, spending hours at the hairdresser, shopping for clothes, shoes, and other items? Or do we focus on character, loving God and others, and bearing witness to God by the way we live?

In the present case, Peter's primary point of application is a Christian wife's witness to her unbelieving husband (always a trying issue), but the principle extends even beyond such situations (cf. Paul's words in 1 Tim. 2:9–10, which extend to women in the church in general and call for modesty, self-control, and good works rather than a focus on "braided hair and gold or pearls or costly attire," the same triad as in the present passage). As Peter points out, a focus on "the hidden person of the heart" and "a gentle and quiet spirit" reveals "imperishable [*aphthartos*, used previously in 1:4, 23, continuing the contrast between abiding and temporal things in this letter] beauty" which "in God's sight is very precious" (3:4; *polytelēs*, used elsewhere in the NT only in Mark 14:3, with reference to the expensive perfume used by Mary of Bethany in anointing the feet of Jesus, and in 1 Tim. 2:9).

In other words, women should be more concerned about what *God* thinks than about what other *people* (including men) think! As a scriptural analogy and precedent, Peter adduces the way in which "the holy women who hoped in God used to adorn themselves"—by submitting to their own husbands—and he cites the specific example of Sarah, who "obeyed" Abraham and called him "lord" (3:6; cf. Gen. 18:12). This is to be understood not as blind subservience but as respectful submissiveness to a godly husband (which Abraham, though not perfect, was). By following Sarah's example—doing good and being unafraid—such women will be her "children" (3:6).

Unlike in the other cases (no instruction for governors or masters), Peter includes a brief word to (Christian) husbands in closing out the house table in 3:7 (note the transition, "Likewise," similar to 3:1). Husbands should live (more literally, "dwell together," *synoikeō*) with their wives (implied), literally, "according to knowledge" (*kata gnōsin*). The obvious question is, "Knowledge *of what?*" In context, the answer most likely is the fact that wives are, literally, "the weaker vessel, the feminine one" (*gynaikeios*; unique in the NT). What husbands are to know (that is, understand and keep in mind as they relate to their wives) is that their wives are, in some sense, "weaker." Whether this applies to physical strength only or more broadly to women over against men in general is a topic on which scholars disagree. If we take our cue from Peter's first-century framework rather than modern psychology or cultural sensibilities, perhaps he had in mind that women are generally more dependent on their husband because, as the creation narrative tells us, God made the woman specifically for the man, as Paul acknowledges as well (1 Cor. 11:8–9; cf. Gen. 2:15–23). In this regard, the woman is oriented toward her husband and serves as his "suitable helper" (cf. Gen. 2:18, 20). When the serpent approached the woman apart from her husband, she fell into transgression (Gen. 3:1–5; cf. 1 Tim. 2:14). In any case, a husband will do well to be considerate toward his wife rather than treating her harshly (cf. Col. 3:19). Peter adds two important factors. First, women are not only the weaker vessels but also, and more importantly, "fellow heirs of the grace of life." Second, if husbands are inconsiderate toward their wives, their prayers (most likely referring to the husbands' prayers) will be hindered (3:7).

Peter concludes the household code in 2:13–3:7 with a brief summary statement, introduced by "Finally" (*to telos*), in 3:8–12. He calls all of his readers to be like-minded (*homophrones*; not elsewhere in the NT), sympathetic (*sympatheis*; not elsewhere in the NT), loving (*philadelphoi*; not elsewhere in the NT), compassionate (*eusplangchnoi*; elsewhere in the NT only in Eph. 4:32), and humble (*tapeinophrones*; not elsewhere in the NT).[17] The exhortation not to "repay evil for evil or reviling for reviling" in 3:9 reiterates the similar injunction in conjunction with Christ's example in 2:23 (cf. Rom. 12:17). To the contrary, Peter urges his readers to bless their opponents, just as Jesus had taught his followers to love their enemies, do good to those who hated them, "bless" those who cursed them, and pray for those who persecuted them (Matt. 5:44; Luke 6:27). In this way, believers will "obtain [literally, "inherit"] a blessing" (3:9; cf. 1:4).[18] Peter closes this section by, once again, providing scriptural support for his exhortation, in the present case with a lengthy quotation from Psalm 34 (vv. 12–16), a psalm he previously cited at 2:3 (Ps. 34:8). This quote provides a positive outlook and orientation for those who suffer persecution, as they are encouraged to control their tongue, turn away from evil and do good, pursue peace, and look to the Lord in prayer.

Suffering for Righteousness' Sake (3:13–22)

In 3:13, Peter then moves beyond the household code and emphatically makes the additional and related point that he is not talking about suffering

---

17. Note the closure provided by the first and last word containing the suffix *-phrones*, "-minded." Note also that the five characteristics listed in 3:8 provide the positive correlative to the five negative characteristics the readers are told to shed in 2:1.

18. See the excellent discussion of this phrase in Karen H. Jobes, *1 Peter*, BECNT (Grand Rapids: Baker Academic, 2005), 218–20.

for doing what is wrong (some people might suffer deservedly) but suffering for doing what is right. He starts out 3:13 with a rhetorical question, apparently expecting a "no" answer—"Now who is there to harm you if you are zealous for what is good?" Implied answer: "No one!"—but then 3:14, a rare instance of the optative mood, expresses in deliberative fashion a possibility (perhaps remote at the time): that Christians might "suffer for *righteousness'* sake." If Peter had written later in Nero's reign after major persecution got underway (Nero reigned AD 54–68, and persecution got more severe in the last few years of his reign), one wonders if he would have still used the optative. In an allusion to Isaiah 8:12–13, Peter calls on his readers to "have no fear of them, nor be troubled," but instead to honor (literally, "set apart," *hagiazō*) Christ the Lord as holy in their hearts, "always being prepared to make a defense [*apologia*; cf. Acts 22:1; 25:16] to anyone who asks [them] for a reason for the hope that is in [them]," yet "with gentleness and respect [*phobos*, "fear"]" (3:14–15).[19] The principle enunciated here is similar to Peter's counsel to wives of unbelieving husbands in 3:1–6 above. In this way, believers will have a good conscience (cf. 2:19 above and 3:21 below), and those who slander them (cf. 2:1, 12) will by their "good behavior in Christ" be put to shame (3:16). As my old pastor used to say, "Just outlive 'em!" Concluding the section that started with 3:13, Peter then reiterates the principle of suffering for doing what is right rather than for doing what is wrong (3:17).

In 3:18–19, similar to 2:21–22, Peter proceeds to elaborate by drawing his readers' attention once again to Christ. "For Christ," he writes, "also suffered once for sins, the righteous for the unrighteous, that he might bring us to God, being put to death in the flesh but made alive in the Spirit [or spirit]" (3:18). While the word *pneumati* could be translated "Spirit" or "spirit," "Spirit" is more likely, because the prepositional relative clause that follows in 3:19 introduced by "in whom" is difficult to construe if one translates "spirit" (note that the ESV translates "spirit" here but "Spirit" in the parallel passage 1 Tim. 3:16). Peter's point here seems to be that believers, when suffering for doing what is right, should take their cue from Jesus, who likewise suffered, "the righteous for the unrighteous"—that is, Jesus's suffering was redemptive and for the benefit of others; in fact, it was for the benefit even of the very people who were the cause of his suffering! What's more, his suffering had a clear purpose—"that he might bring us to God." It's hard to escape the conclusion that Peter here hints at the fact that the suffering of Christ's followers, likewise, has a redemptive component *if they suffer for doing what is right*: by so doing, they might bring others to God, just like Jesus did. This

---

19. Cf. the reference to believers' "living hope" at 1:3; see also 1:21.

invests righteous suffering with great redemptive potential and ennobles it, raising it far above any sense of meaninglessness and despair. Suffering, if done for Christ, has a purpose. It has profound meaning, as it absorbs the evil of others and converts it into a blessing instead—just as Christ's death did on the cross (in a primary, unique, and exclusive sense, of course; all Christian suffering is derivative of his).

Verse 19 then continues the cadence of 3:18: "in which [or in whom] he [Jesus] went and proclaimed to the spirits in prison." Jesus—presumably after his resurrection—went and made proclamation to imprisoned spirits (presumably demonic ones).[20] The word translated "proclaimed" (*kerysso*) is not being used in the technical sense of "preaching the gospel" but more generally as "making proclamation" as a herald (*keryx*). The term "spirits" (*pneuma* in the plural) in the NT virtually always refers to angelic beings— whether fallen or unfallen—not the human departed.[21] But who are these imprisoned spirits? And what is the content of Jesus's proclamation to them? Peter continues that these spirits were in prison "because they formerly did not obey, when God's patience waited in the days of Noah, while the ark was being prepared, in which a few, that is, eight persons, were brought safely through water" (3:20).[22] The passage raises a number of questions that are best taken up in Q&A format:

- *Who are these spirits?* Most likely, they are demons—fallen angels— who disobeyed in the days of Noah (cf. Gen. 6:1–4) and procreated with human women. The relevant passage in Genesis 6 was the subject of extensive speculation in intertestamental literature such as in the book of 1 Enoch.
- *Why these spirits?* It's hard to know for sure, but perhaps because they committed a particularly egregious sin—namely, as mentioned under the previous bullet point, having sexual intercourse with women and

---

20. Note that the Greek word translated "went" (*poreuomai*) merely indicates a journey but not necessarily (or even likely) a descent (the Greek word for "going down" would be *katabainō*). So rightly Storms, "1 Peter," 339, with reference to Paul J. Achtemeier, *1 Peter*, Hermeneia (Minneapolis: Fortress, 1996), 257.

21. The sole exception being Heb. 12:23.

22. The preposition "through" (*dia*) can also mean "by means of" (instrumental sense). If the latter meaning is intended, this would mean that Noah and his family were saved from the universal flood by means of water. This, in turn, would be taken to depict believers' salvation as symbolized by the waters of baptism. See the brief discussion in Storms, "1 Peter," 342, with reference to R. T. France, "Exegesis in Practice: Two Examples," in *New Testament Interpretation: Essays on Principles and Methods*, ed. I. Howard Marshall (Grand Rapids: Eerdmans, 1977), 273–74.

procreating hybrid offspring (Gen. 6:2, 4: "the sons of God . . . took as their wives any they chose . . . and they bore children to them"). Also, judging by Peter's second epistle, there were false teachers who apparently disputed the historicity of the universal flood in Noah's day (2 Pet. 3:6), which may explain why Peter focuses specifically on circumstances surrounding the flood.

- *Where are or were they?* These demonic spirits were in prison when Jesus went to them after his resurrection, though exactly where is not entirely clear. Some early creeds (e.g., the Apostles' Creed) affirm Christ's descent into hell.[23] In any case, they were confined, perhaps in a temporary holding location, awaiting final judgment (cf. 2 Pet. 2:4; Jude 6; Rev. 20:7–15).

- *When did Christ make this proclamation?* Christ did not make proclamation to those imprisoned spirits in the days of Noah as the preexistent Christ. More likely, the spirits disobeyed in the days of Noah, but Jesus made proclamation to them following his resurrection (v. 18) and prior to his ascension (v. 22).

- *What did Christ proclaim to these spirits?* Now that he had been crucified, and subsequently risen from the dead, Jesus most likely would have made proclamation of his victory over death and over Satan (cf. Col. 2:15). This triumphant announcement of victory would have put demons on notice that their demise was close at hand.

- *How does Peter know this?* We simply don't know. This information is not attested anywhere else in the NT.

While the interpretation of 3:18–20 may be bewildering at first, as it raises many complex interpretive issues and covers material not elsewhere attested in

---

23. In Latin, this is known as *descensus ad inferos*. For a more detailed discussion, see Andreas J. Köstenberger, L. Scott Kellum, and Charles L. Quarles, *The Cradle, the Cross, and the Crown: An Introduction to the New Testament*, 2nd ed. (Nashville: B&H Academic, 2016), 851–53. See also J. Ramsey Michaels, *1 Peter*, WBC 49 (Waco: Word, 1988), 194–222; and Thomas R. Schreiner, *1, 2 Peter, Jude*, NAC 37 (Nashville: Broadman & Holman, 2003), 184–90. The classic study is W. J. Dalton, *Christ's Proclamation to the Spirits: A Study of 1 Peter 3:18–4:6*, AnBib 23 (Rome: Pontifical Biblical Institute, 1965), who argues that 1 Pet. 3:18–4:6 is a literary unit referring to Christ's proclamation of victory over angelic powers at his ascension. Wayne Grudem, in *First Epistle of Peter*, TNTC (Grand Rapids: Eerdmans, 1988), 203–39, provides an extensive argument that Jesus, in the Spirit, spoke to Noah's contemporaries through Noah, preceding the flood. More recently, see Chad T. Pierce, *Spirits and the Proclamation of Christ*, WUNT 2/305 (Tübingen: Mohr Siebeck, 2011), who provides a tradition and redaction analysis of 1 Pet. 3:18–22, exploring the influence of 1 Enoch and other relevant strands of pre-Petrine traditions including the Book of Watchers. Justin W. Bass, *The Battle for the Keys: Revelation 1:18 and Christ's Descent into the Underworld* (Eugene, OR: Wipf & Stock, 2014), attempts to make a case for Jesus's descent into Hades following the crucifixion yet prior to the resurrection.

the NT, one important observation provides a vital interpretive framework—namely, that the sequence of Peter's presentation here follows a temporal, *chronological* order:

- *crucifixion* ("put to death in the flesh," v. 18)
- *resurrection* ("made alive in the Spirit," v. 18; "the resurrection of Jesus Christ," v. 21)
- *proclamation* to spirits in prison ("he went and proclaimed," v. 19; flashback in v. 20; digression on baptism in v. 21)
- *ascension* ("gone into heaven," v. 22)

If this chronological reading is accurate, verses 19–21, as seen above, fall between the *resurrection* and the *ascension*.

The other important interpretive principle to keep in mind is that Peter here didn't merely engage in obtuse theologizing but sought to encourage his readers. A cogent interpretation of these verses thus needs to include a cogent *purpose* why Peter would have imparted this information to his readers. We know that Peter's readers were suffering and that Peter was preparing them for even more intense suffering in the future (cf. 4:12 below). Most likely, then, the present passage is part of Peter's overall purpose of encouraging believers amid their suffering. By telling them that Jesus, after his resurrection, already went and announced his victory over death to the spirit world, those believers would be greatly heartened in their suffering, knowing that just as Jesus was vindicated by resurrection following his crucifixion, so they, too, would be vindicated if they persisted in the face of unjust suffering.

Peter's assertion (in the form of an apparent digression) in 3:21—"Baptism now saves you"—is difficult, since elsewhere the NT makes clear that baptism does not in itself save anyone (contra the notion of baptismal regeneration). Rather, baptism represents an outward expression of an inward reality that has already taken place—namely, inward cleansing and renewal accompanying forgiveness of sins upon repentant conversion and the placing of one's trust in Christ's sacrifice on the cross (see esp. Rom. 6:4). The antitype of "salvation" ("which corresponds to this") here is clearly Noah's preservation from God's wrath through the flood (*diasōzō*). Peter may have added this parenthesis to show the relevance of his teaching for believers who had previously been baptized. Such believers are linked with Noah and his family in that they were saved through the flood, corresponding typologically to the waters of baptism. In conjunction with this, Peter also asserts that baptism is an "appeal" or "pledge" (*eperōtēma*) to God. How are we to best understand this term—appeal or pledge? The word is not found elsewhere in the NT, but second-century papyri favor the rendering "pledge." If, then, "good conscience" is taken as an objective genitive ("a pledge to God *for* a good conscience"), Peter is saying here that baptism constitutes a pledge to maintain a good conscience (3:21; cf. 3:16: "having a good conscience"). This aspect of baptism is almost universally neglected in the church today.

Peter finishes this section by adding that believers can make this pledge at baptism "through the resurrection of Jesus Christ, who has gone into heaven [ascension] and is at the right hand of God, with angels, authorities, and powers having been subjected to him" (3:21–22). "Having gone" (*poreutheis*) in 3:22 picks up where 3:19 (*poreutheis*) left off. It is possible that 3:18–19, which, as mentioned, exhibits poetic cadence, stems from preformed tradition (cf. 1 Tim. 3:16, which similarly features a contrast between "flesh" and "Spirit"; cf. 4:6 below). If so, however, this doesn't necessarily make this a piece of baptismal liturgy, as is often supposed. In either case, verses 20–21 are most likely Peter's elaboration, digression, or parenthesis building on 3:18–19, with 3:22 possibly resuming and concluding the poetic cadence marking 3:18–19.

Living for the Will of God (4:1–6)

Starting with a grammatical construction known as a genitive absolute (in which both the subject and the main verb are set off from the remainder of the sentence), 4:1 then picks up on the statement made in 3:18, where Peter wrote, "For Christ also suffered once for sins." Here, in 4:1, Peter writes similarly, "Since therefore Christ suffered in the flesh." In the previous instance, Peter reinforced the importance of suffering for doing what is right by citing Christ's example of suffering "once for sins, the righteous for the unrighteous, that he might bring us to God" (3:18), followed by a remarkable christological section. Now, Peter uses a similar assertion, "Since therefore Christ suffered in the flesh," to urge his readers to arm themselves (*hoplizō*, unique in the NT) with the same mindset (*ennoia*; elsewhere in the NT only in Heb. 4:12). This exhortation encapsulates Peter's primary purpose of writing the entire letter: equipping believers to suffer in a Christlike manner. The reason Peter gives for encouraging the same mindset as Christ's when dealing with suffering is this: "For whoever has suffered in the flesh has ceased from sin [cf. 3:18: "For Christ also suffered *once* for sins"], so as to live for the rest of the time in the flesh no longer for human passions but for the will of God" (4:1–2; of course, this doesn't imply that Christ himself ever sinned). Paul put it this way: "I have been crucified with Christ. It is no longer I who live, but Christ who lives in me. And the life I now live in the flesh I live by faith in the Son of God, who loved me and gave himself for me" (Gal. 2:20).

While 4:1–2 is forward-looking, speaking of how believers are to live the rest of their "time [*chronos*] in the flesh"—no longer for "human passions" (*epithymia*; cf. 2:11)—4:3 is backward-looking, reflecting on "the time [*chronos*] that is past." In the past, Peter's converted gentile readers carried out "the will [*boulēma*] of the Gentiles"; now they are to live for "the will [*thelēma*] of God." Peter sketches the previous lifestyle of these gentile believers prior to their conversion by way of six characteristics: "sensuality, passions, drunkenness, orgies, drinking parties, and lawless idolatry" (4:3). Peter presupposes—or at least urges—maturity on the part of his readers. His point here is that those who would respond to suffering in a Christlike manner must have made a decisive break with the past; as Jesus taught, whoever wants to follow him must put his hand to the plow and not look back (Luke 9:62).

In 4:4, which in the original seamlessly flows from verse 3, Peter insightfully observes that his readers' former *friends* and associates are "surprised" (*xenizō*) that the believers no longer "run with them" into the same "flood" of debauchery (*asōtia*; note that three of the seven characteristics listed are related to drinking), and consequently these former companions malign the readers, former gentiles who have now turned from idolatry to serve the living God (note that the word "malign" renders *blasphēmeō*, which is used elsewhere for blasphemy of God himself).[24] Later, in verse 12, using the same word (*xenizō*), Peter writes that his *readers* should not be surprised at the oncoming fiery trial.

The egregious wrong of lawless gentiles maligning their former friends for turning to God unsurprisingly triggers Peter's remark that the readers' opponents will not escape scot-free; "they will give account to him who is ready to judge the living and the dead" (i.e., all people; 4:5). This somber reminder of future divine judgment serves to encourage the readers to continue to stand firm and to stiffen their resolve to follow Christ even when suffering unjustly, rather than relapsing into their former way of life.

Concluding this section, Peter adds that it is for this very purpose that the gospel was preached (*euangelizō*) "even to those who are dead." There are some apocryphal books (e.g., 2 Maccabees) that speak of prayers for the dead (cf. the reference to baptism for the dead in 1 Cor. 15:29), though the NT clearly doesn't hold out any possibility of a postmortem (after-death) opportunity for people to repent: "And just as it is appointed for man to die once, and

---

24. Where ESV has "join them in the same flood," the NLT translates "plunge into the flood," cited favorably by Greg W. Forbes, *1 Peter*, EGGNT (Nashville: B&H Academic, 2014), 140.

after that comes judgment . . ." (Heb. 9:27). For this reason, those who are "dead" are most likely those who had the gospel preached to them during their lifetime but who are now dead. Apparently, those people responded favorably to the gospel and accepted it and have gone on ahead before the readers.

The result is that, "though judged in the flesh the way people are [*kata anthrōpous*], they [can] live in the spirit the way God does [*kata theon*]" (4:6). The readers' pagan neighbors and former friends judged them by purely human standards; yet God's standard of judgment is entirely different. Note how this section ends the way it began: with a reference to "the flesh" (4:1–2: "Since therefore Christ suffered *in the flesh* . . . for whoever has suffered *in the flesh* . . . so as to live for the rest of the time *in the flesh* . . ."; 4:6: "though judged *in the flesh* . . . , they might live in the Spirit [or spirit]"). In this way, Peter contrasts our human, earthly life as being lived for one's passions with it being lived in the Spirit (cf. 3:18), including responding to suffering in a Christlike manner.

Serving as Stewards of God's Grace (4:7–11)

For the second time (cf. "Finally" in 3:8), Peter seems to be trying to wrap up this letter when he writes, "The end of all things is at hand," and "Above all . . ." (4:7–8), not to mention that he concludes this section with a resounding "Amen" (4:11). Yet, as we can see, 4:12 starts a final section, where Peter returns once more to the topic of suffering for doing what is right (see below). Peter's reference to the "end of all things"—encompassing Jesus's second coming and God's final judgment—again reflects the pervasive perspective adopted and commended by Peter throughout the letter: that readers' present suffering takes place against the backdrop and under the umbrella of the imminent "revelation of Jesus Christ" (i.e., his second coming, marking "the end of all things"; cf. 1:7, 13).

In light of this sobering reminder of Christ's return and God's judgment (cf. 4:5), Peter urges his readers "therefore" to be "self-controlled" (*sōphronēsate*; cf. Rom. 12:3; Titus 2:6) and "sober-minded" (*nēpsate*, from *nēphō*, used in 1:13 in parallelism with *teleios*, "mature"; the same exhortation is repeated in 5:8 below; cf. 1 Thess. 5:6, 8; 2 Tim. 4:5) for the sake of "prayers" (cf. the reference to insensitive husbands' prayers being hindered in 3:7). While in English "self-control" may bring to mind a more narrow control of one's sexual appetites and perhaps one's penchant toward overeating or excessive consumption of alcohol, in Greek the term is broader and encompasses one's mindset. Thus in 3:8, Peter urged a mindset of unity and humility (*phron-*), and in 4:1 he called for the same mindset as Christ's in the face of suffering (*ennoia*).

What Peter has in mind here, I believe, is a stance of tough-minded realism that knows that God is in control even if and when circumstances seem to indicate differently, a mindset that is certain of future spiritual realities such as Christ's return and God's final judgment (cf. Heb. 11:1). Armed with such a mindset, by faith, suffering believers can therefore keep doing what is right even when facing adverse reactions from the unbelieving world. This is also confirmed by the way in which self-control and sober-mindedness are said to have as their purpose believers' "prayers" to God. Self-control is thus not merely an exercise in willpower or human strength of resolve; rather, it is a function of a full-orbed, realistic framework of the world as it really is—including the (at present) unseen world (cf. 1:8–9).

"Above all" (*pro pantōn*), Peter continues, believers should engage in a triad of vital activities: brotherly love, hospitality, and mutual service. First, they should have "earnest" *love* for one another (*ektenēs*, unique in the NT, but cf. the use of the adverb in 1:22 above; see also 3:8), because "love covers a multitude of sins" (4:8; cf. James 5:20, a likely allusion to Prov. 10:12). This exhortation echoes Peter's words toward the beginning of the letter: "Having purified your souls by your obedience to the truth for a sincere brotherly love, love one another earnestly [*ektenōs*] from a pure heart" (1:22).

Second, believers should exhibit hospitality (*philoxenoi*; literally, "love of strangers," elsewhere in the NT mentioned as a requirement for elders: 1 Tim. 3:2; Titus 1:8)[25] and do so "without grumbling" (*gongysmos*; cf. John 7:12; Acts 6:1; Phil. 2:14; avoiding the mindset of the Israelites wandering in the wilderness following the exodus: John 6:41, 43, 61; 1 Cor. 10:10; cf. Num. 16:11–25). That is, they should do so cheerfully and willingly rather than merely as those fulfilling a burdensome obligation. This is in keeping with Peter's continued insistence on Christians living motivated by grace and in an environment permeated by grace (e.g., 2:19–20; 3:7; 4:10).

Third, as each believer has received a "gift" (*charisma*) from God, all should exercise their gifts as "good stewards" (*oikonomoi*) of the "varied" or multifaceted (*poikilos*; cf. 1:6; see also James 1:2) grace of God (cf. 3:7).[26] Believers should exercise their spiritual gifts in *serving* (*diakoneō*) one another, whether in speaking the "oracles [*logia*] of God" or serving in the strength God supplies (*chorēgeō*) rather than in their own strength (4:10–11).[27] This is one of several passages in the NT that speak of believers

---

25. Note the possible wordplay with *xenizō*, "think it strange" (ESV: "are/be surprised") in 4:4 and 12.

26. The fact that "gift" is singular need not imply that every Christian has only one spiritual gift.

27. The Greek word *diakoneō* occurs elsewhere in Peter's writings only in 1 Pet. 1:12.

exercising their spiritual gifts in the church (cf. Rom. 12:1–8; 1 Cor. 12, 14; Eph. 4:11–16).[28]

In this section, again, Peter's focus is on action—living out one's Christian faith based on a sound, realistic mindset and a strong, unwavering commitment to follow Christ even in the face of adversity. The goal is that "in everything God may be glorified through Jesus Christ." Peter concludes this second major unit in his letter—though not yet the letter itself—with a doxology, "To him [in context, Jesus Christ] belong glory and dominion forever and ever," followed by a resounding "Amen" (4:11; see the similar, albeit shorter, doxology at 5:11, the actual ending of the letter: "To him be the dominion forever and ever. Amen").

Exhortation to Suffer as Christians in All Humility (4:12–5:11)

Apparently with a sense of urgency, Peter adds a final section, introduced, like the previous major unit beginning in 2:11, by the address "Beloved" (4:12). The opening command, "Do not be surprised [*xenizō*] . . . as though something strange [*xenos*] were happening to you," intriguingly harks back to the use of the same verb in the previous section (4:4), where Peter told his readers that their former gentile friends and neighbors were "surprised" that the believers no longer joined them in their lascivious lifestyle. Here, however, it is not others who are surprised at the readers but the readers themselves who are told not to be surprised at something—that is, the ominous "fiery trial" (*pyrōsis*, elsewhere in the NT only in Rev. 18:9, 18, signifying the judgment of the "great city" Babylon) that Peter predicts will soon come upon them to "test" (*peirasmos*) them.

At the beginning of the letter, Peter had likewise spoken of "various trials" (*peirasmos*) that awaited the readers (1:6–7); now he seems to be speaking of something even more specific and intense (in the singular) by referring to a "fiery trial" (the word *pyrōsis* is a derivative of the word *pyr*, "fire").[29] It would be only normal human nature to be taken aback when a fierce trial suddenly appears, and so Peter gives those believers a heads-up so that when the trial comes, they will expect it and not be thrown off. This will enable them to respond in a Christlike manner and thus glorify God.[30] Like James (1:2–4), Peter urges his readers to actually "rejoice"—not in the adversity itself but

---

28. The Greek word *chorēgeō* occurs elsewhere in the NT only in 2 Cor. 9:10.

29. The cognate verb *pyroō* is used in Eph. 6:16 to refer to the "*flaming* darts of the evil one" and in 2 Pet. 3:12 to refer to the coming "day of God" when "the heavens will be set on fire and dissolved, and the heavenly bodies will melt as they *burn.*"

30. As Thomas Schreiner (*1, 2 Peter, Jude*, 219) memorably puts it, Christian suffering is "not a sign of God's absence, but of his purifying presence."

"insofar as [they] share Christ's sufferings"—a truly supernatural, biblically informed response. In this way, they will also be able to rejoice at the second coming, "when his glory is revealed" (4:13).

In his second letter, Peter will refer to his eyewitness recollection of the transfiguration, defending himself against charges that his teaching on the second coming of Christ is spurious: "For we did not follow cleverly devised myths [as he was accused of doing] when we made known to you the power and coming of our Lord Jesus Christ [the second coming], but we were eyewitnesses of his majesty [at the transfiguration]. For when he received honor and glory from God the Father, and the voice was borne to him by the Majestic Glory, 'This is my beloved Son, with whom I am well pleased,' . . . we were with him on the holy mountain" (2 Pet. 1:16–18). In other words, Peter knows that Jesus will come in glory (and a second time), because he saw him come in glory the first time—at the transfiguration! There, Peter was one of only three witnesses, along with James and John the sons of Zebedee (Matt. 17:1–8; Mark 9:2–8; Luke 9:28–36).

Peter previously talked about Christ's sufferings in 3:17–18 (see discussion above) and 4:1; now he speaks of believers "sharing in" (*koinōneō*) the "of Christ" sufferings ("of Christ" is emphasized in the original Greek; 4:13). This suggests that the sufferings of Christ are not merely a thing of the past; rather, they continue in the Christian community. Thus, Jesus had asked Saul (later Paul) on the road to Damascus, "Saul, Saul, why are you persecuting me?" (Acts 9:4) when Saul was persecuting the church, and later Paul even wrote, "Now I rejoice in my sufferings for your sake, and in my flesh I am filling up what is lacking in Christ's afflictions" (Col. 1:24). This reveals the amazing identification of Christ with his church and the privilege believers have been given to share in the redemptive and atoning work of Christ, albeit in a derivative way (only Jesus died atoningly for humanity's sins on the cross!). Interestingly, then, Jesus's return is here presented as the occasion when his full glory will be revealed.

Again, Peter pronounces a blessing on those who are reviled (*oneidizō*, only here in Peter's writing; cf. James 1:5; the noun *oneidismos* is used in Heb. 10:33; 11:26; 13:13) for "the name of Christ." The passage echoes Jesus's similar teaching in the Sermon on the Mount, "Blessed are you when others revile you and persecute you and utter all kinds of evil against you falsely on my account" (Matt. 5:11 // Luke 6:22; cf. Matt. 27:44; note that both the word *makarios*, "blessed," and the word *oneidizō*, "revile," are used in both 1 Pet. 4:14 and Matt. 5:11).[31] Jesus's prediction that his followers would be persecuted

31. Cf. 3:14, where Peter echoes Jesus's statement in Matt. 5:10–11, "Blessed are those who are persecuted for righteousness' sake, for theirs is the kingdom of heaven. Blessed are you when others revile you."

was being fulfilled, and Peter echoes the blessing Jesus pronounced on those who were being reviled on account of his name. The reason why believers are blessed when they bear up under persecution is that the "Spirit of glory and of God" rests upon them, an unusual designation for the Holy Spirit, echoing the theme of "glory" in verse 13 (it is also unusual in the NT for a writer to refer to the Spirit as "resting" on, as opposed to indwelling, believers). Having the Spirit of God—the glorious Holy Spirit—rest upon oneself is indeed a great blessing from God. Peter here provides a trinitarian framework for suffering: those who share Christ's sufferings and are reviled for the name of Christ have the Spirit of glory and of God rest upon them!

Again, Peter drives home the point that believers should not suffer for doing what is wrong—as a murderer, thief, or evildoer, or as a meddler (*allotrioepiskopos*, a term probably coined by Peter himself as it is not attested previously in Greek literature; 4:15; cf. 3:17).[32] While the initial triad (murderer, thief, evildoer) clearly denotes criminal activity, the fourth and final term, "meddler," set off by a second "as" (*hōs*), may be less criminal but annoying nonetheless; no one likes a person who meddles in the affairs of others. By contrast, Peter continues, if anyone suffers as a "Christian" (*Christianos*, elsewhere in the NT only in Acts 11:26; 26:28)—that is, as one who openly and fearlessly identifies with the name of Christ—this person should not be ashamed (cf. Rom. 1:16) but should glorify (*doxazō*) God in that name. Again, Peter proceeds to lodge an assertion followed by a quotation of OT Scripture. First, the assertion: "For it is time for judgment to begin at the household of God; and if it begins with us, what will be the outcome for those who do not obey the gospel of God?" (4:17). Then, the citation of Scripture: "If the righteous is scarcely saved, what will become of the ungodly and the sinner?" (cf. Prov. 11:31: "If the righteous is repaid on earth, how much more the wicked and the sinner!"). The backdrop for Peter's statement here may be the expectation of the beginning of messianic woes (cf. 2 Pet. 3:8–13). Peter's closing statement sums up the gist of the entire unit: "Therefore let those who suffer according to God's will entrust their souls to a faithful Creator while doing good" (4:19; cf. 2:23–25).

Winding down the letter, Peter moves toward a conclusion by exhorting (*parakalō*; cf. 2:11) the elders in the churches to which he writes as a "fellow elder and a witness [*martys*] of the sufferings of Christ, as well as a partaker

---

32. Made up of the words *allotrios*, "belonging to another," and *episkopos*, "overseer," so, literally, "overseer of the affairs belonging to another." Cf. the (probable) use of the verb *episkopeō* in 5:2 below. See the lengthy discussion in Forbes, *1 Peter*, 158–59. See also Jeannine K. Brown, "Just a Busybody? A Look at the Greco-Roman Topos of Meddling for Defining *allotrioepiskopos* in 1 Peter 4:15," *JBL* 125 (2006): 549–68.

[*koinōnos*] in the glory that is going to be revealed" (5:1; an example of the "Granville Sharp rule," where an article governs two or more singular nouns that are not proper names). Whereas Peter has called his readers to "share Christ's sufferings" (4:13), he himself is a "witness of Christ's sufferings"—that is, he personally witnessed the events surrounding the crucifixion of the Messiah (cf. 2 Pet. 1:16: "eyewitnesses of his majesty"). This lends Peter an enormous amount of credibility and authority in exhorting his fellow elders.[33] What's more, those who share in Christ's sufferings will also share in his glory, following the familiar biblical path "through suffering to glory" (cf. 1:11; see also Acts 14:22; Heb. 12:2). When Peter told Jesus during the latter's earthly ministry, "See, we have left everything and followed you," Jesus replied, "Truly, I say to you, there is no one who has left house or brothers or sisters or mother or father or children or lands, for my sake and for the gospel, who will not receive a hundredfold now in this time, houses and brothers and sisters and mothers and children and lands, with persecutions, and in the age to come eternal life" (Mark 10:28–30; cf. Matt. 19:27–29).

The main command to Peter's fellow elders follows in 5:2: "Shepherd the flock . . . exercising oversight." What is notable in this passage (5:1–2) is the interchangeable use of the term "elder" (*presbyteros*) and the verbs "to shepherd the flock of God" (*poimainō*; i.e., pastor), and "exercising oversight" (*episkopeō*—i.e., serving as overseer [though not found in all manuscripts]; cf. 2:25: "the Shepherd and Overseer of your souls"). This threefold designation of one and the same office conforms to standard NT usage (cf. Acts 20:17, 28; 1 Tim. 3:1; 5:17; Titus 1:5–9); only later were those offices divided and church leadership came to be exercised in the form of a two-tiered hierarchy, with bishops serving as regional overseers over churches pastored by presbyters or priests. It is moving to see here how Peter—who after denying Jesus three times prior to the crucifixion was recommissioned by the risen Christ and charged with "tending and feeding his sheep" (John 21:15–19; cf. 18:15–18, 25–27)—is now himself charging elders to "shepherd the flock," continuing the chain of ministry from Jesus to Peter to NT elders (though this, of course, does not make Peter the first pope, much less one who is infallible).

It is noteworthy that elders are here told both to shepherd and to exercise oversight; this would seem to suggest that a church leadership model that uses elders more like a board of trustees or executive board of a corporation to exercise oversight—making major decisions affecting the church—but delegates the shepherding role to others (such as deacons or paid church staff)

---

33. It is hard not to notice the amazing humility conveyed by Peter—the great and preeminent apostle—calling the elders in the churches to which he writes his "fellow elders."

falls short of the biblical mandate. Peter's instruction to these elders on how they should shepherd and exercise oversight is given in the form of three contrasting "not . . . but" statements:

- "not under compulsion, but willingly" (v. 2)
- "not for shameful gain, but eagerly" (v. 2)
- "not domineering . . . but being examples [*typoi*] to the flock" (v. 3)

No one should pastor a church while driven by a lust for power or greed. While rarely would anyone openly admit to using a religious office to have power over others or to enrich oneself financially, it is sadly possible to cover up such motives under a sanctimonious, altruistic façade while thinly disguising one's true motives. Alternatively, mixed motives may be at work—church leaders may try to serve the Lord while still pursuing their own ambitions. However, as Jesus stated, "No one can serve two masters. . . . You cannot serve God and money" (Matt. 6:24). Yet another scenario might be that a pastor starts out well and with the right motives but gradually slides into improper motives through yielding to temptation or weakness of moral character. No one is immune from being deceived by the devil, which is one reason why Paul impresses on Timothy the need to be careful when choosing elders and cautions against appointing new converts to the faith (1 Tim. 3:6–7).

Peter has addressed the "elders" (identifying himself as a "fellow elder"), who are to "shepherd the flock" (5:1–2). Now he refers to the "chief Shepherd" (*archipoimēn*, not elsewhere in the NT; 5:4), the Lord Jesus Christ himself. Earlier, Peter wrote, "For you were straying like sheep, but have now returned to the Shepherd and Overseer of your souls" (2:25). During his earthly ministry, Jesus called himself the "good shepherd" (John 10:11, 14), in contrast to Israel's religious leaders, whom (at least by implication) he called "thieves," "robbers," and "hirelings" who enriched themselves at the expense of others but cared nothing about the "sheep" entrusted to them (John 10:1, 12–13; cf. Ezek. 34, esp. vv. 1–9). While some may have considered Peter the "chief shepherd," Peter humbly deflects this designation from himself and redirects it to Jesus. He is only an undershepherd and fellow shepherd along with the other elders of the church. While he has a certain apostolic role (similar to that of the apostle Paul), his exhortation to his fellow elders is to them as equals rather than being given by one who occupies a position of institutional authority over them.

Once again, Peter adopts an eschatological outlook, motivating his readers by the prospect of the return of Christ—the appearing of the Chief

Shepherd—and the accompanying reward, "the unfading [*amarantinos*; cf. *amarantos* in 1:4] crown of glory" (5:4). This is probably not a "glorious crown" but to be understood epexegetically as "a crown—that is, glory." Note the frequency of "glory" language in this final major unit, which adds up to a panoply of glory projected by Peter on the canvas of his readers' outlook on life, and particularly on their present trials and sufferings. As they share (*koinōneō*) in Christ's sufferings, they will rejoice when his glory is revealed (4:13); at present, they are blessed because the Spirit of glory rests upon them (4:14); Peter himself is a partaker (*koinōnos*) in the glory to be revealed (5:1); and when Jesus returns, believers will receive their unfading reward of glory. The present is shot with suffering; the future will be shot with glory—in fact, even now we have a glimpse of glory in that the glorious Holy Spirit rests upon us and we anticipate the glorious return of our Lord Jesus Christ!

Verse 5, then, reads like an addendum to the house table of 2:13–3:7, including the introductory "Likewise" (*homoiōs*; cf. 3:1, 7), except that here Peter first addressed elders—those in authority—and then those who are younger and who are to be subject to the elders (again, the word is *hypotassō*, "submit"; cf. 2:13, 18; 3:1). In conclusion, Peter calls on all of his readers to "clothe" themselves (*engkomboomai*, unique in the NT) with humility—again, providing scriptural support in the form of Proverbs 3:34 (the same passage is cited in James 4:6). If believers humble themselves under the "mighty hand of God," he will exalt them at the proper time (5:6; most likely, at the future vindication and judgment; again, compare the similar exhortation in James 4:10).[34] This humility is exemplified by a sense of dependence on God as believers cast (*epiriptō*, elsewhere in the NT only in Luke 19:35: "throwing their cloaks on the colt") their every care (*merimna*; outside the Gospels only in 2 Cor. 11:28) on him because they know that he cares for them. If prayers to God are like throwing one's garment on a donkey, this means once we've thrown our coat on the colt, it is no longer we who carry it but the donkey! Likewise, once we've cast our cares on the Lord in faith, he will carry them, and it is no longer we who need to do so. This should result in incredible relief and gratitude for the God "who daily bears our burdens" (Ps. 68:19).

The command in 5:8 to be "sober-minded" and "watchful" echoes the similar command in 4:7 to be "self-controlled and sober-minded" because "the end of all things is at hand." Jesus similarly called on believers to be alert in several parables anticipating his return (Matt. 25). Here, Peter supplies an additional reason why it is vital that believers watch out: their adversary

---

34. Storms ("1 Peter," 356) notes that "mighty hand" harks back to OT passages such as Exod. 3:19; 13:3, 9, 14, 16; Deut. 3:24; 4:34; Ezek. 20:34.

(*antidikos*, "opponent"; cf. Matt. 5:25; Luke 12:58; 18:3), the devil, "prowls" (literally, "walks"; the word is *peripateō*) around like a "roaring lion" (most likely an allusion to Ps. 22:13) in search for someone he can devour. And devour someone he most likely will—spiritually speaking—but make sure it isn't you! Rather, we must resist the devil, standing firm in our faith, because we know that we're not alone in our spiritual struggle against the enemy: the same kinds of sufferings (*pathēma*) are perfected or completed (*epiteleō*; cf. 2 Cor. 7:1; Phil. 1:6) by Christians all over the world (*adelphotēs*; literally, "brotherhood"; elsewhere in the NT only at 2:17: "Love the brotherhood").

In closing, Peter (I follow the original word order) assures his readers, "The God of all grace, who called you to his eternal glory in Christ, after you have suffered for a little while, will himself restore, confirm, strengthen, and establish you" (5:10). It is hard to think of a more encouraging ending to this letter. Peter affirms that God is exceedingly gracious (subjective genitive). He doesn't deal with us as we deserve and showers us with blessings rather than condemnation. The ultimate expression of God's grace is that rather than sending us to hell and eternal separation from him, he has called us to his eternal glory in Christ. How fantastic is that! It's almost inconceivable. So, even though we may now be perplexed and hard-pressed, suffering "for a little while," God *himself* (how emphatic) will put us on sure and solid eternal footing.

With words employed like a fireworks grand finale, Peter affirms this by stringing together a rapid-fire series of no less than four virtual synonyms, all future-tense verbs: God will "restore" (*katartizō*; cf. Gal. 6:1; 1 Thess. 3:10; Heb. 13:21), "confirm" (*stērizō*; cf. Rom. 1:11; 16:25; 1 Thess. 3:2, 13; 2 Thess. 2:17; 3:3; James 5:8; 2 Pet. 1:12; Rev. 3:2), "strengthen" (*sthenoō*, only here in the NT and rare in Greek literature), and "establish" (*themelioō*; cf. Matt. 7:25; Eph. 3:17; Col. 1:23; Heb. 1:10) us.[35] Together with the theme of "glory" highlighted in our discussion at 5:4 above, this final upbeat reassurance paints an eschatological rainbow that forms a bright backdrop against which the readers' present and future suffering is set. Peter began this letter by reassuring his readers they have a "living hope" (1:3). He now gives them hope by assuring them of their future glory and deliverance.

Letter Closing: By Silvanus, from Rome, with Mark (5:12–14)

The concluding portion of Peter's first letter contains a rather concise final greeting as well as several interesting pieces of information surrounding the

---

35. See the discussion in Forbes, *1 Peter*, 180.

sending of the letter and its audience. First, Peter mentions that he has written this letter "briefly" "by Silvanus" (i.e., Silas; cf. 2 Cor. 1:19; 1 Thess. 1:1; 2 Thess. 1:1). "Briefly" (*di' oligon*; cf. Heb. 13:22: *dia bracheōn*) seems modest as this is one of the longer NT letters (certainly much longer than truly brief NT letters such as Philemon, 2–3 John, and Jude, though not as long as Hebrews). Silas could have been Peter's secretary or amanuensis but more likely served as letter carrier.[36] Interestingly, Silas served as letter carrier for the decree of the Jerusalem Council (Acts 15:22–23, 32). The contents of the letter are globally sketched as encouraging the readers to "stand firm" in the "true grace of God" (5:12). The one who is "in Babylon" (i.e., Rome),[37] "also chosen" (the feminine gender suggests that this is the church in Rome, as "church," *ekklēsia*, is feminine in the Greek), is said to send her greetings, along with Peter's spiritual "son," Mark the evangelist, cousin of Barnabas and one-time travel companion of Barnabas and Paul (5:13; cf. Acts 12:25; 13:13). The greeting with a "kiss of love" is the likely equivalent to Paul's "holy kiss" (Rom. 16:16; 1 Cor. 16:20; 2 Cor. 13:12; 1 Thess. 5:26).[38] The concluding greeting is "peace" (Greek equivalent of Hebrew *shalom*; cf. 1:2) to all who are "in Christ" (5:14), reminiscent of Pauline nomenclature.

1 Peter: Commentaries

Achtemeier, Paul J. *1 Peter*. Hermeneia. Minneapolis: Fortress, 1996.

Beare, Francis Wright. *The First Epistle of Peter*. Oxford: Blackwell, 1970.

Best, Ernest. *1 Peter*. NCB. Grand Rapids: Eerdmans, 1971, 1982.

Davids, Peter H. *The First Epistle of Peter*. NICNT. Grand Rapids: Eerdmans, 1990.

Dubis, Mark. *1 Peter: A Handbook on the Greek Text*. BHGNT. Waco: Baylor University Press, 2010.

Elliott, John H. *1 Peter: A New Translation with Introduction and Commentary*. AB 37. New York: Doubleday, 2000.

Feldmeier, Reinhard. *The First Letter of Peter: A Commentary on the Greek Text*. Translated by Peter H. Davids. Waco: Baylor University Press, 2008.

Forbes, Greg W. *1 Peter*. EGGNT. Nashville: B&H Academic, 2014.

Goppelt, Leonhard. *A Commentary on 1 Peter*. Translated by J. E. Alsup. Grand Rapids: Eerdmans, 1993.

Green, Joel B. *1 Peter*. THNTC. Grand Rapids: Eerdmans, 2007.

36. See the introduction above.

37. In addition to referring metaphorically to the current world power, Rome, "Babylon" also serves as a metaphor for displacement (as in the Babylonian exile suffered by Israel in OT times), which contributes the final bookend to a letter that started with a reference to the readers as "elect exiles" (1:1; cf. 1:17; 2:11). Cf. Forbes, *1 Peter*, 185.

38. Cf. the references to love sprinkled across the letter (1:22; 2:17; 3:8).

Grudem, Wayne. *1 Peter*. TNTC. Grand Rapids: Eerdmans, 1988.

Harink, Douglas. *1 and 2 Peter*. BTCB. Grand Rapids: Brazos, 2009.

Jobes, Karen H. *1 Peter*. BECNT. Grand Rapids: Baker Academic, 2005.

Kelly, J. N. D. *A Commentary on the Epistles of Peter and of Jude*. HNTC. New York: Harper & Row, 1969.

Marshall, I. Howard. *1 Peter*. IVPNTC. Downers Grove, IL: InterVarsity, 1991.

McKnight, Scot. *1 Peter*. NIVAC. Grand Rapids: Zondervan, 1996.

Michaels, J. Ramsey. *1 Peter*. WBC 49. Waco: Word, 1988.

Richard, Earl J. *Reading 1 Peter, Jude, and 2 Peter: A Literary and Theological Commentary*. Macon, GA: Smyth & Helwys, 2000.

Schreiner, Thomas R. *1, 2 Peter, Jude*. NAC 37. Nashville: Broadman & Holman, 2003.

Senior, Donald P. *1 Peter, Jude, and 2 Peter*. SP 15. Collegeville, MN: Liturgical Press, 2003.

Storms, C. Samuel. "1 Peter." In *ESV Expository Commentary*, vol. 12, *Hebrews–Revelation*, edited by Iain M. Duguid, James M. Hamilton Jr., and Jay Sklar, 287–361. Wheaton: Crossway, 2018.

1 Peter: Articles, Essays, and Monographs

Balch, David L. *Let Wives Be Submissive: The Domestic Code in 1 Peter*. SBLMS 26. Ed. J. Crenshaw. Chico, CA: Scholars Press, 1981.

Batten, Alicia J., and John S. Kloppenborg, eds. *James, 1 and 2 Peter, and Early Jesus Traditions*. LNTS 478. London: Bloomsbury T&T Clark, 2014.

Blazen, Ivan T. "Suffering and Cessation from Sin according to 1 Peter 4:1." *AUSS* 21 (1983): 27–50.

Bockmuehl, Markus. *Simon Peter in Scripture and Memory: The New Testament Apostle in the Early Church*. Grand Rapids: Baker Academic, 2012.

Bond, Helen K., and Larry W. Hurtado, eds. *Peter in Early Christianity*. Grand Rapids: Eerdmans, 2015.

Boring, Eugene M. "First Peter in Recent Study." *WW* 24 (2004): 358–67.

Brown, J. P. "Synoptic Parallels in the Epistles and Form-History." *NTS* 10 (1963–1964): 27–48.

Brown, Raymond E., Karl P. Donfried, and John Reumann, eds. *Peter in the New Testament*. Minneapolis: Augsburg, 1973.

Burtness, J. H. "Sharing the Suffering of God in the Life of the World." *Int* 23 (1969): 277–88.

Campbell, Barth L. *Honor, Shame, and the Rhetoric of 1 Peter*. SBLDS 160. Atlanta: Scholars Press, 1998.

Carson, D. A. "1 Peter." In *Commentary on the New Testament Use of the Old Testament*, edited by G. K. Beale and D. A. Carson, 1015–61. Grand Rapids: Baker Academic, 2007.

Clemen, C. "The First Epistle of Peter and the Book of Enoch." *Expositor* 6, no. 4 (1902): 316–20.

Cross, Frank L. *1 Peter: A Paschal Liturgy*. London: Mowbray, 1954.

Cullmann, Oscar. *Peter: Disciple, Apostle, Martyr.* Translated by F. V. Wilson. Philadelphia: Westminster, 1962.

Dalton, William J. *Christ's Proclamation to the Spirits: A Study of 1 Peter 3:18–4:6.* AnBib 23. Rome: Pontifical Biblical Institute, 1965.

Danker, Frederick W. "1 Peter 1:24–2:17: A Consolatory Pericope." *ZNW* 58 (1967): 93–102.

Davids, Peter H. "A Silent Witness in Marriage: 1 Pet. 3:1–7." In *Discovering Biblical Equality: Complementarity without Hierarchy,* edited by Ronald W. Pierce and Rebecca Merrill Groothuis, 224–38. Downers Grove, IL: InterVarsity, 2004.

———. *A Theology of James, Peter, and Jude: Living in Light of the Coming King.* BTNT. Grand Rapids: Zondervan, 2014.

———. "What Glasses Are You Wearing? Reading Hebrew Narratives through Second Temple Lenses." *JETS* 55 (2012): 763–71.

Dryden, J. de Waal. *Theology and Ethics in 1 Peter: Paraenetic Strategies from Christian Character Formation.* WUNT 2/209. Tübingen: Mohr Siebeck, 2006.

Dubis, Mark. "Research on 1 Peter: A Survey of Scholarly Literature since 1985." *CBR* 4 (2006): 199–239.

Elliott, John H. *The Elect and the Holy: An Exegetical Examination of 1 Peter 2:4–10 and the Phrase βασίλειον ἱεράτευμα.* NovTSup 12. Leiden: Brill, 1966.

———. *1 Peter: Estrangement and Community.* Chicago: Franciscan Herald, 1979.

———. *A Home for the Homeless: A Sociological Exegesis of 1 Peter, Its Situation and Strategy.* Philadelphia: Fortress, 1981.

———. "Rehabilitation of an Exegetical Stepchild: 1 Peter in Recent Research." *JBL* 95 (1976): 243–54.

Filson, Floyd V. "Partakers with Christ: Suffering in First Peter." *Int* 9 (1955): 400–412.

Furnish, Victor P. "Elect Sojourners in Christ: An Approach to the Theology of 1 Peter." *PSTJ* 28 (1975): 1–11.

Gross, Carl D. "Are the Wives of 1 Pet. 3:7 Christian?" *JSNT* 35 (1989): 89–96.

Gundry, Robert H. "Further 'Verba' on 'Verba Christi' in First Peter." *Bib* 55 (1974): 211–32.

———. "'Verba Christi' in I Peter: Their Implications concerning the Authorship of 1 Peter and the Authenticity of the Gospel Tradition." *NTS* 13 (1966–1967): 336–50.

Harner, Philip B. *What Are They Saying about the Catholic Epistles?* Mahwah, NJ: Paulist Press, 2004.

Heil, John Paul. *1 Peter, 2 Peter, and Jude: Worship Matters.* Eugene, OR: Cascade, 2013.

Helyer, Larry R. *The Life and Witness of Peter.* Downers Grove, IL: IVP Academic, 2012.

Hengel, Martin. *Saint Peter: The Underestimated Apostle.* Grand Rapids: Eerdmans, 2010.

Hill, D. "On Suffering and Baptism in 1 Peter." *NovT* 18 (1976): 181–89.

Holdsworth, J. "The Sufferings in 1 Peter and 'Missionary Apocalyptic.'" *Studia Biblica* 3 (1980): 225–32.

Horrell, David G. *1 Peter.* NTG. New York: T&T Clark, 2008.

Huther, J. E. *Critical and Exegetical Handbook to the General Epistles of Peter and Jude.* Translated by D. B. Croom and P. J. Gloab. Edinburgh: T&T Clark, 1881.

Jobes, Karen H. "The Syntax of 1 Peter: Just How Good Is the Greek?" *BBR* 13 (2003): 159–73.

Lapham, F. *Peter: The Myth, the Man and the Writings: A Study of Early Petrine Text and Tradition*. JSNTSup 239. Sheffield: Sheffield Academic, 2003.

Martin, Troy W. *Metaphor and Composition in 1 Peter*. SBLDS 131. Atlanta: Scholars Press, 1992.

Mason, Eric F., and Troy W. Martin, eds. *Reading 1–2 Peter and Jude: A Resource for Students*. SBLRBS. Atlanta: Society of Biblical Literature, 2014.

Mbuvi, Andrew Mutua. *Temple, Exile and Identity in 1 Peter*. LNTS 345. London: T&T Clark, 2007.

Michaels, J. Ramsey. "Eschatology in I Peter III.17." *NTS* 13 (1966–1967): 394–401.

———. "Jewish and Christian Apocalyptic Letters: 1 Peter, Revelation, and 2 Baruch 78–87." In *SBL Seminar Papers* 26 (1987): 268–75.

Niebuhr, Karl-Wilhelm, and Robert W. Wall. *The Catholic Epistles and Apostolic Tradition: A New Perspective on James to Jude*. Waco: Baylor University Press, 2009.

Nienhuis, David R., and Robert W. Wall. *Reading the Epistles of James, Peter, John, and Jude as Scripture: The Shaping and Shape of a Canonical Collection*. Grand Rapids: Eerdmans, 2013.

Perkins, Pheme. *Peter: Apostle for the Whole Church*. Minneapolis: Fortress, 2000.

Piper, John. "Hope as the Motivation of Love: 1 Peter 3:9–12." *NTS* 26 (1980): 212–31.

Richards, E. Randolph. "Silvanus Was Not Peter's Secretary: Theological Bias in Interpreting διὰ Σιλουανοῦ ἔγραψα in 1 Pet. 5:12." *JETS* 43 (2000): 417–32.

Sargent, Benjamin. *Written to Serve: The Use of Scripture in 1 Peter*. LNTS 547. London: Bloomsbury T&T Clark, 2015.

Schattenmann, J. "The Little Apocalypse of the Synoptics and the First Epistle of Peter." *TT* 11 (1954–1955): 193–98.

Schutter, W. L. *Hermeneutic and Composition in First Peter*. WUNT 2/30. Tübingen: Mohr Siebeck, 1989.

Selwyn, Edward Gordon. *The First Epistle of St. Peter*. New York: Macmillan, 1946, 1969.

Senior, Donald. "The Conduct of Christians in the World (1 Pet. 2:11–3:12)." *RevExp* 79 (1982): 427–38.

Sleeper, C. F. "Political Responsibility according to 1 Peter." *NovT* 10 (1968): 270–86.

Sly, Dorothy I. "1 Peter 3:6b in the Light of Philo and Josephus." *JBL* 110 (1991): 126–29.

Steuernagel, V. "An Exiled Community as a Mission Community: A Study Based on 1 Peter 2:9, 10." *ERT* 10 (1986): 8–18.

Sylva, D. "The Critical Exploration of 1 Peter." In *Perspectives on First Peter*, edited by C. H. Talbert, 17–36. Macon, GA: Mercer University Press, 1986.

Talbert, Charles H., ed. *Perspectives on First Peter*. Macon, GA: Mercer University Press, 1986.

Thompson, J. W. "'Be Submissive to your Masters': A Study of 1 Pt 2:18–25." *ResQ* 9, no. 2 (1966): 66–78.

Thurén, Lauri. *Argument and Theology in 1 Peter: The Origins of Christian Paraenesis*. SBLDS 114. Atlanta: Scholars Press, 1995.

van Unnik, W. C. "The Teaching of Good Works in I Peter." *NTS* 1 (1954–1955): 92–110.

Villiers, J. L. de. "Joy in Suffering in 1 Peter." *Neot* 9 (1975): 64–86.

Watson, Duane Frederick. "The Petrine Epistles: Recent Developments and Trends." In *The Face of New Testament Studies: A Survey of Recent Research*, edited by Scot McKnight and Grant R. Osborne, 373–90. Grand Rapids: Baker Academic, 2004.

Watson, Duane Frederick, and Terrance Callan. *First and Second Peter*. Paideia. Grand Rapids: Baker Academic, 2012.

Webb, Robert L., and Betsy Bauman-Martin, eds. *Reading First Peter with New Eyes: Methodological Reassessments of the Letter of First Peter*. LNTS 364. New York: T&T Clark, 2007.

Williams, Martin. *The Doctrine of Salvation in the First Letter of Peter*. SNTSMS 149. Cambridge: Cambridge University Press, 2011.

Williams, T. B. *Good Works in 1 Peter: Negotiating Social Conflict and Christian Identity in the Greco-Roman World*. WUNT 1/337. Tübingen: Mohr Siebeck, 2014.

———. *Persecution in 1 Peter: Differentiating and Contextualizing Early Christian Suffering*. NovTSup 245. Leiden: Brill, 2012.

Witherington, Ben, III. "Not So Idle Thoughts about *eidōlothyton*." *TynBul* 44 (1993): 237–54.

Workman, Herbert B. *Persecutions in the Early Church*. Oxford: Oxford University Press, 1980.

CHAPTER FOUR

2 Peter

Introduction

Author, Audience, Date, and Genre

While some question the Petrine authorship of 2 Peter, the letter claims to have been written by the apostle Peter, and there is little reason to doubt this identification.[1] First, the opening self-identification, "Simon Peter," is even more personal than that in Peter's first epistle, where the author identifies himself simply as "Peter." Second, the author claims to have been an eyewitness of Jesus's transfiguration (1:16–18) which, according to the Gospel witness, was attended only by Peter and the two sons of Zebedee, John and James (Matt. 17:1–8; Mark 9:2–8; Luke 9:28–36). Third, the author specifically claims, "This is now the second letter that I am writing to you" (3:1), linking the present letter explicitly to Peter's first epistle.

It is true that there are some differences in style between 1 and 2 Peter, but these may be explained by the use of an amanuensis in 1 and/or 2 Peter, or various other factors, including that 2 Peter 2 in all likelihood adapts significant portions of Jude.[2] Some have suggested that 2 Peter falls into the

---

1. On the question of the Petrine authorship of 2 Peter, see Michael J. Kruger, "The Authenticity of 2 Peter," *JETS* 42 (1999): 645–71. On the question of genre, see Mark D. Mathews, "The Genre of 2 Peter: A Comparison with Jewish and Early Christian Testaments," *BBR* 21 (2011): 51–64. On patristic references to 2 Peter, see Robert E. Picirilli, "Allusions to 2 Peter in the Apostolic Fathers," *JSNT* 33 (1988): 57–83.

2. See Andreas J. Köstenberger, L. Scott Kellum, and Charles L. Quarles, *The Cradle, the Cross, and the Crown: An Introduction to the New Testament*, 2nd ed. (Nashville: B&H Academic, 2016), 857–63, esp. table 18.5 (pp. 862–63); Terrance Callan, "Use of the Letter of Jude by the Second Letter of Peter," *Bib* 85 (2004): 42–64; and Lauri Thurén, "The Relationship

testamentary genre, in which a later follower writes what purports to be a now deceased person's final words, but this theory is unnecessary (not to mention the lack of evidence for ancient pseudonymous *epistles*) and, in any case, contradicts the above-mentioned claims staked by the letter itself. It is therefore best to suppose that the apostle Peter wrote both 1 and 2 Peter and that 2 Peter was written a few years after 1 Peter, most likely in the mid-60s AD, not long before Peter's martyrdom under Nero in AD 65/66.[3]

The primary occasion of 2 Peter seems to be the denial of Jesus's return by some detractors who held that God never intervenes in human history, which Peter counters by asserting that he already saw Jesus's glory at his *first* coming—at the transfiguration—which makes the expectation of Jesus's *second* coming in glory eminently plausible. Not only this, God did, demonstrably and as attested by authoritative Scripture, intervene in past human history through the universal flood, which disproves these detractors' supposition. As Peter points out, the apparent delay needs to be seen in light of the fact that with God a thousand years is like a single day, and so divine and human calendars are vastly different. While God may seem to have delayed regarding Jesus's second coming, the second coming will certainly take place in God's appointed time.

Structure

The letter opening, as mentioned, identifies Simon Peter as the author. Unlike in 1 Peter, no mention is made of a specific target audience. The opening continues with a well-wish of "grace and peace" (1:2). The body of the letter commences with an exhortation to pursue a series of Christian virtues (1:3–7) and a series of reasons given for this exhortation (1:8–11). In what follows, Peter affirms that he writes these things by way of reminder in view of his imminent "departure" (i.e., his martyrdom; 1:15). Peter stakes his authority squarely on the fact that he saw the glorified Christ, a subject to which he will return in the latter part of his letter (chap. 3). In this way, Peter places himself on par with the OT prophets, who did not speak by their own authority but rather "spoke from God as they were carried along by the Holy Spirit" (1:21).

In chapter 2, Peter at length denounces false teachers who "will secretly bring in destructive heresies" (2:1); in all probability Peter here adapts portions

---

between 2 Peter and Jude: A Classical Problem Resolved?," in *The Catholic Epistles and the Tradition*, ed. Jacques Schlosser, BETL 176 (Leuven: Peeters, 2004), 451–60.

3. See also George H. Boobyer, "The Indebtedness of 2 Peter to 1 Peter," in *New Testament Essays: Studies in Memory of T. W. Manson*, ed. A. J. B. Higgins (Manchester: University of Manchester Press, 1959), 34–53.

of Jude's letter, which likely predates 2 Peter (see discussion below). This is also suggested by Peter's removal of all non-OT material from Jude and his added references to positive OT figures alongside Jude's negative ones.[4] In chapter 3, Peter then seems to get around to addressing the main reason why he wrote the letter—namely, the false teachers' denial of the reality of the second coming. Each of the final four paragraphs, all in chapter 3, include the address "beloved" (*agapētoi*), which is found in verses 1, 8, 14, and 17. The letter closes with an exhortation to "grow in the grace and knowledge of our Lord and Savior Jesus Christ," and a final doxology (3:18).

Structure of 2 Peter

2 Peter	Content
1:1–2	Opening
1:3–21	Exhortation to Christian virtue and assertion of Peter's prophetic authority
2:1–22	Denunciation of false teachers' character and motivation
3:1–18	Denunciation of false teachers' denial of Jesus's second coming; conclusion

Source: Andreas J. Köstenberger, L. Scott Kellum, and Charles L. Quarles, *The Cradle, the Cross, and the Crown: An Introduction to the New Testament*, 2nd ed. (Nashville: B&H Academic, 2016), table 18.6 (p. 883).

Peter's likely adaptation of sections of Jude's letter in 2 Peter 2 can be diagrammed as follows:

Jude	2 Peter 2
Angels (v. 6)	Angels (v. 4)
Sodom and Gomorrah (v. 7)	Sodom and Gomorrah (v. 6)
Archangel Michael (v. 9)	Archangel Michael, not named (v. 11)
Balaam (v. 11)	Balaam (v. 15)
	Noah (v. 5)
	Lot (v. 7)
Israel in the wilderness (v. 5)	
Cain (v. 11)	
Korah (v. 11)	

We see that whereas Jude includes only negative characters in his list of those who engaged in immoral and rebellious activity in OT times, Peter thins out those references (omitting Israel in the wilderness as well as Cain and Korah) while adding positive characters such as Noah and Lot. Peter also

---

4. On the use of Second Temple literature, see Peter H. Davids, "The Use of Second Temple Traditions in 1 and 2 Peter and Jude," in *The Catholic Epistles and Tradition*, ed. Jacques Schlosser, BETL 176 (Leuven: Peeters, 2004), 409–31.

omits references to the Assumption of Moses and 1 Enoch, both of which are likely cited in Jude. This results in a more balanced presentation and eliminates the potentially troubling references to apocryphal literature. On balance, it is more plausible to conceive of Jude writing first and of Peter making those kinds of changes than of Peter writing first and then Jude eliminating all positive characters, adding more negative characters, and inserting extrabiblical references. In addition, Jude and 2 Peter 2 feature a considerable number of verbal similarities, such as that between "have crept in unnoticed" (Jude 4) and "secretly bring in destructive heresies" (2 Peter 2:1); that between "who pervert the grace of our God into sensuality and deny our only Master and Lord" (Jude 4) and "even denying the Master who bought them" (2 Peter 2:1); the references to angels, "darkness," and "judgment" (Jude 6 and 2 Peter 2:4); the reference to "Sodom and Gomorrah" serving as an "example" (Jude 7 and 2 Peter 2:6); and numerous other similarities.[5]

Central Message

The major theme in 2 Peter, as mentioned, is the apparent delay of the *parousia*, Jesus's second coming. Peter identifies himself as an eyewitness of Jesus's glory at his first coming and thus affirms the certainty of Jesus's glorious return, despite an apparent delay. In view of Jesus's return, Peter urges his readers to pursue a series of Christian virtues that will render them neither ineffective nor unproductive (1:8) and calls on them to confirm their calling and election by so doing (1:10). Peter contributes to the NT canon the reference to the *process* of inspiration guiding the OT prophets (1:19–21), which not only continues the reference to the activity of OT prophets in Peter's first letter (1:10–12) but also dovetails with Paul's affirmation of the *product* of inspiration—namely, Holy Scripture (the OT and, by extension, the NT as well), in 2 Timothy 3:16–17. Remarkably, Peter also refers to Paul's letters as Scripture, at a time when portions of the NT were still being written (3:15–16).

The Pursuit of Christian Virtues and the Certainty of Jesus's Second Coming (1:1–21)

Letter Opening (1:1–2)

The opening of Peter's second letter exhibits two changes from that of the first: (1) the author identifies himself as "Simon Peter" rather than merely

5. See my contribution on Jude in Köstenberger, Kellum, and Quarles, *The Cradle, the Cross, and the Crown*, 882–83.

"Peter," a more personal expression; and (2) Peter calls himself not only an "apostle" but also a "servant" (*doulos*) of Jesus Christ (1:1). This strikes a more intimate and humble tone, as "Simon Peter" is Peter's full name, and "servant" indicates a subordinate relationship. The opening address continues on a humble note as Peter writes "to those who have obtained a faith of equal standing with ours." Their faith in Christ provides all Christians with equal standing before God. Peter is no more saved or no more a believer than any other member of the congregation to which he writes (or any of us today). Is it possible that you and I have a faith of equal standing to that of the great apostle Peter, who was Christ's preeminent apostle, became the leader of the early church, and died a martyr's death? Yes, of equal standing—because God looks at us not in light of who we are in ourselves or what we have done for him, but in light of what Christ has done for us. What we do for him is done out of gratitude for what he has done for us, without accruing merit for ourselves or making us somehow superior to "lesser Christians" in our midst. Nevertheless, the Bible also teaches that those who serve Christ faithfully will one day receive a reward from God (e.g., 1 Pet. 5:4; 2 Tim. 4:8).

How did believers attain such faith of equal standing with the apostle Peter? They did so "by the righteousness of our God and Savior Jesus Christ" (1:1). *Jesus* is believers' righteousness. As Paul put it, "For our sake [God] made him to be sin who knew no sin, so that in him we might become the righteousness of God" (2 Cor. 5:21). This is what Christians believe: that Jesus died on the cross—"the righteous for the unrighteous" (1 Pet. 3:18)—so that those who trust in Jesus attain salvation by grace (cf. v. 2) through faith (v. 1). Peter had borne eloquent testimony to this fact in his first letter in the context of his exhortation for Christians to follow in Christ's footsteps as they themselves suffered for their faith. Jesus, he wrote, in language reminiscent of Isaiah's depiction of God's suffering servant, "committed no sin, neither was deceit found in his mouth. . . . He himself bore our sins in his body on the tree, that we might die to sin and live to righteousness. By his wounds you have been healed. For you were straying like sheep, but have now returned to the Shepherd and Overseer of your souls" (1 Pet. 2:22–25; cf. Isa. 52:13–53:12; see also 1 Pet. 3:18; 4:1). Jesus died on the cross for us as our sinless substitute. As a result, believers—depicted as straying sheep—have now returned to their Shepherd and Creator.

What is more, not only does Peter identify Jesus as "our righteousness"; he also identifies him as "our God and Savior." Writing, as is most likely, just prior to his martyrdom in approximately AD 66, Peter here acknowledges Jesus as both God and Savior. While calling Jesus "Savior" would be expected, calling Jesus "God" is striking. The Jewish people were known in the surrounding ancient Near Eastern and Greco-Roman world as those who fiercely adhered to monotheism, a belief that there is only one God, in contrast to the polytheistic worship of the other nations. The Greek pantheon (panoply of gods), later imitated by the Romans—who weren't all that creative in making up their own set of deities (their strengths lay elsewhere, such as in jurisprudence and statesmanship)—consisted of a great variety of gods, so much so that the apostle Paul when visiting Athens noticed that "the city was full of idols" and even an inscription "To the unknown god" (Acts 17:16, 23). Afraid that they might omit worship of some unknown deity, the Athenians had erected an altar to a god they didn't even know—just in case!

Now what is so remarkable is that the first Jewish followers of Jesus—Peter and the other members of the Twelve included, all of whom were Jews—worshiped not only Yahweh (God the Father, the God of Abraham, Isaac, Jacob, and Moses) as God but *Jesus* as well. As early as immediately following the resurrection, Thomas, one of the Twelve, fell at Jesus's feet and exclaimed, "My Lord and my God!" (John 20:28). On the face of it, this blatantly conflicted with Jewish monotheism as it acknowledged Jesus, not merely Yahweh, as God.[6] Yet Thomas, Peter, John, and the other disciples seemed completely unperturbed by this. What we see here is the early seeds of what later would become a full-fledged trinitarianism, the Christian belief that God is one God in three persons—Father, Son, and Holy Spirit.[7] Peter's phrase "our God and Savior Jesus Christ" closely parallels Paul's similar reference to Christians' hope in the glorious future return of "our great God and Savior Jesus Christ" (Titus 2:13). Thus, both Peter and Paul attest to the early Christian worship of Jesus not merely as Savior but also as God.

---

6. For a detailed discussion, see Andreas J. Köstenberger, chap. 1 in *Father, Son and Spirit: The Trinity and John's Gospel*, by Andreas J. Köstenberger and Scott R. Swain, NSBT 24 (Downers Grove, IL: InterVarsity, 2007). See also Richard Bauckham, *God Crucified: Monotheism and Christology in the New Testament* (Grand Rapids: Eerdmans, 1999); Bauckham, *Jesus and the God of Israel: God Crucified, and Other Studies on the New Testament's Christology of Divine Identity* (Grand Rapids: Eerdmans, 2008); Michael F. Bird, Craig A. Evans, Simon J. Gathercole, Charles E. Hill, and Chris Tilling, *How God Became Jesus: The Real Origins of Belief in Jesus' Divine Nature: A Response to Bart Ehrman* (Grand Rapids: Zondervan, 2017); Larry W. Hurtado, *Lord Jesus Christ: Devotion to Jesus in Earliest Christianity* (Grand Rapids: Eerdmans, 2005); Hurtado, *Ancient Jewish Monotheism and Early Christian Jesus-Devotion: The Context and Character of Christological Faith*, Library of Early Christology (Waco: Baylor University Press, 2017); and Christopher J. H. Wright, *The Mission of God: Unlocking the Bible's Grand Narrative* (Downers Grove, IL: InterVarsity, 2006), chaps. 3–4.

7. The essence of trinitarian faith can be found already in passages such as Matt. 28:19, which speaks of baptism "in the name of the Father and of the Son and of the Holy Spirit." Closer to home, see the opening of Peter's first letter: "according to the foreknowledge of *God the Father*, in the sanctification of *the Spirit*, for obedience to *Jesus Christ* and for sprinkling with his blood" (1 Pet. 1:2).

The opening well-wish or greeting expands on the greeting found in Peter's first letter, "May grace and peace be multiplied to you," adding the phrase "in the knowledge of God and of Jesus our Lord" (1:2), further indicating the parallelism between God the Father and the Lord Jesus Christ (cf. 1:1). Here, Peter expresses his hope and prayer ("may be multiplied," *plēthuntheiē*, is in the optative—or "wish"—mood in the original language; cf. 1 Pet. 1:2; Jude 2) that the recipients of his letter may experience the abundance of grace and peace that is theirs in their growing, experiential knowledge of God as it is mediated through their faith-enabled relationship with their Lord Jesus Christ. This desire is similarly expressed in the closing bookend and final verse of the letter, where Peter writes, "But grow in the grace and knowledge of our Lord and Savior Jesus Christ. To him be the glory both now and to the day of eternity. Amen" (3:18). Peter will shortly develop the way in which believers can grow in their knowledge of God in and through their relationship with Jesus Christ in the body of the letter (see 1:3–11 below).

Exhortation to Christian Virtue and Assertion of Peter's Prophetic Authority (1:3–21)

Peter starts out his second letter with a bang. He boldly asserts that believers have been granted everything pertaining to life and godliness—everything they need to live a godly life—through their knowledge of the one who called them by (or to) his own glory and excellence. That person he has just identified in the previous verse when he referred to "the knowledge of God and of Jesus our Lord" (1:2). Through our knowledge of God in the Lord Jesus Christ, God has given us all that we need to live a godly life! Note that we've been given all the spiritual tools to live a godly life only in and through our relationship with Jesus Christ; this contrasts with alternative pursuits of holiness in Eastern religions through meditation, mystical communion with the divine, or other supposed paths to the summit of spirituality. As Paul wrote in his letter to the Colossians, such practices "have indeed an appearance of wisdom in promoting self-made religion and asceticism and severity to the body, but they are of no value in stopping the indulgence of the flesh" (Col. 2:23). The fullness of God is found only in Christ; everything is by, through, and in him (Col. 1:15–20; cf. 2:6–23).

Thus, divine grace extends not only to believers' salvation but also to launching them onto the road of sanctification and Christian growth. Not only is salvation by grace; sanctification is by grace as well! Note that Peter, in opening his first letter, speaks of "the sanctification of the Spirit" (1 Pet. 1:2) and that he opened the present letter with the wish that "grace and peace be multiplied to" his readers (1:2). That grace is being "multiplied"—made even more abundant—in believers' knowledge of God and of the Lord Jesus Christ! Because God is all-powerful ("his divine power"), he is able to grant (*dōreomai*, in the NT only in 1:3, 4 and Mark 15:45, in the latter passage with reference to Pilate granting Jesus's corpse to Joseph of Arimathea) believers all things they need to live a godly life (1:3) as well as his "precious [*timios*; cf. 1 Pet. 1:19] and very great [*megistos*, unique in the NT] promises" (1:4). Believers are chosen (1 Pet. 1:1) and called by God (2 Pet. 1:3), not merely to be delivered from a life of sin, death, and eternal destruction but also to a "living hope" (1 Pet. 1:3), an eternal inheritance, and a bright and blessed future (1 Pet. 1:4). While "precious and very great promises" is a general reference, specificity is introduced in that the very same word for "promise" (*epangelma*) is found elsewhere in the entire NT only later in the present letter in 3:13, where Peter writes, "But according to his *promise* we are waiting for a new heaven and a new earth in which righteousness dwells." These "precious and very great promises" most likely refer to God's eschatological promise of a new heaven and a new earth filled with righteousness.

In the present, believers are called to live a life of "godliness" (*eusebeia*, 1:3; cf. 1:6, 7; 3:11). In the Greco-Roman world, this meant living a life of piety and religious devotion; in NT parlance, this meant sanctification in the Holy Spirit—that is, growth in Christlikeness, exemplified by exhibiting a list of distinctly Christian virtues (see 1:5–7 below)—and in the true knowledge of God. What's more, God has called believers to this life of moral excellence and Christian virtue "by his own glory and excellence" (1:3; cf. 1:5; cf. Isa. 42:8, 12).[8] While "glory" (*doxa*) is commonly used in the NT, "excellence" (*aretē*) is less frequent (found elsewhere in the NT only in 1 Pet. 2:9 and Phil. 4:8). There is some question as to whether the dative case here is to be interpreted as believers being called "to" or "by" God's own glory and excellence, though perhaps the latter is more likely. Or both could be in view. God is glorious and excellent, and he calls believers by and to his own glory and excellence. In Peter's first letter, he cited from the Levitical holiness code: "You shall be holy, for I am holy" (1 Pet. 1:16; cf. Lev. 11:44). Here he urges his readers, "Be morally excellent as I am morally excellent." The former may be a more Jewish way of expressing this truth, while the latter may be couched in more Hellenistic terms, though the import of both exhortations is similar: Peter calls his readers to be distinct from the surrounding culture and characterized by integrity and impeccable character.

8. See the discussion in Matthew S. Harmon, "2 Peter," in *ESV Expository Commentary*, vol. 12, *Hebrews–Revelation*, ed. Iain M. Duguid, James M. Hamilton Jr., and Jay Sklar (Wheaton: Crossway, 2018), 372.

In relation to that culture, it is God's will that believers become "partakers [*koinōnoi*] of the divine [*theios*, elsewhere in the NT only in 2 Pet. 1:3, 4, and Acts 17:29 in Paul's address in Athens] nature [*physis*], having escaped the corruption that is in the world because of sinful desire" (1:4). Much discussion has centered on the phrase "partakers of the divine nature"; the early church gradually developed the notion of *theosis*, the belief that humans, in a sense, were becoming infused with the divine.[9] Most likely, Peter's meaning here is simply that believers receive the Holy Spirit (cf. 1 Pet. 1:2) and in this way partake of God's very own nature—a truly amazing thought to contemplate. In an operation somewhat converse to that in Jesus, who, being God, took on human flesh in the incarnation (John 1:1, 14), humans receive the indwelling Spirit of God upon conversion and in this way partake of the divine nature. They have "escaped from the corruption that is in the world." This refers both to present corruption and future destruction; the same cluster of words is used for the false teachers: "escape" (*apopheugō*) occurs elsewhere in the NT only in 2:18 and 20, while "corruption" (*phthora*) is found in 2:12 and 19 (the term regularly has an end-time dimension in the NT; cf. Rom. 8:21; 1 Cor. 15:42, 50; Gal. 6:8). This shows that Peter's present exhortation is given against the backdrop of the threat of the false teachers who are trying to lead his readers astray (see discussion of chap. 2 below). The world is doomed to destruction as it is controlled by "(sinful) passion or desire" (*epithymia*, very frequent in Peter's writings: 1 Pet. 1:14; 2:11; 4:2, 3; 2 Pet. 1:4; 2:10, 18; 3:3). The reference to the world's corruption sets an end-time frame for Peter's letter that is maintained throughout the epistle and comes to the fore especially in the third chapter, which is given to a denunciation and refutation of the false teachers' denial of the Christian teaching of the second coming of Christ.

Verse 5 is introduced by the phrase "For this very reason." Which reason? The answer to this question is not entirely clear; perhaps it is a combination of the fact that God has given believers all they need to live a godly life through their relationship with Jesus Christ (on the positive side) and their need to embark and continue on the path of sanctification—partaking of the divine nature—to escape the world's corruption. Peter's exhortation is that his recipients "make every effort" (*spoudē*; cf. Jude 3) to "add to their faith" a list of Christian virtues elaborated in 1:5–7. The rare word "make" or "supply" (*epichorēgeō*, elsewhere in the NT only in 2 Cor. 9:10; Gal. 3:5; Col. 2:19) is used in both 1:5 and 1:11 and frames the entire section on the pursuit of Christian virtues; the word "supplement" (*pareispherō*) is unique to this

9. For a study of the ancient background, see James M. Starr, *Sharers in the Divine Nature: 2 Peter 1:4 in Its Hellenistic Context*, ConBNT 33 (Stockholm: Almqvist & Wiksell, 2000).

passage. "Make every effort" stands in apparent tension with Peter's previous emphasis on divine grace (1:2: "grace"; 1:3, 4: "granted"); rightly understood, Peter presents believers as grounded in divine grace and, on this basis, exhorts them to strenuously devote themselves to the pursuit of Christian virtues.

"Supplement your faith" also at first seems curious in that it seems to run against the grain of salvation by faith alone (*sola fide*).[10] If we are saved by faith alone through grace alone, it may be asked (cf. Eph. 2:8–9), how can Peter urge his readers to "supplement" their faith? However, one thinks here of James's words, "You see that a person is justified by works and not by faith alone" (James 2:24). And even Paul, who is adamant that salvation is by faith alone apart from works, writes that believers should "work out [their] salvation with fear and trembling" (Phil. 2:12). What these passages suggest is that divine grace is aimed at eliciting a response of faith, and faith, in turn, should be demonstrated by action prompted by faith. In this sense, then, Christians should make every effort to supplement their faith with Christian virtues (see *aretē*, translated "excellence" in the ESV in 1:3 but "virtue"—twice—in 1:5). Virtue—understood as moral excellence—thus "supplements" our faith in that it proves it to be genuine and is the supernatural outworking of the fruit of our salvation in terms of tangible characteristics that are godlike. In this way, believers exhibit godliness and show themselves to be partakers of the divine nature. Just as God has called us "by his own glory and excellence" (1:3), so we glorify God with our pursuit of Christian virtues, cultivating moral excellence (1:5). Paradoxically, therefore, those who are most appreciative of divine grace will be those who strive the hardest to pursue Christian character. Grace, truly understood, does not lead to complacency but to believing action.

Peter's list of virtues in 1:5–7 thus steps upward in the form of a staircase of virtues as in figure 4.1.[11]

Paul features seven virtues that constitute the fruit of the Spirit starting with love and ending with self-control (Gal. 5:22–23). Peter features seven virtues ending with love and likewise including self-control. By comparison, Paul accentuates more keenly that these are fruit produced by the Spirit,

10. One of the four or five *solas* of the Protestant Reformation. See on this the discussion of the relationship between faith and works in James 2 above.

11. Peter here employs a literary feature known as *sorites*, in which one element builds on the preceding one. See also Rom. 5:3–5; cf. Harmon, "2 Peter," 373, citing Peter H. Davids, *The Letters of 2 Peter and Jude*, PNTC (Grand Rapids: Eerdmans, 2006), 177–78. For an exposition of 2 Peter 1:3–11, see Andreas J. Köstenberger, *Excellence: The Character of God and the Pursuit of Scholarly Virtue* (Wheaton: Crossway, 2011), chap. 2. On a devotional note, see Köstenberger, "Something to Think About: Cultivating Christian Virtues," in Köstenberger, Kellum, and Quarles, *The Cradle, the Cross, and the Crown*, 867. See also J. Daryl Charles, *Virtue amidst Vice: The Catalog of Virtues in 2 Peter 1*, JSNTSup 150 (Sheffield: Sheffield Academic, 1997).

Figure 4.1
Staircase of virtues in 2 Peter 1:5–7

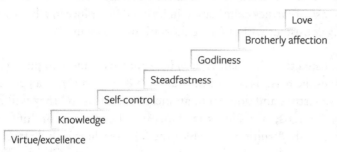

whereas Peter urges believers to climb the staircase of Christian virtues, as it were, by making a deliberate, committed effort to supplement their faith.

- "Virtue" or "excellence" is first in the list presumably because it is a sort of umbrella term for all the remaining virtues (similar to "above reproach" serving as an umbrella term in Paul's list of qualifications for church leaders; cf. 1 Tim. 3:2; Titus 1:6).
- "Knowledge" has already been mentioned in 1:2 and 1:3 as the knowledge of God and of the Lord Jesus Christ who called us by their own glory and excellence.
- "Self-control" (*engkrateia*), as mentioned, is also a fruit of the Spirit mentioned by Paul (Gal. 5:23; elsewhere in the NT only in Acts 24:25, where Paul speaks to governor Felix about righteousness, self-control, and the coming judgment; see also 1 Cor. 7:9; 9:25).
- "Steadfastness" or endurance (*hypomonē*) is a common trait of proven character, showing resilience in the face of adversity, including persecution (elsewhere in the General Epistles also in Heb. 10:36; 12:1; James 1:3, 4; 5:11; and frequently in Paul's writings).
- "Godliness" (*eusebeia*) was previously mentioned at the outset in 1:3 as an overall characteristic of a God-pleasing life (see discussion there).
- "Brotherly affection" (*philadelphia*) and "love" (*agapē*) fittingly conclude the list of virtues, underscoring the supremacy of love in the Christian life (cf. 1 Cor. 13:13). In his first letter, Peter wrote, "Having purified your souls by your obedience to the truth for a sincere brotherly love [*philadelphia*], love one another [*agapaō*] earnestly from a pure heart" (1 Pet. 1:22). Later, he similarly urged his readers to "love the brotherhood" (1 Pet. 2:17) and added, "Finally, all of you, have unity of mind, sympathy, brotherly

love, . . ." (1 Pet. 3:8), and, "Above all, keep loving one another earnestly, since love covers a multitude of sins" (1 Pet. 4:8). This shows that Peter's staircase of virtues culminating in brotherly love/love in 2 Peter 1 is perfectly consistent with Peter's exhortations to love in 1 Peter.

Having listed the Christian virtues he wants his readers to pursue, Peter now supplies the reason for his exhortation (1:8, *gar*, "for"). If a person possesses these virtues and does so in an increasing measure, they will not be "ineffective" (*argos*; cf. 1 Tim. 5:13; Titus 1:12; James 2:20) or "unfruitful" (*akarpos*; literally, "fruitless"; used for the false teachers in Jude 12; see also Eph. 5:11; Titus 3:14) in their knowledge of the Lord Jesus Christ. This suggests that it is possible for a person to be a genuine believer and yet be lacking in effectiveness or fruitfulness in their Christian life. The word "unfruitful" echoes Jesus's words in his parable of the sower and the soils in conjunction with the one who fails to receive the word due to the "cares of the world and the deceitfulness of riches and the desires for other things" (Mark 4:19; cf. Matt. 13:22). Jesus's allegory of the vine and the branches comes to mind as well: "I am the vine; you are the branches. Whoever abides in me and I in him, he it is that bears much fruit, for apart from me you can do nothing. If anyone does not abide in me he is thrown away like a branch and withers. . . . By this is my Father glorified, that you bear much fruit and so prove to be my disciples" (John 15:5–6, 8). Peter would have heard both teachings of Jesus decades earlier and likely echoes them in his exhortation to his readers here.

Conversely, anyone who lacks these qualities (the seven virtues listed in 1:5–7) is so nearsighted as to be blind, a poignant illustration for those of us who are nearsighted almost to the point of being blind. Spiritually speaking, such people have forgotten their cleansing from former sins (1:9). Peter's closing exhortation in conjunction with the pursuit of Christian virtues, therefore, is that his readers be all the more diligent (literally, "make every effort," *spoudazō*, conveying a sense of urgency; cf. 2 Tim. 2:15) to confirm their "calling" (*klēsis*; cf. Phil. 3:14: "upward call"; 2 Tim. 1:9: "holy calling"; Heb. 3:1: "heavenly calling") and "election" (*eklogē*; cf. Rom. 9:11; 11:5, 7, 28; 1 Thess. 1:4). These references underscore God's sovereignty, grace, and love in election. None of us deserve salvation; God's grace is bestowed freely out of sheer generosity and goodness; and most of all, God's calling and election are evidence of his divine love for sinners.

Peter adds that those who practice these qualities can't go wrong! They will never fall (*ptaiō*; 1:10; cf. James 2:10; 3:2).[12] Practicing those virtues makes

---

12. While "fall" may literally refer to losing one's footing, here the figurative meaning "fall away" may be intended (cf. Jude 24; see discussion in Harmon, "2 Peter," 376).

perfect (cf. Matt. 5:48). In this way, believers will be richly furnished with entrance into the eternal kingdom of "our Lord and Savior Jesus Christ" (another instance of the Petrine use of a Granville Sharp–type construction in which one article governs two singular, nontitular nouns indicating a unity of persons, in the present case "Lord" and "Savior"). This, then, is the *goal* of Christians' pursuit of virtues while they are on this earth: a rich entrance into God's eternal heavenly kingdom in and through the Lord Jesus Christ. Logically, therefore, the goal or end ought to shape our present actions and pursuits. The development of and growth in Christian character should be a priority in our individual lives, in our parenting, and in the church. Discipleship, likewise, should not merely be defined as a list of Christian disciplines, no matter how vital, but should be joined with character development as well. Our Christian lives should not primarily be measured in *what we do* but in *who we are*. As followers of the Crucified One, Christians ought to exhibit a growing degree of Christlikeness (Rom. 8:29).

In the second half of the chapter, then, Peter frames his instruction as a "reminder" (1:12, 13) given as long as he is still "in this body" (1:13). He knows that his martyrdom is imminent, as Jesus predicted (1:14; cf. John 21:19). While his readers, if they follow his instruction, will be provided a rich "entrance" (*eisodos*; cf. Heb. 10:19) into God's kingdom (1:11), Peter's "departure" (*exodos*; cf. Luke 9:31 with regard to Jesus's "departure"; literally for Israel's exodus from Egypt, Heb. 11:22) is near (1:15). As long as he will be with them, he will "make every effort" (*spoudazō*; note the inclusio with 1:5; cf. 1:10; 3:14; Eph. 4:3; 2 Tim. 2:15; Heb. 4:11) to impress the importance of pursuing Christian character qualities upon his readers so that when he is gone, they will recall what he said (1:15). In this way, Peter's second and final letter takes on a testamentary character, a kind of final legacy expressing his solemn instructions at the end of his life.[13]

The conjunction *gar* ("for") in 1:16 establishes a transition and connection with the previous paragraph, in 1:12–15, where Peter essentially says that he has written the present letter as a reminder while still being alive. Most likely, the connection pertains to Peter's credibility, on which the impact of his reminders is staked. When "we"—that is, Peter and the other apostles—made known to the readers the "power" and "coming" of the Lord Jesus Christ

---

13. In the OT, cf. the book of Deuteronomy; in the NT, cf. Jesus's farewell discourse in John 13–17; in Second Temple Jewish literature, see The Testaments of the Twelve Patriarchs. For primary sources, see James H. Charlesworth, *The Old Testament Pseudepigrapha*, vol. 1, *Apocalyptic Literature and Testaments* (Garden City, NY: Doubleday, 1983). See also L. Scott Kellum, "Farewell Discourse," in *Dictionary of Jesus and the Gospels*, ed. Joel B. Green, Jeannine K. Brown, and Nicholas Perrin, 2nd ed. (Downers Grove, IL: InterVarsity, 2013), 266–69.

(*parousia*, a technical NT term for the second coming of Christ), they had not followed (aorist participle, *exakolouthēsantes*) "cleverly devised myths" (the perfect participle *sesophismenois*, translated "cleverly devised," suggests the present state of a full-fledged fictional account without basis in fact). In 2 Timothy 3:15, the only other NT occurrence of the word *sophizō*, the word has a positive connotation: The Scriptures are able to "make" Timothy "wise" unto salvation through faith in Christ.

Here, Peter defends himself against accusations of myth making: apparently, he and his apostolic associates had been accused by their opponents of having fabricated the "myth" of Christ's return without any basis in fact. Peter counters that, to the contrary, he and the apostles were "eyewitnesses" (*epoptai*, only here in the NT; but see the use of the verb *epopteuō* in 1 Pet. 2:12 and 3:2; see also *autoptai* in Luke 1:2) of Jesus's "majesty" (*megaleiotētos*; elsewhere in the NT only in Luke 9:43 and Acts 19:27). Peter, along with James and John (the sons of Zebedee), was in the select group who witnessed the heavenly voice on "the holy mountain" pronouncing Jesus to be God's beloved, well-pleasing Son at Jesus's glorious transfiguration, an event recounted in all three Synoptic Gospels (1:18; cf. Matt. 17:1–8; Mark 9:2–8; Luke 9:28–36). On that occasion, Jesus "received honor and glory from God the Father" who himself is described in terms of "Majestic Glory" (*megaloprepēs*, unique in the NT; 1:17). Peter's line of reasoning, therefore, seems to proceed as follows: He is confident that his prediction of Jesus's future glorious return will come to pass because he has *already* seen Jesus in his majestic glory—when he witnessed Jesus being gloriously transformed during his earthly ministry! This dramatically enhances Peter's credibility and constitutes decisive pushback against those who claim Peter's teaching regarding Jesus's second coming is a mere fabrication—a "myth."

In this way, Peter joins the long line of prophetic revelation of God's future purposes as documented in the OT. Consequently, Peter urges his readers "to pay attention as to a lamp shining in a dark place, until the day dawns and the morning star rises in your hearts" (1:19), appropriating an OT passage pointing forward to the coming of the Messiah (Num. 24:14–19).[14] As Peter forcefully asserts, no biblical prophecy originates merely in the prophet's own interpretation (*epilysis*, 1:20; cf. the use of the verb *epilyō* in Mark 4:34 with reference to Jesus's *explanation* of parables). Rather, people "spoke from God as they were carried along by the Holy Spirit" (1:21).[15] Thus, Peter here

14. Cf. the reference to Jesus's "Majestic Glory" in v. 17. For an excellent discussion of v. 19 and the OT echoes found there, see Harmon, "2 Peter," 382–83.

15. Harmon ("2 Peter," 384) notes that in the Greek, the phrase "by the Holy Spirit" is fronted for emphasis.

affirms the divine inspiration of the OT prophetic Scriptures and puts his own prophetic prediction of Jesus's second coming in this long line of prophecy (cf. Heb. 1:1–3). In his first letter, Peter wrote that concerning the salvation to be brought through the Messiah, "the prophets who prophesied about the grace that was to be yours searched and inquired carefully, inquiring what person or time the Spirit of Christ in them was indicating when he predicted the sufferings of Christ and the subsequent glories. It was revealed to them that they were serving not themselves but you, in the things that have now been announced to you through those who preached the good news to you by the Holy Spirit sent from heaven" (1 Pet. 1:10–12). As in 2 Peter 1:21, where the apostle refers to prophets being "carried along by the Holy Spirit," here likewise he speaks of the operation of the "Spirit of Christ" in the OT prophets as they predicted the sufferings and subsequent glories of the Messiah. Now, in the present passage, Peter squarely places himself and his own prediction of Christ's future glorious return within this trajectory and matrix of prophecy.

Denunciation of False Teachers' Character and Motivation (2:1–22)

Peter now transitions from aligning himself with (true) OT prophets to the presence of false teachers in the congregation(s) to which he writes. He says just as there were genuine prophets in Israel, so there were also false prophets (*pseudoprophētai*; cf. Jesus's warning in the Sermon on the Mount [Matt. 7:15] and his prediction in the Olivet Discourse [Matt. 24:11, 34; Mark 13:22]; see also Jesus's reference to false OT prophets in Luke 6:26; and cf. 1 John 4:1). Similarly, Peter predicts that there will be false teachers (*pseudodidaskaloi*; only here in the NT) among his recipients.[16] These teachers will introduce heresies (*haireseis*; only here in this sense in the NT)[17] designed to cause destruction, but, ironically, they will in fact bring swift destruction upon themselves (2:1; cf. 2:3). In so doing, they will even deny the Master (*despotēs*; cf. Jude 4) who bought (*agorazō*; not elsewhere in the General Epistles) them (2:1). This is a puzzling reference that could be taken to imply that those false teachers were once genuinely saved but subsequently lost their salvation. However, this is not a necessary conclusion. Alternatively, Jesus only *potentially* bought these individuals, but they ended up rejecting him permanently and thus incurred severe eternal divine

16. For similar predictions of end-time apostasy, see 1 Tim. 4:1–5; 2 Tim. 3:1–9; 1 John 4:1–6; Jude 5–23. Note that 2 Peter 2 most likely adapts portions of Jude for Peter's own purposes.

17. Paul twice uses the word with the more general meaning "disputes" (1 Cor. 11:19; Gal. 5:20). In Acts, the word occurs several times with the meaning "sect," as in Pharisees or Sadducees or even Christianity (Acts 5:17; 15:5; 24:5, 14; 26:5; 28:22).

judgment.[18] The reference to the false teachers' greed (*pleonexia*; cf. 2:14) and to their exploitation (*emporeuomai*, elsewhere in the NT only in James 4:13) of some of Peter's readers with false (*plastos*, only here in the NT) words implies that false teachers were financially motivated and bent on taking advantage of unsuspecting victims. Peter is certain that the teachers' condemnation has long been decreed and will swiftly ensue (2:3; cf. 2:1). In the remainder of the chapter, Peter adapts portions from Jude 5–23.[19] In what follows, Peter, like Jude, uses the midrashic (Jewish commentary) technique of adducing OT examples of individuals or groups who were guilty of rebellion similar to that of the false teachers. In the case of these offenders, the Hebrew Scriptures already record the divine judgment they met. The false teachers in his day, Peter proceeds to argue by way of typology, will meet a similar judgment because they are guilty of the same kind of rebellion against God. Peter's argument here is based on the premise that God and his judgment are consistent: similar offense, similar punishment. In support, Peter adduces the following in chronological OT order:

1. rebellious angels who sinned and were cast out of heaven (2:4; cf., possibly, 1 Pet. 3:19–20)[20]

2. the ancient world—except for Noah and his family—that perished in the flood (2:5; cf. Gen. 6–9; Heb. 11:7)

3. the cities of Sodom and Gomorrah, which were reduced to ashes—except for Lot (2:6–10; cf. Gen. 19)

What these examples show is that God is certain to punish rebellion; at the same time, he is just to exempt those—such as Noah or Lot—who are righteous (2:9–10a). In the following verses, Peter adapts a wholesale denunciation of these false teachers from Jude (2:10b–22), including yet another OT example of an individual who incurred divine judgment:

4. the prophet Balaam, who was rebuked by a donkey (2:15–16; cf. Num. 22)

18. See Thomas R. Schreiner, "'Problematic Texts' for Definite Atonement in the Pastoral and General Epistles," in *From Heaven He Came and Sought Her: Definite Atonement in Historical, Biblical, Theological, and Pastoral Perspective*, ed. David Gibson and Jonathan Gibson (Wheaton: Crossway, 2013), 387–92. For NT passages teaching or at least impinging on the subject of eternal security, see, e.g., John 10:27–29; 15:16; Rom. 5:9–10; 8:38–39; Eph. 1:4–14; 2:1–10; Col. 1:12–14; 2 Thess. 2:13–14; 2 Tim. 1:12; 2:19; 1 John 3:1–3; 5:10–13.

19. See the discussion of Jude in chapter 7 of this volume.

20. The underlying Greek word *tartaroō* literally means "hold captive in Tartarus," a place in the underworld where, according to Greek mythology, rebellious beings were held captive. Cf. Harmon, "2 Peter," 388n52, citing Douglas J. Moo, *2 Peter, Jude*, NIVAC (Grand Rapids: Zondervan, 1996), 108.

Concluding his denunciation, Peter quotes Proverbs 11:22 with reference to the false teachers: just as a dog returns to its own vomit, and a sow, once washed, returns to its mud, so these heretics, true to their nature, revert back to their original condition. As the saying goes, you can't put lipstick on a pig! Or, as Proverbs 11:22 has it, "Like a gold ring in a pig's snout is a beautiful woman with no discretion." What this example shows is that these false teachers, while appearing to be regenerate, were never truly transformed in their heart of hearts, in the core of their being. Rather, by their immoral lifestyle, they proved that any apparent conversion had never truly occurred (cf. 1 John 2:19). In a similar vein, the reference to their denial of "the Master who bought them" in 2:1 likely does not imply their regeneration and subsequent apostasy and loss of salvation.

Denunciation of False Teachers' Denial of Jesus's Second Coming; Conclusion (3:1-18)

This third and final chapter in Peter's second letter is what the entire letter has been leading up to. In the first chapter, Peter hinted at the main issue at hand when he defended himself against the charge of concocting "cleverly devised myths" when predicting the second coming of Christ (1:16). The entire second chapter was devoted to the presence of "false teachers" amid the congregation whose swift destruction Peter predicted in keeping with the similar judgment meted out on those who in OT times committed similar transgressions (2:1; cf. 2:4–16). But it is here, in the third chapter, that Peter addresses the false teachers and their erroneous teaching most directly and explicitly.

Peter notes that this is the second letter he is writing to his readers and that in both of them he is setting them on notice and putting them on the alert. He calls on them to recall the words spoken beforehand by the "holy prophets" and the command of the apostles: the last days will witness the appearing of scoffers (*empaiktai*; in the NT only here and in Jude 18; cf. 2 Tim. 3:1). This (apparently oral) prophecy of the apostles is cited explicitly in Jude's epistle: "In the last time there will be scoffers, following their own ungodly passions" (Jude 18); Peter here provides a close paraphrase. Jude described those people as divisive and worldly individuals who were "devoid of the Spirit" (Jude 19). Rather than serving the Lord, these scoffers served their own appetites (*epithymia*, 3:3).

What are these false teachers scoffing at? They're scoffing at Peter's teaching of Jesus's imminent return.[21] Apparently, their skepticism was grounded

---

21. Contra Edward Adams, "Where Is the Promise of His Coming? The Complaint of the Scoffers in 2 Peter 3.4," *NTS* 51 (2005): 106–22, who contends that these individuals scoffed not

in the philosophical premise that God doesn't intervene in human history: "Where is the promise of his coming?" they said. "For ever since the fathers fell asleep, all things are continuing as they were from the beginning of creation" (3:4). Peter's riposte is immediate and decisive: What about creation? Did God not create the universe? Does this not constitute a major divine intervention in human history? And what about the universal flood? Does this not constitute a major divine intervention in human history documented in Scripture (3:5–6; cf. Gen. 6–9; 1 Pet. 3:20)? In the same way as God created the universe, Peter continues to contend, the ungodly will one day be judged on the day of judgment (3:7).

In part, Peter asks his readers to ponder whether the false teachers' opposition stems from their failure to appreciate the infinitude of God, resulting in vastly different methods of timekeeping: for God, one day is like a thousand years, and vice versa (3:8; cf. Ps. 90:4).[22] The reason why God may appear to be slow to keep his promise of Christ's return is not that he is unreliable or that the fulfillment of his promises is uncertain (cf. Rom. 9:6; see also Deut. 7:10; Isa. 46:13; Hab. 2:3). Rather, God shows great patience and gives people time to repent (3:9; cf. Rom. 2:4, where Paul makes the exact same argument; see also 1 Tim. 2:3–4). He is "a God merciful and gracious, slow to anger, and abounding in steadfast love and faithfulness, keeping steadfast love for thousands, forgiving iniquity and transgression and sin" (Exod. 34:6–7). In the end, however, Peter continues, echoing Jesus's teaching, the day of the Lord will come suddenly and unexpectedly—like a thief (*kleptēs*)—triggering a massive eschatological conflagration of cosmic proportions (3:10; cf. Matt. 24–25; the word "thief" occurs in Matt. 24:43).[23]

At this, Peter turns to his readers and states the obvious conclusion: in light of such terrible and certain future judgment, what sort of people ought they to be? They should live holy and godly lives (cf. 1:3; and see the list of Christian virtues in 1:5–7, on which see discussion above) as they wait for and even hasten the coming "day of God" (elsewhere called the "day of the Lord").[24]

---

at the delay of the *parousia* but rather at the assumption that God's end-time promises involved the prospect of cosmic destruction. See Richard J. Bauckham, "The Delay of the Parousia," *TynBul* 31 (1980): 3–36, who argues that 2 Peter 3—the most explicit treatment of the delay in the NT—is closely dependent on a Jewish apocalyptic source (Apocalypse of Baruch).

22. There is a deliberate connection between Peter's opponents who "deliberately overlook" God's previous interventions (v. 5) and Peter's readers who are urged to "not overlook" that God's timetable is different from human ways of reckoning time (v. 8).

23. For background on Peter's reference to "the day of the Lord" in v. 10, see Harmon, "2 Peter," 404–5.

24. See Peter's call to holiness in his first letter (1 Pet. 1:15–16; cf. Lev. 19:2) and his references to the believing community as a "holy priesthood" and a "holy nation" (1 Pet. 2:5, 9).

Not only are believers waiting for Christ's return, Peter notes; they are also awaiting the fulfillment of God's promise of "new heavens and a new earth in which righteousness dwells" (3:13; cf. 1:4). Both by referring to the importance of godliness and by referring to God's promises, Peter therefore returns to his opening remarks, in which he stressed his readers' need to pursue godly virtues and moral excellence in keeping with God's "precious and very great promises" (1:4).

After a final call to diligence (*spoudazō*) as they await the fulfillment of God's promises (3:14), Peter urges his readers to appreciate God's patience in keeping with the (sometimes hard-to-understand) teaching found in Paul's letters (3:15–16). Contrary to some modern critical scholars who have sought to drive a wedge between Paul and Peter (such as nineteenth-century scholar F. C. Baur and some of his followers in the Tübingen School), Peter here calls Paul "our beloved brother" and pays tribute to Paul's theological stature by acknowledging that some of Paul's teachings are difficult to grasp. Yet the problem lay not with Paul's relationship with Peter or with Paul's teaching itself but with the devious schemes of the false teachers who—being "ignorant" and "unstable"—twisted them and thus incurred their own destruction (3:16; cf. 2:1–3).

What's more, Peter in effect even puts Paul's letters on par with "the other Scriptures," an amazing acknowledgment in light of the fact that the ink was barely dry on Paul's epistles. This shows that virtually no time elapsed between the writing of key NT documents and their recognition by the early church as on par with OT Scripture.[25] Peter's readers should take care not to be carried away and lose their own footing. Rather, in keeping with Peter's opening words, they should earnestly pursue growth in Christlikeness and spiritual sanctification—grow "in the grace and knowledge of our Lord and Savior Jesus Christ" (another Petrine instance of the Granville Sharp rule; cf. 1:1 and discussion above). The letter closes with a brief doxology addressed to Jesus, to whom glory is due both now and forever. Amen.

2 Peter: Commentaries

Bauckham, Richard. *Jude, 2 Peter*. WBC 50. Waco: Word, 1983.

Charles, J. Daryl. *1–2 Peter, Jude*. BCBC. Scottdale, PA: Herald, 1999.

Davids, Peter H. *The Letters of 2 Peter and Jude*. PNTC. Grand Rapids: Eerdmans, 2006.

———. *2 Peter and Jude: A Handbook on the Greek Text*. BHGNT. Waco: Baylor University Press, 2011.

25. See Köstenberger, Kellum, and Quarles, *The Cradle, the Cross, and the Crown*, chap. 1.

Giese, C. P. *2 Peter and Jude.* Concordia Commentary. St. Louis: Concordia, 2012.

Green, Gene L. *Jude and 2 Peter.* BECNT. Grand Rapids: Baker Academic, 2008.

Green, Michael E. *The Second Epistle of Peter and the Epistle of Jude: An Introduction and Commentary.* Rev. ed. TNTC. Grand Rapids: Eerdmans, 1987.

Harink, D. *1 and 2 Peter.* BTCB. Grand Rapids: Brazos, 2009.

Harmon, Matthew S. "2 Peter." In *ESV Expository Commentary,* vol. 12, *Hebrews–Revelation,* edited by Iain M. Duguid, James M. Hamilton Jr., and Jay Sklar, 363–410. Wheaton: Crossway, 2018.

Kelly, J. N. D. *A Commentary on the Epistles of Peter and of Jude.* HNTC. New York: Harper & Row, 1969.

Mbuvi, Andrew M. *Jude and 2 Peter: A New Covenant Commentary.* NCCS. Cambridge: Lutterworth, 2016.

Moo, Douglas J. *2 Peter, Jude.* NIVAC. Grand Rapids: Zondervan, 1996.

Neyrey, Jerome H. *2 Peter, Jude: A New Translation with Introduction and Commentary.* AB 37C. New York: Doubleday, 1993.

Reese, Ruth A. *2 Peter and Jude.* THNTC. Grand Rapids: Eerdmans, 2007.

Richard, E. J. *Reading 1 Peter, Jude, and 2 Peter: A Literary and Theological Commentary.* Macon, GA: Smyth & Helwys, 2000.

Schreiner, Thomas R. *1, 2 Peter, Jude.* NAC 37. Nashville: Broadman & Holman, 2003.

Senior, Donald P. *1 Peter, Jude, and 2 Peter.* SP 15. Collegeville, MN: Liturgical Press, 2003.

Strange, D. *An Exegetical Summary of 2 Peter.* 2nd ed. Dallas: SIL International, 2008.

Webb, Robert L. *The Letters of Jude and Second Peter.* NICNT. Grand Rapids: Eerdmans, forthcoming.

Witherington, Ben, III. *Letters and Homilies for Hellenized Christians.* Vol. 2, *A Socio-Rhetorical Commentary on 1–2 Peter.* Downers Grove, IL: InterVarsity, 2008.

2 Peter: Articles, Essays, and Monographs

Adams, Edward. "Where Is the Promise of His Coming? The Complaint of the Scoffers in 2 Peter 3.4." *NTS* 51 (2005): 106–22.

Batten, Alicia J., and John S. Kloppenborg, eds. *James, 1 and 2 Peter, and Early Jesus Traditions.* LNTS 478. London: Bloomsbury T&T Clark, 2014.

Bauckham, Richard J. "The Delay of the Parousia." *TynBul* 31 (1980): 3–36.

Boobyer, George H. "The Indebtedness of 2 Peter to 1 Peter." In *New Testament Essays: Studies in Memory of T. W. Manson,* edited by A. J. B. Higgins, 34–53. Manchester: University of Manchester Press, 1959.

Brown, Raymond E., Karl P. Donfried, and John Reumann, eds. *Peter in the New Testament.* Minneapolis: Augsburg, 1973.

Callan, Terrance. "Use of the Letter of Jude by the Second Letter of Peter." *Bib* 85 (2004): 42–64.

Carson, D. A. "2 Peter." In *Commentary on the New Testament Use of the Old Testament,* edited by G. K. Beale and D. A. Carson, 1015–61. Grand Rapids: Baker Academic, 2007.

Charles, J. Daryl. *Virtue amidst Vice: The Catalog of Virtues in 2 Peter 1.* JSNTSup 150. Sheffield: Sheffield Academic, 1997.

Cullmann, Oscar. *Peter: Disciple, Apostle, Martyr.* Translated by Floyd V. Wilson. Philadelphia: Westminster, 1962.

Danker, Frederick W. "2 Peter." In *The General Letters*, edited by Gerhard Krodel, 84–93. Proclamation. Minneapolis: Fortress, 1995.

———. "2 Peter: A Solemn Decree." *CBQ* 40 (1978): 64–82.

Davids, Peter H. *A Theology of James, Peter, and Jude: Living in Light of the Coming King.* BTNT. Grand Rapids: Zondervan, 2014.

———. "The Use of Second Temple Traditions in 1 and 2 Peter and Jude." In *The Catholic Epistles and Tradition*, edited by Jacques Schlosser, 409–31. BETL 176. Leuven: Peeters, 2004.

deSilva, David A. *The Jewish Teachers of Jesus, James, and Jude: What Earliest Christianity Learned from the Apocrypha and Pseudepigrapha.* Oxford: Oxford University Press, 2012.

Gilmour, Michael J. *The Significance of Parallels between 2 Peter and Other Early Christian Literature.* AcBib 10. Atlanta: Society of Biblical Literature, 2002.

Green, E. M. B. *2 Peter Reconsidered.* London: Tyndale, 1961.

Harner, Philip B. *What Are They Saying about the Catholic Epistles?* Mahwah, NJ: Paulist Press, 2004.

Heil, John Paul. *1 Peter, 2 Peter, and Jude: Worship Matters.* Eugene, OR: Cascade, 2013.

Helyer, Larry R. *The Life and Witness of Peter.* Downers Grove, IL: IVP Academic, 2012.

Hengel, Martin. *Saint Peter: The Underestimated Apostle.* Grand Rapids: Eerdmans, 2010.

Huther, J. E. *Critical and Exegetical Handbook to the General Epistles of Peter and Jude.* Translated by D. B. Croom and P. J. Gloab. Edinburgh: T&T Clark, 1881.

Jobes, Karen H. *Letters to the Church: A Survey of Hebrews and the General Epistles.* Grand Rapids: Zondervan, 2011.

Kruger, Michael J. "The Authenticity of 2 Peter." *JETS* 42 (1999): 645–71.

Lapham, Fred. *Peter: The Myth, the Man and the Writings: A Study of Early Petrine Text and Tradition.* JSNTSup 239. Sheffield: Sheffield Academic, 2003.

Martin, Ralph P. "The Theology of Jude, 1 Peter, and 2 Peter." In *The Theology of the Letters of James, Peter, and Jude*, by Andrew Chester and Ralph P. Martin, 63–163. Cambridge: Cambridge University Press, 1994.

Mason, Eric F., and Troy W. Martin, eds. *Reading 1–2 Peter and Jude: A Resource for Students.* SBLRBS. Atlanta: Society of Biblical Literature, 2014.

Meier, Sam. "2 Peter 3:3–7: An Early Jewish and Christian Response to Eschatological Skepticism." *BZ* 32 (1988): 255–57.

Niebuhr, Karl-Wilhelm, and Robert W. Wall. *The Catholic Epistles and Apostolic Tradition: A New Perspective on James to Jude.* Waco: Baylor University Press, 2009.

Nienhuis, David R., and Robert W. Wall. *Reading the Epistles of James, Peter, John, and Jude as Scripture: The Shaping and Shape of a Canonical Collection.* Grand Rapids: Eerdmans, 2013.

Perkins, Pheme. *Peter: Apostle for the Whole Church.* Minneapolis: Fortress, 2000.

Picirilli, Robert E. "Allusions to 2 Peter in the Apostolic Fathers." *JSNT* 33 (1988): 57–83.

Smith, Terence V. *Petrine Controversies in Early Christianity: Attitudes towards Peter in Christian Writings of the First Two Centuries.* WUNT 2/15. Tübingen: J. C. B. Mohr, 1985.

Snyder, John I. *The Promise of His Coming: The Eschatology of 2 Peter.* San Mateo, CA: Western Book, 1986.

Thurén, Lauri. "The Relationship between 2 Peter and Jude: A Classical Problem Resolved?" In *The Catholic Epistles and the Tradition*, edited by Jacques Schlosser, 451–60. BETL 176. Leuven: Peeters, 2004.

Watson, Duane Frederick. *Invention, Arrangement, and Style: Rhetorical Criticism of Jude and 2 Peter.* SBLDS 104. Atlanta: Scholars Press, 1988.

Watson, Duane Frederick, and Terrance Callan. *First and Second Peter.* Paideia. Grand Rapids: Baker Academic, 2012.

Watson, Duane Frederick, and Robert L. Webb, eds. *Reading Second Peter with New Eyes: Methodological Reassessments of the Letter of Second Peter.* LNTS 382. London: T&T Clark, 2010.

Wenham, David. "Being 'Found' on the Last Day: New Light on 2 Peter 3.10 and 2 Corinthians 5.3." *NTS* 33 (1989): 477–79.

CHAPTER FIVE

1 John

Introduction

Author, Audience, Date, and Genre

The apostle John is best known for writing the Fourth Gospel, but he also wrote three NT letters, not to mention the book of Revelation. John, the son of Zebedee, was not only one of the twelve apostles of Jesus; he was one of three disciples in Jesus's inner circle along with his brother James, as well as Peter (Matt. 17:1; 26:37; Mark 5:37). What is more, in his Gospel, John stakes a claim of having been Jesus's closest earthly follower. Not only was John at Jesus's side at the Last Supper; he witnessed the crucifixion and was among the first to see the empty tomb and later repeatedly saw the risen Christ (John 13:23; 19:35; 20:8; 21:24). "And the Word became flesh and dwelt among us," John writes in his Gospel, "and we have seen his glory, glory as of the only Son from the Father, full of grace and truth" (1:14). John's first letter opens with a similar claim of eyewitness testimony: "That which was from the beginning, which we have heard, which we have seen with our eyes, which we looked upon and have touched with our hands, . . . that which we have seen and heard we proclaim also to you . . ." (1 John 1:1, 3).

Scholars at times speak of a "Johannine community" allegedly standing behind the Johannine writings.[1] However, the only "Johannine community"

---

1. See esp. J. Louis Martyn, *History and Theology in the Fourth Gospel*, 3rd ed., NTL (Louisville: Westminster John Knox, 2003); but see the critiques by Jonathan Bernier, *Aposynagōgos and the Historical Jesus in John: Rethinking the Historicity of the Johannine Expulsion Passages*, Biblical Interpretation Series 122 (Leiden: Brill, 2013); and Edward W. Klink III, *The Sheep of the Fold: The Origin and Audience of the Gospel of John*, SNTSMS 141 (Cambridge: Cambridge University Press, 2010). For a history of the debate, see D. A. Lamb, *Text, Context and*

attested in the literature is the congregations to which John wrote his three NT letters. It is to these communities that John writes about his firsthand knowledge of Jesus, so that they too "may have fellowship" with him; and indeed, he adds, his fellowship is "with the Father and with his Son Jesus Christ" (1:3). In 2 and 3 John, John calls himself "the elder," most likely alluding to his advanced age at the time of writing; John was the only member of the Twelve who didn't suffer a martyr's death (except for Judas, of course) but rather died of natural causes at a ripe old age. First John, as mentioned, doesn't really start out like a letter but, similar to Hebrews, begins more like an oral address or perhaps like a literary preface (no ancient letter template, "From . . . to . . . grace and peace" here). It doesn't end like a letter, either. The last sentence is simply, "Little children, keep yourselves from idols" (5:21)—though, as in his Gospel, near the end John does cite his purpose for writing when he says, "I write these things to you who believe in the name of the Son of God that you may know that you have eternal life" (5:13).

John also played a vital role in the early church's mission. None other than the apostle Paul, the eventual leader of that mission, ranks John among the "pillars" of the early church alongside James (the half-brother of Jesus) and Peter (Gal. 2:9). As we've seen, John is frequently paired with Peter, both during the latter stages of Jesus's ministry (John 13–21) and in the early stages of the newly established Christian community (Acts 3–4; 8). We don't have a detailed itinerary of John's whereabouts in the first century, but several decades later, according to second-century tradition, John is apparently based in the important city of Ephesus in Asia Minor, where he writes his Gospel (most likely first), followed by his three letters, and finally the book of Revelation. These five writings are united by considerable stylistic unity and demonstrably come from the same author—the apostle John—though they are of three different genres: historical narrative (the Gospel), epistolary literature (the letters), and apocalyptic literature (Revelation; more on this below).

As briefly touched upon, John's writings come near the end of NT revelation and were most likely penned close to the end of the first century as the last NT writings to be composed. We can tentatively date the Gospel to the 80s or early 90s AD based on several clues contained within the text of the narrative: (1) the lack of mention of the Sadducees, who faded from view following the Jewish revolt against Rome in AD 66–73; (2) hints that the Jerusalem temple has been destroyed and the assertion that Jesus is the Messiah and the temple's replacement (2:18–22; cf. 4:23–24); (3) references

---

the Johannine Community: A Sociolinguistic Analysis of the Johannine Writings, LNTS 477 (London: Bloomsbury T&T Clark, 2014).

to the Sea of Galilee as the Sea of Tiberias, a change in nomenclature that, according to extrabiblical literature, took place in the latter half of the first century (6:1; 21:1); (4) the remarkable account of Thomas's confession of Jesus as "my Lord and my God" (20:28), which may play off Emperor Domitian's insistence to be similarly identified (Domitian reigned AD 81–96); and other factors. If John, therefore, wrote his Gospel sometime in the 80s or early 90s AD, and if he wrote his letters not too long after the Gospel, this would place the writing of the letters (probably in the order 1, 2, and 3 John) sometime in the mid- to late 80s or early 90s as well, followed by Revelation in the mid-90s AD (per our discussion below).

Structure

We've already discussed the fact that 1 John neither starts nor ends like a letter. What, then, is the likely structure of 1 John?[2] Again, the letter seems to defy easy compartmentalization. Among the above-mentioned writings (Hebrews, James, 1 and 2 Peter), perhaps its structure is closest in character to that of James, who, as mentioned, strings together rather loosely a series of exhortations or warnings on a variety of topics to a broad audience (no specific individuals are named). Similarly, John names no specific individuals but rather speaks in more general terms to older and younger believers, especially in chapter 2 ("children," "fathers," "young men"; 2:12–14).

After the opening preface (1:1–5), John settles into a mode of issuing various kinds of exhortations, possibly informed by the recent departure of antagonists who at one time were members of the church but by their leaving proved that they had not been truly part of God's church all along (2:19).

It may be possible to infer from John's words some of the false teachings of these opponents. This is likely especially regarding the common refrain in chapter 1, "If we say . . ." (1:6, 8, 10; see also "Whoever says . . . ," 2:4). Apparently, the opponents taught that there was no necessary connection between what a person believed and how they lived. While professing orthodox doctrine,

---

2. Matthew D. Jensen, "The Structure and Argument of 1 John: A Survey of Proposals," *JSNT* 35 (2012): 54–73, surveys proposals for the structure and argument of 1 John according to five constituent elements (thematic, source-critical, literary, text-linguistic, and rhetorical) and how these units are related to one another (not at all, association of ideas, cyclic or spiral, parallels to John's Gospel, chiastic), concluding that no consensus has been reached. See also L. Scott Kellum, "On the Semantic Structure of 1 John: A Modest Proposal," *FM* 23 (2008): 34–82, who proposes the following semantic structure of 1 John: prologue; overview (peaking at 2:12–17 and 18–27); ethics; theology (prominent sections 4:1–6 and 7–12); conclusion. Ray Van Neste, "1–3 John," in *ESV Expository Commentary*, vol. 12, *Hebrews–Revelation*, ed. Iain M. Duguid, James M. Hamilton Jr., and Jay Sklar (Wheaton: Crossway, 2018), 418–20, identifies as many as fifteen literary units with numerous subunits.

or even claiming special spiritual insight, these opponents indulged in an immoral lifestyle, as did Jude's opponents, whom Jude calls "ungodly people, who pervert the grace of our God into sensuality" (Jude 4; cf. 1 John 1:6–7).

Also, the opponents may have claimed to be without sin or denied the reality of sin altogether (cf. 1:8–2:2). As a result, they didn't practice confession of sins (cf. 1:9) and lacked appreciation for the propitiation of sins (averting of God's wrath) procured for true believers by the Lord Jesus Christ (2:1–2).

Finally, such detractors and imposters did not truly believe that Jesus was the Messiah, though they likely paid some sort of lip service to such belief, which made their teaching all the more deceptive (see, e.g., 2:22; 4:2; 5:1).[3] Not only did such misguided individuals fail to attain regeneration themselves; they likely intimidated rank-and-file believers in those congregations with their claims of higher knowledge and superior spirituality, even shaking believers' assurance of salvation.

In response, John writes to the believers who remained after the secessionists' departure: "You have been anointed by the Holy One, and you all have knowledge" (2:20). Most likely he says this to counter the claim of those false teachers that they alone possessed special "knowledge" not available to the average Christian. Over against these false teachers, John assures his readers, "The anointing that you received from him abides in you, and you have no need that anyone should teach you" (2:27). This dual reference to the "anointing" believers have received almost certainly pertains to their new birth through the Holy Spirit and the subsequent enlightenment they received, awakening them to the realization of the true identity of Jesus and enabling them to discern spiritual truth. In this regard, they needed no teachers—certainly not the false teachers who were not even regenerate themselves!

To sum up, then, we may say that John wrote his first letter to reassure true believers that they did know who Jesus was, that they did have the Holy Spirit, and that they did possess salvation and eternal life. Conversely, he denounced the false teachers and excoriated them for their lack of belief in Jesus the Messiah, whose teachings and activities he had presented at great length in his Gospel, which likely preceded John's letters and whose central claim those false teachers denied.

In light of the preceding discussion, we may sketch the flow of John's first letter as follows. During the course of writing, John repeatedly returns to his favorite topics, most pronounced of which is believers' obligation to love one another as Christ has loved them (the "new commandment"). Subsections of

---

3. See Daniel R. Streett, *They Went Out from Us: The Identity of the Opponents in First John*, BZNW 177 (Berlin: de Gruyter, 2011).

John's letter are often introduced with addresses such as "My children" (or simply "Children") or "Beloved," something we've seen already in James's and Peter's letters above. At other times, subsections are introduced with statements pertaining to John's purpose for writing: "I am writing [or "have written"] these things to you."

Structure of 1 John

1 John	Introductory Phrase	Content
1:1-10	That which was from the beginning	Opening denunciation of false teachers
2:1-6	My little children	On Jesus's propitiation and keeping his commandments
2:7-11	Beloved	The "new commandment" to love one another
2:12-14	I am writing/have written to you	Messages to older and younger believers
2:15-17	Do not love the world	Do not love the world
2:18-27	Children	Departure of the secessionists a sign of the last days, pitting Christ vs. antichrists
2:28-3:1	Little children	Abide in him
3:2-6	Beloved	Purify yourselves
3:7-12	Little children	Children of God vs. children of the devil
3:13-17	Do not be surprised, brothers	The world's hatred
3:18-20	Little children	Do not love in word only but also in deed
3:21-24	Beloved	Love one another
4:1-6	Beloved	Test the spirits
4:7-10	Beloved	Love one another
4:11-21	Beloved	Perfect love
5:1-12	Everyone who believes that Jesus is the Christ	Jesus is the Christ
5:13-21	I write these things to you	Assurance of eternal life (except for sin leading to death)

Central Message

John's first letter is predicated upon belief in the message of his Gospel—that Jesus is the Christ, the Son of God (John 20:30–31; cf. 1 John 2:24; 4:2; 5:1). False teachers—operating in the spirit of the antichrist—have arisen denying such belief, deceiving many. John writes to reiterate the truth of the Christian gospel message—which is based on reliable apostolic eyewitness testimony—in his pastoral role and out of a shepherd's concern. He calls out the wolves who have torn at the sheep and desires to protect the sheep from doctrinal predators.

None other than the apostle Paul had told the Ephesian elders that after his departure, "Fierce wolves will come in among you, not sparing the flock; and from among your own selves will arise men speaking twisted things, to draw away the disciples after them. Therefore be alert" (Acts 20:29–31). It appears that Paul's prediction had come true, and John found himself in a position to address the havoc wreaked by these errant elders in the Ephesian church after their departure.

Church leaders in our day, likewise, should be alert and address any damage caused by those who spread false teachings in the body of Christ, so that true believers are not swayed or led astray.

As mentioned, there are numerous similarities between John's Gospel and letters. The table on the following page is illustrative rather than exhaustive. The similarities not only include similar phrases but also reflect a similar worldview (including multiple polarities such as "light and darkness" or "love and hate") that sets John's Gospel and letters apart from other NT writings.

Introduction: The Apostolic Witness to Jesus (1:1–4)

John's first letter opens, like the Gospel, with a reference to "the beginning" (*archē*; 1:1; cf. John 1:1).[4] The Gospel begins with the assertion that "in the beginning was the Word, and the Word was with God, and the Word was God." Picking up seamlessly on this assertion, John in his first letter bears witness to "that which was from the beginning." Also, just as in the Gospel the identity of the Word is only gradually disclosed as Jesus Christ (John 1:17), so here John uses the neuter, not masculine, gender in referring to "that which was from the beginning, which we have heard, which we have seen with our eyes, which we looked upon and have touched with our hands," though the reader is easily able to infer that the four instances of the neuter relative pronoun all refer to none other than the Lord Jesus Christ, to whom John's Gospel previously bore witness.

In the Gospel, the author maintained, "We have seen [*theaomai*] his [the incarnate Word's] glory" (John 1:14). Similarly, the author here uses the plural "we"—most likely to refer to the apostolic witness, including, but not limited to, himself—and asserts that he and his fellow apostles have enjoyed the most thorough and intimate acquaintance with the Lord Jesus Christ: they've heard him speak and teach; they've seen him with their own eyes (they were firsthand

---

4. Matthew D. Jensen, *Affirming the Resurrection of the Incarnate Christ: A Reading of 1 John*, SNTSMS 153 (Cambridge: Cambridge University Press, 2012), notes that the letter opening (1:1–4) provides the framework for interpreting the letter and contends that the most plausible context is an intra-Jewish controversy over Jesus's messiahship.

Similarities between John's Gospel and Letters

Similarity	John's Gospel	John's Letters
Jesus is the Christ, the Son of God	20:30-31	1 John 2:22; 4:15; 5:1; 2 John 7
God sent his only Son into the world	3:16, 18	1 John 4:9-10, 14
Believers are born of God	1:12-13; 3:3, 5	1 John 2:29; 3:9; 4:7; 5:1, 4, 18
Believers are God's children	1:12-13; 8:39-58	1 John 3:1-2
Believers have passed from death into life	5:24	1 John 3:14
Frequent use of Father-Son language	1:18; 5:19-47	1 John 1:3; 2:22-23
Light and darkness language	1:4-9; 3:19-21; 8:12; 12:35, 46	1 John 1:5-7; 2:8-11
Jesus is engaged in cosmic struggle with the devil	12:31; 13:2; 14:30; 16:11	1 John 3:8, 10
Jesus laid down his life for believers	10:15, 17-18; 15:13	1 John 3:16
The importance of remaining in him and his word	8:31; 15:4-10, 16	1 John 2:6, 24; 3:24; 4:16; 2 John 9
The new commandment of love	13:34-35	1 John 2:7-8; 2 John 5
The importance of believing for eternal life	3:16; 20:30-31	1 John 5:10-13
Concluding purpose statement	20:30-31	1 John 5:13

eyewitnesses); they've looked at him (*theaomai* means "perceive," "observe"); and they've touched him with their own hands (one thinks here especially of the memorable occasion narrated at the end of John's Gospel when Jesus tells Thomas to touch his crucifixion wounds; cf. John 20:27; cf. 20:25).

There is, therefore, no question that "that which was from the beginning" is none other than the preexistent Lord Jesus Christ, the Word-become-flesh, God-in-the-flesh, who had made the Father known (John 1:18). John's first letter is thus a fitting sequel to the Gospel's narration of the Son's revelation of the Father in his words and deeds, ultimately in his finished work at the cross, the place where Jesus revealed the Father's love for his own (19:30; cf. 3:16; 13:1). All these references to the apostles' (including the author's) intimate knowledge of Jesus ought to boost the readers' confidence in the reliability of that witness. The apostles literally know what (or whom) they're talking about!

This establishes the connection between Jesus—the central person in the apostles' message—and the gospel message itself, more broadly conceived as the good news of salvation in Christ (the likely referent of the neuter relative pronouns in 1:1; cf. 1:5: "This is the message," *angelia*). Also, just as in the Gospel, John here refers to Jesus somewhat obliquely in terms of "life": the apostles' witness concerns "the word of life" (1:1); that "life" was manifested, and they've seen it and testify to it and proclaim the "eternal life" that previously was with the Father and subsequently was manifested in their midst (1:2).

The opening verses of John's first letter are thus a very solemn declaration that the apostolic message is of utmost importance and comes with the highest credibility, authority, and authenticity: the apostolic gospel is grounded in personal knowledge of Jesus Christ that the readers can accept and believe. This is very important, because neither the first readers of 1 John nor we today have had the privilege of physically hearing, seeing, or touching Jesus. All of us have placed our faith in Jesus because of the apostolic witness. If that witness is reliable, our faith is secure; if it is tenuous, our faith is on a shaky foundation. What's more, if received, the apostolic witness fosters fellowship among believers (1:3) and brings joy to the original eyewitnesses (1:4).[5]

Denouncing the False Teachers' Immoral Lifestyle and Denial of Sin (1:5–10)

Having established a close connection with the Gospel, the author continues to speak in terms reminiscent of the opening words of the Gospel. He has already spoken in terms of life (1:1–2; cf. John 1:4); now he speaks of God in terms of light (1:5–7; cf. John 1:5–9). The Genesis narrative tells us that God spoke, "'Let there be light,' and there was light." John here attests that God himself is light; there is no darkness in him at all. This metaphorically refers to God's holiness and moral excellence. By implication, anyone who would have fellowship with God must likewise be holy and morally excellent. This belies the claim, refuted by John in 1:6, of having fellowship with God while living in sin. Not that believers are holy in and of themselves; rather, the blood of Jesus, shed at the cross, cleanses them from all sin (1:7).

Anyone who denies their own sinfulness, John continues, is therefore self-deceived (1:8). While Christians have been forgiven on the basis of trusting in Christ's finished cross-work for salvation, they must still confess their sins (cf. James 5:16). As Jesus explained to Peter when washing his feet in the upper room, he didn't need a full bath (Peter was already saved), but he did need Jesus to wash his feet, symbolizing the cleansing from sin that even believers need to remain in fellowship with God (John 13:6–10). If they confess their sins, God is faithful and just—on the basis of what Christ has

---

5. See William W. Combs, "The Meaning of Fellowship in 1 John," *DBSJ* 13 (2008): 3–16.

done for them—to forgive and cleanse them (1:9). Denying one's own sinfulness is therefore tantamount to making God out to be a liar and is contrary to God's Word (1:10).

Addressing the False Teachers' Denial of Sin and Immoral Lifestyle (2:1-6)

In chapter 2, John tackles in reverse order the two related problems raised in the first chapter, addressing first the problem of the false teachers' denial of sin and then turning to their immoral lifestyle (see outline at the end of this section). The phrase "My little children, I am writing these things to you" marks a transition while at the same time elaborating on the author's previous point (2:1). In fact, John clarifies that his previous comments regarding the reality of sin even in believers' lives was not meant in any way to encourage a cavalier attitude toward sin, along the lines of, "If I sin, God will forgive me." Along similar lines, Paul wrote to the Romans: "What then? Are we to sin because we are not under law but under grace? By no means!" (Rom. 6:15).

In the present case, John categorically states that his intent in writing was to urge believers not to sin. If they do, however—as they surely will, because their sin nature still remains—they now have an "advocate" (*paraklētos*, the only time in John's writings where this term is used with reference to Jesus; elsewhere the term is used with reference to the Holy Spirit; cf. John 14:16, 26) with God the Father: "Jesus Christ the righteous" (2:2). Not only is God righteous (1:9), but Jesus is righteous as well. The fact that God is faithful and righteous means that he accepts the substitutionary sacrifice of Jesus his Son on behalf of sinners.

As John writes, "He [Jesus] is the propitiation [*hilasmos*; elsewhere in the NT only in 4:10; cf. *hilastērion* in Rom. 3:25; Heb. 9:5; cf. *hilaskomai* in Luke 18:13; Heb. 2:17] for our sins," adding, "and not for ours only but also for the sins of the whole world" (2:2). "Propitiation" means the turning away of God's wrath toward sin. As John writes in his Gospel, "Whoever believes in the Son has eternal life; whoever does not obey the Son shall not see life, but the wrath of God remains on him" (3:36). Conversely, anyone who believes "does not come into judgment, but has passed from death to life" (5:24). This means that Jesus's sacrifice is *potentially* able to atone for the sins of the entire world, though it does so *effectively* only for those who trust Christ and accept his sacrifice on their behalf.[6]

---

6. In apparent contradiction of the third tenet of Calvinism, the "L" in TULIP—namely, "limited atonement."

In apparent chiastic fashion, as mentioned, John proceeds to address the problem with which he started. He has already addressed the false teachers' denial of their own sinfulness (and thus also their denial that they need a remedy for sin—namely, the atonement and propitiation accomplished by Christ's cross-death on their behalf); now he returns to the related problem of their immoral lifestyle, which belies their profession of faith. John previously wrote that anyone who claims to be without sin makes *God* a liar (1:10); now he says that anyone who professes to know God but fails to keep his commandments is a liar *himself* (2:4). In fact, if anyone lives a Christlike life, this furnishes evidence that they are truly his follower. Conversely, if anyone lives in immorality, one may legitimately question whether such a person is truly a Christian, even if they claim they are (2:5–6).

Two Problems Addressed in 1 John 1:5–2:6

Problem 1	Immoral lifestyle (1:5–7)
Problem 2	Denial of sin (1:8–10)
Problem 2	Denial of sin (2:1–3)
Problem 1	Immoral lifestyle (2:4–6)

The New Commandment (2:7–11)

In 2:5, John wrote that "the love of God" is perfected in those who keep his commandments (echoing Jesus's teaching). Now he is developing this thought further in reference to Jesus's statement that he gave his followers a "new commandment"—to love one another as he loved others (John 13:34–35). John labels this as both a new commandment and yet not a new commandment, presumably because the command to love one's neighbor was already given in the OT (Lev. 19:18, cited in Matt. 22:39 and parallels; an old commandment), and yet Jesus upped the ante by requiring his followers to love one another *as he had loved them* (a new commandment). Again, John makes this statement in reference to the false teachers, who apparently claimed to "be in the light" (i.e., professed to be Christians) and yet "hated their brother" (2:9–11). This, John points out, is inconsistent with professing faith in the one who loved us so much that he gave his life for us on the cross and who told his followers to love one another as he had loved them. In a paradoxical turn of phrase, John writes that such a person is in moral darkness—he moves about in the dark and can't see where he's going, "because the darkness has blinded [!] his eyes" (2:11).

Messages to Older and Younger Believers; Do Not Love the World (2:12–17)

John now turns to specific instructions for different groups of believers identified by age or life stage of maturity ("children"—"fathers"—"young men"). In the first three instances, he uses the present-tense form of *graphō*, "I am writing" (2:12–13). Then, in his second set of instructions to the same groups, he switches to the aorist (global) tense form of the same word, "I write" (2:13c–15). According to Greek verbal aspect—that is, the way in which a given action is subjectively perceived by a given writer or speaker—John first casts his writing in the imperfective (ongoing) aspect before changing his perspective to the perfective (global or universal) aspect. That is, he first portrays the writing as ongoing and then portrays it in a more matter-of-fact, descriptive manner.[7]

John's Special Messages to Different Groups in 1 John 2:12–14

1 John	Group	Message
2:12	Little children	Your sins are forgiven for his name's sake
2:13		You know the Father
2:13	Fathers	You know him who is from the beginning
2:14		You know him who is from the beginning
2:13	Young men	You have overcome the evil one
2:14		You are strong, the word of God abides in you, and you have overcome the evil one

The message for mature believers is constant: you know the Lord. The message for new believers is progressive: your sins are forgiven, and you know the Father. The message for young men is also progressive and developed the most: you are strong, God's Word lives in you, and you've overcome Satan, "the evil one." All three sets of messages are extremely encouraging and reassuring. Especially young men will be greatly encouraged to know that they can be strong in God's grace, that through the indwelling Spirit they have God's Word living in them (as they've previously read and memorized it), and that, while not having achieved sinless perfection (which is unattainable in this life and awaits the eternal state), they have achieved substantial victory over Satan and thus can live as those who, in Paul's words, are "more than conquerors through him who loved us" (Rom. 8:37).

7. On Greek verbal aspect, see chap. 7 in Andreas J. Köstenberger, Benjamin L. Merkle, and Robert L. Plummer, *Going Deeper with New Testament Greek* (Nashville: B&H Academic, 2016), and the additional resources cited there.

Without transition, John exhorts (one assumes) not merely young men but all believers not to "love the world or the things in the world" (2:15). Materialism—being attached to one's possessions and material things—is antithetical to a believer's spiritual focus and orientation, which prioritizes one's hope and prospect of life beyond the grave and thus eschews undue attachment to material things, which detracts from one's ability to follow the Lord wherever he might lead and call a person to go on mission with and for him. Love of the world and love of the Father are mutually exclusive; if our affections are fixed on the Father, we will love the world less and subordinate our desires for material wealth and prosperity to our service of him and love for him.

John gives two reasons to substantiate his contention that believers should shun love of this world: (1) the things of this world—the triad "the desires of the flesh and the desires of the eyes and pride of life" (the same triad that led Eve to transgress God's command at the fall; cf. Gen. 3:6)—are not from the Father; (2) the world is passing away, whereas those who do God's will are going to live forever (2:16–17). As Jesus said, "No one can serve two masters, for either he will hate the one and love the other, or he will be devoted to the one and despise the other. You cannot serve God and money" (Matt. 6:24; cf. Matt. 6:25–34). In his Gospel, John writes that "*God so loved the world, that he gave his only Son*" (John 3:16). Here, he urges believers *not to love the world*. Are these two passages contradicting each other? Not at all. In the second passage, God loved the world in all its sinfulness and sent his Son to die for us; in the first passage, we're told not to love the world in the sense of getting attached to it rather than God.

The False Teachers as Antichrists (2:18–27)

As previously in 2:1 ("My little children") and 2:7 ("Beloved"), John indicates a change of topic with the introductory expression, "Children" (2:18). "It is the last hour" immediately indicates a turn to a very serious topic.[8] His readers have heard that the antichrist (in the singular) is coming, the final evil individual who will set himself up in opposition to Christ but who will ultimately fail. But already now, John tells his readers, many antichrists (in the plural) have appeared. These many figures, forming a long trajectory of spiritual opposition to God and his purposes, will culminate in the climactic

8. See G. K. Beale, "The Old Testament Background of the 'Last Hour' in 1 John 2,18," *Bib* 92 (2011): 231–54, who proposes Dan. 8:12 as the primary background passage for "the last hour" in 1 John 2:18.

figure called "the antichrist," who will epitomize evil and opposition to God and his Christ (see the discussion of the book of Revelation below).

In light of this, John now squarely addresses a situation that in all probability would have been fresh in his readers' minds. Most likely, they were still reeling from the recent departure of false teachers, possibly even elders in that church or group of churches, who had wreaked havoc in the church with their teaching. "They went out *from* us," John writes—that is, those people had until recently been members, if not leaders, of that church in good standing. But, John continues, "they were not [truly] *of* us." He explains that if those individuals "had been of us, they would have continued with us. But they went out, that it might become plain that they all are not of us" (2:19).

In other words, by their leaving, these false teachers revealed that they had never been true members of that church, and in fact were not even true Christians, in the first place—otherwise, John contended, they would still be members of that church at the time he wrote the letter. John is writing this primarily to reassure his readers that if they were shaken by the departure of the false teachers, maybe even questioning their own assurance of salvation, they need not doubt their own salvation. The reason for this is that they have an "anointing" (*chrisma*) from "the Holy One" (presumably God or the Holy Spirit).

John, perhaps ominously, adds, "and you all have knowledge" (2:20).[9] This may imply that the false teachers—who had now left—had claimed special insight not accessible to ordinary believers, which may have intimidated those believers and made them question whether they were in fact true Christians (or at least may have made them feel like second-tier Christians, inferior to those who claimed special knowledge). Not so, seems to be what John is telling those believers—you have the Holy Spirit, and thus you all know (2:20–21)! The prototypical Christian heresy, John contends, is the denial that Jesus is the Messiah. In fact, John's entire Gospel was written to demonstrate that Jesus is the Messiah and Son of God (cf. John 20:30–31).[10]

---

9. Some believe that John wrote to oppose an early Christian heresy known as "Gnosticism" (from the Greek word for "to know"), which held that people were saved by special knowledge rather than by the blood of Christ. In fact, this would explain much of John's response to the false teaching. However, Gnosticism as a full-fledged Christian heresy did not form until the second century AD, so that most scholars today speak of an early form of gnostic teaching or proto-Gnosticism (a precursor). Others have challenged the Gnostic background of 1 John; see esp. Streett, *They Went Out from Us.*

10. Cf. Matthew D. Jensen, "John Is No Exception: Identifying the Subject of εἰμί and Its Implications," *JBL* 135 (2016): 341–53, who argues that the subject of εἰμί in John 20:31; 1 John 2:22; 4:15; 5:1; and 5:5 is the articular noun and that the five clauses answer the Jewish question about the identity of "the Christ, the Son of God."

What's more, John also asserts the essential and unbreakable unity of Father and Son (cf. John 10:30); denying one is thus tantamount to denying the other (2:22–23). The readers should therefore hold on to the teaching they heard "from the beginning" and so remain in both Father and Son and receive eternal life (2:24; cf. 1:1; 2:14; again, cf. John 20:30–31). Concluding this section about the false teachers, John makes clear that his purpose for writing is to warn his readers against the false teachers who are trying to deceive them (2:26).

Once more (cf. 2:20), John assures them of the "anointing" they received (2:27)—the Holy Spirit—who teaches them about everything; thus they have no need for any (false) teachers who pretend to be the recipients of special knowledge. If you have the Holy Spirit, John essentially tells his readers, you have all you need; he will be your teacher. Of course, this doesn't mean that there is no room for human teachers and pastors; God gave the church teachers and pastors (Eph. 4:11) to equip believers in the Word of God and for the work of the ministry. John's point here is merely that believers have no need for teachers who claim to have special, extrabiblical knowledge that in effect contradicts what the Bible is saying.

Remain in Him and Purify Yourselves (2:28–3:6)

Repeating Jesus's teaching from the Gospel, John urges his readers to "abide in him" so that they need not shrink back in shame at his return (*parousia*; 2:28). This places their present lives within an end-time context and renders maintaining the readers' spiritual union with Christ in the Holy Spirit absolutely vital. Again reassuring his readers, John asserts that since Jesus is righteous, they can know that everyone who likewise does what is righteous has been spiritually reborn (2:29). As in his Gospel, the "apostle of love" marvels at the love God has lavished on his children in Christ: they're called God's children, and this is what they truly are (3:1; cf. John 1:12). If they're rejected by the world, that's because people in the world don't know God (3:1).

Not only are his readers God's children now; it hasn't yet been "revealed" (*phaneroō*) what they will be, but when Christ will be "revealed" (*phaneroō*; i.e., at the second coming), they'll be like him because they'll see him just as he is (3:2). This is truly an amazing prospect! For this reason, everyone who has this hope (*elpis*) purifies himself (*agnizō*; cf. James 4:8; 1 Pet. 1:22) just as Christ is pure (i.e., holy and free from sin; *agnos*; cf. 1 Tim. 5:22; Titus 2:5; James 3:17; 1 Pet. 3:2). John explains that sin is lawlessness,[11] and Jesus "was

---

11. Colin G. Kruse, "Sin and Perfection in 1 John," *FM* 23 (2005): 23–33, contends *anomia* in 3:4 doesn't conceive of sin as violation of the Mosaic law but rather as opposition to and

revealed" (*phaneroō*; i.e., came for the first time) to take away sins (cf. John 1:29, 36); in fact, there is no sin in him (3:4–5).[12] For this reason, no one who remains in Jesus continues in sin. Conversely, anyone who continues in sin doesn't truly know Jesus (3:6).

The Children of the Devil and the Hatred of the World (3:7–17)

Reiterating and further developing his earlier point (cf. 2:29), John tells his readers that a person's conduct reveals their true identity: those who do what is right are righteous as Jesus is; those who characteristically sin show that they are children of the devil (3:8). By making his statement categorically in black-and-white fashion in his vintage spiritual radicalism, John emphasizes that there is ultimately no middle ground: either a person has been spiritually reborn and as a result characteristically does what is right (though not without sin), or they're controlled by their sinful nature and thus show that they're still under the control of the devil, who "has been sinning from the beginning" (3:8). This refers both to Satan's sin at the beginning of time (cf. Gen. 3) and to the fact that Satan's very nature has been irredeemably corrupted by sin.

Again, John here echoes the teaching of Jesus, who made the exact same argument vis-à-vis his opponents decades earlier during his earthly ministry (cf. John 8:31–47). The very reason why Jesus came, John observes, was to destroy the devil's works (3:8). If anyone has been born of God, he cannot continue living in sin because God's "seed" (*sperma*) remains in him (presumably, the Holy Spirit). The simple diagnostic tool John gives his readers is therefore this: anyone who doesn't characteristically live a righteous life is not truly a believer—nor, John adds, is anyone who doesn't love his "brother" (most likely, his fellow believer, though possibly also his fellow human beings, whether Christians or not; 3:10).

At the beginning of this letter, John wrote, "This is the message we have heard from him . . . : *that God is light, and in him is no darkness at all*" (1:5). Now, John writes similarly, "For this is the message that you have heard from the beginning: *that we should love one another*" (3:11). In fact, John asserted both of these truths in his Gospel (1:4, though there with reference to Jesus; 13:35–36). From these twin theological truths, John deduces that (1) claiming to be a Christian and indulging in an immoral lifestyle is an impossibility and

---

rebellion against God, similar to that of Satan; those who claim to know God, yet persist in sin, don't truly know God but are in league with Satan. The use of *anomia* provides an important criterion for distinguishing the "children of God" from the "children of the devil."

12. In the original, the statement is even more emphatic, as the word order reads literally, "*sin* [emphasized] in him there is not."

(2) claiming to be a Christian while failing to care for one's fellow believers is an impossibility as well.

Believers shouldn't be like Cain, who murdered his brother Abel because he resented him for his righteous deeds (3:12; cf. Gen. 4:8).[13] Nor should they be surprised that the world hates them (3:13). They know they've "passed out of death into life" (3:14; cf. John 5:24) because they love others. Conversely, if they don't love, they remain in a state of spiritual death. Whoever hates others, spiritually speaking, is a murderer (!), and no murderer has eternal life (3:15). Jesus showed what true love looks like when he gave his life for us; we should do the same for others (at least figuratively speaking; 3:16). Yet whoever has it in his power to help a person in need and closes his heart toward him shows that he doesn't have God's love in himself (3:17).[14]

Love One Another in Deed and Truth (3:18-24)

Building on his challenging question in the previous verse, John urges his readers to practice their Christian faith by expressing their love for others in tangible ways (3:18). Once again striking a note of reassurance and encouragement, he tells his readers that even where their hearts may condemn them, their omniscient God is greater than their hearts. And if their hearts *don't* condemn them, and they do what he commands, they can have confidence in prayer. Boiling down the Christian faith to its core essentials, John writes that God's commandment is this: believe in Jesus Christ, God's Son, and love one another, in keeping with Jesus's own command (3:23). In this way, believers will remain in God, and he in them—through the Holy Spirit, whom God has given to believers (3:24).

The Need for Discernment (4:1-6)

The recent departure of the false teachers (2:19) ought to be a lesson for these believers. For this reason, John urges them not to "believe every spirit" but to test (*dokimazō*; cf. 1 Thess. 5:21) the spirits to determine whether they are in fact from God; for there are many false prophets (*pseudoprophētai*; cf. Acts 13:6; 2 Pet. 2:1) in the world, in keeping with Jesus's prediction (4:1; cf. Matt. 24:11, 24; Mark 13:22). The obvious question is, What should be on the test? John at once supplies the answer: every spirit that confesses Jesus as

---

13. The reference to Cain and his brother is one of the few explicit instances of the use of the OT in John's letters.

14. Jesus had made the same point in the parable of the good Samaritan (Luke 10:25–37).

Messiah—"that Jesus Christ has come in the flesh"—in keeping with John's core message conveyed in his Gospel (cf. John 20:30–31), is from God, while every spirit that denies that Jesus is Messiah is not from God (4:2–3). In essence, "spirit" in this paragraph refers either to the Holy Spirit or to demonic spirits.

This is a very simple diagnostic strategy indeed. In fact, the core of every Christian heresy and departure from orthodoxy centers on a denial of the Bible's teaching regarding Jesus's person and/or work: his full humanity and/or his full divinity, his cross-work, or some other doctrine related to Jesus.[15] In this way, these false prophets exhibit the "spirit of the antichrist," an end-time figure who will come and set himself up boldly as a counterfeit Messiah and oppose the true Messiah and God himself (4:3; Paul calls him "the man of lawlessness," 2 Thess. 2:1–12). But while the appearance of the antichrist (in the singular) is yet to come, the *spirit* of the antichrist is already at work in false teachers and prophets who stake false claims about themselves and about Jesus Christ—that spirit, John asserts, "is in the world already" (4:3).

Again, John quickly switches to a mode of encouragement, reassuring his readers that they are from God (i.e., they're born of God and are his true spiritual children) and thus have overcome those who exhibit the spirit of the antichrist—for God, who is in them through his Holy Spirit, is greater than the spirit in the world (4:4). These false prophets are of the world and speak of the world, and thus the world listens to their teaching. Conversely, John and the apostles—and the readers as well—are from God, so true believers listen to them while people in the world don't (4:5–6). This is the diagnostic test by which we know if another person is controlled by the "Spirit of truth" or "the spirit of error"—whether they listen to us and our message about Jesus Christ, the Messiah (4:6).[16]

God Is Love: Perfect Love (4:7–21)

As at previous junctures in the letter (2:7; 3:2), and especially in this section of the letter (see 3:21; 4:1 above; 4:11 below), John addresses his recipients with the designation "Beloved," which is entirely fitting as his exhortation

15. See Andreas J. Köstenberger, "Orthodoxy," in *The Encyclopedia of Christian Civilization*, 4 vols., ed. George Thomas Kurian (Oxford: Blackwell, 2011), 1735–43.

16. Note that similar language—"the spirit of truth and the spirit of error"—is also found in the Dead Sea Scrolls. For discussions of parallels, see T. A. Hoffman, "1 John and the Qumran Scrolls," *BTB* 8 (1978): 117–25; and Marie-Émile Boismard, "The First Epistle of John and the Writings of Qumran," in *John and the Dead Sea Scrolls*, ed. James H. Charlesworth (London: J. Chapman, 1972), 156–65.

is bound up with the assertion that God is love and that believers ought to live a life of love.[17] God is the source of love, and whoever truly loves the way God does thereby proves that he is spiritually reborn and knows God (4:7). Conversely, anyone who doesn't love thereby proves that he doesn't know God because God isn't merely the *source* of love; he *is* love in his essential being (4:8). If anyone therefore lives outside the sphere of love, he also lives outside the sphere of God.

Yet God's love is not merely a feeling or a matter of believing assertion; God backed up his love with action, just as believers are urged to do (3:18), in that he "sent his only Son [*huios monogenēs*] into the world" to give us life (4:9; cf. John 1:14, 18; 3:16, 18). As John wrote in his Gospel, "God so loved the world, that he gave his one and only Son, that whoever believes in him should not perish but have eternal life" (John 3:16). The crucified Christ thus provides a concrete demonstration of God's love. Just as Jesus has "given a full account" of God (John 1:18) and just as whoever looks at Jesus looks at the Father (John 14:9), whoever looks at Jesus's life and his propitiatory sacrifice on the cross (4:10; cf. 2:2) looks at the God of love, the God who himself is love.

To clarify: it is not that *we* loved *God*, but that *he* loved *us*—"We love because he first loved us" (4:19; cf. 4:10). In light of God's love for each of us, we should extend that same kind of love toward others (4:11). In his Gospel, John wrote that "no one has ever seen God; the only God, who is at the Father's side, he has made him known" (John 1:18). Here, he writes, in sort of a sequel, "No one has ever seen God; if we love one another, God abides in us and his love is perfected in us" (4:12) (the word for "perfected" is *teteleiōmenē*; cf. Jesus's cry on the cross, "It is finished," *tetelestai*; John 19:30). While no one can see God because he is spirit—though we shall be like him because we shall see him as he is (3:2)—people can see God through the love believers have for one another.

In the early church, believers voluntarily shared their possessions (Acts 4:32–37), and the church father Tertullian famously wrote that unbelievers said of first-century Christians, "'Look,' they say, 'how they love one another . . . and how they are ready to die for each other.'"[18] Jesus himself told his followers, "By this all people will know that you are my disciples, if you have love for one another" (John 13:35). That said, it is truly astonishing that John

---

17. On John's theology of love, see Andreas J. Köstenberger, *A Theology of John's Gospel and Letters: The Word, the Christ, the Son of God*, BTNT (Grand Rapids: Zondervan, 2009), chap. 13. For a succinct listing of dimensions of love in 1 John, see I. H. Marshall, *New Testament Theology: Many Witnesses, One Gospel* (Downers Grove, IL: InterVarsity, 2004), 539.

18. Tertullian, *Apologeticum* 39.7, in *Tertullian: Apology. De Spectaculis*, trans. T. R. Glover, Loeb Classical Library 250 (New York: Putnam's Sons, 1931), 177.

can write that God's love is *perfected* in believers. In his love, God sent his one and only Son; in his love, that Son—Jesus—gave his life for us on the cross; and in his love, and in the Holy Spirit (cf. Rom. 5:5), believers can love one another and thus God's love can be perfected in them!

It is to this Spirit that John turns next. The Spirit in us is yet another tangible piece of evidence that we are God's children (4:13). John previously spoke of believers having been "anointed by the Holy One" (2:20, 27). What is more, John and the apostles bear witness that the Father has sent the Son as "the Savior of the world" (4:14; cf. John 4:42). In fact, anyone who confesses Jesus as Messiah (4:2) and Son of God (4:15) abides in spiritual union with God, and thus also in (his) love (4:16). In this way, "God" and "love" are virtually synonymous (though of course God has numerous other attributes as well). What is more, love perfected among believers also results in confidence on judgment day; perfect love casts out fear (4:17–18; cf. 4:12).

John concludes his train of thought in this section by reiterating the vital importance of brotherly love as proof of the genuineness of one's Christian confession (4:20–21; cf. 3:17–18). Possibly alluding to the false teachers who had recently departed from the congregation (cf. 2:19), John writes that "if anyone says, 'I love God,' and hates his brother, he is a liar; for he who does not love his brother whom he has seen cannot love God whom he has not seen" (4:20). Loving God and loving others are therefore inseparable, as none other than Jesus himself taught, in keeping with OT teaching (4:21; see Matt. 22:35–40 // Mark 12:28–34 // Luke 10:25–28; cf. Deut. 6:5; Lev. 19:18).

Jesus Is the Christ (5:1–12)

As John moves toward a conclusion, he focuses again on evidence that a given person has been reborn spiritually, and he reassures genuine believers that they in fact have eternal life.[19] The new birth has been experienced by all those who believe that Jesus is the Messiah and Son of God (cf. 4:2, 15; 5:5), in keeping with the overriding message of the Gospel (John 20:30–31). Loving God means obeying his commandments, in contrast to the false teachers, who claimed to know and love God while failing to obey his commands (cf. 1:5–6). For true believers, John asserts, obeying God's commands is not burdensome (*barus*), in contrast to the scribes and Pharisees in Jesus's day, who tied up "heavy [*barus*] burdens, hard to bear," and laid them on people's shoulders while themselves being unwilling to bear them (Matt. 23:4).

19. See Matthew Barrett, "Does Regeneration Precede Faith in 1 John?," *MAJT* 23 (2012): 5–18, who argues that texts such as 1 John 5:1 teach that regeneration precedes faith.

The reason for this is that the person who has been spiritually reborn has, like Jesus, overcome (*nikaō*; cf. 2:13, 14; 4:4) the world (5:4–5; cf. John 16:33), for the darkness cannot overcome the light (John 1:4–5). In Christ, our faith (*pistis*, the only instance of the noun "faith" in John's Gospel and letters; everywhere else, the verb *pisteuō*, "to believe," is used) enables us to have spiritual victory (*nikē*, not elsewhere in the NT) over Satan and his domain of darkness. Ending the paragraph the way he began, John poses the rhetorical question, "Who is it that overcomes the world except the one who believes that Jesus is the Son of God?" (5:5; cf. 5:1). The implied answer: "No one." But the one who does believe that Jesus is the Son of God does!

The next portion (5:6–12) is devoted to the testimony concerning Jesus Christ, similar to the Gospel, which features a series of (seven) witnesses to Jesus. In the present unit, the noun "testimony" (*martyria*) or the verb "to testify" or "to bear witness" (*martyreō*) occurs nine times in the span of seven verses. In 5:6–8, John asserts that there are three "witnesses" that testify to Jesus. He came not only "by water"—presumably referring to Jesus's baptism at the inception of his messianic ministry—but also "by blood"—his crucifixion. These, then, are two witnesses—water and blood, symbolizing Jesus's baptism and crucifixion—to which a third is added, the Spirit, who is the truth.[20] In this way, God himself has borne testimony concerning his Son—greater than human testimony—which imparts eternal life to all who believe (5:9–12).

Assurance of Eternal Life (5:13–21)

Similar to the Gospel, this letter features a purpose statement near the end: "I write these things to you who believe in the name of the Son of God that you may know that you have eternal life" (5:13; cf. John 20:30–31). This, then, provides the key to understanding John's overall purpose for writing this letter: reassuring his recipients who believe that Jesus is the Messiah and Son of God (as set forth in the Gospel) that they indeed have eternal life (cf. John 3:16).[21] Although the false teachers may have shaken their confidence, perhaps by claiming special supernatural insight, John has assured them that they have

20. Commentators differ in their interpretation of the meaning of "water" and "blood" in this passage. In addition, many versions contain a lengthy but late textual variant, the so-called *Comma Johanneum*, which is almost certainly not original. See Andreas J. Köstenberger, L. Scott Kellum, and Charles L. Quarles, *The Cradle, the Cross, and the Crown: An Introduction to the New Testament*, 2nd ed. (Nashville: B&H Academic, 2016), 920n113.

21. Christopher D. Bass, *That You May Know: Assurance of Salvation in 1 John*, NACSBT (Nashville: B&H, 2008), provides an inductive biblical theology of assurance in 1 John, concluding that assurance is grounded in the work of Christ and supported by obedience.

an "anointing" from God—the Holy Spirit—who teaches them all they need to know (2:20, 27). Whatever the false teachers may have told them, if they are born of God and have the Spirit, they have eternal life.

Not only are believers assured of eternal life; they also have confidence (*parrēsia*; cf. 2:28; 3:21; 4:17) in the here and now that God will answer their prayers (5:15; cf. John 14:13–14). These prayers, of course, are those offered in Jesus's name—Jesus, who is exalted and at the Father's side—and according to his will, to advance his kingdom mission on earth. God will be faithful to supply the believing community with everything it needs to carry out the mission to which he has called it in Christ and for which he has empowered it by the Holy Spirit (cf. John 20:21–22). In this way, believers are taken into the trinitarian loving, united mission, which cannot and will not fail, because it is based on Jesus's finished cross-work—completed in keeping with the will of God the Father, who sent his Son—and empowered by the Holy Spirit, who undergirds believers' witness in the unbelieving, sinful, evil world around them (cf. John 15:26–27).[22]

In conjunction with his statement concerning believers' confidence of answered prayer, John proceeds to issue a brief disclaimer. Such prayer pertains to anyone who has committed "a sin not leading to death." John ominously adds, "There is sin that leads to death; I do not say that one should pray for that" (5:16). Of course, all sin is wrong, but not all sin leads to death—though apparently there is a sin that is so egregious that it does (5:17). Scholars have debated what exactly this sin might be, though consensus has proven elusive. There are several related questions to adjudicate in arriving at a proper interpretation of this difficult passage.[23]

(1) Who is the "brother" referred to in verse 16? Is it a fellow believer (as in the majority of cases in 1 John), or is the reference more broadly to any other human being (cf. 3:17)? If the former, this would mean that a believer could commit a sin so egregious that it results in death, whether in physical or spiritual death (if the latter, he could lose his salvation, which seems unlikely in light of other places in John's writings where John unequivocally affirms the eternal security of the believer; cf., e.g., John 10:28–29).

(2) What kind of "death" is referred to repeatedly in verses 16 and 17? Is it physical or spiritual death? If the former, this would mean that a person

22. On John's mission theology, see esp. Andreas J. Köstenberger, *The Missions of Jesus and the Disciples according to the Fourth Gospel* (Grand Rapids: Eerdmans, 1998).

23. For further detail, see the standard commentaries listed in the bibliography below. For a helpful basic discussion, see John R. W. Stott, *The Letters of John*, rev. ed., TNTC (Grand Rapids: Eerdmans, 1988), 189–93. See also Randall K. Tan, "Should We Pray for Straying Brethren? John's Confidence in 1 John 5:16–17," *JETS* 45 (2002): 599–609.

who commits this sin dies physically as a result of this sin; if the latter, there would be no further room for repentance and salvation, and therefore no more prayers would be needed or encouraged, as these could not be answered.

(3) What is the actual "sin leading to death"? There are several possibilities. Jesus mentioned "blasphemy against the Holy Spirit," which could not be forgiven, most likely his opponents' attribution of Jesus's miracles to the power of Satan (Mark 3:28–30 and parallels). In this way, Jesus argued, his opponents blasphemed the Spirit who empowered Jesus's miracles—and with these words, Jesus implied the deity of the Holy Spirit. Jesus didn't perform his miracles in his own strength, which meant that attributing them to Satan didn't merely blaspheme Jesus; he did them in the power of the Spirit. Therefore, slanderously misidentifying the power behind Jesus's miracles in effect was a way to call the Spirit "Satan"—an offense that, according to Jesus, was unforgivable. This was an extremely serious and powerful shot across the bow in Jesus's confrontation with his opponents who would later go on to have him crucified. Yet, I believe, this sin is inextricably bound up with Jesus's earthly ministry and so is no longer a sin that can be committed by believers today. Therefore, John must have been talking about another kind of sin.

We also see in Paul's letter to the Corinthians that some people in that church failed to wait for their fellow believers in celebrating the Lord's Supper; they impatiently went ahead or otherwise ate and drank the Lord's Supper in an unworthy manner (1 Cor. 11:17–34). As a result, Paul notes, "many of you are weak and ill, and some have died" (v. 30). Apparently, the sin of some in the Corinthian church related to the observance of the Lord's Supper was so egregious that they died a physical death.[24] This presumably didn't mean they lost their salvation; it meant that they died physically, just like believers might die for a number of reasons without losing their spiritual salvation. So, it is possible that John is speaking here about believers (understanding "brothers" in a narrow sense) committing a sin so egregious that it results in physical death (understanding "death" literally rather than spiritually).

Another possibility is that the reference is to an unbeliever (taking "brother" in a broad sense) committing a sin so egregious that it leads to either physical (less likely) or spiritual death, so that prayer is no longer called for. It may indeed be possible for an unbeliever to reject God's self-disclosure and his offer of salvation in Christ in such a way as to make it exceedingly dif-

---

24. Another possible, though admittedly extreme, example is that of Ananias and Sapphira, who lied to the Holy Spirit and were struck dead (Acts 5).

ficult, if not virtually impossible, for such a person to repent and be saved. The warning passages in the book of Hebrews seem to fall in this category. There, the author warns his readers against persistent unbelief such as that displayed by Israel's wilderness generation; as a result, people ended up being barred from entry into the promised land. By analogy, the author urged his readers (who likewise had received a considerable amount of divine revelation) not to "neglect such a great salvation" (Heb. 2:3–4). In fact, anyone who in effect "recrucifies" Christ has lost all hope of salvation (Heb. 6:4–6). Similarly, John may here speak of an unbeliever having rejected God and Christ in such an egregious manner that future repentance and salvation are impossible, and as a result John may be advising against praying for them. The sobering reality is that no one should keep brazenly sinning, presuming they can always repent later. Such a person may one day cross the threshold beyond which their eternal condemnation is certain and not even prayer can any longer be effective.

In the end, we may not have sufficient information to determine with certainty what John had in mind when he spoke of a "sin that leads to death." To summarize the available interpretive options, John could be referring to a believer sinning, leading to spiritual death (causing his loss of salvation), a rather unlikely option (cf. John 10:28–29); he may be referring to a believer sinning, leading to physical death (cf. 1 Cor. 11:17–34), which is possible; or he may be referring to an unbeliever sinning, leading to physical (unlikely) or spiritual death (though not the blasphemy of the Holy Spirit, which cannot be committed today; cf. warning passages in Hebrews), which is possible and perhaps most likely.

Interpretations of "Sin That Leads to Death" (1 John 5:16-17)

1. Believer sins, leading to spiritual death (loss of salvation): unlikely
2. Believer sins, leading to physical death: possible
3. Unbeliever sins, leading to physical death: unlikely
4. Unbeliever sins, leading to spiritual death
   a. Blasphemy of Holy Spirit: cannot be committed today
   b. Warning passages: possible and perhaps most likely

Following John's statement pertaining to the assurance of answered prayer (except in cases where a person has committed the mysterious "sin that leads to death"), verses 18, 19, and 20 each start with the phrase "we know" (*oidamen*). John thus concludes the letter—not a conventional epistolary ending—with three certainties believers can enjoy:

- They know that anyone who has been spiritually reborn doesn't continue in sin, but "he who was born of God" (Jesus) protects him, and "the evil one" (Satan) won't be able to touch him.
- They know that they are "from God" (i.e., God's children), while the entire world is under the power and control of "the evil one."
- They know that the Son of God has come and given them insight (*dianoia*) to know the true God in his Son, the Lord Jesus Christ, who himself is "the true God and eternal life," one of the loftiest affirmations of Jesus's deity in all of the NT.

Almost as an afterthought, John adds, "Little children, keep yourselves from idols" (5:21).[25] He previously urged his readers not to love the world or the things in the world (2:15). God—and thus John as well—is supremely concerned about our hearts. He wants our affections to be exclusively devoted to him rather than to be misdirected toward any idol or false object or worship. In these final verses, John thus shows clear awareness that believers' lives are lived in the context of intense spiritual warfare for their hearts, souls, and minds, in a world controlled by Satan, "the evil one." This calls for spiritual protection, fierce loyalty to Christ (whose blood covers believers' sins), a keen awareness of spiritual realities such as believers' spiritual rebirth, and the active presence of the Holy Spirit.

See after 2 and 3 John for a combined bibliography of 1, 2, and 3 John.

---

25. See Benjamin L. Merkle, "What Is the Meaning of 'Idols' in 1 John 5:21?," *BSac* 169 (July–August 2012): 328–40, who argues that those who don't pass the threefold test of belief, righteousness, and love are in danger of idol worship, creating a false religion.

CHAPTER SIX

2 and 3 John

Introduction

Author, Date, and Genre

Since John's other two letters—commonly referred to as 2 and 3 John—are both considerably shorter than 1 John, we'll discuss them together in this chapter. What unites both letters is the fact that they open with the same designation, "The elder," unlike 1 John, which lacks such a designation and subsumes the author under the apostolic "we" (e.g., 1 John 1:1–4). As briefly mentioned in our discussion of 1 John above, in light of the stylistic unity and early church tradition we have every reason to believe that the person writing 1 John is none other than the apostle John, the author of the Gospel, and that "the elder" writing 2 and 3 John is that same apostle, here alluding to his advanced age as well as his responsibility of oversight of these congregations ("elder" in the original can mean both "church leader" and "old man").

Some distinguish between John the apostle and John the elder, as if the latter were a different person from the former, but this distinction is based on a doubtful reference in one church father's writings (Papias, by way of Eusebius) that is open to a variety of interpretations.[1] Much simpler and more likely is the conclusion that one individual—John the apostle—wrote not only the Gospel but also all three letters (as well as Revelation; see below).

---

1. See the discussion in Andreas J. Köstenberger, L. Scott Kellum, and Charles L. Quarles, *The Cradle, the Cross, and the Crown: An Introduction to the New Testament*, 2nd ed. (Nashville: B&H Academic, 2016), 353, with further reference to D. A. Carson and Douglas J. Moo, *An Introduction to the New Testament*, 2nd ed. (Grand Rapids: Zondervan, 2005), 233–34.

Thus not only do 2 and 3 John have a common author, but that author assumes the same stance toward his readers, that of "elder" statesman in the church, whether formally or more informally (i.e., John most likely was not an actual "presbyter" or "bishop" in a later, second- or third-century sense). These similarities aside, 2 John is addressed to "the elect lady and her children, whom I love in truth" (2 John 1), whereas 3 John is addressed to "the beloved Gaius, whom I love in truth" (3 John 1). Most commentators believe, correctly I think, that the "elect lady and her children" to whom John addresses his second letter are not a literal woman and her children (indeed, it would be slightly odd for John to affirm his love for an actual woman at the outset of the letter) but that the expression refers metaphorically to a mother church and her daughter churches.

Not only are the recipients of 2 and 3 John different; the circumstances surrounding these two letters are different (albeit related) as well. In 2 John, the issue seems to be that of extending hospitality to visiting teachers. This is epitomized by the elder's pronouncement in verses 10–11: "If anyone comes to you and does not bring this teaching, do not receive him into your house or give him any greeting, for whoever greets him takes part in his wicked works." Itinerant preachers in the ancient world relied on the hospitality of others, and John is adamant that believers not provide a base of ministry for heretics. In 3 John, John writes to strengthen the hand of "the beloved Gaius." Apparently, John had written to this church before (v. 9), but a dictatorial individual named Diotrephes, "who [liked] to put himself first," had failed to recognize John's authority. What's more, he had refused hospitality to genuine Christian teachers and even had stopped those who did show them hospitality and put them out of the church (v. 10)!

As mentioned in the discussion of 1 John above, all three of John's letters were probably written in the late 80s or early 90s AD, most likely following the writing of John's Gospel, which seems presupposed. While 1 John is rather lengthy and doesn't follow the typical epistolary format, both 2 and 3 John conform to the standard letter template of the day and are quite similar to everyday letters that would have been written and would have fit on a single papyrus sheet. Most likely, similar to the Gospel and 1 John, these letters were written in the vicinity of Ephesus. Like 1 John, 2 and 3 John would have been written to congregations under John's jurisdiction or at least overall influence, churches that by and large respected him (Diotrephes notwithstanding) because of his apostolic stature and long-standing testimony to Christ.

Structure

Unlike the structure of 1 John, that of 2 and 3 John, respectively, is comparatively simple. Second John opens with the standard formula, "Sender to recipient, greeting," or, in 2 John's case, "The elder to the elect lady and her children, . . . Grace, mercy, and peace . . . " (2 John 1–3). The body extends from verse 4 to verse 11 and includes an encouragement to love, a reference to "many deceivers" and anticipations of the antichrists that "have gone out into the world" who do not confess Jesus as the Messiah (v. 7), an exhortation not to "[go] on ahead" but to "[abide] in the [apostolic] teaching" (v. 10), and a warning not to receive traveling teachers who don't preach the true Christian gospel (vv. 10–11). The letter closes with the "elder" expressing hope of an upcoming visit and extending a final greeting (vv. 12–13).

Third John starts out with an even terser introduction following the template, "Sender to recipient" (no opening greeting; v. 1). Similar to the paragraph breaks in 1 John (see outline on page 173), the respective sections of 3 John are introduced by the address "Beloved" (vv. 2, 5, 11) or a reference to what John has written ("I have written something to the church," v. 9). The first such section utters the customary wish for good health and recalls a previous occasion "when the brothers came and testified to [Gaius's] truth" (v. 3). The second subunit then affirms the recipient in extending hospitality to visiting teachers (vv. 5–8). After interjecting a paragraph on the unpleasant opposition put up by Diotrephes (vv. 9–10), John returns to positive instruction and commends a man named Demetrius (vv. 11–12). As does 2 John, 3 John closes with a reference to the elder's express desire to visit the church in person soon, and brief final greetings.

Structure of 2 John

2 John	Content
1–3	Opening greeting
4–11	Warning not to extend hospitality to itinerant false teachers
12–13	Closing greeting ("Though I have much to write to you")

Structure of 3 John

3 John	Content	Introductory Phrase
1	Opening greeting	
2–4	Opening well-wish and commendation	Beloved
5–8	Continued commendation of faithfulness	Beloved
9–10	Denunciation of dictatorial Diotrephes	I have written something
11–12	Commendation of Demetrius	Beloved
13–15	Closing greeting	I had much to write to you

Central Message

The central message of 2 John is that believers shouldn't extend hospitality to itinerant false teachers and thereby give them a platform for their operation. They should be discerning and only support those servants of Christ who teach sound doctrine and are worthy of church support.

The central message of 3 John is that believers should continue to extend hospitality to genuine servants of Christ, who faithfully preach the gospel. In this way, 3 John encourages and affirms on the positive side what 2 John warns against on the negative side, and 2 and 3 John together present a unified message: support orthodox teachers but shun heretical ones!

2 John: Don't Provide a Base for False Teachers

Opening Greeting (1–3)

John's second epistle, as mentioned, follows the standard format for ancient letters and consists of a brief introduction (1–3), a body whose main burden is to urge the readers not to extend hospitality to itinerant false teachers (4–11), and a closing greeting (12–13). The "elder"—most likely the apostle John—is writing to the "elect lady and her children" (presumably, a mother church and several daughter churches). Most conspicuous is John's repeated mention of "truth" in the opening verses (twice in v. 1 and once each in vv. 2, 3, and 4), which ominously foreshadows his concern that false teachers not be given safe haven and a platform for their heretical operations in believers' homes. Thus John writes that he "loves" the churches to which he writes "in truth," and not only he but all who "know the truth," on account of "the truth" that remains in them (John and his readers) and will be with them forever (vv. 1–2). The opening well-wish of grace, mercy, and peace in God the Father and Jesus Christ his Son, likewise, is extended "in truth and love" (v. 3). Then, at the outset of the body of the letter, John expresses his great joy upon finding that some of these believers were "walking in the truth" (v. 4).

Body of the Letter (4–11)

At this point, John asks the "dear lady" to whom he writes (most likely, the mother church) to live by the "new commandment" which is really not a new commandment, namely to love one another (v. 5; cf. 1 John 2:7–8). John at once clarifies that love is no license to sin but is inextricably tied to keeping Jesus's commandments, just as Jesus told his followers: "You are my friends if you do what I command you" (John 15:14) and "If you keep my commandments, you will abide in my love" (John 15:10). Living the Christian life is thus not reliance on "cheap grace" or freedom to do whatever one wants; it is being held to a higher standard, which is ultimately grounded in Christ's selfless, sacrificial love for others. This "new commandment," in turn, encompasses and includes all other obligations a Christian might have. Believers have heard this commandment "from the beginning"; now they should live by it (vv. 5–6; cf. 1 John 1:1; 2:7, 13, 14, 24; 3:8, 11).

That said, John now turns to the primary reason for writing—namely, the "many deceivers" (*planoi*) who have "gone out into the world" and who fail to confess "the coming of Jesus Christ in the flesh" (most likely, a shorthand for believing that Jesus is the Messiah and Son of God; cf. John 20:30–31). This, at heart, is the essence of the antagonism of the "deceiver" (*planos*) and the "antichrist" (in the singular). In his first letter, John warned about the operation of the spirit of the antichrist in conjunction with the departure of false teachers, which apparently had left believers shaken, confused, and in need of reassurance (cf. 1 John 2:18–27; 4:1–6). Apparently, false teachers such as these were still threatening the true confession of Jesus in the churches to which John wrote, so that he feels compelled to renew his warning against these individuals.

In particular, John's concern for these believers is that they may not lose what he and his fellow apostles have worked so hard for and that these believers will receive their full reward (*misthos*; elsewhere in John's Gospel and letters only in John 4:36; see also Rev. 11:18; 22:12). During his earthly ministry, Jesus said to some who appeared to have believed him, "*If you abide in my word*, you are truly my disciples" (John 8:31). Sadly, those individuals in short order turned out not to be true followers of him at all. Similarly, John writes here that whoever "goes on ahead [*proagō*] and does not abide in the teaching of Christ, does not have God" (v. 9). Conversely, anyone who does has both Father and Son. Having arrived at his climactic exhortation, therefore, John urges his readers that if anyone comes to them and "does not bring this teaching," they should not welcome him into their house (*oikia*) or even greet him (*chairein*), for by so doing they would share (*koinōneō*) in their evil works (vv. 10–11).

Closing Greeting (12–13)

John concludes his brief letter by announcing an upcoming visit and by sending greetings. The visit will enable him and these believers to converse face-to-face (literally, "mouth to mouth"), which was preferable to written communication. He sends greetings from "the children of your elect sister"— that is, believers in a related daughter church (vv. 12–13).

3 John: Continue to Provide a Base for True Teachers

Opening Greeting (1–4)

This is now the third and final letter written by the apostle John preserved and included in our NT canon. Like the second letter, John's third epistle is likewise said to come from "the elder," presumably referring to the apostle's advanced age at the time of writing. Unlike the second letter, which is written to an entire congregation, 3 John is addressed to a specific individual, a man named Gaius of whom nothing is known apart from what we learn from the present letter. Similar to 2 John, 3 John opens with a reference to the elder loving the recipient "in truth" (v. 1; cf. 2 John 1). The opening wish for good health, both physically and spiritually, reproduces standard epistolary convention in the first century (v. 2). John continues by mentioning his joy when other believers came to him and brought a good report about Gaius's faithful ministry ("your truth, as indeed you are walking in the truth"; v. 3). John's added comment, "I have no greater joy than to hear that my children are walking in the truth" (v. 4), seems to imply that Gaius may be John's spiritual "child," which could mean either that he was converted directly through John's ministry or that John had adopted him as his son in the faith.

Body of the Letter (5–12)

As does verse 2 (the letter opening), verse 5 (the beginning of the body of the letter) starts with the word "beloved" (*agapēte*), referring to Gaius, the recipient of the letter. John goes on to strongly affirm Gaius's efforts on behalf of those brothers, even though they were strangers (*xenoi*), whom he had shown love and sent on their journey "in a manner worthy of God" (vv. 5–6). These brothers—apparently, itinerant evangelists—had embarked on their mission for the sake of "the name" (a shorthand for Jesus Christ) and accepted nothing from "the Gentiles" (i.e., unbelievers; v. 7), which is why they were eminently worthy of church support and of being treated as partners in the work of the gospel—"fellow workers [*synergoi*] for the truth" (v. 8).

Thus, Gaius had done the right and noble thing—supporting those who preached the gospel, even though they were strangers, by extending hospitality to them. While 2 John is aimed at depriving false teachers of a platform in believers' homes, 3 John is aimed at commending a certain individual (Gaius) for supporting faithful teachers of the gospel in their ministry. Apparently, John had previously written to the church, but another man, by the name of Diotrephes, had rejected John's authority, because, as John wistfully remarks, he "loves to put himself first" (*philoprōteuō*, not elsewhere in the NT). Of course, the way of Christ is diametrically opposite—denying oneself and putting others' interests above one's own (Matt. 16:24; Mark 8:34; Luke 9:23; Phil. 2:3–4).

This dictatorial, even rebellious, individual named Diotrephes, John expands, is "talking wicked nonsense" (!) against John and his associates ("talking nonsense" translates the word *phlyareō*, which is unique in the NT; the related adjective *phlyaros* is rendered "gossip" in 1 Tim. 5:13). What's more, not only is Diotrephes spreading malicious gossip about John's intentions and motives; he also refuses to welcome those whom John has sent and even stops others in the church who want to do so. In fact, he even kicks them out of the church! Clearly, that man had quite an attitude and was entirely unfit to lead a church. One thinks of Peter's words to the elders of another church: "Shepherd the flock of God that is among you, exercising oversight, not under compulsion, but willingly, as God would have you; not for shameful gain, but eagerly; *not domineering over those in your charge*, but being examples to the flock" (1 Pet. 5:2–3).

For a third time, John indicates the transition to a new paragraph by the word "beloved," again referring to Gaius (cf. vv. 2, 5). John instructs this dear brother not to imitate evil but to do good. He adds that "whoever does evil has not seen God," presumably referring to the fact that Diotrephes, judging by his atrocious, repugnant behavior, was likely not even a Christian. The silver lining in that whole situation seems to have been another individual named Demetrius, who was well spoken of by everyone, including by "the truth itself" as well as "the elder" (John). Echoing the conclusion to his Gospel, John states, "You know that our testimony is true" (v. 12; cf. John 21:24). That said, we know very little about Demetrius apart from this positive commendation. Perhaps he was the bearer of the letter?

Closing Greeting (13–15)

The closing greeting is closely reminiscent of that in 2 John. John reiterates that he hopes to come for a personal visit in the near future and sends greetings from "the friends" (*philoi*) to "the friends," "by name." All this reveals the close, even intimate nature of relationships among fellow believers in the body of Christ in the early Christian community.

1–3 John: Commentaries

Akin, Daniel L. *1, 2, 3 John*. NAC 38. Nashville: Broadman & Holman, 2001.

Bray, Gerald, ed. *James, 1–2 Peter, 1–3 John*. ACCS 11. Downers Grove, IL: InterVarsity, 2000.

Brown, Raymond E. *The Epistles of John*. AB 30. Garden City, NJ: Doubleday, 1982.

Bruce, F. F. *The Epistles of John*. Grand Rapids: Eerdmans, 1979.

Bultmann, Rudolf. *The Johannine Epistles*. Hermeneia. Translated by R. P. O'Hara with Lane C. McGaughy and Robert Funk. Philadelphia: Fortress, 1973.

Burge, Gary M. *The Letters of John*. NIVAC. Grand Rapids: Zondervan, 1996.

Edwards, Ruth B. *The Johannine Epistles*. NTG. Sheffield: Sheffield Academic, 1996.

Jobes, Karen H. *1, 2, and 3 John*. ZECNT. Grand Rapids: Zondervan, 2014.

Kruse, Colin G. *The Letters of John*. PNTC. Grand Rapids: Eerdmans, 2000.

Lieu, Judith M. *I, II, III John: A Commentary*. NTL. Louisville: Westminster John Knox, 2008.

Marshall, I. Howard. *The Epistles of John*. NICNT. Grand Rapids: Eerdmans, 1978.

Painter, John. *1, 2, and 3 John*. SP 18. Collegeville, MN: Liturgical Press, 2002.

Parsenios, George L. *First, Second, and Third John*. Paideia. Grand Rapids: Baker Academic, 2014.

Schnackenburg, Rudolf. *The Johannine Epistles: A Commentary*. New York: Crossroad, 1992.

Schuchard, Bruce G. *1-3 John*. Concordia Commentary. St. Louis: Concordia, 2012.

Smalley, Stephen S. *1, 2, 3 John*. WBC 51. Waco: Word, 1984.

Stott, John R. W. *The Letters of John*. Rev. ed. TNTC. Grand Rapids: Eerdmans, 1988.

Strecker, Georg. *The Johannine Letters: A Commentary on 1, 2, and 3 John*. Hermeneia. Translated by Linda M. Maloney. Minneapolis: Fortress, 1996.

Thompson, Marianne M. *1-3 John*. IVPNTC. Downers Grove, IL: InterVarsity, 1992.

Van Neste, Ray. "1-3 John." In ESV *Expository Commentary*, vol. 12, *Hebrews–Revelation*, edited by Iain M. Duguid, James M. Hamilton Jr., and Jay Sklar, 411–99. Wheaton: Crossway, 2018.

Yarbrough, Robert W. *1-3 John*. BECNT. Grand Rapids: Baker Academic, 2008.

1–3 John: Articles, Essays, and Monographs

Allman, James E. "First John 1:9: Confession as a Test, but of What?" *BSac* 172 (April–June 2015): 203–21.

Barrett, Matthew. "Does Regeneration Precede Faith in 1 John?" *MAJT* 23 (2012): 5–18.

Bass, Christopher D. *That You May Know: Assurance of Salvation in 1 John*. NACSBT. Nashville: B&H, 2008.

Beale, G. K. "The Old Testament Background of the 'Last Hour' in 1 John 2,18." *Bib* 92 (2011): 231–54.

Cantey, Daniel L. *1 John: On Docetism and Resurrection*. Eugene, OR: Wipf & Stock, 2017.

Carson, D. A. "1–3 John." In *Commentary on the New Testament Use of the Old Testament*, edited by G. K. Beale and D. A. Carson, 1063–68. Grand Rapids: Baker Academic, 2007.

Combs, William W. "The Meaning of Fellowship in 1 John." *DBSJ* 13 (2008): 3–16.

Dodd, C. H. "The First Epistle of John and the Fourth Gospel." *BJRL* 21 (1937): 129–56.

Griffith, Terry. *Keep Yourselves from Idols: A New Look at 1 John*. JSNTSup 233. London: Sheffield Academic, 2002.

———. "A Non-Polemical Reading of 1 John: Sin, Christology and the Limits of Johannine Christianity." *TynBul* 49 (1998): 253–76.

Hill, Charles E. *The Johannine Corpus in the Early Church*. Oxford: Oxford University Press, 2004.

Jensen, Matthew D. *Affirming the Resurrection of the Incarnate Christ: A Reading of 1 John*. SNTSMS 153. Cambridge: Cambridge University Press, 2012.

———. "'Jesus Is the Christ': A New Paradigm for Understanding 1 John." *RTR* 75 (2016): 1–20.

———. "John Is No Exception: Identifying the Subject of εἰμί and Its Implications." *JBL* 135 (2016): 341–53.

———. "The Structure and Argument of 1 John: A Survey of Proposals." *JSNT* 35 (2012): 54–73.

Kellum, L. Scott. "On the Semantic Structure of 1 John: A Modest Proposal." *FM* 23 (2008): 34–82.

Köstenberger, Andreas J. *A Theology of John's Gospel and Letters: The Word, the Christ, the Son of God*. BTNT. Grand Rapids: Zondervan, 2009.

Kruse, Colin G. "Sin and Perfection in 1 John." *FM* 23 (2005): 23–33.

Law, Robert. *The Tests of Life: A Study of the First Epistle of John*. 3rd ed. Grand Rapids: Baker, 1979. First published 1914 by T&T Clark (Edinburgh).

Lieu, Judith. "Us or You? Persuasion and Identity in 1 John." *JBL* 127 (2008): 805–19.

Longacre, Robert E. "Towards an Exegesis of 1 John Based on the Discourse Analysis of the Greek Text." In *Linguistics and New Testament Interpretation*, edited by D. A. Black, 271–86. Nashville: Broadman, 1992.

Merkle, Benjamin L. "What Is the Meaning of 'Idols' in 1 John 5:21?" *BSac* 169 (July–August 2012): 328–40.

O'Neill, J. C. *The Puzzle of 1 John: A New Examination of Origins*. London: SPCK, 1966.

Poythress, Vern S. "Testing for Johannine Authorship by Examining the Use of Conjunctions." *WTJ* 46 (1984): 350–69.

Streett, Daniel R. *They Went Out from Us: The Identity of the Opponents in First John*. BZNW 177. Berlin: de Gruyter, 2011.

Stubblefield, Benjamin S. Book review of *That You May Know: Assurance of Salvation in 1 John*, by Christopher D. Bass, *JETS* 53 (2010): 183–85.

Tan, Randall K. "Should We Pray for Straying Brethren? John's Confidence in 1 John 5:16–17." *JETS* 45 (2002): 599–609.

Thomas, John Christopher. "The Literary Structure of 1 John." *NovT* 40 (1998): 369–81.

von Wahlde, Urban C. *The Gospel and Letters of John*. 3 vols. Grand Rapids: Eerdmans, 2010.

CHAPTER SEVEN

Jude

Introduction

Author, Audience, Date, and Genre

Jude's letter is little known and often neglected. Some have called it "the stepchild" of the NT. Such neglect is not surprising, as Jude's letter is mostly devoted to a rather scathing denunciation of false teachers.[1] Nevertheless, there are also positive features, most notably the exhortation at the outset for his readers to "contend for the faith that was once for all delivered to the saints" (v. 3) and the closing benediction, "Now to him who is able to keep you from stumbling . . ." (vv. 24–25). At a closer look, even the largely negative body of the letter contains many interesting features and lessons to be learned. We'll therefore do well to recognize that God included Jude's letter in the Bible for a reason and we should give the letter the respect it deserves.

That said, one can hardly dispute that Jude ranks among the more "minor voices" in the NT. Unlike the authors of the other letters discussed above—James, Peter, John—Jude is not considered one of the pillars in the early church. While his brother James can confidently start out his letter by identifying himself merely as "James, a servant of God and of the Lord Jesus Christ," expecting his readers to know which of several men with that name is writing this letter, Jude meekly identifies himself as "Jude, a servant of Jesus Christ *and brother of James*" (v. 1). Thus we know that as James's brother, Jude is

---

1. Note, however, that Jude has received increasing attention in recent years. See the literature cited in Andreas J. Köstenberger, L. Scott Kellum, and Charles L. Quarles, *The Cradle, the Cross, and the Crown: An Introduction to the New Testament*, 2nd ed. (Nashville: B&H Academic, 2016), 873n172.

also Jesus's half-brother (Joseph and Mary being their parents) and thus belongs to the earthly family of Jesus. In this way, he shares in the stature that was awarded the family of Jesus in the days of the early church.[2]

We don't know exactly when Jude wrote his letter. If, as is likely and argued by the vast majority of commentators, Peter in 2 Peter adapts large portions of Jude's letter for his own purposes, Jude's letter must have been written prior to 2 Peter.[3] That isn't saying much, however, as most likely 2 Peter was only written in the mid-60s AD. Beyond this, the Jewish nature of Jude's letter—he is steeped not only in the OT but also in several pseudepigraphical writings (i.e., writings not traditionally included in the OT)—places him in even closer proximity to James (who, as discussed above, wrote very early and serves as an exemplar of early Jewish Christianity). Thus it is possible, if not likely, that Jude was written sometime in the 50s AD, which would allow sufficient time for Peter to become aware of the letter and to adapt portions of it in his second letter.[4]

Both the provenance and destination of the letter are unknown. We don't know where Jude wrote it or who his recipients were. What we do know, first, is that Jude candidly acknowledges at the outset that the letter he wrote was not the letter he originally intended to write. His original purpose was to write to them about the salvation he and they had in common, yet he "found it necessary to write appealing to [them] to contend for the faith that was once for all delivered to the saints" (v. 3). Second, we also know quite a bit about the false teachers whom Jude seeks to expose. We know that these people had "crept in unnoticed" into the congregation (v. 4). Jude calls them "hidden reefs at your love feasts, as they feast with you without fear" (v. 12), indicating that they were present at the church's community meals that formed part of their gatherings.

We also know that their key error was that they "pervert[ed] the grace of our God into sensuality" (v. 4); that is, they invoked God's grace so as to indulge in an immoral way of living. In particular, they engaged in sexual immorality, most likely including homosexual acts, as Sodom and Gomorrah had done at feasts (v. 7). Jude's favorite word for describing the opponents is "ungodly" (v. 4); this is likely why he cites from the book of Enoch, which

2. Richard J. Bauckham, *Jude and the Relatives of Jesus in the Early Church* (Edinburgh: T&T Clark, 1990).

3. On the use of Jude in 2 Peter, see Terrance Callan, "Use of the Letter of Jude by the Second Letter of Peter," *Bib* 85 (2004): 42–64; Lauri Thurén, "The Relationship between 2 Peter and Jude: A Classical Problem Resolved," in *The Catholic Epistles and the Tradition*, ed. Jacques Schlosser, BETL 176 (Leuven: Peeters, 2004), 451–60.

4. So, e.g., Richard Bauckham, *Jude, 2 Peter*, WBC 50 (Waco: Word, 1983), 13.

in one short verse contains as many as four references to ungodliness ("to convict all the *ungodly* of all their deeds of *ungodliness* that they have committed in such an *ungodly* way, and of all the harsh things that *ungodly* sinners have spoken against him"; v. 15). We also know that these false teachers were "devoid of the Spirit" (v. 19). Imagine that—calling yourself a Christian and committing homosexual acts! According to Jude, people who do such things are subject to God's severe judgment.

Structure

Jude starts out his letter with the standard opening formula, "Sender to recipient, greetings," or specifically in his case, "Jude, . . . to those who are called, beloved . . . and kept for Jesus Christ: May mercy, peace, and love . . ." (vv. 1–2). Both the opening-section verses 3–4 and the concluding-section verse 20 are addressed to the readers as "Beloved" (*agapētoi*), an address we've also seen surface repeatedly in the letters written by James, Peter, and John above.

The body of the letter extends from verse 5 to verse 19 and proceeds in what many scholars call a Jewish "midrash" or "pesher"—a commentary utilizing various thematically appropriate passages from the Hebrew Scriptures and Second Temple Jewish writings.[5]

These midrashic elements in the body of Jude's letter present themselves as follows:

Jude	Source	Jude	Midrash
5–7	Hebrew Scripture	8–10	In the same way, these people
11	Hebrew Scripture	12–13	These people are
14–15	1 Enoch	16	These people are
17–18	Apostolic prophecy	19	These people are

Reproduced from my contribution on Jude in Andreas J. Köstenberger, L. Scott Kellum, and Charles L. Quarles, *The Cradle, the Cross, and the Crown: An Introduction to the New Testament*, 2nd ed. (Nashville: B&H Academic, 2016), 885.

The major underlying premise in Jude's use of midrash is this: like crime, like punishment. That is, when we look at people in OT times who committed

---

5. See E. Earle Ellis, "Prophecy and Hermeneutic in Jude," in *Prophecy and Hermeneutic in Early Christianity: New Testament Essays*, WUNT 1/18 (Tübingen: Mohr Siebeck, 1978), 221–36, who notes Jude's midrashic method involving the use of prophetic types as central to his rhetorical strategy, structured in the form of source and commentary. See also Bauckham, *Jude and the Relatives of Jesus*, 233, who likens Jude's exegetical method to that of the Qumran community extant in the Dead Sea Scrolls.

the kinds of sins committed by the false teachers in the first century AD, we see what kind of divine judgment such sins incurred. For example, Sodom and Gomorrah engaged in homosexual acts, and both cities were utterly destroyed by God (v. 7). When Korah and his followers rebelled, the ground swallowed them up alive (v. 11).

Jude's argument is clear: Just as those who engaged in sexual immorality and egregious rebelliousness in OT times incurred God's severest judgment, so the false teachers who likewise are sexually immoral and rebellious will incur an equivalent judgment from God. For anyone who believed in the authority of Scripture (and even for those who did not), any such argument would have had considerable potency and rhetorical persuasiveness.

Specifically, Jude's letter most likely presents itself in the form of a chiasm— that is, an ABCDD'C'B'A' pattern. The structure of the letter, therefore, can be diagrammed as follows:[6]

A   Greeting (1–2)
  B   Occasion (3–4)
    C   Reminder (5–7)
      D   The heretics (8–13)
      D' The quote from 1 Enoch (14–16)
    C' Reminder (17–19)
  B' Exhortation (20–23)
A' Doxology (24–25)

Central Message

Jude's central message is that false teachers will be severely punished. God's people should be on the alert and call out such false teachers, who will be known not only by their false teaching but also by their way of life, which fails to match their (false) Christian profession. God's people, watch out for false teachers! And false teachers, watch out for God's judgment! What's more, while Jude holds out little hope for the false teachers themselves, he has great compassion, care, and concern for the victims of those false teachers, as becomes clear in his concluding exhortation for believers to "have mercy on those who doubt" and to "save others by snatching them out of the fire" (vv. 22–23).

---

6. Adapted from Köstenberger, Kellum, and Quarles, *The Cradle, the Cross, and the Crown*, 884. For a slightly different chiastic structure, see Bauckham, *Jude, 2 Peter*, 5–6. See also J. T. Dennison, "The Structure of the Epistle of Jude," *Kerux* 29 (2014): 3–7.

Opening Greeting (1–2)

The author identifies himself in two ways: (1) as a "servant [*doulos*] of Jesus Christ" and (2) as the "brother of James" (v. 1). Jude's identity as a servant of Christ is primary, though as a secondary designation Jude, who is less well known than his brother, links himself with James. "James" and "Judas" or "Jude" were both common names in first-century Palestine; among Jesus's twelve apostles, two bore the name "James" (or "Jacob") and two were named "Judas."[7] There were several additional men named James who featured prominently in the days of Jesus and the early church. There is virtually no doubt that the two individuals referred to here are two of the four half-brothers of Jesus whom the NT identifies as "James and Joseph and Simon and Judas" (i.e., Jude; Matt. 13:55). It is possible that in the Matthean passage the brothers are listed in order from oldest to youngest; if so, James would have been the firstborn (not counting Jesus, of course) and Jude the youngest. Jude is not mentioned elsewhere in the NT, whether the NT epistles or the book of Acts, though as the present letter reveals, he was an active part of the early Christian community.

In characteristic triadic fashion, Jude addresses his letter to believers who are (1) called, (2) beloved in God the Father, and (3) kept for—or by, or in—Jesus Christ (v. 1). Literally, the address in the original Greek reads, "to those in-God-the-Father-beloved-and-in-Jesus-Christ-kept called." In other words, Jude makes the overarching point that believers are called (presumably, by God) and that, as those called, they are beloved in (or by) God and kept in (or by, or for) Jesus Christ. It would be extremely encouraging for these believers—who, as will shortly become evident, are confronted with false teachers in their midst—to be reassured at the outset of the letter that they are called, beloved by God, and kept by or for Jesus Christ. In each case, God is the primary actor: he called those believers, he loves them, and he (or Jesus Christ) keeps them for himself and for that final day. Not only are believers called; they are also loved and guarded by none other than God himself, the one who is sovereign, all-powerful, and eternal (cf. v. 25). The opening greeting, "May mercy, peace, and love be multiplied to you," starts with a wish for "mercy," which may be a significant adaptation and alteration of the standard greeting, as more frequently the greeting is "grace and peace," combining the Greek *charis* and Hebrew *shalom*. This is supported by the fact that the theme of mercy features prominently in the conclusion, where it is mentioned three times in as many verses (vv. 21, 22, 23), alongside the motif of spiritual preservation (v. 24).

---

7. These were James son of Zebedee (brother of John), James son of Alphaeus, Judas son of James, and Judas Iscariot. See Matt. 10:2–4; Mark 3:16–19; Luke 6:14–16; Acts 1:13.

The Occasion (3–4)

In keeping with his opening designation of the recipients as "beloved in God the Father" (v. 1), Jude addresses them as "Beloved" (v. 3). Intriguingly, Jude signals at the outset that he had a change of plans as to his purpose for writing. His original purpose was a positive one—that is, to encourage his readers about their "common salvation"; yet—no doubt because of the threat of the false teachers (cf. v. 4)—he decided it was more urgent to write appealing (*parakaleō*) to them to "contend [*epagōnizomai*] for the faith once for all delivered to the saints" (v. 3). As a result, only the last few verses of the letter are positive and constructive (cf. vv. 17–25), while the bulk of the letter is devoted to exposing and denouncing the false teachers (vv. 5–16; see introduction above). Jude at once elaborates on the reason for his change of plans: the fact that certain individuals have "crept in" (*pareisdy[n]ō*), apparently "unnoticed" (i.e., by stealth), and have upset the congregation. Jude asserts that, first, these individuals were "long ago designated [*prographō*; literally, "written up beforehand"] for this condemnation." In other words, just as the recipients are called by God (v. 1), these false teachers are marked out for final judgment.

Second, they are "ungodly people" (*asebēs*, Jude's "favorite" word for the false teachers, is used both in quotes of the book of 1 Enoch and in the apostolic prophecy in vv. 14–15, 18) who "pervert [literally, "exchange"] the grace of our God[8] into sensuality and deny our only Master and Lord, Jesus Christ" (v. 4). Thus, these individuals have engaged in an unholy exchange, trading God's grace—his wonderful free gift of salvation in Christ—for living for their own pleasure. The term "sensuality" (*aselgeia*) denotes lack of restraint of one's bodily appetites, whether in the form of gluttony or sexual immorality (cf. 2 Cor. 12:21; Gal. 5:19; Eph. 4:19; apparently appropriated by 2 Pet. 2:7; see discussion on 2 Pet. above). They taught and practiced a form of "cheap grace," contending that because God is gracious, they were free to do as they pleased—an utter perversion of the true meaning of grace. As Paul wrote to the Romans, "What then? Are we to sin because we are not under law but under grace? By no means! Do you not know that if you present yourselves to anyone as obedient slaves, you are slaves of the one whom you obey, either of sin, which leads to death, or of obedience, which leads to righteousness?" (Rom. 6:15–16). As Jude devastatingly observed, this unholy exchange on the part of the false teachers constituted a total denial of "our only Master and Lord Jesus Christ."[9] John, in

8. "Our God" may imply that he is the God of Jude and his readers but not that of the false teachers.

9. An instance of the Granville Sharp rule where "Master and Lord" both designate the person of Jesus Christ. Again, note the personal pronoun "our," including Jude and his readers but not the false teachers.

his first letter, had similarly pointed out over against the threat of false teachers that the true test of one's identity (or lack thereof) in Christ was one's actual moral lifestyle (cf., e.g., 1 John 1:5–10).

When Jude, along with other NT writers, pointed out that grace was never meant to set aside God's righteous requirements and expectations, he built on the understanding that the OT law was good, and the problem was not with the law itself but with people's inability to keep the law because of their sinful nature. When Christ, therefore, came to take our sin upon himself and to pay the just penalty for our sin, he set us free from the power of sin and introduced us to the realm of God's grace—not so that we could now sin with impunity and no negative consequences but so that we could now live righteous lives in the power of the Holy Spirit. True believers understand this and in the Spirit desire to live holy, God-pleasing lives; yet unregenerate, insincere opportunists such as Jude's opponents only use the biblical teaching of grace as an excuse for sinning while trying to have their cake and eat it too—claiming to be Christians saved by grace while engaging in sexual immorality. As Jude rightly notes, the future judgment of such individuals is assured, because their conduct makes a mockery of God's grace and Christ's sacrifice.[10]

A Reminder (5–7)

Jude proceeds to remind his readers of three examples of God's judgment recorded in Scripture: (1) the wilderness generation at the exodus (unbelief; v. 5), (2) fallen angels (rebellion against authority; v. 6), and (3) Sodom and Gomorrah (sexual immorality and "unnatural desire"; v. 7; cf. Gen. 19; Rom. 1:26–27).[11] The judgment, respectively, was (1) destruction, (2) eternal chains, and (3) eternal fire (note that Jude here speaks not merely of literal, material fire but of the eternal "fire" of everlasting punishment). As mentioned in the introduction above, Jude here engages in a form of commentary ("midrash") that identifies previous examples recorded in OT Scripture of individuals who sinned and as a result were judged by God, and then he turns to the false teachers who were committing similar sins and thus would face similar judgment.

---

10. See Robert L. Webb, "The Eschatology of the Epistle of Jude and Its Rhetorical and Social Functions," *BBR* 6 (1996): 139–51, who argues that Jude's eschatology highlights past, present, and future judgment and proposes that the rhetorical and social function of Jude's end-time focus is to convince his readers that they won't be judged and to persuade them to judge the false teachers and separate themselves from them.

11. On the use of triplets in Jude, see J. Daryl Charles, "'Those' and 'These': The Use of the Old Testament in the Epistle of Jude," *JSNT* 38 (1990): 109–24.

Old Testament Examples of Sin and Judgment in Jude 5-7

Jude	OT Example	Sin	Punishment
5	Israel's wilderness generation	Unbelief	Destruction
6	Fallen angels	Rebellion	Eternal chains
7	Sodom and Gomorrah	Sexual immorality	Eternal fire

The Heretics (8-13)

The analogy between these OT examples and the false teachers is highlighted by the introductory phrase in verse 8: "Yet in like manner these people also" (see comments on structure in the introduction above). We may infer from Jude's comments here that the heretics claimed special knowledge through dreams. Not only did they engage in immoral conduct and rebel against authority (cf. v. 4 above); they apparently blasphemed angels. At this, Jude cites a pseudepigraphical account from a now-lost passage in a work called *The Assumption of Moses* in which the archangel Michael has a dispute with Satan about the body of Moses.[12] By way of background, the OT indicates that Moses's burial place was unknown (Deut. 34:5–6). In the NT, the Gospels show Moses, along with Elijah, appearing with Jesus at the latter's glorious transfiguration (Matt. 17:1–8; Mark 9:2–8; Luke 9:28–36).

The assumption in some apocryphal literature was that perhaps Moses, if capable of appearing in bodily form at a later time, similar to Elijah, never died. That said, Jude's primary point is that while Michael was in the right, even he, the highest of angels, didn't dare rebuke the devil—Satan being a *fallen* angel notwithstanding—but rather let the Lord do so (v. 9; cf. Zech. 3:1–2). By contrast, these false teachers not only blasphemed angelic creatures; they committed another triadic set of offenses (v. 11): (1) walking "in the way of Cain" (who murdered his brother Abel; Gen. 4); (2) seeking selfish gain in keeping with "Balaam's error" (Num. 22–24; cf. Rev. 2:14); and (3) rebelling like Korah and his companions and therefore perishing (Num. 16). As in the previous triad of examples (vv. 5–7), Jude establishes a typology of sin and judgment from OT examples and applies it to the false teachers along the maxim "similar crime, similar punishment."[13]

---

12. Michael is depicted elsewhere in Scripture as leading the armies of God against Satan and his forces (Dan. 10:21; 12:1; Rev. 12:7; cf. Dan. 10:13). The phrase, "The Lord rebuke you!" in Jude 9 echoes Zech. 3:2 where God rebukes Satan who had accused Joshua the high priest.

13. Cf. Bauckham, *Jude, 2 Peter*, 5, who observes that Jude "applies Scripture to the last days not only as prophecy, but also as typology."

Old Testament Examples of Sin and Judgment in Jude 11

Jude	OT Example	Sin	Punishment
11	Cain	Fratricide	Futile labor; being a fugitive and wanderer
11	Balaam	Greed, treachery	Rebuked by a donkey
11	Korah	Ringleader in rebellion	Ground swallowed him alive

Jude then turns directly to a denunciation of the false teachers, whom he calls "hidden reefs at your love feasts, as they feast with you without fear" (v. 12). This rather chillingly suggests that they were present at *agapē* meals, "love feasts" or communal meals following the church service. They shamelessly threatened to shipwreck the faith of some like a hidden iceberg may cause an ocean liner to sink. At this, Jude unleashes a withering series of invectives, calling the heretics "shepherds feeding themselves; waterless clouds, swept along by winds; fruitless trees in late autumn, twice dead, uprooted; wild waves of the sea, casting up the foam of their own shame; wandering stars, for whom the gloom of utter darkness has been reserved forever" (vv. 12–13).[14] The opponents were self-seeking, failed to bear spiritual fruit, promised but didn't deliver, and were unregenerate, riddled with shame, and doomed to judgment.

The Prophecies from Enoch and the Apostles (14–19)

Jude backs up his denunciation of the false teachers with a prophecy from 1 Enoch (vv. 14–16; cf. 1 Enoch 1:9)—the climax of the entire epistle—and another (otherwise unattested) prophecy by the apostles (vv. 17–18; alluded to in 2 Pet. 3:2–3, who is probably dependent on Jude; see discussion above).[15] Like the above-mentioned Assumption of Moses (v. 9), 1 Enoch is not part of the OT Scriptures but belongs to the pseudepigraphical literature surrounding the mysterious figure of Enoch, "the seventh from Adam." It appears that the book was held in sufficiently high esteem among the recipients that Jude

14. For background, see Matthew S. Harmon, "Jude," in *ESV Expository Commentary*, vol. 12, *Hebrews–Revelation*, ed. Iain M. Duguid, James M. Hamilton Jr., and Jay Sklar (Wheaton: Crossway, 2018), 515–16.

15. On the use of pseudepigraphical material in Jude, see J. Daryl Charles, "Jude's Use of Pseudepigraphical Source-Material as Part of a Literary Strategy," *NTS* 37 (1991): 130–45. On the use of 1 Enoch in Jude, see esp. Matthew Black, "The Maranatha Invocation and Jude 14, 15 (1 Enoch 1:9)," in *Christ and Spirit in the New Testament: Fs. C. F. D. Moule*, ed. Barnabas Lindars and Stephen S. Smalley (Cambridge: Cambridge University Press, 1973), 189–96; Gene L. Green, *Jude and 2 Peter*, BECNT (Grand Rapids: Baker Academic, 2008), 26–33, 101–8; and Carroll D. Osburn, "The Christological Use of 1 Enoch 1:9 in Jude 14, 15," *NTS* 23 (1976–77): 334–41.

chose to cite a pertinent passage from it (just like someone today might cite C. S. Lewis) to drive home his point that the false teachers' judgment for their ungodliness had been predicted and would soon come to pass.

While the prophecy from 1 Enoch focuses on the certainty of God's future judgment on the false teachers' ungodliness, the following prophecy from the apostles focuses on the prediction that in the last time there would be false teachers who would follow their own "ungodly passions" (v. 18). What unites both quotes is the use of the word "ungodly," which has previously been used to describe the heretics. All the way from Enoch to the apostles, God's judgment on the ungodly has been predicted and will surely be meted out on the false teachers. Not only are they divisive and worldly; they lack the Spirit (v. 19). With this, Jude concludes his devastating denunciation of the opponents, as was his purpose for writing (cf. vv. 3–4).

Exhortation (20–23)

In contrast to the false teachers ("But you," v. 20), Jude urges his readers to keep themselves in the love of God (v. 21, the main command; cf. v. 2) by (1) building themselves up (*epoikodomeō*) in their "most holy faith"—the same faith for which they are to contend (cf. v. 3); (2) praying in the Holy Spirit; and (3) waiting for Christ's mercy (cf. v. 2). Not only are they to *wait* for God's mercy to be extended to *them*; they are to *show* mercy toward any in the congregation who doubt (*diakrinō*; note the intensive middle; vv. 21–22), in keeping with Jesus's Beatitude, "Blessed are the merciful, for they shall receive mercy" (Matt. 5:7).[16] Beyond having mercy on some, the readers should try to save others by "snatching" (*harpazō*) them "out of the fire" (presumably symbolizing hell, their eternal destiny if they remain unsaved; contrast the reference to "eternal life" in v. 21). In many of its other NT occurrences, the word "snatch" means a person is picked up or seized and taken (at times supernaturally) to a different location (cf. John 6:15; 10:12, 28, 29; Acts 8:39; 23:10; 2 Cor. 12:2, 4; Rev. 12:5).

This dramatic rescue operation is called for because the false teachers are "hidden reefs" at the love feasts of the congregation (cf. v. 12) and actively seeking to pull people away from the "most holy faith" to their version of "cheap grace" and immorality (cf. v. 4). When believers show mercy toward those who doubt, however, Jude adds, they should do so with holy fear, "hating even the garment stained by the flesh" (v. 23). While entering a burning building and saving a person from being consumed, they must take heed lest

16. See Darian Lockett, "Objects of Mercy in Jude: The Prophetic Background of Jude 22–23," *CBQ* 77 (2015): 322–36.

they themselves perish in the fire. They must be strong enough to rescue those who are perishing and eschew even the paraphernalia of license and sin, or else they will defile themselves in the process. The same principle applies to those today who seek to save those who are engaging in an immoral lifestyle or some other perversion or bondage. When you save a drowning person, you need to make sure they're not pulling you down with them but instead you're pulling them up with you to safety. Jude's imagery here is gripping, as he likens evangelism to rescuing people from a burning building where they would otherwise perish; this calls for great urgency, alertness, and courage.

Doxology (24–25)

Jude closes his letter with one of the finest examples of doxology in the entire NT: "Now to him who is able to keep you from stumbling and to present you blameless before the presence of his glory with great joy, to the only God, our Savior, through Jesus Christ our Lord, be glory, majesty, dominion, and authority, before all time and now and forever. Amen" (vv. 24–25). Once again, he fittingly puts the spotlight on God, who is able to keep Jude's readers from stumbling and to present them blameless before God on that final day. He is "the only God, our Savior, through Jesus Christ our Lord," and to him be "glory, majesty, dominion, and authority" for all eternity. Amen.

Jude: Commentaries

Bauckham, Richard J. *Jude, 2 Peter*. WBC 50. Waco: Word, 1983.

Charles, J. Daryl. *1–2 Peter, Jude*. BCBC. Scottdale, PA: Herald, 1999.

Davids, Peter H. *The Letters of 2 Peter and Jude*. PNTC. Grand Rapids: Eerdmans, 2006.

———. *2 Peter and Jude: A Handbook on the Greek Text*. BHGNT. Waco: Baylor University Press, 2011.

Elliott, John H. *I–II Peter/Jude*. ACNT. Minneapolis: Augsburg, 1982.

Giese, C. P. *2 Peter and Jude*. Concordia Commentary. St. Louis: Concordia, 2012.

Green, Gene L. *Jude and 2 Peter*. BECNT. Grand Rapids: Baker Academic, 2008.

Green, Michael E. *The Second Epistle of Peter and the Epistle of Jude: An Introduction and Commentary*. Rev. ed. TNTC. Grand Rapids: Eerdmans, 1987.

Harmon, Matthew S. "Jude." In *ESV Expository Commentary*, vol. 12, *Hebrews–Revelation*, edited by Iain M. Duguid, James M. Hamilton Jr., and Jay Sklar, 501–23. Wheaton: Crossway, 2018.

Kelly, J. N. D. *A Commentary on the Epistles of Peter and of Jude*. HNTC. New York: Harper & Row, 1969.

Kraftchick, Steven J. *Jude, 2 Peter*. ANTC. Nashville: Abingdon, 2002.

Mbuvi, Andrew M. *Jude and 2 Peter: A New Covenant Commentary*. NCCS. Cambridge: Lutterworth, 2016.

Moo, Douglas J. *2 Peter, Jude*. NIVAC. Grand Rapids: Zondervan, 1996.

Neyrey, J. H. *2 Peter, Jude: A New Translation with Introduction and Commentary*. AB 37C. New York: Doubleday, 1993.

Reese, Ruth A. *2 Peter and Jude*. THNTC. Grand Rapids: Eerdmans, 2007.

Richard, E. J. *Reading 1 Peter, Jude, and 2 Peter: A Literary and Theological Commentary*. Macon, GA: Smyth & Helwys, 2000.

Schreiner, Thomas R. *1, 2 Peter, Jude*. NAC 37. Nashville: Broadman & Holman, 2003.

Senior, D. P. *1 Peter, Jude, and 2 Peter*. SP 15. Collegeville, MN: Liturgical Press, 2003.

Webb, Robert L. *The Letters of Jude and Second Peter*. NICNT. Grand Rapids: Eerdmans, forthcoming.

Witherington, Ben, III. *Letters and Homilies for Hellenized Christians*. Vol. 2, *A Socio-Rhetorical Commentary on Hebrews, James and Jude*. Downers Grove, IL: InterVarsity, 2007.

Jude: Articles, Essays, and Monographs

Bauckham, Richard J. *Jude and the Relatives of Jesus in the Early Church*. Edinburgh: T&T Clark, 1990.

Birdsall, J. Neville. "The Text of Jude in P72." *JTS* 14 (1963): 394–99.

Boobyer, George H. "The Verbs in Jude 11." *NTS* 5 (1958): 45–47.

Callan, Terrance. "Use of the Letter of Jude by the Second Letter of Peter." *Bib* 85 (2004): 42–64.

Carson, D. A. "Jude." In *Commentary on the New Testament Use of the Old Testament*, edited by G. K. Beale and D. A. Carson, 1069–79. Grand Rapids: Baker Academic, 2007.

Charles, J. Daryl. "Jude." In *Hebrews–Revelation*. Vol. 13 of *The Expositor's Bible Commentary*, rev. ed., edited by Tremper Longman III and David E. Garland, 539–69. Grand Rapids: Zondervan, 2005.

———. *Literary Strategy in the Epistle of Jude*. Scranton, PA: University of Scranton Press, 1993.

Davids, Peter H. *A Theology of James, Peter, and Jude: Living in Light of the Coming King*. BTNT. Grand Rapids: Zondervan, 2014.

———. "The Use of Second Temple Traditions in 1 and 2 Peter and Jude." In *The Catholic Epistles and Tradition*, edited by Jacques Schlosser, 409–31. BETL 176. Leuven: Peeters, 2004.

deSilva, David A. *The Jewish Teachers of Jesus, James, and Jude: What Earliest Christianity Learned from the Apocrypha and Pseudepigrapha*. Oxford: Oxford University Press, 2012.

Ellis, E. Earle. "Prophecy and Hermeneutic in Jude." In *Prophecy and Hermeneutic in Early Christianity: New Testament Essays*, 221–36. WUNT 1/18. Tübingen: Mohr Siebeck, 1978.

Greenlee, J. Harold. *An Exegetical Summary of Jude.* 2nd ed. Dallas: SIL International, 2008.

Gunther, John J. "The Alexandrian Epistle of Jude." *NTS* 30 (1984): 549–62.

Heil, John Paul. *1 Peter, 2 Peter, and Jude: Worship Matters.* Eugene, OR: Cascade, 2013.

Hiebert, D. Edmond. "Selected Studies from Jude, Part 2: An Exposition of Jude 12–16." *BSac* 142 (1985): 245–49.

———. "Selected Studies from Jude, Part 3: An Exposition of Jude 17–23." *BSac* 142 (1985): 355–66.

Huther, J. E. *Critical and Exegetical Handbook to the General Epistles of Peter and Jude.* Translated by D. B. Croom and P. J. Gloab. Edinburgh: T&T Clark, 1881.

Jobes, Karen H. *Letters to the Church: A Survey of Hebrews and the General Epistles.* Grand Rapids: Zondervan, 2011.

Kubo, Sakae. "Jude 22–23: Two-Division Form or Three?" In *New Testament Criticism: Its Significance for Exegesis,* edited by Eldon J. Epp and Gordon D. Fee, 239–53. Oxford: Clarendon, 1981.

Landon, Charles. *A Text-Critical Study of the Epistle of Jude.* JSNTSup 135. Sheffield: Sheffield Academic, 1996.

Martin, Ralph P. "The Theology of Jude, 1 Peter, and 2 Peter." In *The Theology of the Letters of James, Peter, and Jude,* by Andrew Chester and Ralph P. Martin, 63–163. Cambridge: Cambridge University Press, 1994.

Mason, Eric F., and Troy W. Martin, eds. *Reading 1–2 Peter and Jude: A Resource for Students.* SBLRBS. Atlanta: Society of Biblical Literature, 2014.

Mayor, Joseph B. *The Epistles of Jude and II Peter.* Grand Rapids: Baker, 1979.

Niebuhr, Karl-Wilhelm, and Robert W. Wall. *The Catholic Epistles and Apostolic Tradition: A New Perspective on James to Jude.* Waco: Baylor University Press, 2009.

Nienhuis, David R., and Robert W. Wall. *Reading the Epistles of James, Peter, John, and Jude as Scripture: The Shaping and Shape of a Canonical Collection.* Grand Rapids: Eerdmans, 2013.

Osburn, Carroll D. "Discourse Analysis and Jewish Apocalyptic in the Epistle of Jude." In *Linguistics and New Testament Interpretation,* edited by David Alan Black, 287–319. Nashville: Broadman, 1992.

Painter, John, and David A. deSilva. *James and Jude.* Paideia. Grand Rapids: Baker Academic, 2012.

Ross, John M. "Church Discipline in Jude 22–23." *ExpTim* 100 (1989): 297–98.

Thurén, Lauri. "Hey Jude! Asking for the Original Situation and Message of a Catholic Epistle." *JSNT* 43 (1997): 451–65.

Watson, Duane Frederick. *Invention, Arrangement, and Style: Rhetorical Criticism of Jude and 2 Peter.* SBLDS 104. Atlanta: Scholars Press, 1988.

Webb, Robert L. "The Eschatology of the Epistle of Jude and Its Rhetorical and Social Functions." *BBR* 6 (1996): 139–51.

Webb, Robert L., and Peter H. Davids, eds. *Reading Jude with New Eyes: Methodological Reassessments of the Letter of Jude.* LNTS 383. London: T&T Clark, 2009.

CHAPTER EIGHT

Revelation

Introduction

Author, Audience, Date, and Genre

The book of Revelation poses a stiff challenge to the interpretive skills and abilities of its readers. The meaning of the book beckons to be properly extracted by careful attention to the matrix of history, literature, and theology embedded in it. Historical research is required as the book is in the first instance addressed to real first-century churches and believers for whom its message must have been meaningful and applicable. The book is littered with subtle and not-so-subtle historical data that ground Revelation in its end-of-first-century original setting. At the same time, the book exhibits a careful pattern of composition and narrative flow that calls for all the literary efforts a reader can muster. Grounded in history and expressed in literary terms, the book conveys a theological message that shows God, the Lord Jesus Christ, and the Spirit of God engaged in a fierce battle against Satan and his demonic forces that involves the churches in Asia Minor at the end of the first century and ultimately spans across the church age until the end of time.

Revelation contains countless references to realities the churches in John's day would have readily understood.[1] Yet while the book's message is grounded in historical references, it is not exhausted by the original historical referents. Rather, by way of typology, we are shown typical characteristics of a given

---

1. For examples, see Andreas J. Köstenberger, L. Scott Kellum, and Charles L. Quarles, *The Cradle, the Cross, and the Crown: An Introduction to the New Testament*, 2nd ed. (Nashville: B&H Academic, 2016), 944–50. For details, see Colin J. Hemer, *The Letters to the Seven Churches of Asia in Their Local Setting*, JSNTSup 11 (Sheffield: JSOT Press, 1986).

217

church, manifestations of the devil's work, or other phenomena as they unfold in an escalating manner across history, culminating in the climactic expression of evil at the coming of the antichrist and finally Christ himself, followed by God's judgment and the eternal state. That said, it is amazing how much of the visionary material in Revelation is cast in terms reminiscent of OT apocalyptic material. While God is giving these visions to John, he is expecting him to recognize these images as he sees these visions. Consequently, John uses OT language to describe what he sees. This language, in turn, places a considerable demand on us as readers to be cognizant of those OT visions, and it calls for greater familiarity on our part with OT prophetic literature, especially those portions that are highly symbolic and apocalyptic in nature.

The author of the book of Revelation is John, the seer (1:9). This is none other than the evangelist (John the apostle, writer of the Gospel) and John "the elder" (author of John's letters, written by the same John). The location of these visions is identified as the island of Patmos, off the coast of Greece, where John was at the time he received these oracles (1:9). The immediate recipients of these visions and of the book that records them are the seven churches mentioned in chapters 2 and 3, churches in Asia Minor located along a postal route connecting them.[2] The date of composition likely is approximately AD 95, making this the last NT book to be written. Canonically speaking, the book brings tremendous closure to the Christian canon, which started with the book of Genesis. Thus, like a magnificent rainbow, the Bible spans human history from beginning to end.

The genre of the book is that of prophetic-apocalyptic epistle.[3] That is, the book largely consists of real visions given to John by God, providing direct divine revelation about the present (from John's vantage point) and future of humanity, both believing and unbelieving, as history slowly but surely moves toward a climax and conclusion. While the book is presented in the form of an *epistle* (as the first and last chapter attest), its essential character is prophetic-apocalyptic. What this means is that apocalyptic is essentially a subset of biblical *prophecy*, by which a prophet or seer engages in forthtelling (speaking into the present) as well as foretelling (predicting the future). *Apocalyptic* primarily entails the giving of such revelation in the form of visions, which contain extensive symbolism in which a given symbol represents an actual historical figure or event. The challenge, then, is to discern the referent of a

---

2. Hemer, *Letters to the Seven Churches*, 15.

3. Richard Bauckham, *The Theology of the Book of Revelation*, NTT (Cambridge: Cambridge University Press, 1993), 1–2, calls Revelation "an apocalyptic prophecy in the form of a circular letter to seven churches in the Roman province of Asia" (2). See also the classic article by George E. Ladd, "Why Not Prophetic-Apocalyptic?," *JBL* 76 (1957): 192–200.

particular symbol, or, alternatively, the presence of typology, in which case a symbol may have multiple referents.[4]

The resulting literary work is referred to as "apocalypse" (the first word of the book in the original Greek, *apokalypsis*). Though found in the OT only in portions of books, such as Isaiah, Ezekiel, Daniel, and Zechariah, apocalyptic blossomed into a full-fledged literary genre during the Second Temple period (the period between the Testaments) and is represented by works such as 4 Ezra, 2 Baruch, and 1 Enoch.[5] Apocalyptic works proceed within a narrative framework and feature angelic mediators, otherworldly creatures, and vivid visions of the end of time.[6] Viewed from such a narrative framework, the climax of the book is the triumphant return of Christ, the supreme King and Ruler of the universe, who is depicted as riding on a white horse and as clothed in a robe dipped in blood, symbolizing his crucifixion (19:11–16). The book thus conveys the victory of Jesus over all his enemies, including Satan, the highest fallen angel, whose rebellion is at last put down when the final judgment is rendered.

Structure

Structural proposals for the book of Revelation are legion.[7] And yet delineating the basic structure of the book may not be quite as difficult as it may appear if one takes one's cue from the four-times-repeated phrase "in the Spirit" (1:10; 4:2; 17:3; 21:10), each instance of which designates a separate vision

---

4. I.e., the "great prostitute" in chap. 17 can signify Rome as well as "empire" more broadly, plus constitute a climactic reference to a specific future empire or city. For relevant interpretive issues, see Andreas J. Köstenberger and Richard D. Patterson, *Invitation to Biblical Interpretation* (Grand Rapids: Kregel, 2011), chap. 11. Cf. Thomas R. Schreiner, "Revelation," in *ESV Expository Commentary*, vol. 12, *Hebrews–Revelation*, ed. Iain M. Duguid, James M. Hamilton Jr., and Jay Sklar (Wheaton: Crossway, 2018), 531, who helpfully distinguishes between four levels of communication in Revelation: (1) the linguistic level, that is, the text itself; (2) the actual visions John saw as described in the text; (3) the referential level, that is, the specific figures and events conveyed in those visions; and (4) the symbolic level, using images to convey end-time realities. Schreiner embraces a combination of the preterist (fulfillment entirely or primarily in the first century), idealist (fulfillment primarily symbolic), and futurist (fulfillment primarily in future history) approaches to Revelation (see 544–46, esp. table 9.2). He expresses a "slight preference" for the amillennial position, the notion that the millennium—the 1,000-year reign of Christ mentioned in Rev. 20:2, 5, and 7—is to be taken as a symbolic reference (see 723–25).

5. See the collection in James H. Charlesworth, ed., *The Old Testament Pseudepigrapha*, vol. 1, *Apocalyptic Literature and Testaments* (Garden City, NY: Doubleday, 1983).

6. For a standard definition, see John J. Collins, "Introduction: Towards the Morphology of a Genre," *Semeia* 14 (1979), 9; Adela Yarbro Collins, "Introduction: Early Christian Apocalypticism," *Semeia* 36 (1986), 7.

7. See the survey of major structural proposals in Köstenberger, Kellum, and Quarles, *The Cradle, the Cross, and the Crown*, 956–60.

playing out in a particular location (see table below).[8] That said, the idea of "four visions" doesn't mean they're thoroughly distinct. In other words, they aren't four separate, self-contained visions but four parts of a unified whole.[9]

Structure of the Book of Revelation

Revelation	Unit	Location
1:1–8	Prologue	
1:9–3:22	Vision 1: The glorified Christ, message to the churches	Isle of Patmos
4:1–16:21	Vision 2: The divine court, trial of the nations	Heaven
17:1–21:8	Vision 3: Destruction of Babylon, return of Christ	Desert
21:9–22:5	Vision 4: Believers' reward, new creation	Mountain
22:6–21	Epilogue	

For a detailed table, see Andreas J. Köstenberger, L. Scott Kellum, and Charles L. Quarles, *The Cradle, the Cross, and the Crown: An Introduction to the New Testament*, 2nd ed. (Nashville: B&H Academic, 2016), 965–66.

One observation that is readily apparent is that the visions are of unequal length, with the second vision taking up the lion's share of the entire book. However, this does not invalidate the proposed outline. In fact, it demonstrates that the main focus of the book is on the divine judgment of the nations and the commensurate vindication of believers at the end of human history.

Specifically, this judgment is conveyed in a threefold pattern represented metaphorically in terms of seven seals, trumpets, and bowls: the judgments are first revealed (opening of seals, 6:1–14), subsequently announced (blowing of trumpets, 8:1–9:19), and finally executed (pouring out of bowls, 16:1–21). Through this pattern of (partial) repetition, the message of God's judgment on the unbelieving world is reiterated and reinforced.[10] Of course, beneath this simplified presentation of the structure of the book of Revelation lurk many twists and turns that will be further traced in the discussion below.

Central Message

The cluster of major themes in the book revolves around the notion of theodicy—that is, the vindication of the righteousness of God in the face of the apparent triumph of evil in John's day.[11] This is conveyed particularly in the form of the Roman emperor cult and also in the "Nero *redivivus* [Latin

---

8. For a detailed table, see Köstenberger, Kellum, and Quarles, *The Cradle, the Cross, and the Crown*, 965–66.

9. For a strong argument for the overarching unity of Revelation, see Richard Bauckham, *The Climax of Prophecy: Studies on the Book of Revelation* (London: T&T Clark, 1993), 1–37.

10. Cf. Schreiner ("Revelation," 543, 546), who notes the recursive structure of Revelation.

11. Grant R. Osborne, "Theodicy in the Apocalypse," *TrinJ* 14 (1993): 63–77.

for "revived"] myth"—that is, the popular belief that Emperor Nero (reigned AD 54–68) would return from the east leading the invading Parthian army (as mentioned in the Roman writer Suetonius's biography of Nero).[12]

The opposition against God and his people is epitomized by various figures representing the evil Roman Empire, such as the "great prostitute" sitting on a scarlet beast whose seven heads represent seven mountains, a thinly veiled reference to Rome, which was widely known in antiquity as the city on seven hills, as attested in the writings of a wide range of Roman authors such as Virgil, Horace, Cicero, and Suetonius. The references to "Babylon" in the latter part of Revelation (14:8; 16:19; 17:5; 18:2, 10, 21) also clearly point in the direction of Rome (cf. 1 Pet. 5:13, already discussed above; see also 4 Ezra, 2 Baruch, and Sibylline Oracles).

Revelation is thus primarily addressed to suffering Christians who need to be reassured that, contrary to how it may appear at the moment, evil will not forever triumph, but God will eventually vindicate believers and judge the unbelieving world.[13] This would help Christians persevere until the end and strengthen their faith in God and his ultimate deliverance in Christ at his return. In addition, Revelation is directed toward complacent Christians who may be tempted to compromise their witness by idolatrous participation in the world system in order to escape persecution.[14]

Prologue (1:1–8)

The opening phrase, "The revelation of Jesus Christ," announces what will constitute the heart of the book: the second coming of Christ. Unlike his first coming, which was lowly and seemingly inconspicuous, culminating in his ignominious and apparently shameful death on a cross, Jesus's return will be triumphant and highly visible, representing his public vindication and the vindication of his followers. Not only is Jesus the *object* of this momentous revelation; he is also its *subject*, the one who himself is the messenger of that

---

12. Suetonius, *Nero* 49.3; see 57.1. See Köstenberger, Kellum, and Quarles, *The Cradle, the Cross, and the Crown*, 935–39. See also J. Nelson Kraybill, *Imperial Cult and Commerce in John's Apocalypse*, JSNTSup 132 (Sheffield: Sheffield Academic, 1996).

13. On suffering and martyrdom in the churches to which the book is addressed, see Eckhard J. Schnabel, "The Persecution of Christians in the First Century," *JETS* 61 (2018): 544–45.

14. See further below. See also the discussion in Michael J. Gorman, *Reading Revelation Responsibly: Uncivil Worship and Witness; Following the Lamb into the New Creation* (Eugene, OR: Wipf & Stock, 2011), chap. 3. For a mini-theology of Revelation discussing the reality of evil, the suffering of the saints, the sovereignty of God, God's protection of his people, God's justice in judgment, the deity and the cross of Christ, the centrality of worship, and the new creation, see Schreiner, "Revelation," 532–41.

revelation ("The revelation . . . which God gave *him*"; 1:1). The recipients of this revelation are his "servants," who include his "servant" John the seer. These things, from the perspective of eternity, "must soon take place," even though from an earthly vantage point the end of history may seem long in coming. As Peter reminds his readers, with the Lord a thousand years are as one day (2 Pet. 3:8; cf. Ps. 90:4). As he did in his Gospel (21:24–25; cf. 19:35), John, by writing the book of Revelation, "bore witness to the word of God and to the testimony of Jesus Christ." While in his Gospel he recorded his eyewitness testimony of what he and his fellow apostles saw—"We have seen his glory" (John 1:14)—in the present work John records the God-given visions he saw about what would happen at the end. While the genre of the Gospel is historical narrative, the present book conveys the future by way of apocalyptic symbols.

The prologue establishes the composite genre of the present literary work. In fact, as mentioned, the book combines three genres rolled into one: an apocalypse ("The revelation [*apokalypsis*] of Jesus Christ"; 1:1), a prophecy ("the words of this prophecy"; 1:3), and a letter ("John to the seven churches that are in Asia: Grace to you and peace"; 1:4). As apocalyptic literature, the book depicts the return of Christ in a series of striking images. As a letter, the book is addressed to real churches in a specific location (Asia Minor, modern-day Turkey) at a particular time in history (ca. AD 95) with a message that must have been intelligible to its original audience. As a type of prophetic literature, the book sustains a strong connection with the OT prophets. The phrase "the things that must soon take place" (1:1), for example, is reminiscent of the book of Daniel (e.g., Dan. 2:28–29). Thus while the present work is future oriented, it also has an important present dimension. Rather than containing a mere outline of the future, the book, as prophetic literature, also speaks to people in the here and now. What's more, the book is given not merely for the purpose of information but also calls for obedient, faithful application. Consequently, an opening blessing is pronounced on those who read, hear, *and keep* what is written in this book (1:3).[15]

While 1:1–3 constitutes a *prophetic* prologue, 1:4–8 represents an *epistolary* prologue, indicating both the author, John—already mentioned in 1:1 as the recipient of the visions contained in the book but now identified as the literary author of the book to its original intended audience—and the recipients, believers in seven specific churches in Asia Minor (cf. chaps. 2–3).[16] In addition, the epistolary introduction doesn't merely cover chapters 2–3; the entire book

15. This is the first of seven blessings scattered throughout the book (1:3; 14:13; 16:15; 19:9; 20:6; 22:7, 14). See table 9.4 in Schreiner, "Revelation," 551.

16. While the churches are literally seven in number, in addition it is likely that the number "seven," as regularly in John, also conveys a sense of perfection or completeness. In this way,

is the message God has for these churches. This is underscored by parallels between the opening and closing of the book. The opening, "John to the seven churches" (1:4), is mirrored by the closing "I, John, am the one who heard and saw these things" (22:8). The opening reference to "the things that must soon take place" (1:1) corresponds to the closing "Behold, I am coming soon" (22:7, 12). Finally, the opening assurance, "Blessed is the one who reads aloud the words of this prophecy, and blessed are those who hear, and who keep what is written in it" (1:3), is matched by the closing affirmation, "Blessed is the one who keeps the words of the prophecy of this book" (22:7).[17]

The opening greeting, "Grace . . . and peace," represents the standard Christian greeting, combining the Greek *charis* (grace) and Hebrew *shalom* (peace; 1:4). This is followed by a trinitarian reference to God the Father, "who is and who was and who is to come" (i.e., who is eternal), "the seven spirits who are before his throne" (a likely reference to the Holy Spirit), and Jesus Christ, "the faithful witness, the firstborn of the dead, and the ruler of kings on earth" (1:4–5a), three designations that convey his crucifixion, resurrection, and exaltation.[18] The doxology in 1:5b–6, which concludes with a resounding "Amen," attributes eternal glory and dominion to Christ, "who loves us and has freed us from our sins by his blood and made us a kingdom, priests to his God and Father."[19] Conflating two OT prophetic passages, the seer announces, "Behold, he is coming with the clouds [cf. Dan. 7:13], and every eye will see him, even those who pierced him" (Zech. 12:10, cited in John 19:37), resulting in universal mourning, an assertion affirmed even more emphatically with "Amen"—that is, "Yes!" (1:7).[20] While Jesus's death is never narrated in Revelation—presupposing the Gospels—it stands as a central assumption behind the book (cf., e.g., the references to the Lamb that was slain in 5:6–9).

The prologue ends with the thumping threefold self-designation of God as the "Alpha and the Omega," the one "who is and who was and who is to come," and "the Almighty" (1:8). God is the Alpha and Omega—the first and last letters in the Greek alphabet—the eternal God who has no beginning or end in time. He is also "the Almighty," the all-powerful God who will bring human history

---

therefore, Christ's message to these seven churches typologically also conveys his message to the universal church across the church age prior to his return.

17. Note also the curse in 22:18–19 on those who add to or take away from the words of the prophecy.

18. See chap. 2, "The One Who Is and Was and Is to Come," in Bauckham, *Theology of the Book of Revelation*.

19. Cf. Exod. 19:6. "Loves" is in the present-tense form, conveying the ongoing nature of Christ's love for us, while "freed" and "made" are in the aorist-tense form, conveying the global, universal dimension of Christ's actions on our behalf.

20. See the discussion in Schreiner, "Revelation," 556–57.

to its predetermined end according to his sovereign plan.[21] While God the Father doesn't speak much in Revelation, this is his normal self-identification when he does speak. Thus the book establishes at the very outset God's sovereignty and matchless power, which will be parodied by the beast and Satan, who, along with the second beast (the "false prophet"), are described in similar "trinitarian" terms. In this way, John signals that this is a book of theodicy (from *theos*, "God," and *dikaios*, "righteous")—that is, a defense of the righteousness of God's judgment of the unbelieving world, as well as a word of reassurance to suffering believers that they will eventually be vindicated at Christ's return.

Vision 1: The Glorified Christ, Message to the Churches (1:9–3:22)

The Vision of the Exalted Christ (1:9–20)

Whereas the prologue *declares* John's prophetic authority, the rest of chapter 1 *narrates* that authority, giving us John's prophetic commission. In the opening verse, we learn three things about John: (1) he was on the island of Patmos "on account of the word of God and the testimony of Jesus," whether in exile (*relegatio ad insulam*, "banishment to an island") or preaching the gospel (1:9);[22] (2) it was the Lord's Day—that is, Sunday, the day marking Jesus's resurrection; and (3) John was "in the Spirit"; that is, God gave John a vision conveyed by the Holy Spirit (1:10). John, the seer, identified here not only as "your brother" but also in triadic terms as the readers' "partner in the tribulation and the kingdom and the patient endurance that are in Jesus," is given the command to write down in a book the things he has seen and send it to seven churches in Asia (1:11). At this, he turns and sees the glorified Christ (1:12–16) and promptly falls at his feet (the standard response in Scripture to an encounter with the divine supernatural; 1:17).

The passage bears striking resemblance to Daniel's prophetic commission, at which the OT prophet sees a stunning vision, falls on his face, is comforted, and is given heavenly revelation (Dan. 10).[23] Together, 1:11 and 1:19 frame the literary unit and serve to narrate and flesh out John's divine commission, with

21. Schreiner ("Revelation," 558) notes that "Almighty" (*pantokratōr*) in the Septuagint (LXX), the Greek version of the Old Testament, is often a translation of the Hebrew expression for "the LORD of hosts," depicting God as commanding the heavenly angelic armies. In the book of Job, "Almighty" is a translation of the Hebrew *Shaddai* (e.g., Job 11:7; 22:17, 25; 23:16), designating God as all-powerful amid intense suffering, which provides a fitting application to Revelation.

22. See further Mark Wilson, "Geography of the Island of Patmos," in *Lexham Geographic Commentary on Acts through Revelation*, ed. Barry J. Beitzel (Bellingham, WA: Lexham, 2019), 619–28.

23. See G. K. Beale, *The Book of Revelation*, NIGTC (Grand Rapids: Eerdmans, 2013), 213.

1:11 specifying the identity of the seven churches,[24] and 1:19 recording John's commission to write down the things he has seen, both "those that are and those that are to take place after this." Everything the reader is about to be told is what John was told to prophesy and write about, and the entire book is for God's people throughout history—applying to John's original readers, the church throughout history, and God's people until the end of time all the way until Christ's return (without implying that every reader will experience everything depicted in the book).

Verses 12–20 identify the source of the loud voice who gave John his commission—none other than the glorified Lord Jesus Christ. Turning, John sees seven golden lampstands (echoing Zechariah's vision of a golden lampstand in Zech. 4), which, the readers are told later, represent the seven churches to whom the book is addressed (1:12; cf. 1:20). In the midst of those lampstands, John sees "one like a son of man" (echoing again Dan. 7:13; cf. Rev. 1:7), whose appearance is then described in striking and majestic terms reminiscent of Daniel's terrifying vision of a man of the following description (cf. Dan. 10:5–6):

- clothed with a long robe (Dan. 10:5: "clothed in linen")
- a golden sash around his chest (Dan. 10:5: "belt of fine gold . . . around his waist")
- hair white like white wool, like snow (cf. Dan. 7:9: "clothing . . . white as snow"; "hair of his head like pure wool")
- eyes like fire (Dan. 10:6: "eyes like flaming torches")
- feet like burnished bronze (Dan. 10:6: "arms and legs like the gleam of burnished bronze")
- a voice like the roar of many waters (Deut. 10:6: "the sound of his words like the sound of a multitude"; cf. Ezek. 1:24; 43:2)
- in his right hand seven stars (representing the seven angels of the churches, 1:20)
- from his mouth a double-edged sword (Isa. 49:2: "mouth like a sharp sword"; cf. Isa. 11:4)[25]
- face like the sun shining in full strength (cf. Exod. 34:29; Matt. 17:2 [the transfiguration]: "his face shone like the sun")

24. Listed in the order Ephesus, Smyrna, Pergamum, Thyatira, Sardis, Philadelphia, and Laodicea, the likely postal route on which actual letters would have been delivered to these cities in the first century. See fig. 8.2 below.

25. Cf. table 9.5 in Schreiner, "Revelation," 560.

Just pause and take a moment and try to picture this magnificent vision John saw! Particularly striking is the way in which Christ shares the same symbol as the Ancient of Days in Daniel 7:9. No wonder the seer falls flat on his face at the sight of the exalted Christ. And yet Christ puts his right hand on the seer and tells him not to fear, identifying himself as the risen Christ who has overcome death. Like God the Father, he is "the first and the last" (1:17; cf. 1:8) and the "living one." Unlike God the Father, Jesus actually died, but came back to life, and now is alive forever, and holds the keys to death (1:18). On this basis, Jesus has authority to reveal to John what will take place in the future prior to, at, and subsequent to the second coming of Christ. What is more, Jesus reveals to John the "mystery" of the seven golden lampstands and the seven stars, identifying them, respectively, as the seven churches and their seven angels, which provides a perfect segue to what is about to follow.

The Letters to the Seven Churches (2:1–3:22)

Chapters 2 and 3, then, feature the letters to the seven churches in Asia Minor conveyed to John by the exalted Christ:

Church	Characteristic of Christ	Commendation	Accusation	Admonition	Warning	Promise
Ephesus (2:1–7)	Holds seven stars, walking among lampstands	Works, endures, examines false apostles, rejects teaching of Nicolaitans	Abandoned first love	Repent, remember, return	Remove lampstand	Eat from tree of life in paradise
Smyrna (2:8–11)		Faithfully endured tribulation, poverty, slander		Be faithful unto death		Never harmed by second death
Pergamum (2:12–17)	Sharp double-edged sword out of his mouth	Held on to Christ's name, didn't deny faith in him	Some hold to teachings of a false prophet and Nicolaitans	Repent	Fight them with his sword from his mouth (words)	Hidden manna and white stone with new name
Thyatira (2:18–29)	Eyes like fire, feet of burnished bronze	Ever greater works, love, faithfulness, service, endurance	Some hold to teachings of false prophets, commit sexual immorality	Repent, don't hold to teachings of false prophetess Jezebel	Cast false prophetess and followers to bed of suffering	Authority over nations

Church	Characteristic of Christ	Commendation	Accusation	Admonition	Warning	Promise
Sardis (3:1–6)	Holds seven spirits and seven stars		Reputation of being alive but spiritually dead	Be alert, strengthen what remains, remember what you heard, repent	Come against them like a thief	Dressed in white, name secure in book of life
Philadelphia (3:7–13)	Holy and true, holds key of David	Works, little strength, not denied his name, obedient, endurance		Hold on to what you have		Pillar in God's sanctuary, name of God and of God's city on them
Laodicea (3:14–22)	Amen, faithful and true witness, ruler of creation		Lukewarm, complacent, self-deceived; spiritually poor, blind, naked	Receive refined gold, pure clothes, eye ointment	Rebuke those he loves, restore fellowship	Sit on throne with Father and Son

Adapted from Andreas J. Köstenberger, L. Scott Kellum, and Charles L. Quarles, *The Cradle, the Cross, and the Crown: An Introduction to the New Testament*, 2nd ed. (Nashville: B&H Academic, 2016), 976–77.

Each of the letters is addressed to the "angel" (*angelos*) of a particular church, which may refer to (1) the pastor or church leader, (2) a literal messenger or letter bearer, (3) a guardian angel of the church or an angel to whom a given church is assigned, or (4) some sort of heavenly counterpart of the church. Perhaps a combination of the last two views is the most likely option.[26] If so, Jesus addresses these messages to each of the churches by way of an angel who has been assigned some sort of spiritual care for a given church body, conveying the sense that churches operate within the framework of a supernatural set of realities. Overall, the address fits the revelatory pattern of moving from God the Father to his Son, the Lord Jesus Christ, who conveys his message(s) through the Spirit (depicted as the sevenfold spirit) through a given angel through John the seer to the respective church.[27]

26. Grant R. Osborne, *Revelation Verse by Verse*, Osborne New Testament Commentaries (Bellingham, WA: Lexham, 2016), 42.

27. Cf. Köstenberger, Kellum, and Quarles, *The Cradle, the Cross, and the Crown*, 973.

Figure 8.1
The pattern of revelation in the book of Revelation

God → Jesus Christ → Holy Spirit → Angels → John → Churches

In chapters 2 and 3, Jesus's self-declaration is related to what John has just seen (cf. 1:9–20). The promises to the seven churches are picked up again in the vision of the new heaven and the new earth (e.g., 2:7: "I will grant to eat of the tree of life"; 22:2, 14: "the right to the tree of life"), where promises of eschatological reward are depicted as being fulfilled. The book thus narrates eschatological fulfillment at the end of the biblical canon, providing closure, often in the form of literary inclusios (a passage bookended by a repeated phrase). As David deSilva has aptly noted, Revelation can "afflict the comfortable just as much as comfort the afflicted."[28] Thus we find in the letters to the seven churches both words of encouragement issued to those churches that suffer persecution and words of admonition directed toward those that suffer from complacency and compromise. There is no middle ground; God's people must have no part with Jezebel or the Nicolaitans (see below). Neither must they compromise their faith when being hard-pressed by Rome and the emperor. People will follow either the Lamb or the beast. Depending on their current state of allegiance, readers of this book will receive either great comfort or a stern warning to repent. The theme and language of overcoming—often by dying—requires perseverance until the end.[29] The apocalyptic paradox, then, is that believers overcome spiritually by being overcome physically. Similarly, today there is ultimately no middle ground, as people are faced with the stark choice of casting their allegiance either with Christ or with the world. Following Christ may come at great cost, but Revelation makes clear that it is the path of victory.

LETTER 1: TO THE CHURCH IN EPHESUS (2:1–7)

The early history of the church at Ephesus is well documented in Scripture. The book of Acts records how Paul established the church in Ephesus (Acts 19) and how, as he affirms in his farewell to the elders of the church, he preached the gospel there for three years (20:31). Later, Paul dispatched Timothy to the church there in order to confront false teachers (1 Tim. 1:3).

---

28. David A. deSilva, *Seeing Things John's Way: The Rhetoric of the Book of Revelation* (Louisville: Westminster John Knox, 2009), 34.

29. Cf. 5:5, where the Lamb is described as "the Lion of the tribe of Judah, the Root of David," who "has conquered"; and see 12:11, where God's people are said to "have conquered him [Satan] by the blood of the Lamb and by the word of their testimony."

Figure 8.2
The seven churches of Revelation

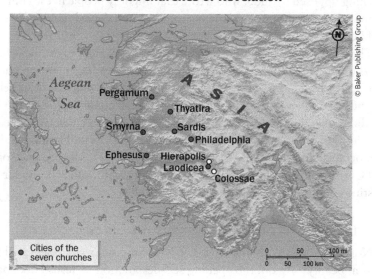

The entire Johannine corpus, according to early church tradition, seems to have originated in and around Ephesus, which is why it comes as no surprise that the first of the letters to the seven churches is addressed to the church at Ephesus.[30]

At the outset of his letter to the church at Ephesus, Jesus affirms his authority over the angels and his presence in the midst of his churches (2:1). In characteristic fashion, Jesus first commends the church for what is praiseworthy: its works, toil, and endurance (further elaborated in triadic fashion in 2:3) and its exposure of false apostles (2:2; cf. 2 Cor. 11:13). Then, Jesus reproves the church for having forsaken its "first love" (2:4). He calls the church to repentance and threatens to remove its lampstand (2:5), which may refer to the church's demise. At this, Jesus mentions one more positive point: the church's hatred of the "works of the Nicolaitans" (2:6).

The Nicolaitans are mentioned also in the letter to the church at Pergamum (2:15), yet nowhere else in Scripture, and the origins and beliefs of this group are shrouded in mystery. From the context in the letter to Pergamum, we may infer that among their teachings and practices were that of eating food sacrificed to idols and sexual immorality (2:14). This would seem to indicate

---

30. For a thorough treatment, see Paul R. Trebilco, *The Early Christians in Ephesus from Paul to Ignatius* (Grand Rapids: Eerdmans, 2004). See also David A. deSilva, "The Social and Geographical World of Ephesus," in Beitzel, *Lexham Geographic Commentary*, 537–53.

a disregard for the morality that was required of Christians, similar to the teaching opposed by Jude, who wrote that ungodly people in the church perverted "the grace of our God into sensuality" and denied their "only Master and Lord, Jesus Christ" (Jude 4).[31]

The letter closes with Jesus's promise that he will grant to the one who conquers (*nikaō*) the privilege of eating from the "tree of life" in the "paradise of God" (2:7; cf. Gen. 2:9; 3:22). This is another way of saying that these believers will be granted eternal life in the new creation, a common Johannine idiom for those who will receive salvation and be allowed to enter God's heavenly kingdom (e.g., John 3:16). Eating from the tree of life will sustain believers' immortality, and they will be able to enjoy eternity in the presence of God and Christ in an environment unstained by sin, death, and evil, similar to the pristine conditions in paradise prior to the fall.

LETTER 2: TO THE CHURCH IN SMYRNA (2:8–11)

North of Ephesus lay the ancient city of Smyrna, a city celebrated for its natural beauty.[32] Again, the opening self-designation of Jesus harks back to the vision of the exalted Christ in chapter 1: he is "the first and the last, who died and came to life" (2:8). This affirms both Jesus's deity and his eternity and refers to his crucifixion and resurrection. First off, Jesus commends the church for its forbearance under tribulation (*thlipsis*; see further 2:10 below) and its poverty (parenthetically noting that they are rich spiritually, in marked contrast to the church in Laodicea, which claimed to be rich while in reality being poor; cf. 3:17–18). Apparently, much of the tribulation the church is suffering has to do with the slander of those in a "synagogue of Satan" (2:9), a reference that recurs in the letter to the church at Philadelphia (3:9).

Most likely, the reference here is to those who were ethnically Jewish but who persecuted (Jewish) Christians who worshiped Jesus as the Messiah and Son of God (cf. John 20:30–31). The book of Acts indicates that often the fiercest opposition to the Christian preaching of the resurrected Jesus came from Jewish quarters, just as Jesus himself was put to death at the instigation of the Sanhedrin, the Jewish supreme court. The NT consistently makes the point that Jewish ethnic privilege has been superseded by the priority of faith—a true "Jew" is one who is one inwardly, not one who can claim proper

---

31. Hemer, *Letters to the Seven Churches*, 39, calls the group "libertarian."

32. For background, see Hemer, *Letters to the Seven Churches*, 57–60. The city's current name is Izmir in modern Turkey. There may be a connection between Smyrna and myrrh, which may help explain the emphasis on suffering in this letter (Hemer, *Letters to the Seven Churches*, 58–59). See also David A. deSilva, "The Social and Geographical World of Smyrna," in Beitzel, *Lexham Geographic Commentary*, 629–37.

ethnic credentials but is spiritually unbelieving and unregenerate.[33] Remarkably, Jesus has no complaint with this church.[34]

In the face of fierce Jewish opposition, Jesus encourages the church at Smyrna to stand firm as some church members are about to be thrown into prison (2:10).[35] He calls on believers to be faithful even "unto death," so that they will receive their eternal reward (the "crown of life"; 2:10; cf. 3:11). In the same vein, James writes, "Blessed is the man who remains steadfast under trial, for when he has stood the test he will receive the crown of life" (James 1:12). Similarly, Paul spoke of the "crown of righteousness" (2 Tim. 4:8; cf. 1 Cor. 9:25; Phil. 4:1; 1 Thess. 2:19) and Peter of the "crown of glory" (1 Pet. 5:4). True followers of Christ will be tested and receive a reward if they remain faithful and pass the test. They will not be hurt by the "second death" (2:11).

Letter 3: To the Church in Pergamum (2:12–17)

Farther north along the postal route in the Roman province of Asia Minor is the city of Pergamum.[36] The third letter is addressed to the angel of the church there. Jesus's opening identification likens his words to a "sharp two-edged sword" (*rhomphaia*, 2:12, mentioned again in 2:16; cf. 1:16). Later references to this sword are poignantly found at the triumphant return of Christ as a rider on a white horse in 19:15 and 21. The simile powerfully impresses on the reader the fact that Jesus's words are to be taken seriously. They are to instill fear of destruction if not heeded.

The message to the church at Pergamum ominously begins by referring to the church's dwelling place as "where Satan's throne is" located (2:13). The city is a stronghold of Satan. One recent victim of Satan in that place apparently was a man named Antipas, identified as "my faithful witness, who was killed among you" (2:13)—that is, who suffered martyrdom for the Christian faith.[37] On the positive side, believers in Pergamum didn't deny the faith during

---

33. See, e.g., Rom. 2:28; Gal. 6:15; Phil. 3:3. See already the controversy between Jesus and the Jewish leaders as to who truly was a "child of Abraham" (John 8:33–58).

34. This makes the church at Smyrna one of only two churches in chaps. 2–3 that escape reproach; the other is the church at Philadelphia (3:7–13).

35. Reference is made to "ten days" of tribulation. While it is impossible to be certain, this may simply indicate that the suffering will be limited to an intermediate period of time. See Hemer, *Letters to the Seven Churches*, 69–70.

36. See David A. deSilva, "The Social and Geographical World of Pergamum," in Beitzel, *Lexham Geographic Commentary*, 638–54.

37. Schnabel, "Persecution of Christians in the First Century," 545, writes, "The statement that Antipas was killed 'in your city' leaves open whether Antipas was a member of the church in Pergamum or whether he was a member of the church in another city in the region whose legal case was heard in Pergamum, which was one of the judicial centers of the province." The reference to Antipas draws connections to Jesus, the faithful witness (1:5; 3:14; cf. 1:2, 9; 12:17;

those trying times. On the negative side, however, there were some there who held to the teaching of Balaam and others who adhered to the beliefs of the Nicolaitans (cf. discussion at 2:6 above).[38]

What makes discerning the reference to Balaam difficult is that his advice to Balak is not made explicit in the OT narrative, though 2:14 suggests that his counsel related to eating food sacrificed to idols and to sexual immorality (Num. 25:1–2; 31:16; cf. 1 Cor. 8:1–13; 10:20–30). Apparently the "woman Jezebel," a female false teacher, promulgated similar teachings in the church at Thyatira, down the road (2:20). In later Jewish literature, including Philo and Josephus, it was commonly held that Balaam was responsible for Israel's sin with the Moabite women. The sin in Pergamum similarly had to do with an abuse of freedom (antinomianism or libertinism).[39]

The letter to the church at Pergamum ends on a mysterious note, with references to "the hidden manna" and a "white stone" being given to those who conquer, the stone having a new name written on it, known only to the recipient (2:17). The reference to the "hidden manna" may allude to Exodus 16:32–34, where Moses instructs his brother Aaron to set aside a portion of manna so as to preserve it for future generations, which led to extensive speculation in later Jewish literature as to its whereabouts.[40] Apparently, the Messiah was expected to provide manna for God's people just like Moses had done (John 6:31). The "white stone" symbolizes the "new name" given to believers.[41]

LETTER 4: TO THE CHURCH IN THYATIRA (2:18–29)

Not far from Pergamum, to the southeast on the same postal route, lay the city of Thyatira.[42] The church there is the recipient of the longest of the seven letters in Revelation. While the city is rarely mentioned in ancient literature, the NT indicates that the first Christian convert in the province of Macedonia, Lydia, a seller of purple clothing, hailed from Thyatira (Acts 16:14). Jesus's opening characteristics include his penetrating eyes (like flames of fire; cf. 1:14) and his strong feet (like burnished bronze; cf. 1:15). By way of commendation, Jesus acknowledges believers' works, love, faith, service, and endurance,

---

19:10; 22:20) and the one who died (5:6), as well as God's people more broadly, who are pictured as bearing faithful witness unto death (6:9; 12:11; 17:6).

38. See the discussion in Osborne, *Revelation Verse by Verse*, 87–94.

39. See Osborne, *Revelation Verse by Verse*.

40. See Schreiner, "Revelation," 578.

41. The background of this symbol is hard to pinpoint. Hemer (*Letters to the Seven Churches*, 96–102) lists as many as seven options. See also the discussion in Grant R. Osborne, *Revelation*, BECNT (Grand Rapids: Baker Academic, 2002), 147–49.

42. For pertinent background information, see Hemer, *Letters to the Seven Churches*, 106–11. See also Mark Wilson, "The Social and Geographical World of Thyatira," in Beitzel, *Lexham Geographic Commentary*, 655–64.

yet then immediately turns to a major grievance: the church's toleration of "that woman Jezebel," who claims to be a prophetess while teaching Jesus's "servants" to engage in sexual immorality (*porneuō*) and to eat food that has previously been offered to idols (*eidōlothyta*). Intriguingly, these are the same two sins also mentioned in the previous letter, to the city of Pergamum up the road, in conjunction with the "teaching of Balaam" (2:14).

The original Jezebel was the wicked, Baal-worshiping wife of the OT king Ahab known for her "whorings and sorceries"; she was the nemesis of the OT prophet Elijah (1 Kings 16:31; 2 Kings 9:22). Women did serve as prophetesses in OT times, including Moses's sister Miriam (Exod. 15:20–21), Deborah (Judg. 4:4–5), and Huldah (2 Kings 22:14), not to mention Isaiah's wife (Isa. 8:3). This "woman Jezebel" who had arisen in the church at Thyatira apparently was a self-styled prophetess and teacher who espoused a libertine message touting Christian freedom.[43] It seems the church in the area was infested with false teaching, both in Thyatira and in neighboring Pergamum. Eating food offered to idols and sexual immorality were often connected in the ancient world due to "sacred" temple prostitution.

In the present instance, apparently this woman had been given an opportunity to repent but had refused to do so (2:21). Jesus announces that he will afflict her with sickness and bring tribulation upon those who commit spiritual adultery with her (2:22). The severity of Jesus's denunciation shows how seriously he takes false teaching, especially in that it is linked with idolatry—the worship of "gods" other than the one true God—and immoral, ungodly, and unholy behavior. In fact, he goes on to describe the woman's teaching as "what some call the 'deep things of Satan'" (2:24; contrast 1 Cor. 2:10: "the deep things of God"), indicating that ultimately Satan himself is behind this heresy. At the beginning, Satan instigated the fall of humanity (Gen. 3:1–7); more recently, he entered Judas the betrayer in order to bring about the crucifixion of Jesus (John 13:2, 27). Now, Satan attacked the church in the form of false teachers, spreading what Paul elsewhere calls "teachings of demons" (1 Tim. 4:1), as expressions of the spirit of the antichrist, who would wage a climactic assault on God's people.

Whether by spreading heresy, causing division, or tempting church leaders and getting them to stumble, Satan seeks to undermine the church's witness to the Lord Jesus Christ and render it ineffective. Yet Jesus's promise stands that the gates of hell will not be able to withstand the conquering advance of his spiritual army: "I will build my church, and the gates of hell shall not prevail

---

43. More specifically, Hemer suggests that "presumably Jezebel argued that a Christian might join a guild and participate in its feasts without thereby compromising his faith." *Letters to the Seven Churches*, 123.

against it" (Matt. 16:18). The church must follow the Great Commission of her risen Lord: "Go therefore and make disciples of all nations, baptizing them in the name of the Father and of the Son and of the Holy Spirit, teaching them to observe all that I have commanded you" (Matt. 28:19–20). To the church in Thyatira, the exalted Jesus issues the promise that he will give it "authority over the nations" (2:26) even as he has received authority from God the Father (2:27) in keeping with the prediction in the messianic psalm,

> The LORD said to me, "You are my Son;
> today I have begotten you.
> Ask of me, and I will make the nations your heritage,
> and the ends of the earth your possession.
> You shall break them with a rod of iron
> And dash them in pieces like a potter's vessel." (Ps. 2:7–9)

However, what is remarkable here is that the referent is not the Messiah but his conquering, overcoming, faithful followers, who will share in his authoritative rule. Finally, Jesus says he will give the "morning star" to those who conquer. As with the "white stone" in the previous letter, the reference is mysterious, though perhaps in light of the earlier reference to Balaam in 2:14 there may be an allusion here to the "star . . . out of Jacob" in Balaam's prophecy (Num. 24:17).[44]

LETTER 5: TO THE CHURCH IN SARDIS (3:1–6)

Slightly southeast of Thyatira along the same road, the traveler came to Sardis. According to Greek tradition, this is where king Midas lost his golden touch. In AD 17, Sardis, along with nearby Philadelphia (see below), was hit by a massive earthquake. The city recovered, but its glory days were gone.[45] At the outset of the letter to the church at Sardis, Jesus identifies himself as the one who has the "seven spirits of God" (i.e., the Holy Spirit; cf. 1:4; Zech. 4:10: "seven . . . eyes of the LORD") and the "seven stars" (the same designation as in 2:1; i.e., the angels of the churches; cf. 1:16, 20), asserting both his spiritual insight and his authority over the churches.[46]

Jarringly, the letter doesn't start out with the usual commendation (even when problems are addressed later) but moves straight to exhortation. This

---

44. Hemer, *Letters to the Seven Churches*, says that the symbol "has never been satisfactorily explained" (125). For various proposals and interpretive options, see 125–26; and Osborne, *Revelation* (BECNT), 168.

45. For the ancient background, see Hemer, *Letters to the Seven Churches*, 129–34. See also David A. deSilva, "The Social and Geographical World of Sardis," in Beitzel, *Lexham Geographic Commentary*, 655-73.

46. Regarding the "seven spirits of God," see the discussion in Hemer, *Letters to the Seven Churches*, 142.

is a church that is reputed to be spiritually alive when in fact it is spiritually dead. All Jesus can tell this church is to wake up! That is, nominal believers must repent and be genuinely converted. The exhortation to "strengthen what remains" and the command to vigilance in 3:2–3 may allude to well-known occasions when the citadel in Sardis had succumbed due to lack of alertness by the local citizenry.[47] Also, an integral part of the history of Sardis was the fate of Croesus, whose life was "a classic story of pride before a fall, of misplaced trust in riches, and of lack of vigilance."[48]

At the same time, there were apparently some in the church at Sardis who were spiritually regenerated and had not compromised their faith. In dealing with the godless world around them, they had "not soiled their garments" and compromised their faith (cf. James 1:27; Jude 23). Those who had not succumbed to the world's pressure would be clothed in "white garments," and their name would never be erased from the "book of life" (3:5, an allusion to Exod. 32:32–33). White garments are a symbol of purity, while the book of life conveys the possession of eternal life in God's presence. Also, Jesus would acknowledge them before his Father and the angels (3:5, echoing Jesus's words in Matt. 10:32; Luke 12:8).

LETTER 6: TO THE CHURCH IN PHILADELPHIA (3:7–13)

The next missive is addressed to the close-by city of Philadelphia (Greek for "brotherly love").[49] Other than the epistle to the church at Smyrna, this is the only letter not containing a rebuke. Like Sardis, Philadelphia suffered from the AD 17 earthquake and was slow to recover. The city boasted numerous vineyards, and the Greek god of wine, Dionysius, was a prominent deity. A recent edict by the Roman emperor Domitian in AD 92 to destroy over half of the vineyards would have harmed Philadelphia's economy.[50] At the beginning of the letter, Jesus identifies himself as the one who is both holy and true and who holds the "key of David, who opens and no one will shut, who shuts and no one opens" (an allusion to Isa. 22:22). While originally referring to Eliakim, who controlled access to King David's house, the present reference may be to God's sovereign act of opening the church to gentiles despite Jewish resistance while refusing entry to ethnic Jews who rejected Jesus as Messiah.[51]

---

47. Hemer, *Letters to the Seven Churches*, 144.
48. Hemer, *Letters to the Seven Churches*, 150; see also 131–33.
49. See Mark Wilson, "The Social and Geographical World of Philadelphia," in Beitzel, *Lexham Geographic Commentary*, 674–83.
50. Hemer, *Letters to the Seven Churches*, 158–59.
51. F. J. A. Hort, *The Apocalypse of St John I–III* (London: Macmillan, 1908), 34, cited in Hemer, *Letters to the Seven Churches*, 161.

The letter to the church in Philadelphia is full of encouragement and support. Jesus assures believers that he knows their works and that he has set before them an open door no one can shut. While weak, the church has kept Jesus's word and confessed him before others (3:8). As in the letter to the church at Smyrna (2:9), Jesus refers to "the synagogue of Satan," Jews who not only rejected Jesus as Messiah but persecuted Christians, particularly fellow Jews who embraced the Christian faith. Jesus promises that he will vindicate his followers and subdue their enemies (3:9). What's more, he will keep those believers from the trial that those in the world will soon encounter (3:10).[52] All that those believers need to do is "hold fast to what [they] have," as Jesus will come soon (3:11). Those who conquer will be made pillars in the temple of God, and they will be identified with the name of God, the name of the new Jerusalem (cf. 21:9–22:5), and the new name of Jesus (3:12; cf. Isa. 62:2; Ezek. 48:35).[53]

LETTER 7: TO THE CHURCH IN LAODICEA (3:14–22)

The seventh and final letter is addressed to the church in Laodicea, the city farthest inland, southeast of Philadelphia and almost directly east of Ephesus.[54] In the letter to the Colossians, Paul writes, "When this letter has been read among you, have it also read in the church of the Laodiceans, and see that you also read the letter from Laodicea" (Col. 4:16). Unfortunately, however, this letter from Laodicea has not been preserved. In the present letter to Laodicea, the threefold opening self-identification of Jesus is "the Amen, the faithful and true witness, the beginning of God's creation" (3:14). The Hebrew word *amen* means "it is firm"; that is, God's will cannot be thwarted. Jesus is the faithful and true witness to God par excellence. And he is the beginning of God's creation—not in the sense that he himself is part of creation but in that he preexisted from eternity prior to creation. As Paul wrote in his letter to the Colossians, Jesus is "the firstborn of all creation. For by him all things were created. . . . All things were created through him and for him. And he is before all things, and in him all things hold together" (Col. 1:15–17).

As in the case of the church at Sardis, Jesus goes straight to denunciation, starting with the same phrase: "I know your works" (3:15; cf. 3:1). Against the backdrop of Laodicean culture, Jesus laments that the church is neither hot nor cold but lukewarm, hence he will spit her out of his mouth—harsh words, but Jesus backs up his denunciation with incontrovertible evidence.

52. This passage most likely does not refer to a pretribulation rapture of the church. Schreiner ("Revelation," 545) notes that there is no evidence in Revelation that the church is raptured prior to chapter 4, nor is there a sharp Israel/church distinction in the book.

53. See the discussion in Hemer, *Letters to the Seven Churches*, 167.

54. See Cyndi Parker, "The Social and Geographical World of Laodicea," in Beitzel, *Lexham Geographic Commentary*, 684–96.

The indictment is almost certainly contextualized to the city of Laodicea. A short six miles away, in nearby Hierapolis, were famous hot springs where "hot, sparkling waters rise from deep pools on the city-plateau, which they cross in narrow raised channels . . . and spill over the escarpment edge in white cascades through stepped pools of snowy incrustation. The cliff is in full view of Laodicea. . . . The waters are said to be 95°F."[55] At the same time, "cold, pure water is a notable feature of Colossae."[56] Thus, in contrast to her neighbors, whose waters were either therapeutically hot or refreshingly cold, Laodicea's spiritual condition was lukewarm.

In fact, the church claimed to be rich, but its material prosperity masked great spiritual poverty (3:17). Similar to the church at Sardis, which had a reputation of being alive while being spiritually dead (3:1), the church in Laodicea was in great need of spiritual renewal and revival, of repentance and regeneration. Shockingly, Jesus was standing at the door and knocking at the door of the church from the outside! If anyone heard his voice and opened the door, he would come in and eat with him (3:20). This was a rather desperate situation. The church was nominally Christian but lacked any real spiritual vitality, similar to many mainline churches in the West today. Jesus counsels the church to buy *from him* gold refined by fire, white garments, and eye salve. These items, too, seem to be contextualized to the city of Laodicea, which served as a center of banking and boasted a vibrant textile industry as well as a noted medical school.[57] The savvy bankers in Laodicea needed to buy spiritual gold from Jesus; the city's fashion-conscious needed to buy white garments; and ophthalmologists needed to buy eye salve from Jesus to restore their spiritual vision.

Despite his stinging rebuke, Jesus's words are motivated by love: "Those whom I love, I reprove and discipline; so be zealous and repent" (3:19). In closing, Jesus holds out the reward to anyone who conquers and overcomes. Jesus will grant him to sit with him on his throne and rule with him, as he also conquered and sat down with his Father on his throne (3:21). This is truly an amazing prospect for those who follow the Lamb who was slain, the Lion of Judah, who will return in victorious splendor.

While each of the letters addresses a specific church in Asia Minor at the end of the first century in its unique historical setting, the seven churches of Revelation display a range of spiritual symptoms and conditions that are representative of churches in every culture and every age. Believers in every generation have a need to bear faithful witness to Christ and to avoid spiritual compromise with the godless, surrounding culture. The church must remain

---

55. Hemer, *Letters to the Seven Churches*, 187.
56. Hemer, *Letters to the Seven Churches*, 188.
57. The background is discussed in Hemer, *Letters to the Seven Churches*, 196–201.

vigilant in the face of false teaching seeking to infiltrate the church or already present within its walls. Satan will continue to attack the church, but believers, in all their weakness, can seek refuge under the protection of the all-powerful God, who in Christ has already won the victory on our behalf.

Vision 2: The Divine Court, Trial of the Nations (4:1–16:21)

Narrative Survey and Interpretive Challenges

The next vision—the second in the book following the vision of the exalted Christ and his letters to the seven churches—spans a total of thirteen chapters and is by far the longest of the four visions contained in Revelation. Following the opening throne-room scenes in chapters 4–5, its primary focus is God's judgment of the unbelieving world, which is initially revealed by the breaking of the seven seals in chapter 6 and is formally announced with the sounding of the seven trumpets in chapters 8–9 (though the seventh trumpet is not sounded until 11:14–18) and finally shown as being carried out through the outpouring of the seven bowls in chapter 16.

Due to the complexity of the second vision, it will be helpful to provide (1) a basic outline and (2) an initial discussion of various interpretive approaches taken in the context of a narrative survey of the vision, with special focus on the three septets of judgment and the three major interludes interrupting the narrative sequence. After this, we will move through the basic contents of the vision in customary fashion, though due to the complexity of the second vision, a detailed discussion is impossible here; readers are referred to the standard commentaries listed in the bibliography below.[58]

Structure of John's Second Vision (Revelation 4–16)

Revelation	Contents
4–5	The throne-room scene
6	The seven seals
7	Interlude 1: God's people sealed
8–9	The seventh seal and the seven trumpets
10–11	Interlude 2: The little scroll, the two witnesses, and the seventh trumpet
12–15	Interlude 3: Holy war
16	The seven bowls

58. Regarding major interpretive approaches to Revelation, see Köstenberger, Kellum, and Quarles, *The Cradle, the Cross, and the Crown*, 966–73. If the following discussion is too confusing or not needed, the reader may want to go straight to the section "The Throne-Room Scene (4:1–5:14)," below.

Three Views

The big interpretive question regarding this longest vision of the book is this: what to do with the three septets of judgment, conveyed by the symbolism of seals, trumpets, and bowls.[59] Are these to be interpreted in strictly linear terms as conveying chronological succession (i.e., as twenty-one separate sequential events), in terms of total recapitulation (i.e., seven thrice-repeated events), or somewhere in between these two extremes (see the telescoping view described below)?[60] It is fairly clear that the series of sevens (in the case of the seals, seals 6 and 7) all refer to the coming day of the Lord. The seals are opened, the trumpets blown, and the bowls poured out, all reaching the culminating moment of the day of Yahweh predicted by the OT prophets. The book provides very strong indications that the day of the Lord has arrived, but the Lord himself never appears. While there is an abundance of theophanic language throughout the book, beginning in chapter 4 ("flashes of lightning, and rumblings and peals of thunder," 4:5), as well as Sinai imagery such as eschatological earthquakes (6:12; 11:13; 16:18), expectations of theophanies are rising, but God remains hidden.[61] But then the theophany finally takes place in chapter 19 with the appearance of the rider on the white horse. Thus each of the three sevens builds toward the same climax and ends at the same place.

How do they all line up? This is not entirely clear. Advocates of reading the book in terms of strict chronological succession, as mentioned, argue, rather implausibly, that the sequence is strictly linear, featuring twenty-one consecutive events, while recapitulationists believe each set of sevens in some form revisits the previous cycle of judgments (the difficulty here is how to reconcile differences between corresponding portions in each cycle). The telescoping view, in one of its various permutations, trying to balance progression with overlapping aspects, perhaps more plausibly contends that the first five seals, and then the six trumpets and bowls, refer to the end-time judgment, but that the sixth and seventh seal open the seventh trumpet and bowl. Thus, the sequence would be as follows: seals 1, 2, 3, 4, 5, and 6; trumpets 1, 2, 3, 4, 5, and 6; bowls 1, 2, 3, 4, 5, and 6 (some place seal 6 here); and finally seal, trumpet, and bowl 7.[62]

---

59. The imagery of trumpets and bowls harks back to antecedent salvation history at the exodus.

60. See Köstenberger, Kellum, and Quarles, *The Cradle, the Cross, and the Crown*, 962.

61. See Richard Bauckham, "The Eschatological Earthquake," in *Climax of Prophecy*, 199–209.

62. See charts in Paul M. Hoskins, *The Book of Revelation: A Theological and Exegetical Commentary* (North Charleston, SC: ChristoDoulos, 2017), 25; and Mark Wilson, *Charts on the Book of Revelation: Literary, Historical, and Theological Perspectives* (Grand Rapids: Kregel,

Figure 8.3

Telescoping view of seals, trumpets, and bowls in Revelation

1 2 3 4 5 6	1 2 3 4 5 6	1 2 3 4 5 6	7
Seals	Trumpets	Bowls	Seal, Trumpet, and Bowl
6:1–17	8:6–21	16:1–21	19:11–21

Three Interludes

To complicate matters yet further, chapters 4–16 also contain several interludes. There are three interludes: (1) chapter 7; (2) 10:1–11:14; and (3) chapters 12–14. The main narrative is describing the coming judgment of God, whereas these interludes intermittently ask the question: But what is happening to God's people? The interludes thus serve as a sort of parenthesis helping the readers by anticipating and addressing questions they may be asking. The interludes also clarify the readers' role in relation to the unfolding waves of judgment.[63] God's people are his witnesses. Satan will persecute them, but God will protect them; yet they must remain faithful.

The first interlude, chapter 7, sustains a strong connection with the end of chapter 6, which leaves the reader with the question: Who is able to stand? Chapter 7 answers this question: those who have been sealed with the seal of the Lamb. Throughout, there is a pattern of hearing, then seeing;[64] the seer first hears, but when turning to see, sees not just the people of Israel but a great multitude, the 144,000 typologically representing the eschatological people of God.[65] Chapter 7 also marks the first time the idea of being "marked" appears in the book, drawing on Ezekiel 9, where God sends his angel to mark the righteous in Jerusalem. God's mark represents the protection of his people in the midst of his judgment, just as God marked the faithful of Jerusalem for preservation while the rest were judged. Yet the mark is not a physical but a spiritual mark. Further, it does not spare God's people from suffering or persecution, but from God's judgment. This will help the reader understand Revelation 13, discussed below.

The second interlude, 10:1–11:14, in chapter 10 features another mighty angel descending from heaven with a little scroll and John's prophetic commission;

2007), 78. Hoskins has argued that the seals represent judgments that take place throughout church history, whereas G. K. Beale (*Book of Revelation*, 48, 127–29) suggests that all take place throughout church history in general. Dispensationalists hold that all judgments are still future.

63. See Bauckham, *Climax of Prophecy*, 11–17.

64. See James L. Resseguie, *Narrative Criticism of the New Testament: An Introduction* (Grand Rapids: Baker Academic, 2005), 181–82.

65. See sidebar 20.1 in Köstenberger, Kellum, and Quarles, *The Cradle, the Cross, and the Crown*, 979.

then chapter 11 features two witnesses representing the church, most likely drawing on Moses and Elijah; in addition, the reference to two witnesses in all probability also indicates two individuals who will arise in the end times (see further below). In keeping with the prophet Zechariah, the lampstands represent the witness of the church (cf. chaps. 1–3). There are close literary connections between chapters 11, 12, and 13, which feature the dragon (symbolizing Satan) pursuing the woman (representing God's people). Chapter 11 then portrays God's spiritual protection of his witnesses as they face conflict: they die, but God raises them. Chapters 12–14 take one step back, showing the backdrop of cosmic conflict: the conflict begins in heaven, but then Satan is cast down (possibly at his primordial fall or, perhaps most likely, at the crucifixion) and pursues God's people. On the one hand, Satan is able to conquer them, yet God preserves his people, and they conquer Satan through their deaths. In one very important sense, therefore, Satan has already been defeated. He is confined to the earth, where he wages war on the saints. And his defeat is demonstrated repeatedly as God protects his people spiritually and as they remain faithful in the face of his opposition.

The third interlude, in chapters 12–14 (ending at 15:4), features the church engaged in a holy war against Satan and his minions in the context of three signs. Following a dramatic shift signaled by the introduction, "a great sign appeared in heaven" (12:1), depicting a woman symbolizing Israel. This is followed by a second sign featuring a red dragon symbolizing Satan (12:3). After a period of holy war, a third sign depicts believers' victory over Satan (15:1). Progressively, chapters 12–14 span the period from Christ's earthly ministry to his return. Satan's war on Christ and on God's people is carried on through individuals portrayed as beasts, culminating in two harvests (chap. 14). These chapters thus provide a potted NT salvation history from the cradle, to the cross, to the crown. There is a harvest of the righteous (symbolized by a grain harvest, 14:14–16) and a harvest of the wicked (symbolized by a grape harvest, 14:17–18). Following the third sign in 15:1–4 and a transition (15:5–8), chapter 16, at long last, portrays the outpouring of the seven bowls, signifying the actual occurrence of God's judgment on the unbelieving world, a judgment previously revealed in the seven seals and announced in the seven trumpets.

The Throne-Room Scene (4:1–5:14)

At the outset of the second vision, John is transported "in the Spirit" (4:2) from Patmos to heaven, where he witnesses an extraordinary throne-room scene (cf. Isa. 6:1–4; Ezek. 1:26–28). He sees God seated on his throne, surrounded by twenty-four elders "clothed in white garments, with golden crowns on their heads" (4:4). In front of the throne are seven flaming torches, symbolizing the "seven spirits of God"—that is, the Holy Spirit (4:5).

Also around the throne are four mysterious living creatures in the form of a lion, ox, man, and eagle (4:6–7; cf. Ezek. 1:5, 10).[66] These two groups—the twenty-four elders and the four living creatures—serve as worship leaders and interpreters throughout the book. Most likely, the elders represent the heavenly angelic council, the number 24 possibly deriving from the priestly orders in 1 Chronicles 24:4–5; the living creatures resemble the cherubim and seraphim in Ezekiel 1 and 10 and Isaiah 6.[67]

First, the four living creatures—the inner circle—cry out,

> Holy, holy, holy, is the Lord God Almighty,
>   who was and is and is to come! (4:8; cf. Isa. 6:3)

Antiphonally, the twenty-four elders—the outer circle—cry out,

> Worthy are you, our Lord and God,
>   to receive glory and honor and power,
> for you created all things,
>   and by your will they existed and were created. (4:11)

Then, John sees a scroll with seven seals (5:1; cf. Ezek. 2:9–10). None other than the "Lion of the tribe of Judah, the Root of David" (cf. Gen. 49:9; Isa. 11:1), who "has conquered," "can open the scroll and its seven seals" (5:5), signifying Jesus's enthronement at the Father's right hand as the basis for his authority to reveal God's future judgments. And John sees a Lamb who was slain, with seven horns and seven eyes (symbolizing the Holy Spirit; cf. 1:4; 4:5), taking the scroll, being worshiped by the four living creatures and the twenty-four elders. At this point, multiple worship scenes erupt, praising the Lamb (5:9–14; cf. Ps. 103:20–22).

The Seven Seals (6:1–17)

Then the Lamb opens the seven seals.[68] The first four seals, when opened, each reveal horses with different colors—the famous "horsemen of the Apoca-

---

66. Schreiner ("Revelation," 602) suggests that, cumulatively, these four figures represent all of creation. In Christian iconography these figures were taken to symbolize, in the form of a tetramorph, the four evangelists: most commonly, Matthew as a (winged) man, Mark as a lion, Luke as an ox, and John as an eagle.

67. Osborne, *Revelation Verse by Verse*, 100–103. See also Schreiner, "Revelation," 600.

68. See table 9.7 in Schreiner, "Revelation," 613.

lypse" (cf. Zech. 1:7–11; 6:1–8). Each pertains to earthly judgment along lines similar to the judgment depicted in Jesus's great end-time discourse. The respective colors of the horses are as follows: (1) white (signifying conquest); (2) red (bloodshed); (3) black (famine); and (4) pale green (the color of a corpse, signifying death; 5:2–8; cf. Matthew 24 and parallels).

The remaining seals are moving toward judgment on an even more comprehensive scale in anticipation of the day of the Lord. The fifth seal reveals Christian martyrs crying out for vindication, and then the sixth seal unveils major cosmic upheaval as a portent of the coming universal judgment (6:9–17; cf., e.g., Isa. 34:4; Joel 2:31; see also Matt. 24:29–31). The upcoming judgments reveal God's justice and sovereignty against the backdrop of human depravity. These judgments are meted out in keeping with God's holy and righteous character and in response to the saints' and martyrs' prayers for vindication. Repentance is still possible (cf. 11:13), but time is rapidly running out.

Interlude 1: God's People Sealed (7:1–17)

Following the breaking of the first six seals, which convey God's impending judgment of the unbelieving world, the first major interlude (see narrative survey above) depicts the sealing of God's people (7:3–4). John, the seer, first "hears" the number of the sealed; later, he "sees" them in his vision (cf. 7:9 below).[69] A seal in the ancient world signified ownership and protection. In the NT, believers are said to be "sealed" by the Holy Spirit (Eph. 1:13–14; 4:30; 2 Cor. 1:22). These are symbolically depicted as the 144,000—12,000 from each tribe of Israel (cf. Gen. 35:23–26; the numeric symbolism involves a composite of three perfect numbers: 12 × 12 × 1,000)—though almost certainly the reference is to all Christians, not merely Jews.[70]

At this point, John sees an innumerable crowd from every nation—most likely to be identified with the 144,000—gathered before the throne of God and the Lamb, "clothed in white robes, with palm branches in their hands," and crying out, "Salvation belongs to our God who sits on the throne, and to the Lamb!" (7:9–10). The worship scene includes angels as well as the twenty-four elders and the living creatures, all of whom engage in praise and worship (7:11–12). One of the elders identifies for John those in white robes as those

---

69. James L. Resseguie, *The Revelation of John: A Narrative Commentary* (Grand Rapids: Baker Academic, 2009), 118, 138.

70. Schreiner ("Revelation," 622) notes certain irregularities in the list of twelve tribes: Dan is omitted, while both Joseph and Manasseh are mentioned. Since Manasseh is the offspring of Joseph, it might be expected that Manasseh and Ephraim are included in the list, not Joseph and Manasseh. These liberties support a symbolic interpretation.

who have come out of the "great tribulation" (7:14; cf. Jer. 30:7; Dan. 12:1–2; Mark 13:19)—that is, the conflict spreading throughout history (chaps. 12–14) or the final end-time battle (chaps. 14 and 16).[71] In keeping with the function of interludes in the book, this scene encourages believers to persevere in the midst of tribulation and assures them of ultimate victory. God is protecting them and will vindicate them in the end.

The Seventh Seal and the Seven Trumpets (8:1–9:21)

The Lamb opens the seventh seal, and for a short time ("about half an hour") there is silence in heaven (8:1). What follows is preparations for seven angels to blow seven trumpets announcing the impending judgment of God on the unbelieving world, which may typologically build on Israel's conquest of Jericho (8:2–5; cf. Josh. 6).[72] Then four trumpets are blown in rapid succession (8:6–13), followed by trumpets 5 and 6, which are given more extensive coverage (chap. 9). The various judgments that are announced collectively hark back typologically to the plagues on Egypt prior to the exodus (Exod. 7–10):

- *Trumpet 1*: hail and fire, mixed with blood, signifying the destruction by fire of a third of the earth (cf. Exod. 9:19–35 [the seventh Egyptian plague]; Joel 2:30–31)
- *Trumpet 2*: a great mountain, burning with fire, is thrown into the ocean, a third of which turns into blood, signifying the destruction of a third of sea creatures and ships (cf. Exod. 7:14–21 [the first Egyptian plague]; Jer. 51:25)[73]
- *Trumpet 3*: a great star ("Wormwood") falls from heaven (cf. 6:13; Jer. 9:15), contaminating the waters (a reversal of Moses's miracle at Marah; cf. Exod. 15:23–25), signifying the destruction of a third of the earth's water resources
- *Trumpet 4*: a third of the sun, moon, and stars are struck, dimming a third of each day (cf. Exod. 10:21–23 [the ninth Egyptian plague]; Zeph. 1:15), followed by an eagle flying overhead in midair (cf. 14:6; 19:17) woefully announcing the three remaining trumpets

71. Cf. Schreiner ("Revelation," 625–26), who argues that the entire time preceding Jesus's return is the "great tribulation."

72. Hoskins, *Book of Revelation*, 206. Hoskins discusses this at Rev. 11:19 as the appearance of the ark, connecting this with the Jericho account as well. Cf. table 9.8 in Schreiner, "Revelation," 631.

73. In a Greco-Roman context, the image of a burning mountain may have invoked the fearful memory of the eruption of Mount Vesuvius (AD 79), which reduced the city of Pompeii to ashes.

- **Trumpet 5**: a star falls from heaven[74] and a pit is opened; locusts swarm out, tormenting but not killing unbelievers for five months (cf. Exod. 10:14; Joel 1–2); at this point, the reader is told that "the first woe" is past, but two woes remain (9:12; cf. 11:14)[75]
- **Trumpet 6**: four angels (cf. 7:1) bound at the Euphrates are released to kill a third of the earth's population by troops mounted on powerful, frightening horses, resembling the Parthian army and depicted as a potent force poised to strike[76]

The chapter closes on the ominous note that the surviving remainder of the earth's population still didn't repent from their sins of idolatry, demon worship, or sexual immorality (9:20–21).

Interlude 2: The Little Scroll, the Two Witnesses, and the Seventh Trumpet (10:1–11:19)

On this cliffhanger—with the final seventh trumpet still to come—the narrative continues with another interlude. Another angel emerges from heaven with a little scroll in his hand, one foot on land, the other in the ocean (10:2).[77] He announces that at the sound of the seventh trumpet, God's mystery—a previously undisclosed salvation truth—will be fulfilled just as he announced it to "his servants the [OT] prophets" (10:7, an allusion to Amos 3:7). The scene gives way to John's prophetic commissioning, enacted in the form of the seer eating the little scroll, which is sweet in his mouth but turns bitter

74. This may refer to Satan or a demon (cf. 9:11; 12:5–7; cf. Isa. 14:12–14) or an unfallen angel (cf. 20:1): see the discussion in Osborne, *Revelation Verse by Verse*, who favors the latter, since "it is difficult to conceive of God entrusting the key to the Abyss to the primary inhabitant of the demonic prison house" (159).

75. The name of the king of locusts, the ruler of demons and angel of the abyss (the bottomless pit) is (in Hebrew) Abaddon and (in Greek) Apollyon, both of which mean "Destroyer" (9:11), which epitomizes the judgments signified by the fifth and sixth trumpets. In the OT, "Abaddon" is often used to convey death and destruction (e.g., Job 26:6; 28:22; 31:12; Ps. 88:11; Prov. 15:11; 27:20; see Schreiner, "Revelation," 437).

76. The River Euphrates was a symbol of foreign invasion, as previously in the past enemy powers from the east crossed it to attack Israel, such as the Assyrians, Babylonians, and Persians. The Euphrates also marked the eastern border of the Roman Empire, and the Parthians lived on the other side. See Osborne, *Revelation Verse by Verse*, 167. The Parthians made incursions from the east in both 53 BC and AD 62 (see Schreiner, "Revelation," 639).

77. In John's day, this image would immediately have brought to mind the famous Colossus of Rhodes, one of the "seven wonders" of the ancient world, a giant statue erected in the harbor of the island of Rhodes that symbolized control of both sea and land. While destroyed by an earthquake in 224 BC, its remains were still visible in John's day. Osborne, *Revelation Verse by Verse*, 175.

in his stomach, indicating the unpleasant nature of his task of pronouncing judgment (cf. Ezek. 3). And he is told, "You must again prophesy about many peoples and nations and languages and kings" (10:11), most likely a reference to the remaining visions to follow in chapters 12–22.

Next, he is given a measuring rod and told to measure God's temple (11:1; cf. Ezek. 40:3, 5; Zech. 2:1–5) but not its courtyard, as it is the domain of the nations, who will "trample the holy city" (cf. Dan. 8:9–14) for forty-two months (i.e., three and a half years, a limited and symbolic time, half of the perfect number seven; cf. 1 Kings 17:1; 18:1). But authority will be given to God's two witnesses—likened to olive trees and lampstands (cf. Zech. 4:2–6)—who will prophesy for 1,260 days (the same amount of time—namely, three and a half years; 11:2–3). Most likely, these will be two individuals who come according to the pattern of Moses and Elijah, both of whom performed striking miracles.[78] After this, the beast will wage war against them and kill them (cf. Dan. 7), and their corpses will lie in the streets of the "great city"—symbolically called "Sodom" and "Egypt"—where Jesus was crucified (i.e., Jerusalem).[79] This sets the "old" Jerusalem in stark contrast with the "new Jerusalem" that will be unveiled in the final vision of the book.

But after three and a half days, the two witnesses come back to life (11:11; cf. Ezek. 37:10), and their enemies watch them being taken up to heaven, a possible reference to the rapture (11:12).[80] Then an earthquake shakes the earth, killing seven thousand people, while the rest "[give] glory to the God of heaven," a possible lone reference in the book to genuine repentance (11:13). Thus the "second woe" is past, but one more woe still remains (11:14). At long last, the seventh trumpet is blown (the third "woe"), triggering scenes of worship, as God's judgment is now close at hand and the coming of God's kingdom is near (11:15–16). The twenty-four elders sing a song of worship (11:16–18), God's heavenly temple is opened, and the ark of the covenant becomes visible (cf. 2 Sam. 6:2; Pss. 80:1; 99:1). And all of this is accompanied by powerful signs of theophany, such as thunder and lightning, an earthquake, and massive hail (11:19). The seven seals have been opened, and the seven trumpets have been blown. The stage is set for one final holy war. This scene reminds believers that God preserves them to serve as witnesses even in the face of persecution.

78. Cf. Osborne, *Revelation Verse by Verse*, 186–87. Schreiner ("Revelation," 651–52) thinks the two witnesses symbolically depict the church as a kingdom of priests (cf. Rev. 1:6; 5:10; 20:6).

79. Schreiner ("Revelation," 653) cites several passages where Jerusalem or Judah are likened to Sodom in both the OT (Isa. 1:9–10; 3:9; Jer. 23:14; Lam. 4:6; Ezek. 16:46–56; Amos 4:11) and the NT (Matt. 10:15; 11:23–24; Luke 10:12; Rom. 9:29).

80. Osborne, *Revelation Verse by Verse*, 192–93. The reference is reminiscent of Elijah's being taking up to heaven (2 Kings 2:11) and of Jesus's ascension (Acts 1:9).

Interlude 3: Holy War (12:1–15:8)

The third and final interlude opens with two signs on the earth: a "great sign" of a woman adorned with the sun, moon, and stars, who is giving birth (12:1–2; cf. Gen. 37:9), and "another sign" of a red dragon with seven heads (Dan. 7:4–8)—on which were seven diadems—and ten horns (12:3).[81] The woman—most likely representing not Mary but Israel producing the God-sent Messiah (cf. Isa. 26:18)—gives birth to a son, Jesus, and flees to the wilderness, chased by the dragon, who is intent on devouring the child (cf. Herod's slaughter of infants in Bethlehem, Matt. 2:16). But the woman's son is caught or snatched up to heaven (symbolizing Jesus's resurrection and ascension), and God protects the woman in the wilderness for three and a half years (12:4–6).

Now the location of the (same?) conflict changes from earth to heaven. Michael and his angels fight against the dragon and his minions (cf. Dan. 10:13, 21; 12:1). Satan loses and is cast down from heaven, and his minions with him (12:7–9), which may refer either to Satan's primordial fall (cf. Isa. 14:12–15) or, perhaps more likely, to his defeat at the crucifixion (cf. Luke 10:18).[82] And a loud voice is heard from heaven, rejoicing that now that Satan has been cast out, the kingdom of God and of Christ has come. This is great news for those who have overcome by the "blood of the Lamb and by the word of their testimony" but terrible news for unbelievers who dwell upon the earth, for Satan's fury is intense, as he knows that he only has a short time left (12:10–12). Satan now turns to persecuting the woman and her offspring, but to no avail, as God is protecting them (12:13–17).[83] The reality of spiritual warfare, in which all believers are engaged, is palpable (cf. 2 Cor. 10:3–6; Eph. 6:10–18). The chapter closes ominously with Satan standing on the seashore looking out toward the water.

At this point, John sees rising from the water a *beast*—"the military and administrative head of the empire"[84]—whose description matches almost precisely that of the dragon: ten horns, seven heads, ten diadems (13:1; cf. 12:3; Dan. 7). The ferocious beast combines features of a leopard, bear, and lion

---

81. On the OT background for associating Satan with the mythical figure of a dragon, see Osborne, *Revelation Verse by Verse*, 205.

82. See Osborne, *Revelation Verse by Verse*, 209.

83. The reference to God's protection of the woman for "a time, and times, and half a time" in v. 14 echoes the language of the prophet Daniel (Dan. 7:25) and mirrors the length of time the infamous Seleucid (Greek) ruler Antiochus IV Epiphanes afflicted Israel (reigned 175–164 BC). Schreiner ("Revelation," 665) takes this reference to be symbolic as referring to the period between Jesus's resurrection and return.

84. Osborne, *Revelation Verse by Verse*, 219.

and is given power by the dragon (13:2; cf. Dan. 7:4–7). The beast, a quasi-second person of the unholy trinity (mimicking the relationship between God the Father and the Son), recovers from a fatal wound (mimicking Christ's resurrection), eliciting worship of both the dragon and the beast (13:3–4; cf. 13:12, 14).[85] The beast utters blasphemies against God but holds sway for three and a half years and draws universal worship from all but the saints (13:5–9).[86] This calls for faithfulness and endurance on the part of believers (13:10).

Now, a second beast—"the head of the one-world religion centered on worshiping the beast and the dragon"[87]—rises, though this one emerges from the earth (13:11; cf. Dan. 7:17). This third member of the "unholy trinity" has two horns, like a lamb (cf. Dan. 8:3) but speaks like the dragon. It draws worship to the first beast and performs impressive signs, even making fire come down from heaven as Elijah had done (1 Kings 18:36–39; 2 Kings 1:10–14). The second beast is even empowered to give breath to the image of the first beast, a remarkable feat (cf. Dan. 3:1–6). This seriously turns up the heat on believers, as no one can engage in business unless he has the mark of the beast (Rev. 13:17; cf. 2:9; 3:8). The mark of the beast is a parody of the antecedent passage speaking of God sealing the 144,000 (chap. 7). Yet the mark is not physical but spiritual; the people who have the mark of the beast are those who have followed the beast. As to the beast's identity, its number—which calls for wisdom—is 666 (most likely, in the original instance designating the Roman emperor Nero [reigned AD 54–68]).[88]

The next scene flashing before John's eyes is that of the Lamb standing on Mount Zion, and with him the 144,000 representing the totality of all believers (cf. chap. 7). Those followers of the Lamb are blameless and undefiled, and they sing a song known only by the redeemed (14:1–5). Then John hears

85. The possible background to this is the *Nero redivivus* myth, according to which the Roman emperor Nero, who had committed suicide in AD 68, would come back to life and return at the head of the Parthian army to destroy Rome. See Osborne, *Revelation Verse by Verse*, 224; Köstenberger, Kellum, and Quarles, *The Cradle, the Cross, and the Crown*, 937–39. Schreiner ("Revelation," 532, 666–67) identifies the "unholy trinity" as Satan, the Roman Empire, and false religion.

86. Again, this is reminiscent of Daniel's vision (Dan. 7:8, 20; 11:36), which found initial fulfillment in Antiochus IV Epiphanes (see note 79 above; cf. the "man of lawlessness" in 2 Thess. 2:3–4). See Schreiner, "Revelation," 669.

87. Osborne, *Revelation Verse by Verse*, 219.

88. The letters of the alphabet would be converted into a numeric value, whereby the first letter of the alphabet had a numeric value of 1, the second letter the value 2, and so forth. "Nero Caesar," when spelled in Hebrew (*qsr nrwn*), adds up to the number 666. In that 6 is one less than 7, the perfect number, 666 also conveys imperfection (favored by Schreiner, "Revelation," 672–73, who thinks a reference to Nero is unlikely because of the need to transliterate from Greek to Hebrew and because fear of Nero's return would have lessened by the time Revelation was written).

another angel proclaiming the "eternal gospel"; apparently the church's mission is not quite over, even at this late stage of salvation history (14:6–7; cf. 11:13).[89] A second angel announces the demise of Babylon, the unbelieving world that seduced the inhabitants of the earth with her sexual immorality (14:8; cf. Isa. 21:9). Then, a third angel warns those who would worship the beast and its image (14:9–11). Again, a call is issued for the endurance and faithfulness of the saints (14:12; cf. 13:10), and a blessing pronounced on those who die in the Lord (14:13).

John looks again and sees on a white cloud "one like a son of man" holding a sickle, and a second angel calling on the first angel to reap the harvest on earth, for it is ripe (14:14–16; cf. Joel 3:13). This harvest, as discussed further below, is most likely of believers.[90] The grain harvest is followed by a second, grape harvest (14:17–18; cf. the parable of the wheat and weeds in Matt. 13:24–30). There can be no doubt that this second harvest is of unbelievers, as it is an expression of "the winepress" of God's wrath and results in a vast amount of bloodshed (14:19–20; cf. Isa. 63:3).

Then, John sees a third sign (15:1; cf. 12:1, 3) with two main images: (1) seven angels with seven plagues that complete the outpouring of God's wrath and (2) the saints who conquered standing beside a sea of glass (cf. Ezek. 1:22) with harps in their hands, singing the song of Moses (cf. Exod. 15; Deut. 32) and of the Lamb. They are praising God for his amazing works and his holiness and proclaim that all nations will worship him (15:3–4; cf. Jer. 10:6–7). In a transitional scene (15:5–8), one of the living creatures hands the seven angels seven bowls full of God's wrath, setting the scene for the outpouring of the seven bowls in the next episode.

The Seven Bowls (16:1–21)

Next, John hears a voice coming from the temple urging the angels to pour out the seven bowls of God's wrath (16:1). They do just that, one at a time, typologically building on the Egyptian plagues in Exodus 7–10 (16:2–21):[91]

- **Bowl 1**: painful sores afflict those who bear the mark of the beast and worshiped its image (cf. 14:11; 20:4; see Exod. 8:22–23; 9:4, 6, 9–11 [the sixth Egyptian plague])

89. See esp. Richard Bauckham, "The Conversion of the Nations," in *Climax of Prophecy*, 238–337.

90. This is a minority view; most believe both harvests are of the wicked. But see Osborne, *Revelation Verse by Verse*, 250.

91. See table 9.9 in Schreiner, "Revelation," 687.

- **Bowl 2**: the ocean turns into blood, killing all sea creatures (resembling the first Egyptian plague; cf. 8:8–9 [the second trumpet])

- **Bowl 3**: rivers and springs, likewise, turn into blood (also resembling the first Egyptian plague; cf. Ps. 78:44)

- **Bowl 4**: the sun afflicts people with intense heat, yet no one repents (cf. 8:12 [the fourth trumpet]; and contrast 7:16)

- **Bowl 5**: the beast's kingdom is plunged into darkness (cf. Exod. 10:21–29 [the ninth Egyptian plague]; 8:12 [the fourth trumpet]); no repentance (like Pharaoh), people curse God

- **Bowl 6**: the River Euphrates dries up (cf. Exod. 14:21–22; Josh. 3:13–17), the unholy trinity assembles armies for the great final battle, Armageddon (cf. 9:13–19 [the sixth trumpet])

- **Bowl 7**: a massive earthquake and giant hailstones wreak havoc (Sinai imagery: cf. Exod. 19:16–18), yet people curse God (cf. 6:12–14 [the sixth seal])

We've hit rock bottom. The terrifying judgment on the rebellious world without Christ has been consummated. In the following vision, we'll get a close-up view of the world and its destruction.

Vision 3: Destruction of Babylon, Return of Christ (17:1–21:8)

The Fall of Babylon the Great (17:1–18:24)

The second and longest of the four visions in the book of Revelation has finally come to an end. Chapter 17 is transitional, conveying a sort of pause in the action; narrative continuity is provided by the reference to "one of the seven angels who had the seven bowls," who now becomes the seer's guide for the third and penultimate vision. In a sense, 17:1–19:10 constitutes another interlude. With chapter 16, the divine judgment is finished, but there is not yet an appearance of Yahweh. In chapter 17, then, John travels to earth and is about to learn more about Babylon, the "great prostitute," who typologically symbolizes the unbelieving world apart from Christ. Her earthly splendor is gaudy, her arrogance breathtaking, and her fall precipitous. A stark contrast is presented in the form of a tale of two cities featuring two women, two brides: Babylon on the one hand and the church, the bride of the Lamb, on the other. As with a zoom lens, Babylon's judgment is now depicted in greater detail. Merchants mourn for her, kings grieve over her demise, but heaven rejoices over her destruction.

Structure of the Third Vision in the Book of Revelation (17:1–21:8)

Revelation	Contents
17–18	The fall of Babylon the great
19	The prospect of the marriage supper of the Lamb and the return of Christ
20	The millennial reign of Christ, the devil's demise, and the great white throne judgment
21:1–8	The new heaven and the new earth

Rhetorically, the extended depiction of Babylon's judgment is designed to help John's readers understand why they are commanded to come out of the worldly city. All her beauty is temporary and will soon give way to utter ruin. In fact, what appears attractive in the world's eyes is actually ugly, immoral, and reprehensible when viewed from an eternal, spiritual perspective. The world is thus exposed for what it truly is, and once exposed, it will be severely and irreversibly judged. Those who would be tempted to flirt with the woman depicting all the ephemeral wealth, attractions, and allurements the world has to offer now see her naked and exposed for what she really is. As will be seen, within the book's original historical-cultural setting, the woman portrays the Roman Empire in its material and moral decadence and in its spiritual idolatry and demonic, oppressive force, though typologically the characteristics she displays extend to ungodly cultures of any age.

As intimated in John's introduction to the third vision, the initial and primary subject of the vision is the judgment of the unbelieving world, depicted here as "the great prostitute" situated on many waters, with whom the rulers of the earth perpetrated sexual immorality and who, in turn, rendered earth dwellers dizzy with her "wine" (17:1–2; cf. 17:15; see also 14:8, 10). As John is carried away "in the Spirit," this time into a wilderness, he sees a prostitute seated on a scarlet beast—symbolic of Rome's luxury—replete with blasphemous names (cf. 13:1). The beast has seven heads and ten horns, and the woman is clad in purple and scarlet and decked with gold, jewels, and pearls. In her hand, she is holding a golden cup of abominations and impurities flaunting her sexual immorality (17:3–4; cf. Jer. 51:7). On her forehead, she carries a mysterious sign: "Babylon the great, mother of prostitutes and of earth's abominations" (17:5; cf. 13:16). And the whore is inebriated with the blood of Christian martyrs (17:6; cf. Isa. 49:26; Jer. 46:10; Ezek. 39:18–19).

At this, John marvels as to what the sign might mean, but the angel steps in to explain. The riddle calls for wisdom (17:9; cf. 13:18). As to the beast that "was and is not and is to come," the seven heads represent seven hills—designating Rome (cf. 1 Pet. 5:13), known in the ancient world as the "city on the seven hills"—as well as seven kings, the reign of five of which is past, one is currently reigning, and the reign of the seventh is yet to come but will be brief.[92] The beast on which the woman is seated represents the antichrist who was with Satan, is not here now, but will come at the appointed time yet will be destroyed.[93] The ten horns, for their part, also represent ten kings who are yet to be given power for one hour (symbolic for a short time; cf. 18:10, 17, 19) along with the beast (cf. Dan. 7:7–8, 20–25). These may be client kings who ruled ten provinces under the overall jurisdiction of the Roman emperor but also, beyond this, they represent all the kings of the earth.[94] All of these unite and yield power to the beast, and together they wage war against the Lamb, who emerges triumphant as the supreme Ruler and King.[95] The many waters where the whore is seated—reminiscent of Babylon's location by the Euphrates River (Jer. 51:13)—symbolize all the world's nations, who have been deceived by the great whore (17:15). Yet the ten kings make an alliance with the beast mysteriously *against* the prostitute, rendering her desolate (17:7–17; cf., possibly, 17:5). This "civil war" motif (cf. Ezek. 38:21) would have resonated in Rome, which had a history of civil war, whether in the period between Julius Caesar's death and the beginning of Augustus's reign (44–31 BC) or more recently in the days of Galba, Otho, and Vitellius (AD 68–69) following the suicide of Emperor Nero.[96]

At this point, another angel flies down from the sky, radiant in glory (cf. Ezek. 43:2), who calls out with a loud voice, uttering a dirge concerning Babylon the great prostitute, proclaiming her fall:

92. If Revelation (as is likely) dates to the reign of the Roman emperor Domitian (AD 81–96), he would be the emperor who "now is." Backtracking through the five emperors preceding Domitian would mean the short-lived Galba is the first emperor. Though not literally the first emperor (either Julius Caesar or Augustus), Galba, along with Otho and Vitellius, brought the empire to the brink of disaster, which may make him a fitting starting point.

Alternatively, the symbols could designate empires rather than individual emperors—perhaps Egypt, Assyria, Babylon, Medo-Persia, and Greece as kingdoms of the past and Rome as the current world power. Of course, since these seven "heads," while building on previous historic figures or empires, typologically point to future figures preceding the coming of the antichrist, the identity of these future figures remains to be seen.

Finally, if Revelation was written during Nero's reign, he could be the sixth emperor, who was currently on the throne (see the chart in Osborne, *Revelation Verse by Verse*, 285). Cf. the discussion in Schreiner, "Revelation," 696–99, who favors a symbolic and general solution.

93. Cf. the emergence and demise of the "little horn" in Dan. 7:11, 17–18, 23, 26. See Osborne, *Revelation Verse by Verse*, 282–83.

94. Cf. Osborne, *Revelation Verses by Verse*, 286, who also notes that of these Roman "client kings," only Herod the Great and his grandson Agrippa I actually bore the title "king."

95. The Hebrew superlatives are "Lord of lords" and "King of kings" (17:14; cf. Deut. 10:17; Dan. 2:37, 47).

96. Cf. Osborne, *Revelation Verse by Verse*, 288.

> Fallen, fallen is Babylon the great!
>> She has become a dwelling place for demons,
>> a haunt for every unclean spirit,
>>> a haunt for every unclean bird,
>>> a haunt for every unclean and detestable beast.
> For all nations have drunk
>> the wine of the passion of her sexual immorality. (18:1–3; cf. 14:8;
>>> Isa. 21:9)

The once-great city now resembles a "ghost town, a deserted city inhabited by demons and unclean birds."[97] This illustrates how the once-proud and flourishing empire has become desolate and unfit for human life.

Then John hears another voice from heaven calling on God's people to come out of Babylon, so that they will not share in her sins (cf. Isa. 52:11; Jer. 50:8; Ezek. 20:41). Although the woman is proud, boastful, and self-confident, her destruction will come "in a single day"—death, mourning, famine, and fiery judgment—it's payback time (18:4–8).[98] The kings of the earth who committed spiritual adultery with the woman and lived in great luxury are mourning her demise, wailing over the swift judgment that has come upon the "great city, [the] mighty city, Babylon" (18:9–10; cf. the lament over Tyre in Ezek. 26:17–28 and chapter 27, which provides the blueprint for the laments in this section). The merchants join in the lament (cf. Ezek. 27:27, 36), as no one buys their products anymore, whether luxury goods, grain, animals, or even human slaves (cf. Ezek. 27:12–24).[99] They, too, mourn the sudden demise of the "great city," as do captains and sailors (18:11–20; cf. Ezek. 27:29).

Yet what is a cause of great mourning for those who benefited from the great city's commercial power—kings, merchants, sailors—is cause of great rejoicing in the heavenly realm:

> Rejoice over her, O heaven,
>> and you saints and apostles and prophets,
>> for God has given judgment for you against her! (18:20)

At this, yet another angel flings a great millstone into the ocean and announces that in the same way Babylon will be thrown down and be no more (cf. Jer. 51:53–54). There will be utter devastation and ruin. The contrast between the

---

97. Osborne, *Revelation Verse by Verse*, 292; cf. Isa. 13:21–22; Jer. 50:39; 51:37.

98. Divine retribution proceeds in keeping with the *lex talionis* (the "law of retaliation" stated in Lev. 24:19–21: "eye for eye, tooth for tooth"; cf. Jer. 50:29; Osborne, *Revelation Verse by Verse*, 293–94).

99. See the discussion in Osborne, *Revelation Verse by Verse*, 298–99.

city's flourishing and decadence and her sudden demise couldn't be more stark. One day trade is booming; the next the city is gone. Where there was music, there remains only silence. Joyful weddings are a thing of the past (cf. Jer. 25:10).[100] The day of reckoning has finally arrived. All the atrocities and travesties of justice committed by the political and economic powers of this world have at long last been confronted and addressed. The day that many had thought would never come has finally arrived. Yet while the world mourns, God's people rejoice.

The Return of Christ and the Final Judgment (19:1–20:15)

THE PROSPECT OF THE MARRIAGE SUPPER OF THE LAMB AND THE RETURN OF CHRIST (19:1–21)

The mighty angel's announcement of Babylon's demise now gives way to a mighty "Hallelujah" (Hebrew for "Praise God") chorus in chapter 19. Striking the theme of theodicy, a great crowd in heaven rejoices that "salvation and glory and power belong to our God, for his judgments are true and just" (19:1–2; cf. 16:7). And a second "Hallelujah!" rings out on account of the "smoke" emanating from the great city forever (19:3; cf. 14:11; Isa. 34:9–10). The suffering and martyrdom of God's servants have finally been vindicated, and the world in its egregious immorality and rampant injustice has been judged. Reminiscent of the worship scenes at the outset of the second vision, the twenty-four elders and the four living creatures—"the celestial worship leaders in the book"[101]—join in worship and agree, and a heavenly voice calls on all of God's servants to praise him (19:4–5). At this, a third "Hallelujah!" is heard, rejoicing at the imminent prospect of the marriage supper of the Lamb—the Lord Jesus Christ—with his bride, the church (cf. Matt. 8:11; Luke 14:15; 22:30), who is clothed in "fine linen" representing the righteous deeds of believers (19:6–8; cf. Isa. 61:10). At this, the angel tells John to write that those who are invited to the marriage supper of the Lamb are blessed (cf. Isa. 25:6–8). When John falls down to worship him, the angel rejects all worship and redirects it toward God (19:9–10).

What follows at last unveils the theophany the readers have long been waiting for. John sees heaven open (cf. Ezek. 1:1), and from it emerges a rider on a white horse—the one who is faithful and true (cf. 1:5; 3:7, 14; 16:7; 19:11, 22; 21:5; 22:6), who judges righteously (cf. Isa. 11:4), and who comes to confront and defeat the enemies of God. As in the opening appearance of the exalted

---

100. Osborne (*Revelation Verse by Verse*, 304) perceptively notes the implicit contrast with the "bride of Christ" (19:7–8; 21:2, 9).

101. Osborne, *Revelation Verse by Verse*, 308. Cf. 4:8–11; 5:8, 11, 14; 7:11–17; 11:16; 14:3; 19:4.

Christ in chapter 1, Jesus is described in 19:11–16 with a series of stunning, awe-inspiring images at his return:

- eyes like flames of fire (cf. 1:14; 2:18; cf. Dan. 10:6)
- a plethora of diadems on his head (elsewhere in the NT only in 12:3; 13:1, there, by contrast, with reference to the crowns of the dragon and the beast)
- clothed in a blood-dipped robe (cf. 14:10; Isa. 63:3)
- called "The Word of God" (cf. John 1:1, 14)
- followed by the armies of heaven clothed in fine linen (like the bride; cf. 19:8) riding on white horses (like Jesus; cf. 19:11)
- a sharp sword emanating from his mouth (cf. 1:16; 2:12, 16)
- "Supreme King and Ruler" (cf. 17:14) written on his robe at the thigh level[102]

The following scenes then depict the beginning of a resolution (19:17–21). An angel announces that the final judgment is about to take place and issues an invitation to the grisly "great supper of God"—the antithesis of the marriage supper of the Lamb—feasting on the flesh of God's enemies (19:17–18; cf. Ezek. 39:17–20). At this point, the returning Messiah fully vanquishes the demonic opposition and the kings of the earth (19:19–21), marking the fulfillment of the sixth seal, seventh trumpet, and seventh bowl (see above). The end-time battle is no contest.[103] The beast and the false prophet—who had performed the sign that "deceived those who had received the mark of the beast and those who worshiped its image" (19:20; cf. 13:11–18)—are captured and thrown alive into the lake of fire.[104] All the rest are likewise slain by the sword emanating from the mouth of the rider on the white horse (19:21; cf. 19:15). The kings of the earth—arrayed for battle at 16:14—and the forces of evil are judged, and the kingdom of God—announced at 11:15 ("The kingdom of the world has become the kingdom of our Lord and of his Christ, and he shall reign forever and ever")—is about to arrive.

---

102. See the discussion in Osborne, *Revelation Verse by Verse*, 313–15.

103. OT passages depicting the end-time battle include Isa. 31:4; 59:17–20; 63:1–5; Ezek. 38–39; Dan. 12:1–3; Joel 3:9–16; Zech. 12:3–9; 14:2–9 (listed in Osborne, *Revelation Verse by Verse*, 318).

104. Deception is an important theme in Revelation. In chaps. 2–3, false teachers such as the "woman Jezebel" are denounced for leading believers astray. Subsequently in the book, deception is one of the major functions of Satan and the beasts, who deceive the nations and lead them astray (chaps. 12–13). Yet now the beast and the false prophet are judged, and Satan is bound and can no longer deceive the nations.

The Millennial Reign of Christ, the Devil's Demise, and the Great White Throne Judgment (20:1–15)

Chapter 20 is moving the action forward chronologically, narrating the binding of Satan and Christ's millennial reign with the departed saints.[105] First, an angel holding the key to the pit and a large chain (cf. 9:1) is shown to seize Satan and to bind him for a thousand years (commonly known as the "millennium"). For now, the devil's days of deceiving the nations are over, though when the millennium is over, the devil "must be released for a little while" according to God's sovereign plan (20:1–3). After this, John sees a judgment scene; on the thrones are Christian martyrs and others who didn't bow their knee to the beast and its image and didn't receive its mark on their foreheads or hands (cf. 3:21; Dan. 7:22; Matt. 19:28; 1 Cor. 6:2–3). These departed Christian saints are resurrected—the "first resurrection" (cf. 1 Cor. 15:51–52; 1 Thess. 4:13–18)—and reign with Christ for a thousand years (or, if figurative, an unspecified long period of time). John parenthetically notes that others (most likely unbelievers) weren't resurrected until after the millennium (20:5).[106] Those who share in the first resurrection are blessed, as the "second death"—that is, the divine judgment and consignment to hell—has no power over them (20:6; cf. 20:14; 2:11). As Grant Osborne contends, the purpose of the millennium is twofold: (1) the public vindication of the suffering saints; and (2) the public vindication of the righteousness of God's judgment of the unbelieving world (theodicy).[107] As Osborne remarks, the sobering "truth is that even after a billion years those who are controlled by sin will still hate Christ!"[108]

At the end of the thousand years, Satan is released and marshals the nations of the earth for one last-gasp, ill-fated attempt to overthrow the reign of God and his Christ. A vast army gathers (cf. 16:14) from the four corners of the

105. Schreiner ("Revelation," 726) speaks out against the view that Rev. 20 chronologically follows Rev. 19 because of the apparent universality of God's judgment in Rev. 19. However, Satan is not finally judged until after the millennium (Rev. 20:7–10), followed by the "great white throne" judgment (Rev. 20:11–15), and it may thus reasonably be surmised that the judgment at the end of Rev. 19 was not total.

106. "Came to life" in v. 4 and "first resurrection" in vv. 5 and 6 most likely refer to physical resurrection (cf. Schreiner, "Revelation," 728–29, who notes that the amillennial view holds that a spiritual resurrection is in view). The important interpretive question with regard to the millennium specifically and with regard to the book of Revelation in general is the distinction between symbolism and the spiritual dimension. A vision or message is given in the form of symbols, but that doesn't mean there is no historical referentiality. By pointing out that the message is conveying a spiritual truth in symbolic form, we're not saying a given event or person is not literally true; rather, we're pointing out that this matter is conveyed by a symbol. If the author means that symbol to be understood symbolically, that constitutes the literal meaning.

107. Osborne, *Revelation Verse by Verse*, 331–32.

108. Osborne, *Revelation Verse by Verse*, 332.

earth—Gog (a king) and Magog (the "land of Gog"; cf. Ezek. 38–39)—and marches across a large plain toward the camp and city of the saints, but fire from heaven consumes them, and the devil is cast into a lake of fire where the beast and the false prophet, the other members of the "unholy trinity," already are, to everlasting torment (20:7–10; cf. 19:20–21; Dan. 7:9–11). Now the final judgment—commonly referred to as "the great white throne judgment" (white being a common symbol for purity and holiness)—ensues; now all the remaining dead are raised. In a memorable scene, John writes, "And I saw the dead, great and small, standing before the throne, and books were opened. Then another book was opened, which is the book of life. And the dead were judged by what was written in the books, according to what they had done" (20:12). This may refer to the judgment of believers for the purpose of assigning rewards.[109] After this, the remaining dead—most likely unbelievers (20:15)—are judged, each according to their works (20:13).[110] In the end, Death and Hades themselves are cast into the lake of fire, as is anyone whose name is "not found written in the book of life" (20:14–15; cf. 1 Cor. 15:26).

The New Heaven and the New Earth (21:1–8)

At this point, as if dark storm clouds give way to the rays of the sun, John now sees "a new heaven and a new earth" (21:1; cf. Isa. 65:17; 66:12) as the book transitions from the latter portion of the present vision (19:11–21:8) and moves toward the beginning of the fourth and final vision (21:9–22:5). Most likely, this represents not merely a restored, refurbished world but a new world replacing the old (cf. 2 Pet. 3:10). And he sees the new Jerusalem—which will form the focus of the fourth and final vision below—descending from heaven, "prepared as a bride adorned for her husband" (21:2; cf. Isa. 54:5–6, 11; 61:10). This stands in stark contrast to the old, earthly Jerusalem, which crucified her Lord (11:8). In the holy city (cf. Isa. 52:1), God's covenant vision and promise will at last be fulfilled, culminating the entire scope of salvation history. God will dwell with his people, and they will be his people, and he their God (21:3; cf. Lev. 26:11–12; Jer. 31:33; Ezek. 37:27). No longer will there be a sharp

---

109. While many take 20:12 to refer to the judgment of unbelievers, it is possible that believers are in view here and that the judgment is not condemnation but a judgment of rewards (so, e.g., Osborne, *Revelation Verse by Verse*, 333–34). Of course, 20:4 mentions that the departed saints came to life at the outset of the millennium, though 20:5 says that "the rest of the dead did not come to life until the thousand years were ended." Thus, the dead mentioned in 20:4 may correspond to those referred to in 20:12 (believers), and the dead mentioned in 20:5 may correspond to those referred to in 20:13 (unbelievers). If so, 20:12 would refer to the judgment of believers (rewards), and 20:13 would refer to the judgment of unbelievers (hell).

110. See previous note.

separation between heaven and earth. In that blessed, eternal state, there will be no more tears, death, mourning, or pain (21:4; cf. Isa. 25:8; 30:19; 35:10).

Strikingly, this is the first time (after 1:8) in the book when the one "who was seated on the throne"—God himself—raises his voice. He affirms that he is the one who makes "all things new" (cf. Isa. 65:17) and tells John to write down what he sees, as all of God's "words are trustworthy and true" and thus of vital importance for the church (21:5; cf. 1:11, 19). Just as Jesus cried at the cross, "It is finished" (*tetelestai*, John 19:30), so now the one who sits on the throne—the sovereign God of the ages—tells John, "It is done" (*gegonan*, 21:6). The verbal similarity of this passage to the similar statement in 16:17, "It is done" (*gegonen*), ties the present passage in with the seventh bowl judgment as its obverse. God will quench the thirst of those who are thirsty and give those who conquer their inheritance (21:7)—that is, their eternal reward (cf., e.g., Eph. 1:14; 3:6; Titus 3:7; 1 Pet. 1:4). Parenthetically, John notes that, by contrast, the fiery lake and the second death will be the portion of those who were faithless and immoral (21:8; cf. 20:13–15; this is one of several vice lists in this book and in the NT at large). And on this ominous note, the momentous third vision of the book of Revelation comes to a close, and all that remains is one final glimpse of the eternal state in heaven.

Vision 4: Believers' Reward, New Creation (21:9–22:5)

Heaven as a Holy Sanctuary (21:9–27)

Once more, John is "in the Spirit" (21:10). He is transported to a high mountain, where he has a vision of the new Jerusalem, "the holy city . . . coming down out of heaven from God" (21:10). This is now the fourth and final vision narrated in the book, following the vision of the exalted Christ and his message to the seven churches (chaps. 1–3), the vision of God's judgment on the unbelieving world, which has taken up the lion's share of the book (chaps. 4–16), and the vision of the whore of Babylon, which symbolizes the depravity and decadence of fallen, sinful humanity (chaps. 17–20). This fourth and final vision brings proper closure to the book and, in fact, to the entire canon of Scripture, which began with God's creation and his placement of the first man and the first woman in a pristine garden—and which now ends with the description of the splendor of the celestial city, the eternal destination of the followers of God and of his Christ.[111]

111. See T. Desmond Alexander, *The City of God and the Goal of Creation: An Introduction to the Biblical Theology of the City of God*, Short Studies in Biblical Theology (Wheaton: Crossway, 2018).

Narrative continuity is provided by the fact that it is the seven angels who had the seven bowls conveying the outpouring of God's judgment on the unbelieving world who now set out to show John "the Bride, the wife of the Lamb" (21:9). The typological depiction of the new Jerusalem as Christ's bride symbolizes the union of Christ and his church in the form of a wedding and marriage. What started out as a union between the first man and the first woman in the book of Genesis is now consummated as a spiritual union between Christ and his bride, the church (cf. Eph. 5:31–32). Already in the church age commencing at Pentecost, Christ was the head of the church and the church was his body (e.g., Eph. 5:22–33). Now, the spiritual union between Christ and his church is consummated, rendering their union during the church age a sort of spiritual betrothal or engagement period. Mountains throughout Scripture serve as places of divine revelation, whether Mount Sinai (Exod. 19–20), Mount Nebo (Deut. 34:1–4), Mount Zion (Heb. 12:22; Rev. 14:1), the Mount of Transfiguration (Matt. 17:1–8), or now the place where John has a vision of the new Jerusalem.[112]

The new Jerusalem is described in resplendent, glorious terms (cf. Isa. 6:1–4; Ezek. 43:2–5):

- radiant like the rarest of jewels, like jasper, clear as crystal (21:11)
- surrounded by a high wall with twelve gates, with twelve angels and the names of the twelve tribes, with three gates each in every direction—east, north, south, and west (21:12–13; cf. Ezek. 48:30–35)
- the wall has twelve foundations inscribed with the names of the twelve apostles (21:14)

In what follows, the vast dimensions of the city—laid out in the form of a square—and its gates and walls are given (21:15–17).[113] While the city is described as being out of "pure gold, like clear glass" (21:18; cf. 1 Kings 6:20–22), the wall's foundations are described as being adorned with twelve precious jewels resembling OT priestly garments (21:19–20; cf. Exod. 28:17–20),[114] and the city's gates as adorned with twelve pearls (cf. Isa. 54:11–12). Like the city, the street is pure gold, like clear glass (21:21). Remarkably, there is no temple, as God and the Lamb are the temple (21:22). Also, there is no sun or moon, as the glory of God illumines the city, and the nations walk by its light (21:23–24;

112. Cf. Ezek. 40:1–2. On the mountain motif in Scripture, see Terence L. Donaldson, *Jesus on the Mountain: A Study in Matthean Theology* (Sheffield: JSOT Press, 1985).
113. See Osborne, *Revelation Verse by Verse*, 348–49.
114. See the chart in Osborne, *Revelation Verse by Verse*, 350.

reiterated at 22:5; cf. Isa. 60:3, 5, 11). The gates always remain open (cf. Isa. 60:11), and there is never any night (21:25; reiterated at 22:5). Access is open to nothing unclean but only to those whose names are written in the Lamb's book of life (21:27).

Heaven as the Completed Garden of Eden (22:1–5)

Reminiscent of the original garden of Eden with the tree of life in the midst of the garden and the four rivers Pishon, Gihon, Tigris, and Euphrates (Gen. 2:9–14), the angel proceeds to show John the river of life, "flowing from the throne of God and of the Lamb," as well as the tree of life with twelve kinds of fruit, one for each month (22:1–2; cf. Gen. 3:22). This shows that God is the source and giver of eternal life and of continual nourishment and provision. Thus the images of a garden and of a city are fused in John's vision of the heavenly topography; the vision is also reminiscent of Ezekiel's vision of a life-giving river flowing from the temple, lined abundantly with trees that provide both food and healing (Ezek. 47:7–12).

In their heavenly dwelling, believers will see God's face (!), indicating that the divine-human relationship has now been fully and irreversibly restored.[115] His name will be on their forehead (i.e., they will be completely his), and they will reign with him forever (22:4–5). We seldom think about eternity in our daily lives, but one day the new heaven and the new earth will be very real and palpable, and the things of this world will be past. The book of Revelation holds up a beautiful vision of life forever in the presence of God and Christ that should serve as an encouragement and incentive to continue to follow Christ even in the midst of adversity and opposition.

Epilogue (22:6–21)

Just as the book starts with a prologue (1:1–8), it concludes with an epilogue, as does John's Gospel. The epilogue begins with three affirmations. First, the *angel* affirms the truthfulness of the revelation contained in the book and asserts that "the Lord, the God of the spirits of the prophets [cf. Num. 27:16], has sent his angel to show his servants what must soon take place" (22:6, echoing 1:1–2; see also 1:19; 4:1). Second, *Jesus* himself affirms that he is coming soon and pronounces a blessing on those who keep the prophecy contained in the book (22:7). Third, *John* certifies that he saw the visions

115. Cf. Exod. 33:20; John 1:18; and the discussion in Osborne, *Revelation Verse by Verse*, 359.

recorded in this book (22:8). When he attempts to worship the angelic messenger, the angel refuses and tells John to worship God (22:9). He also tells him not to seal the prophecy, as the time is near (22:10); the wicked should continue to do what is evil, while the righteous should continue to do what is right (22:11; cf. Dan. 12:9–10). A second time, Jesus promises to come soon and to reward each person for what he or she has done (22:12). He is "the Alpha and Omega, the first and the last, the beginning and the end" (22:13; cf. 1:8, 17; 21:6). Another blessing is pronounced on those who "wash their robes" (i.e., cleanse themselves) so as to be able to enter the city and to eat from the tree of life (symbolizing the possession of eternal life in God's presence; 22:14). All who are immoral will be forever shut out (22:15).

At this, Jesus affirms that it is he who sent his angel to testify about the matters contained in the book (22:16; cf. 1:1–2). He is "the root" and descendant of David (cf. Isa. 11:1, 10), "the bright morning star" (22:16; cf. 2:28; Num. 24:17). The Spirit and the bride (i.e., the church) longingly beckon Jesus to come. And the reader, too, is urged to echo their cry, along with all those who are thirsty for the water of life, dispensed at no charge (22:17; cf. Isa. 55:1). Just as a blessing was pronounced earlier on those who keep the prophecy contained in the book (cf. 22:7), so now a warning is issued for those who add or take away any of it (22:18–19; cf. Deut. 4:2; 12:32; 29:20). God's prophecy about end-time events must come to pass, and no one can resist what he has sovereignly ordained. For the third time, Jesus affirms that he will come soon (22:20; cf. 22:7, 12). And the seer replies, "Amen. Come, Lord Jesus!" (22:20). As is appropriate for a work with an epistolary framework, the book concludes with the final well-wish, "The grace of the Lord Jesus be with all. Amen" (22:21).

The epilogue is a final important reminder that while Revelation does cast a vision of what is going to happen in the future, it also tells us how to live as followers of the Lamb in the present. We are called to obedient living and faithful witness, and we can be encouraged because God will sustain and preserve us until he brings about our final salvation at the return of Christ. The book also warns complacent believers who suppose they can be Christ-followers while walking in the ways of the world. Such believers need to realize that they must cast their lot with the persecuted church or they cannot be faithful to the crucified Christ whom they profess to follow. They must eschew all forms of social, economic, political, or religious compromise even if it means persecution. As Jesus himself pointed out during his earthly ministry, no one can serve both God and money (Matt. 6:24). One's allegiance must be either with Christ and the community of believers or with the world, and one's reward or punishment will ensue in accordance with this all-important choice. This is not a matter of outward confession or lip service but of active obedience; actions speak louder than words.

Thus, fittingly, the canon of Scripture has come to an end with a resounding "Amen." God's Word—including the apocalyptic prophecies of the final book in the canon, the book of Revelation—will certainly come to pass and will complete human history, which began with God's creation. God's Word has continued through the fall, the call of Abraham, the exodus and giving of the law through Moses, the promises made to King David of an eternal dynasty, and the first coming of Jesus for salvation; and it will continue until his second coming, for vindication and judgment and to bring about the final state. God has abundantly proven not only his faithfulness but also his abundant mercy and grace toward the people he created. He has proven faithful even where his creatures have been unfaithful. And he has provided in Christ a means of salvation and forgiveness that still stands as a gracious offer to those who have yet to repent of their sins and embrace by faith the sacrifice rendered by Christ on the cross: "And this gospel of the kingdom will be proclaimed throughout the whole world as a testimony to all nations, and then the end will come" (Matt. 24:14).

Revelation: Commentaries

Aune, David E. *Revelation*. 3 vols. WBC 52. Nashville: Nelson, 1997, 1998.

Beale, G. K. *The Book of Revelation*. NIGTC. Grand Rapids: Eerdmans, 1999.

Blount, Brian K. *Revelation: A Commentary*. NTL. Louisville: Westminster John Knox, 2009.

Charles, R. H. *The Revelation of St. John*. ICC. 2 vols. Edinburgh: T&T Clark, 1920.

Duvall, J. Scott, and Mark Strauss. *Revelation*. TTC. Grand Rapids: Baker Books, 2017.

Fee, Gordon D. *Revelation*. NCC. Eugene, OR: Cascade, 2010.

Ford, J. Massyngberde. *Revelation*. AB 38. New York: Doubleday, 1975.

Harrington, Wilfrid J. *Revelation*. SP 16. Collegeville, MN: Liturgical Press, 2008.

Hoskins, Paul M. *The Book of Revelation: A Theological and Exegetical Commentary*. North Charleston, SC: ChristoDoulos, 2017.

Keener, Craig S. *Revelation*. NIVAC. Grand Rapids: Zondervan, 2009.

Koester, Craig R. *Revelation: A New Translation with Introduction and Commentary*. AB 38A. New Haven: Yale University Press, 2014.

Ladd, George E. *A Commentary on the Revelation of John*. Grand Rapids: Eerdmans, 1972.

Mathewson, David L. *Revelation: A Handbook on the Greek Text*. BHGNT. Waco: Baylor University Press, 2016.

Michaels, J. Ramsey. *Revelation*. IVPNTC 20. Downers Grove, IL: InterVarsity, 1997.

Morris, Leon L. *Revelation*. 2nd ed. TNTC. Downers Grove, IL: IVP Academic, 2009.

Mounce, Robert H. *The Book of Revelation*. Rev. ed. NICNT. Grand Rapids: Eerdmans, 1997.

Osborne, Grant R. *Revelation*. BECNT. Grand Rapids: Baker Academic, 2002.

———. *Revelation Verse by Verse*. Osborne New Testament Commentaries. Bellingham, WA: Lexham, 2016.

Patterson, Paige. *Revelation*. NAC. Nashville: B&H Academic, 2012.

Resseguie, James L. *The Revelation of John: A Narrative Commentary*. Grand Rapids: Baker Academic, 2009.

Schreiner, Thomas R. "Revelation." In *ESV Expository Commentary*, vol. 12, *Hebrews–Revelation*, edited by Iain M. Duguid, James M. Hamilton Jr., and Jay Sklar, 525–754. Wheaton: Crossway, 2018.

Wall, Robert W. *Revelation*. NIBC. Grand Rapids: Baker, 1991.

Wilson, Mark W. *Revelation*. ZIBBC. Grand Rapids: Zondervan, 2015.

Witherington, Ben, III. *Revelation*. NCBC. Cambridge: Cambridge University Press, 2003.

Revelation: Articles, Essays, and Monographs

Allen, Garrick V. "Scriptural Allusions in the Book of Revelation and the Contours of Textual Research 1900–2014: Retrospect and Prospect." *CBR* 14 (2016): 319–39.

Aune, David E. "The Apocalypse of John and the Problem of Genre." *Semeia* 36 (1986): 65–96.

Bandstra, A. J. "A Kingship and Priests: Inaugurated Eschatology in the Apocalypse." *CTJ* 27 (1992): 10–25.

Barr, David L. *Reading the Book of Revelation: A Resource for Students*. RBS 44. Atlanta: Society of Biblical Literature, 2003.

Bauckham, Richard. *The Climax of Prophecy: Studies on the Book of Revelation*. London: T&T Clark, 1993.

———. *The Theology of the Book of Revelation*. NTT. Cambridge: Cambridge University Press, 1993.

Bay, Carson. "Lion of the Apocalypse: A Leonine Messiah in the Book of Revelation." *BR* 60 (2015): 65–93.

Beagley, A. J. *The "Sitz im Leben" of the Apocalypse, with Particular Reference to the Role of the Church's Enemies*. BZNW 50. Berlin: de Gruyter, 1987.

Beale, G. K. *John's Use of the Old Testament in Revelation*. JSNTSup 166. Sheffield: Sheffield Academic, 1998.

Beale, G. K., and Sean M. McDonough. "Revelation." In *Commentary on the New Testament Use of the Old Testament*, edited by G. K. Beale and D. A. Carson, 1081–161. Grand Rapids: Baker Academic, 2007.

Blaising, Craig A., and Darrell L. Bock. *Progressive Dispensationalism*. Grand Rapids: Baker, 1993.

Campbell, W. Gordon. *Reading Revelation: A Thematic Approach*. Cambridge: James Clarke, 2012.

Chilton, Bruce. *Visions of the Apocalypse: Receptions of John's Revelation in Western Imagination.* Waco: Baylor University Press, 2013.

Collins, John J. "Introduction: Towards the Morphology of a Genre." *Semeia* 14 (1979): 1–20.

Court, John M. *The Book of Revelation and the Johannine Apocalyptic Tradition.* JSNTSup 190. Sheffield: Sheffield Academic, 2000.

deSilva, David A. *Seeing Things John's Way: The Rhetoric of the Book of Revelation.* Louisville: Westminster John Knox, 2009.

Diehl, Judith A. "'Babylon' Then, Now and 'Not Yet': Anti-Roman Rhetoric in the Book of Revelation." *CBR* 11 (2013): 168–95.

Duvall, J. Scott. *A Theology of Revelation.* BTNT. Grand Rapids: Zondervan, forthcoming.

Friesen, Steven J. *Imperial Cults and the Apocalypse of John: Reading Revelation in the Ruins.* Oxford: Oxford University Press, 2001.

Gorman, Michael J. *Reading Revelation Responsibly: Uncivil Worship and Witness; Following the Lamb into the New Creation.* Eugene, OR: Wipf & Stock, 2011.

Harker, Andrew. "The Affective Directives of the Book of Revelation." *TynBul* 63 (2012): 115–30.

Hays, Richard B., and S. Alkier, eds. *Revelation and the Politics of Apocalyptic Interpretation.* Waco: Baylor University Press, 2012.

Helyer, Larry R., and Ed Cyzewski. *The Good News of Revelation.* Eugene: Wipf & Stock, 2014.

Hemer, Colin J. *The Letters to the Seven Churches of Asia in Their Local Setting.* JSNTSup 11. Sheffield: JSOT Press, 1986.

Herms, Ronald. *An Apocalypse for the Church and for the World: The Narrative Function of Universal Language in the Book of Revelation.* BZNW 143. Berlin: de Gruyter, 2006.

Johnson, Alan F. "Revelation." In *Hebrews–Revelation*, vol. 13 of *The Expositor's Bible Commentary*, rev. ed., edited by Tremper Longman III and David E. Garland, 571–789. Grand Rapids: Zondervan, 2005.

Koester, Craig R. "The Church and Its Witness in the Apocalypse of John." *TTKi* 78 (2007): 266–82.

———. "On the Verge of the Millennium: A History of Interpretation of Revelation." *WW* 15 (1995): 128–36.

Kovacs, Judith, and Christopher Rowland. *Revelation: The Apocalypse of Jesus Christ.* BBC. Oxford: Blackwell, 2004.

Kraus, Thomas J., and Michael Sommer, eds. *Book of Seven Seals: The Peculiarity of Revelation, Its Manuscripts, Attestation, and Transmission.* WUNT 1/363. Tübingen: Mohr Siebeck, 2016.

Kraybill, J. Nelson. *Apocalypse and Allegiance: Worship, Politics, and Devotion in the Book of Revelation.* Grand Rapids: Brazos, 2010.

Kuykendall, Michael. "The Twelve Visions of John: Another Attempt at Structuring the Book of Revelation." *JETS* 60 (2017): 535–55.

Labahn, Michael, and Outi Lehtipuu, eds. *Imagery in the Book of Revelation.* Leuven: Peeters, 2011.

Lioy, Dan. *The Book of Revelation in Christological Focus*. Studies in Biblical Literature 58. New York: Peter Lang, 2003.

Marriner, Keith T. *Following the Lamb: The Theme of Discipleship in the Book of Revelation*. Eugene, OR: Wipf & Stock, 2016.

Mathewson, David. "Assessing Old Testament Allusions in the Book of Revelation." *EvQ* 75 (2003): 311–25.

———. "Revelation in Recent Genre Criticism: Some Implications for Interpretation." *TrinJ* NS 13 (1992): 193–213.

Mayo, Philip L. *"Those Who Call Themselves Jews": The Church and Judaism in the Apocalypse of John*. PTMS 60. Eugene, OR: Pickwick, 2006.

Michaels, J. Ramsey. *Interpreting the Book of Revelation*. GNTE. Grand Rapids: Baker, 1992.

Moyise, Steve. *The Old Testament in the Book of Revelation*. JSNTSup 115. Sheffield: Sheffield Academic, 1995.

———, ed. *Studies in the Book of Revelation*. Edinburgh: T&T Clark, 2001.

Murphy, Frederick J. *Apocalypticism in the Bible and Its World: A Comprehensive Introduction*. Grand Rapids: Baker Academic, 2012.

Naylor, Michael. "The Roman Imperial Cult and Revelation." *CBR* 8 (2010): 207–39.

Osiek, Carolyn. "Apocalyptic Eschatology." *TBT* 37 (1996): 341–45.

Pate, C. Marvin, ed. *Four Views on the Book of Revelation*. Grand Rapids: Zondervan, 1998.

Pattemore, Stephen. *The People of God in the Apocalypse: Discourse, Structure and Exegesis*. SNTSMS 128. Cambridge: Cambridge University Press, 2004.

Porter, Stanley E. "The Language of the Apocalypse in Recent Discussion." *NTS* (1989): 582–603.

Porter, Stanley E., and A. K. Gabriel. *Johannine Writings and Apocalyptic: An Annotated Bibliography*. JS 1. Leiden: Brill, 2013.

Rainbow, Paul A. *Johannine Theology: The Gospel, the Epistles and the Apocalypse*. Downers Grove, IL: InterVarsity, 2014.

———. *The Pith of the Apocalypse: Essential Message and Principles for Interpretation*. Eugene, OR: Wipf & Stock, 2008.

Sandy, D. Brent, and Daniel M. O'Hare. *Prophecy and Apocalyptic: An Annotated Bibliography*. IBRB 4. Grand Rapids: Baker Academic, 2005.

Smalley, Stephen. *Thunder and Love: John's Revelation and John's Community*. Milton Keynes, UK: Word, 1994.

Smith, Brandon D. "The Identification of Jesus with YHWH in the Book of Revelation: A Brief Sketch." *CTR* 14, no. 1 (Fall 2016): 67–84.

Stevens, Gerald L. *Revelation: The Past and Future of John's Apocalypse*. Eugene, OR: Pickwick, 2014.

Sweeney, James P. "Annihilation or Renewal? The Meaning and Function of New Creation in the Book of Revelation." *BBR* 22 (2012): 455–58.

Swete, H. B. *The Apocalypse of St. John*. 3rd ed. London: Macmillan, 1909.

Tavo, Felise. *Woman, Mother and Bride: An Exegetical Investigation into the "Ecclesial" Notions of the Apocalypse*. BTS 3. Leuven: Peeters, 2007.

Tõniste, Külli. *The Ending of the Canon: A Canonical and Intertextual Reading of Revelation 21–22*. LNTS 526. London: Bloomsbury T&T Clark, 2016.

Trail, Ronald L. *An Exegetical Summary of Revelation 1–11*. 2nd ed. Dallas: SIL International, 2008.

Wainwright, Arthur W. *Mysterious Apocalypse: Interpreting the Book of Revelation*. Nashville: Abingdon, 1993.

Whitaker, Robyn J. *Ekphrasis, Vision, and Persuasion in the Book of Revelation*. WUNT 2/410. Tübingen: Mohr Siebeck, 2015.

Whiteley, Iwan. "A Search for Cohesion in the Book of Revelation with Specific Reference to Chapter One." *TynBul* 57 (2006): 309–12.

Wilson, Mark. *Charts on the Book of Revelation: Literary, Historical, and Theological Perspectives*. Grand Rapids: Kregel, 2007.

Yarbro Collins, Adela. *Crisis and Catharsis: The Power of the Apocalypse*. Philadelphia: Westminster, 1984.

———. "Introduction: Early Christian Apocalypticism." *Semeia* 36 (1986): 1–11.

Scripture Index

Old Testament

Genesis

1:20–21 86n16
1:24–25 86n16
2:2–3 18
2:7 89
2:9 230
2:9–14 260
2:15–23 125
2:18 125
2:20 125
3 183
3:1–5 125
3:1–7 233
3:5 75
3:6 180
3:22 230, 260
4 210
4:4–5 50
4:8 184
5:21–24 50
6–9 162, 164
6:1–4 127
6:2 128
6:4 128
12:1–3 30, 83
12:1–4 50
12:2 51
12:8 50
14:18–20 22, 31
15 30
15:6 71, 82, 83, 84
16:1–5 51

18:9–15 51
18:12 115, 124
19 162, 209
21:12 51
22 82, 83
22:1–2 51
22:1–19 51, 82
22:3 51, 82
22:8 52
22:9 82
22:12 52
22:13 52
22:17 30, 51
25:31–34 56
27:27–29 52
27:30–40 56
27:39–40 52
35:23–26 243
37:9 247
48:8–20 52
49:9 242
50:25 52

Exodus

1:15–16 52
2:2 52
2:11–12 53
3:19 139n34
7–10 244, 249
7:14–21 244
8:22–23 249
9:4 249
9:6 249
9:9–11 249

9:19–35 244
10:14 245
10:21–23 244
10:21–29 250
12:22–23 53
13:3 139n34
13:9 139n34
13:14 139n34
13:16 139n34
13:21–22 27
14:15–31 53
14:21–22 250
15 249
15:20–21 233
15:23–25 244
16 27
16:32–34 232
17:7 16
19–20 259
19:5 117
19:5–6 115, 116
19:6 116, 117, 223n19
19:16–18 250
19:16–19 56
20:8–11 18
20:13–14 80
20:16 90
20:17 88
20:18 56
23:19 75n4
24:8 40
25:10–22 37
25:23–40 37
25:40 35, 41

267

Subject Index